Introduction to New and Alternative Religions in America

Introduction to New and Alternative Religions in America

Volume 3: Metaphysical, New Age, and Neopagan Movements

Edited by Eugene V. Gallagher and W. Michael Ashcraft

GREENWOOD PRESS
Westport, Connecticut · London

Library of Congress Cataloging-in-Publication Data

Introduction to new and alternative religions in America / edited by
  Eugene V. Gallagher and W. Michael Ashcraft.
    v. cm.
  Includes bibliographical references and index.
  Contents: v. 1. History and controversies—v. 2. Jewish and Christian traditions—v. 3. Metaphysical,
New Age, and neopagan movements—v. 4. Asian traditions—v. 5. African diaspora traditions and other
American innovations.
  ISBN 0–275–98712–4 (set : alk. paper)—ISBN 0–275–98713–2 (v. 1 : alk. paper)—ISBN 0–275–
98714–2 (v. 2 : alk. paper)— [etc.]
  1. Cults—United States. 2. Sects—United States. 3. United States—Religion—1960– . I. Gallagher,
Eugene V., 1960– . II. Ashcraft, W. Michael, 1955– .
  BL2525.I58 2006
  200.973—dc22   2006022954

British Library Cataloguing in Publication Data is available.

Library of Congress Catalog Card Number: 2006022954
ISBN: 0–275–98712–4 (set)
  0–275–98713–2 (vol. 1)
  0–275–98714–0 (vol. 2)
  0–275–98715–9 (vol. 3)
  0–275–98716–7 (vol. 4)
  0–275–98717–5 (vol. 5)

First published in 2006

Greenwood Press, 88 Post Road West, Westport, CT 06881
An imprint of Greenwood Publishing Group, Inc.
www.greenwood.com

Printed in the United States of America

The paper used in this book complies with the
Permanent Paper Standard issued by the National
Information Standards Organization (Z39.48–1984).

10 9 8 7 6 5 4 3 2 1

Contents

Acknowledgments

This project is the result of a collaborative effort. We the coeditors are grateful to the contributors of this series for sharing their expertise with the general public through these outstanding scholarly essays. They did so for the sake of bringing to a wide reading audience the best information and interpretations now available about a wide range of new religious movements. We are especially grateful to Catherine Wessinger and David Bromley for helping us identify authors and for many other suggestions that have improved this set of volumes.

We the coeditors thank all of these scholars who gave so much to make this set possible. Many of them wrote their essays amid personal hardship and busy professional lives.

We also thank Suzanne Staszak-Silva, our editor at Greenwood, for her advice and guidance as this set went from one stage of development to another.

We are also grateful to our colleagues, at our respective teaching institutions as well as among the wider scholarly community, who offered us personal support and encouragement, much free advice, and many good wishes and kind thoughts.

Finally, we thank our families: our wives, Jennifer Gallagher and Carrol Davenport, and our daughters, Maggie Gallagher and Brittany and Kathleen Ashcraft. We lovingly dedicate this set to those daughters, our hope for the future, whom we love very much.

Introduction

Although new or alternative religious movements, or New Religious Movements (NRMs), have always been part of the American religious landscape, they have not always received broad public attention. Most often, their formation, attraction of members, and growth or decline have occurred beyond the harsh glare of prolonged public scrutiny. In some striking cases, however, a new or alternative religious movement has dominated the news for a period of time, usually because the movement itself, or some of its members, became involved in something that was widely perceived to be illegal, immoral, or simply destructive. For example, in the wake of the 1963 assassination of President John F. Kennedy, Minister Malcolm X of the Nation of Islam became notorious for his comment that Kennedy's murder meant "the chickens had come home to roost." In the 1970s saffron-robed members of the International Society for Krishna Consciousness, also known as Hare Krishna, became so well known for seeking donations and engaging strangers in conversations in public that they were easily lampooned in the comic film "Airplane." In the 1980s, the Rev. Sun Myung Moon, leader of the Unification Church (or Moonies), was found guilty of tax evasion by diverting church funds for his personal use. More recently, in 1993, the U.S. Bureau of Alcohol, Tobacco, and Firearms staged a raid on the home and church of a small group of Bible students outside of Waco, Texas. In addition to the ten lives lost in the botched raid, the 51 day standoff between the students of David Koresh, a group widely known as the Branch Davidians, and agents of the federal government, particularly the Federal Bureau of Investigation, culminated in the loss of 78 lives in a fire that consumed the Mount Carmel Center where the Branch Davidians lived. In 1997 followers of Marshall Applewhite, forming a group called Heaven's Gate, joined him in committing suicide so that they could all progress to what they viewed as "the evolutionary level above human." The list of such incidents could easily be multiplied.

In the late twentieth century as new and alternative religious movements continued to receive public attention for elements of their practice or belief that were highly controversial, a dominant image of such groups began to solidify. That image was fostered by the activism of groups of former members, their families, some professionals in social work and psychology, and various other volunteers. When the opposition to new or alternative religious groups originated with more or less secular individuals, those opponents were generally called anticultists. When opposition originated with Evangelical Protestant Christians, those opponents were usually called countercultists. The tireless work of such activists, anticultist or countercultist, quickly produced a standard understanding of new and alternative religions that united a wide variety of groups under the umbrella category of "cults." In the perceptions of their anticult opponents, cults posed serious threats to vulnerable individuals and, ultimately, to the stability of American society itself. Anticultists and countercultists believed that cults had three prominent characteristics. First, they were led by unscrupulous, manipulative, and insincere individuals who sought only to increase their own power, wealth, and/or sexual enjoyment. Second, cults preyed upon unsuspecting, confused, and vulnerable individuals, often using sophisticated and virtually irresistible tactics of influence. Third, participation in a cult would surely bring harm to individual participants and might also lead them to commit any number of antisocial actions that threatened the public good. The stereotype of the "destructive cult" was aggressively marketed by the loose coalition of anticultists, particularly when disturbing news about any new or alternative religious movement became public. Thus, on the one hand, while a variety of events created a broad interest in learning about individual religious groups, their practices and beliefs, organizational structure, leadership, and many other topics, on the other hand, the predominance of the cult stereotype inevitably skewed the information available, attributed the perceived faults of any one group to all of them, and created expectations that any group labeled a cult must necessarily be worthy of suspicion, scorn, and vigorous opposition. Despite their prodigious efforts at educating the general public, the various anticult and countercult activists have, in fact, promoted much more misunderstanding than accurate understanding of the religious lives of some of their fellow citizens. Consequently, they have helped to create a very hostile environment for anyone whose religious practices do not fit within a so-called "mainstream." The personal and social costs of such religious bigotry may actually be higher than what the activists fear from cults themselves.

This set of volumes on "New and Alternative Religions in America" intends to rectify that situation for the general reader. It aims to present accurate, comprehensive, authoritative, and accessible accounts of various new and alternative religious movements that have been and are active in American society, as well as a set of essays that orient the reader to significant contexts for understanding new and alternative religions and important issues involved in studying them. The presentations are predicated on a simple but fundamental assumption. It is that accurate description and understanding must precede any judgment about the truth, validity, morality, or trustworthiness of any religious group or person. Accurate description demands that the group be presented in terms that it could itself recognize and acknowledge as being at least close to the way it understands itself. Providing an accurate description of the history, organization, practices, and beliefs of a particular group does not, in any way, constitute an endorsement of that group, but it does provide an indispensable baseline for any further discussion. Such a baseline has often been lost in the public discussions of new and alternative religious movements, because their most bizarre, threatening, or even humorous aspects have been exaggerated. What is missing from such caricatured presentations is a sense of how any person could find such apparently ludicrous, lethal, or laughable groups worth joining. Simple dismissal of new or alternative religions as absurd, erroneous, or pernicious misses the social influence that they can have and demonstrably have had. Whatever an outsider's perception of new and alternative religions might be, many clear-thinking and well-intentioned individuals, throughout American history, have associated themselves with such groups. This set is founded on the idea that members' or participants' reasons for their decisions and their accounts of their experiences form the primary data for understanding new and alternative religions. Both hostile and approving accounts of new or alternative religions from outsiders provide a different sort of data, which reveals the social location and often-controversial careers of new and alternative religions. But neither approval nor criticism by external observers should take precedence over the self-understanding of each group as articulated by its members in establishing a baseline of descriptive accuracy.

Readers of this set of volumes will thus encounter both information and analytical frameworks that will help them arrive at an informed and appropriately complicated understanding of new and alternative religious movements in American history and society. Volume 1 provides a set of analytical perspectives on new and alternative religions, including the history of such movements in the United States, the controversies in which they have often become embroiled, the roles of leaders within the groups and the processes by which individuals become members and also leave their groups, the legal and global contexts in which new and alternative religions function, and a variety of prominent themes in the study of new religions, including roles of gender, children, and violence.

The four volumes that follow generally present accounts of individual groups, many of them well known but some much less so. Each chapter presents information about the origin and subsequent development of the group in question, its internal organization including the predominant type of leadership, its most important practices and beliefs, and controversies that have put the group in the limelight. Volume 2 focuses on groups that have developed out of the broad biblical tradition—Judaism and Christianity—and have achieved such a distinctive status as to be considered, at least by some observers, as independent religious groups rather than simple sectarian variations of more mainstream Jewish or Christian traditions. Volume 2 accordingly raises most acutely the problems of definition that are involved in using the admittedly malleable categories of "new" and "alternative" religions.

The description of a religious movement as *new* or *alternative* only begs further questions. Novelty can be in the eye of the beholder, or in the mind of someone claiming to be innovative. That is, religious movements are judged to be new, alternative, or anything else only in particular contexts and by certain audiences. They may claim, for example, to retrieve and correctly interpret or represent past beliefs and practices, which have been neglected or forgotten. But their opponents might view the same claims as dangerous and deviant inventions. New religions themselves often manifest a pronounced ambivalence about their own novelty. A fundamental dynamic in new and alternative religions is that they strive to present themselves as both new and old, as unprecedented and familiar. The novelty of new religions cuts both ways; it can just as easily excite the interest of potential adherents as it can strain their credulity. As they spread their messages to those whose interest, approval, and even acceptance they hope to secure, NRMs proclaim both their challenging novelty and their comforting familiarity.

In their sectarian forms, these movements attempt to recapture the lost purity of an idealized past. Sects typically have prior ties to larger religious organizations from which they have intentionally broken off. They aim to return to the pristine origins of the tradition and reestablish its foundations. Sectarian forms of Christianity frequently exhort their partisans to get "back to the Bible"; contemporary Islamic sects similarly yearn for the purity of the times of the prophet Muhammad. Even the Church of Satan, founded by Anton Szandor LaVey in 1966, has spawned sectarian groups that accuse the original Church of Satan of having abandoned its initial commitments and emphases. Sects thus define themselves both in relation to the broader world and in relation to their specific tradition, both of which are perceived to threaten their purity of belief and practice.

In their typology of responses to secularization, Rodney Stark and William Sims Bainbridge contrast cults to sects. Rejecting the polemical definition of cults spawned by their cultural opponents, they define cults as independent religious traditions. Cults may be imports from another culture or independent products of the society in which they develop. Like sects, cults often find themselves in tension or conflict with broader society, simply by virtue of being new and different. Because they, too, want to locate themselves in relation to an authoritative past, cults also lay some claim to previous tradition. What separates cults from sects in their relation to previous traditions is that cults typically do not have a history of institutional conflict and eventual separation. Cults are marked from their beginnings as new entities. Both sects and cults, then, simultaneously declare their novelty and sink their roots in the past. In order to avoid confusion about the term "cult," which has such negative connotations in contemporary American society, this set will keep to the designations of new and alternative religions, which are widely employed by many scholars even though they are somewhat imprecise. The choice of which groups to include in Volume 2, as with the other volumes, is a judgment call. The guiding principle was not only to provide a representative sample of new and alternative religious groups throughout American history, but also to present the groups in sufficient detail to enable the reader to form a complex understanding of them.

Volume 3 investigates groups in the occult or metaphysical tradition, including nineteenth century Spiritualism, the Theosophical Society begun by Helena Petrovna Blavatsky and Colonel Henry Steel Olcott in the late nineteenth century, and the contemporary New Age movement. Like the groups discussed in the second volume, those in Volume 3 are part of a broad tradition that has deep roots in antiquity. For example, in *The Secret Doctrine* Madame Blavatsky included the ancient Vedic sages of India, the Buddha, and a collection of ancient Greek philosophers among the ancient teachers whose wisdom about the nature of human beings and the nature of god was being given its fullest expression in Blavatsky's modern Theosophical system.

The religious movements discussed in Volume 3 typically present a different organizational profile from those in Volume 2. The groups in Volume 2 have made substantial efforts to maintain boundaries between themselves and their surrounding social environment, demanding exclusive allegiance of their members; vesting authority over practice, doctrine, and group life in charismatic leaders; and offering new and improved interpretations of familiar texts already acknowledged to have broad cultural legitimacy. In contrast, the movements in Volume 3 center on individual teachers who attract shifting groups of students with varying degrees of commitment for varying lengths of time, leave the ability to determine the authority or validity of any pronouncements in the hands of individual seekers, and claim to bring to light extraordinary wisdom from previously unknown or underappreciated sources.

Many of the religions that have appeared to be innovative developments in American religious life have actually been transplanted from other cultures where they have often enjoyed long histories. The openness of the United States to immigrants has always been an important factor in promoting American religious diversity. The 1965 repeal of the 1924 *Asian Exclusion Act,* for example, permitted a variety of Eastern religious teachers to extend their religious activities to the United States. Late in his life, for example, Swami A.C. Bhaktivedanta Prabhupada, the founder of the International Society for Krishna Consciousness, made the United States the focus of his efforts to awaken love for Krishna in as many people as possible. Military personnel returning from service abroad, often with spouses from countries where they had been stationed, also helped to introduce new religious practices and movements to the United States. This was the case, for example, with the form of Japanese Nichiren Buddhism known as Soka Gakkai. Even where it is difficult to provide independent corroboration of claimed international ties, they can nonetheless be claimed. A dramatic example here was the assertion that the elusive figure at the origins of the Nation of Islam, W.D. Fard, arrived in Detroit, Michigan, in 1930 from Mecca in Saudi Arabia. The movements in Volume 4 show clearly that religious innovation in the United States always needs to be considered in a broader, global context. That is no less true of the groups discussed in other volumes as well. For example, Ann Lee's small band of Shakers began in Manchester, England; David Koresh gathered Bible students from Australia, England, and other foreign countries as well as the United States. Theosophy's Madame Blavatsky was a Russian émigré. Finally, the Church of Scientology, like many other new religions that have begun in the United States, conducts a vigorous international missionary program.

The frequent movement of individuals, practices, and ideas across national borders could make a focus on new and alternative religions solely in the United States vulnerable to a myopia that could distort the nature and significance of those movements. That caution holds equally for homegrown and imported religions. Few religions in the contemporary world, no matter what their age or relation to a mainstream, are confined within a single set of national boundaries. Nonetheless, the focus of this set remains on a selection of religions that have had, for one reason or another, a significant impact on religious and social life in the United States. Prominent in that selection is a group of religions that have been independently founded in the United States. For example, although the contemporary revival of Paganism can be traced to the career of Gerald Gardner in England beginning in the 1930s, many influential Pagan thinkers and teachers, such as Z Budapest, Starhawk, and Isaac Bonewits have flourished in the United States. Similarly, the Church of Satan and its subsequent offshoots owe their inspiration to Anton Szandor LaVey, who produced *The Satanic Bible* and other fundamental texts in San Francisco, California, in the 1960s. Also, beginning in the 1950s the prodigious literary output of L. Ron Hubbard gave rise first to the therapeutic system known as Dianetics and then, as his purview broadened, to the Church of Scientology. Other founders of NRMs in the United States, like Marshall Applewhite of the Heaven's Gate group, attracted far fewer adherents than the Church of Scientology but nonetheless carved out a place for themselves in American religious history through their dramatic, and sometimes tragic, actions. Volume 5 thus focuses on both new developments in international movements within the United States, such as the rise of Neo-Paganism, and the conscious construction of new religions, such as the Church of Scientology, by American teachers and organizations.

As this overview suggests, the definition of what counts as a new or alternative religion is frequently open to argument. Many groups that appear dramatically novel to external observers would claim that they are simply being faithful to ancient traditions. Joseph Smith, for example, claimed that the Church of Jesus Christ of Latter-day Saints, or Mormons, was a restoration of primitive Christianity. Groups that claim to be innovative often express their messages in the form of fresh interpretations of ancient texts, as with Swami Prabhupada's effort to present the ancient Indian classic, the Bhagavad-Gita, "as it is"; or Rael's contention that the mentions of "Elohim" in the biblical book of Genesis actually refer to extraterrestrial beings who came to earth in space ships. Because of the subjective nature of the categories —new to whom? alternative to what?—it will always be difficult to delimit precisely which groups definitely do, and do not, "count" as new or alternative. Moreover, in popular discourse, where the category cult is frequently used but appears devoid of anything other than emotional content, and in interreligious arguments, where cult easily expands to include "virtually anyone who is not us," attempts at substantive definitions give way entirely to polemics. Discussion of new and alternative religions in the United States thus always refers to a shifting and vigorously contested terrain where categories like "alternative religion" or "cult" and implicit comparisons like those implied by "new religious movement" are used to establish, reinforce, and defend certain kinds of individual and group identities, even as they threaten, compromise, or erode other kinds of individual or group identities.

No mapping of such terrain can hope to be definitive. Too much is in flux. Those who enter the terrain need trustworthy and experienced guides. The essays in these five volumes provide just such guidance. Experienced, authoritative, and plainspoken, the authors of these essays provide both perspectives on some of the most prominent general features of the landscape and full descriptions of many, but by no means all, of the specific areas within it. Those who want to explore the terrain of new and alternative religions in the United States will find in this set multiple points of entry. They may want to focus on a specific local part of the larger area, such as the Theosophical tradition, the Branch Davidians, or Heaven's Gate. On the other hand, they may want to investigate the characteristic dynamics of the broader field, such as the processes of conversion into and defection from groups or the interactions between new and alternative religions and their cultural opponents. There is much to explore—much more than can even be covered in these five volumes. But this set aims to equip the would-be explorer with enough tools and knowledge to make the exploration rewarding and worthwhile.

Swedenborgianism

Jane Williams-Hogan

INTRODUCTION

Based on the religious writings of Emanuel Swedenborg (1688–1772), the Swedenborgian faith emerged in Europe and North America toward the end of the eighteenth century—a century defined by innovation and revolutionary change. Changes occurred in almost every area of human endeavor: science, philosophy, agriculture, manufacture, politics, and religion. In the clash between the traditional and the modern, some people abandoned the old faiths in the name of science or philosophy, others found comfort in new formulations of the old confessions, and a few sought out radically new religions, today called New Religious Movements (NRMs).

Many of these new faiths did not survive beyond the founding generation. The story of Swedenborgianism is different. Perhaps because Swedenborg's new Christian revelation explores the root cause of the broad intellectual and social changes that ushered in the modern world or because it offers a rational faith compatible with the needs of the new age. In *True Christianity* published in 1770, Swedenborg wrote in number 508: "Now it is permitted to enter with understanding into the mysteries of faith."[1]

Swedenborgianism survived beyond the first generation of believers in the eighteenth century, and over the centuries grew in a variety of cultural soils and climates, although better in some environments than others. By 1800, believers were found in the European nations of England, Sweden, France, Germany, and Russia as well as in the United States. In the nineteenth century, the number of believers grew, taking root in Africa, Australia, Canada, and New Zealand. The number of believers and their locations continued to grow in the twentieth century, and by the beginning of the twenty-first century they are on every continent in the world with the possible exception of Antarctica. In 2005 there are approximately 50,000 members of Swedenborgian religious organizations worldwide. The small number may be due to the doctrinal emphasis on freedom and the teaching that heaven is open to all who live a good life irrespective of their faith.

Swedenborgianism draws its doctrines from the religious writings of Swedenborg. He wrote in *True Christianity* number 779 that the Lord would "establish a new church, ... by means of a man, who is able not only to receive these doctrines in the understanding but also to publish them by the press." For 23 years (1747–1770) Swedenborg wrote and published a new revelation he claimed was from God (he published the books anonymously until 1768). He produced 18 different titles in 30 volumes, but he never attempted to found a church. When he died in 1772, only a handful of readers of his religious writings professed them to be the true word of God. However, 15 years later in 1787, a church based on those teachings was established in London by individuals who never knew Swedenborg or anyone acquainted with him. Since then, other people in other countries have also established churches after reading Swedenborg's writings. Thus, it might be said that, unlike many churches founded by charismatic leaders, who their followers believed to be filled with grace, this church is founded instead through the "charisma of the book."

In order to understand this type of charisma and the basic characteristics of the Swedenborgian faith, this chapter explores the following: Swedenborg's life, Swedenborgian doctrines, the establishment, history, and practices of Swedenborgian Churches, the impact of the Swedenborgian Movement on Western culture, controversies and issues, and the future.[2]

EMANUEL SWEDENBORG

Swedenborg's life was long, productive, and eventful. He published over 128 different works and left manuscripts for another 182.[3] He published poetry and scientific, civic, philosophical, and religious books. He traveled extensively throughout his life, leaving his native Sweden for the eleventh and last time in 1770 at the age of 82. However, his most remarkable journeys were not to European destinations, but were mental and spiritual in nature. He claims he had his spiritual eyes opened, and to "have seen, heard, and felt" in a world beyond the natural.[4] What follows is a brief overview of his extraordinary life.[5] It can be readily divided into three periods: (1) childhood and education; (2) career; (3) religious call and revelator.

Childhood and Education

Swedenborg was born on January 29, 1688 in Stockholm Sweden. He was born Emanuel Swedberg, and became Emanuel Swedenborg in 1719 when and he and his brothers and sisters were ennobled by Queen Ulrika Eleonora (1688–1741). He was the third child and second son of Jesper (1653–1735) and Sara (nee Behm 1666–1696) Swedberg. The Behm and Swedberg families had extensive mine holdings, and were part of Sweden's upper class. This wealth provided an inheritance for Swedenborg in his adult life that gave him the resources to independently publish his own writing.[6] Looking back on his life from the perspective of his "call" and his claim to be a revelator, what is noteworthy about his childhood is the fact that his father was a Lutheran pastor, and he was raised in a religiously conservative home. Although Swedenborg recalled late in life that his parents believed that "angels spoke through me," his first passion in life was science.

He graduated from Uppsala University in 1709, then went on an extended European tour from 1710–1715 to complete his education. The purpose of his trip was to absorb the latest scientific developments. He studied in England, France, Holland, and Germany by reading about new discoveries, attending lectures, and meeting with well-known scholars. In addition, he stayed in the homes of trained craftsmen and learned their trades. In this way he learned engraving and lens grinding among other skills.

Career

Swedenborg came home ready to be of service to his nation. First he published a scientific journal (Sweden's first) with the hope that he could contribute to the intellectual and economic development of his homeland. Six issues of the journal *Daedalus Hyperboreus* were published in 1716 and 1717. He included descriptions of some of the inventions he had developed during his trip.[7]

The journal brought Swedenborg into contact with Sweden's most highly regarded inventor Christopher Polhem (1661–1751) and the king, Charles XII (1682–1718). He was invited to be Polhem's assistant, and together they traveled to Lund to meet the king. Impressed with Swedenborg's talent, the king gave him an appointment as Extraordinary Assessor on the Board of Mines, the oversight agency for Sweden's vital mining industry.

Before assuming his duties as a mine inspector and judge, Charles had several pressing engineering projects that required immediate attention, and Polhem and Swedenborg were engaged to oversee them. The final project entailed the transportation of the king's navy overland for a surprise attack on Norwegian forces at Fredrikshall. This campaign ended with Charles's death on November 30, 1718.

That royal death affected Swedenborg's career. His appointment to the Board of Mines was no longer automatic. He attempted to bolster his claim by learning about mining techniques and practices through direct observation during a trip to Europe in the early 1720s. His diligence and persistence were rewarded. He secured a paid position in 1724. For the next quarter of a century Swedenborg dedicated his public life to the administrative and judicial duties of that position. Less successful in private life, although interested, he never married.

Like others during the Enlightenment, he used the tools of natural philosophy to explore nature, as a mirror of God's order and a vessel for his purposes. His *Basic Principles of Nature,* published in 1734, articulated a nebular hypothesis similar to the later theory of marquis La Place (1749–1827) to account for the creation of our solar system. His initial projects had the same goals as his contemporaries; however, his religious writings were at odds with both the rationalist philosophers and religious enthusiasts.

During this phase of his life, Swedenborg used his time outside of his official position to wrestle with understanding the creation of the universe, the formation of the human being from the soul, and the relationship between creation and God. He published extensively on these topics. He studies the mineral kingdom and the cosmos in search of the creator, and the human body—the soul's domain—in search of the redeemer.

In 1743 he asked for a leave of absence from the Board of Mines to go to The Hague and published what he hoped would be his *magnum opus, the Soul's Domain.* In preparation for this work, Swedenborg compiled notes from various philosophers, classical and contemporary. Among others he cited the works of Plato, Aristiotle, Gottfried Wilhelm Leibnitz (1646–1716), and Christian Wolff (1679–1754). Wolff was of particular interest because of his attempt to reconcile reason with the doctrines of the Christian Church. This had direct bearing on Swedenborg's project to find the soul within the human body. While he did publish two volumes of this work in The Hague in 1744, and another volume in London in 1745, at this same time, he experienced a spiritual crisis that profoundly changed his life.[8]

Religious Call and Revelator

When Swedenborg left Sweden in July 1743, his mind was no doubt focused on the task that awaited him at his journey's end—overseeing the printing of the manuscripts of the *Soul's Domain.* He reveals his excitement and anticipation, when he showed them to Adolph Fredrich (1710–1771) the future king of Sweden. He was certain that this was an important work because he believed that his demonstration of the existence of the soul to the senses might help others to banish the human propensity to unbelief.

In mid-August en route to The Hague via Amsterdam, he began to experience dreams sufficiently extraordinary in nature that he recorded them in his travel journal. For the next year Swedenborg recorded his dreams. The journal was never intended for publication. Nevertheless, it was discovered and authenticated in the 1850s and 99 copies were published in Swedish as *Swedenborgs Drommer* by G. E. Klemming. The journal contains 286 entries, although the first ten are observations made during his trip to Amsterdam. It is perhaps the oldest and longest series of dreams ever recorded. Soon after he began recording his dreams, Swedenborg also began to interpret them.

He believed that his dreams were communications about his state of spiritual health. These dreams penetrated his pretenses and laid bare his vanity, arrogance, sense of superiority, conceit, and pride. In one dream, he is lying beside a pure woman, who he believed was his guardian angel. She told him that he smelled ill. This signaled the beginning of strong temptations, which at times brought him to the edge of despair. Gradually his temptations alternated with feelings of blessedness. For example, on the night after Easter, April 6–7, 1744, Swedenborg heard a loud thunderclap and was cast face down on the floor. He prayed and felt the presence of Jesus Christ, and then he saw him face-to-face. Jesus asked him if he had a clean bill of health. Swedenborg responded, "Lord, you know better than I." "Well do so," he said.[9] This image of a bill of health harkened back to Swedenborg's youth, when he broke the quarantine imposed by London harbor officials, fearful of the plague, on the ship he had taken on his first trip from Sweden to England. Encouraged by friends, he entered London without a "clean bill of health." In Swedenborg's analysis in his journal, God's command signified "love me in reality." When God said, "Well, do so," he was asking Swedenborg to do what he had not done in his youth, when he had acted out of self-interest and could have imperiled the lives of thousands. God now demanded that he love others more than himself. This dream was life altering for Emanuel Swedenborg. As he said,

> I have now learned this in spiritual [things], that there is nothing for it but to humble oneself and to desire nothing else, and this with all humility, than the grace of Christ.... The Holy Spirit taught me this; but I, with my foolish understanding, left out humility, which is the foundation of all.[10]

In one of his last recorded dreams, he was told by Christ not to undertake anything without him.

Although he oversaw the third volume of the *Soul's Domain* through the press in London, he began to write a very different sort of book. Called *The Worship and Love of God* (London, 1745) it is a prose poem written as an offering of love to God. Not long after the publication of the first two parts of this little book (the third part was never finished), Swedenborg returned to Sweden in the summer of 1745 still seeking a focus for his "call."

For the next two years, he continued his work on the Board of Mines. He also delved into the study of the Bible. Bible study was essential because it is God's Word, and he spoke to Swedenborg in it. The Bible was to be his guide and his sole source of divine truth. He had been warned in his dreams not to read theology written by others to prevent contamination.[11] He mastered Hebrew in order to read Hebrew Scriptures (Old Testament) in the original. He attempted to interpret the story of creation and developed a Biblical index through which he hoped to discover the deeper meaning of the text. He read and reread the Bible, he prayed, and he saw visions of the spiritual world. In 1747, he began to record these visionary experiences, somewhat like scientific field notes, in what is now called *Spiritual Experiences*. It was also a multivolume work, written over an 18-year period and left in manuscript form.

In 1747, two events occurred that signaled a shift in Swedenborg's focus. First, he was unanimously nominated to be President of the Board of Mines, an honor that recognized his enormous contribution to the activities of the Board. He declined the offer, however, and instead petitioned the king, Frederick I (1676–1751), to relieve him of his duties, and to grant him a pension of half his salary in retirement in order that he "could finish the work on which I am now engaged."[12] The King accepted his request, as a way to recognize Swedenborg's outstanding civic and intellectual contribution to the nation.[13] To the regret of all his colleagues, Swedenborg took leave of the Board of Mines on July 17, 1747.

He left Sweden almost immediately for Amsterdam. The second event took place on August 7. He recorded it in one of the indices of the Bible he was working on. He wrote, "1747, August 7, old style. There is a change of state in me into the heavenly kingdom, in an image."[14] Swedenborg's followers interpret this to mean that he was now in full communication with the heavens and understood his call.[15]

Swedenborg saw himself as a revelator for a new age. As he interpreted the role, he was not called to be an Old Testament prophet or to be another Christ. He was called to serve the Lord Jesus Christ as a scribe of heaven, faithfully using the doctrine of correspondences to interpret the internal or spiritual sense of the Old and New Testaments and to record for mortal eyes the wonders of heaven and hell. The nature of Swedenborg's prophecy was not to speak new words or share new visions clothed in mystery and symbol, but to write and publish the secrets of heaven and eternal life, making them available for all sincere seekers. He strove to interpret the old symbols, making them accessible for future generations, knowing that those generations would demand clarity and rationality in spiritual things.

The first book that Swedenborg produced, using the doctrine of correspondence, was the *Arcana Coelestia,* or *Heavenly Secrets.* Correspondence, according to Swedenborg, is a relationship of causality, and therefore it denotes a similarity between something spiritual and something physical.[16] For example, truth on the spiritual plane does what water does on the physical plane, it purifies; love enlivens the spirit, just as the heat of the sun causes plants to grow in the natural world. He published the first volume anonymously in London in 1749. The remaining seven volumes were published regularly until 1756.

The manner in which Swedenborg published his religious works mirrored his earlier publishing efforts. Through the resources he had inherited and his salary or pension, Swedenborg had sufficient financial resources at his disposal, enabling him to travel outside of Sweden, hire a printer, and pay for the printing and binding of several hundred copies of his books. He was able to do this for the nine major philosophical volumes he published, as well as for the 18 religious titles. He chose to publish outside of Sweden because of the strict censorship laws found there.

The publication of *Heavenly Secrets* marked the opening of the public phase of Swedenborg's spiritual mission. In the middle of this period (1759), he had a verified clairvoyant experience. He saw a fire break out in Stockholm while at dinner with friends and acquaintances in Göteborg. He reported what he saw to his dinner companions, and the next day he was asked to repeat them for the governor. The following day news came of the fire, and the report of the course of the fire matched his description. Stories concerning this circulated in Europe, so that even Immanuel Kant (1724–1804) was asked to comment on this and other of Swedenborg's clairvoyant experiences by a friend (1763).[17] Nonetheless, he continued to write and publish his religious works anonymously until 1768. Thirteen different titles were produced during this time period.

In 1768 Swedenborg published in Amsterdam *Marriage Love* and signed it "Emanuel Swedenborg, a Swede."[18] In the book, he also advertised his previous religious works and listed a forthcoming title. He may have revealed his identity as the author, at this time, for two reasons: first, by 1768, it was fairly well known that Swedenborg was the author of these works, because stories of his clairvoyant experiences circulated fairly widely; and second, Swedenborg, now 80 years old, may have been aware that acknowledging authorship might be the best way to preserve these books for future generations.[19]

Swedenborg returned to Sweden one last time in 1769 and discovered that two Lutheran pastors and personal friends, who read his books and became convinced of their truth were on trial for heresy in Göteborg. The findings about heresy were inconclusive, and the case was sent to Stockholm for judgment to determine whether the gymnasium teachers had taught and encouraged heresy. After two years the case was dropped, and no action was taken against the men. There was even talk among some clergy about bringing charges against Swedenborg himself, but, perhaps because he had influential friends among the nobility and royalty, that did not happen. Nonetheless, stories circulated, questioning Swedenborg's sanity. Swedenborg expressed no concern about these charges, telling friends in Sweden and England he felt secure with heavenly protection.

Swedenborg left Sweden for the last time in July 1770. He settled in Amsterdam and oversaw the publication of his last work *True Christianity*. The two-volume work was ready in 1771, and he signed it "Emanuel Swedenborg, Servant of the Lord Jesus Christ."[20]

Not long after the publication of *True Christianity*, Swedenborg traveled to London, where he suffered a stroke in December 1771. Although he partially recovered, he remained essentially bedridden. Sometime in early 1772 he received word that John Wesley wanted to meet him (because of his reputation as a seer), but he died on March 29, 1772, before any meeting could take place. On two occasions after his stroke he was asked whether his writings were true, supposedly he said, "I have written nothing but the truth ... and I could have said more, if it had been permitted."[21]

DOCTRINES

Swedenborg left an impressive spiritual legacy of his call and mission in the many volumes he published between 1749 and 1771. His corpus of religious works includes 18 titles in 30 volumes. Some of his works are exegetical in nature, such as *Heavenly Secrets* (London 1749–1756) and *Revelation Unveiled* (Amsterdam 1766); others are based on his spiritual experiences, such as *Heaven and Hell* (London 1758) and the *Last Judgment* (London 1758); another group is doctrinal in nature, such as *Lord* (Amsterdam 1763), *Sacred Scripture* (Amsterdam 1763), *Life* (Amsterdam 1763), *Faith* (Amsterdam 1763); another two are philosophical, *Divine Love and Wisdom* (Amsterdam 1763) and *Divine Providence* (Amsterdam 1763); *Marriage Love* (Amsterdam 1768) might be considered sociological, addressing as it does the foundational love of human societies on earth and in heaven; and finally some are theological in nature, such as *Survey* (Amsterdam 1769) and *True Christianity* (Amsterdam 1771). Despite the variety in both the substance and style,

Swedenborg's essential teachings are found throughout all of them. His corpus presents a universal theology that is supported by his spiritual experiences, biblical exegesis, rational explanation, biblical quotations, and deductive logic.

Fundamental to the whole of his New Christian theology is his claim that the Lord Jesus Christ called him to see the reality of the spiritual world by opening his spiritual eyes, thereby permitting him contact with that world on a regular, almost daily basis. He wrote in the preface to *Heaven and Hell* that he was given this ability in order to prevent the negative attitude of agnostics and atheists "from infecting and corrupting people of simple heart and simple faith."[22] For this purpose, he was not only able to see into heaven and hell, but he was allowed to describe what he saw and heard, "in the hopes of shedding light where there is ignorance, and of dispelling skepticism."[23]

Swedenborg believed that his task was to lay the foundation for a restored and revitalized Christianity. While in agreement with many of the basic tenets of Christianity, his teachings differ from traditional Christianity in several fundamental ways. He offers a new vision of God, human nature, the requirements for salvation, the nature of heaven and hell, marriage, correspondence, and the Last Judgment.

GOD

According to Swedenborg, from the beginning of time and for all eternity God is one. He is "the Lord, who is the God of the universe [and he] is uncreated and infinite," and therefore "he is that essential reality that is called Jehovah and is life itself or life in itself."[24] In him the trinity makes one "as soul, body, and operation make one in man."[25] The divine "esse" constitutes the soul; the "divine human," or the divine nature of the son (Jesus Christ), constitutes the body; and the divine proceeding, or the holy spirit, constitutes the operation. The true essence of the divine is love and wisdom. God's love called forth the creation of a human race, through his wisdom, for the purpose of eternal conjunction with it. Conjunction was the purpose, not union, because it is an activity or process that retains the identity of the participants.

The whole of the finite universe and everything in it was created to be a recipient of life from the Lord; human beings were specifically created with the capacity not only to receive life and love from the Love, but with the additional capacity to return it. God's love desires nothing more that to give of itself, freely and fully. For the return to be complete, it must not only be received, but it must be returned in the spirit in which it was given. That is, it must be both received and returned freely and with conscious rational understanding.

HUMAN NATURE

In order to play their unique role in creation, human beings, according to Swedenborg, have a dual inheritance. They are both natural and spiritual. They are created or are born into the order of the natural world with the capacity to become spiritual. This does not happen automatically, however, but only if they truly desire it and choose to do what is necessary to achieve it. In all of creation, the human race alone was created in the image and likeness of God, as a form of love and wisdom (Swedenborg makes it clear in his religious writings that the earth is not the only home of the human race, and that human beings in the image and likeness of God exist throughout the created universe).[26]

To this end, "God created the human rational mind in accordance with the order of the whole spiritual world, and the human body in accordance with the order of the whole natural world, and this is why everyone was called by the ancients a little heaven or a little cosmos."[27]

THE REQUIREMENTS OF SALVATION

The human race was endowed with the faculty to receive love and wisdom from God and with the freedom and rationality to acknowledge him as the sole source of their life. They are also free to reject him. Human beings may embrace their natural inheritance as the only true reality and, thus, reject their spiritual potential. Or they may choose to acknowledge their spiritual potential, seek the path of regeneration or rebirth, and, in this way, come into their spiritual inheritance.

Human beings are granted the freedom to reject God, according to Swedenborg, because a relationship that is compelled is really no relationship at all. The Lord does not wish to compel people to accept his life, because compulsion is foreign to his essence. Compulsion, by its very nature, is a natural, not a spiritual quality. Human spiritual choices, made with the divine gifts of freedom and rationality, lead a person either to heaven or to hell.

Human beings are born into the fixed reality of time and space, in order that they may choose what they truly love and, thus, who they are. One way leads to heaven, the other to hell. As Swedenborg wrote in the opening sentence of *Divine Love and Wisdom,* "Love is our life Even though the word 'love' is commonly on our tongues,... We are wholly unaware that it is our very life—not just the general life of our whole body and of all of our thoughts, but the life of their every least detail."[28] People reveal what they love in their actions.

According to Swedenborg the Lord wills everyone to heaven, and he provides all people with the means to reach heaven. The religious writings of Swedenborg clearly state that salvation is not dependent on knowing specific doctrines or belonging to any particular faith. It is dependent only upon living a life of useful service based upon universally available truths. However, the Lord saves no one apart from his or her life's work because, according to Swedenborg, the Lord saves in conjunction with the efforts the person made during his or her life in this world.[29]

According to Swedenborg, religion has two universal characteristics: one should acknowledge God and refrain from evil because it is contrary to God.[30] He further states that the Lord provided for some religion to be present nearly everywhere, and that the two universals of religion exist almost everywhere. Thus, everyone who acknowledges God and refrains from evil should have a place in heaven.

THE NATURE OF HEAVEN AND HELL

Swedenborg humanizes heaven and hell as well as what he calls the world of spirits (where people go immediately after death). The spiritual world, he describes, has both form and substance. His work *Heaven and Hell* offered a vivid and compelling picture of the afterlife to countless readers seeking to know the next world. Some are spiritual seekers, while others take solace in its pages after the death of a loved one. The picture is comforting because, although the laws of spiritual life differ from natural life in some very fundamental ways, in appearance the two worlds are very similar.

Swedenborg describes the process of waking after death, the fact that we experience ourselves as substantially as we did on earth, and the process of personal discovery and revelation concerning who each of us really is—that is, how we become what we really love. Those who love the Lord and the neighbor come into heaven, where they engage in useful employments of every kind, while those who deny the Lord and burn with hatred to the neighbor form themselves into hell. Heaven in all its forms, from the highest to the lowest, is created by a life of use to others. Hell, from the darkest to the mildest, is fashioned by a love of self and the world.

Swedenborg, in his discussion of heaven and hell, makes it clear that all spirits, whether in the world of spirits, heaven or hell, were all born on one of the many earths in the universe. Angels were not created as a race apart, and the devil was not formed from an angel of light cast down into hell. The spiritual realms of heaven and hell are peopled by individuals who were born into the natural world on some earth in the universe, lived a life there, and made choices that then created his or her own personal heaven or hell.

Throughout a person's life, the forces of heaven and hell are kept in equilibrium, so everyone is free to choose either heaven or hell for his or her eternal home. There is an intimate and mutually dependent relationship between these two worlds, so that "The human race apart from heaven would be like a chain without a hook; and heaven without the human race would be like a house without a foundation."[31]

Even though human beings live simultaneously in these two worlds during their earthly life, they focus primarily on life here. In the other world, after a time an individual's awareness of the natural world dims. At the end of the process of self-discovery and spiritual examination, the good seek the path to heaven and find a home provided for them. Evil spirits undergo the same process of self-examination. When it is complete, they wander until they find their own special spot in hell.

Swedenborg desired to make it clear that "Death is not the extinction but the continuation of life."[32] Spiritual life is lived in an eternal present. Angels are continually advancing to the springtime of life, as they lovingly serve others.

MARRIAGE

According to Swedenborg, heaven is not filled with ethereal asexual beings, but consists of couples living in loving eternal marriages. Couples in heaven share all the delights of earthly married life, and they feel themselves to be one angel as they work together. Human beings were created male and female not just for the sake of natural reproduction, but for essential spiritual purposes.

Men and women were created so they would differ not just in body and appearance but, according to Swedenborg, also as to their form of mind. Masculinity is a form of truth, and femininity is a form of love. Every truth has its corresponding love, and together they generate a special use. The sacred and eternal nature of marriage is founded on this idea. Swedenborg called monogamous married love "the precious treasure of human life."[33]

Marriage is, in fact, the dominant metaphor found in Swedenborg's theology. Marriage is the concept used to describe the union of love and wisdom within God himself. That union is the source of all creation—that marriage is life itself.

Swedenborg called the marriage relationship the seminary of the human race, and he wrote that because of this, the Lord conferred on it the greatest possible delights and happiness. In fact, Swedenborg states that "into this love are gathered all joys and delights from their first to their last."[34]

Swedenborg's teaching on the central importance of married love for the renewal of Christianity is a clear departure from the Christian ideal of *agape* or brotherly love. Nevertheless, his emphasis on the eternal nature of marriage resonates with many, loving married couples unable to imagine being separated after death.

CORRESPONDENCES

In Swedenborg's published religious writings he frequently mentions the internal or spiritual sense of the Word (his name for the Bible) and the concept of correspondences. Correspondences, for Swedenborg, are the key to the inner meaning of the Word. They are as old as the human race and were the transparent language of the inhabitants of the Golden Age, or, as Swedenborg identifies them, members of the Adamic or Most Ancient Church. These early humans could "read" nature, each other, and the events of their own lives, correspondentially. That is they could grasp

> something spiritual in something earthly, people saw heavenly qualities reflected in the trees, plants, and animals around them. As well as in each other and the events of their lives. Having no spoken or written language, and needing none, they received direct revelations and guidance from God through the mirror of nature, through dreams and visions, and through their contact with angels.[35]

The ability of humanity to understand life through correspondences was lost as a result of the fall. Swedenborg believed that it was his role as revelator to restore them, through revealing the spiritual message of the Bible, long hidden in the historical and literal sense of the Word.

THE LAST JUDGMENT

The writings of Swedenborg outline God's relationship to humanity through an examination of the history of the five churches that they describe as having existed on the earth.[36] The Bible is the source of that history, and the internal or spiritual sense of the literal Biblical narrative revealed in the writings, through the doctrine of correspondences, documents the rise and fall of the first four of the five churches established on earth by God (the fifth is the New Christian Church that Swedenborg claimed was to be established through his revelation). These churches correspond to five states of human spiritual development. Swedenborg identified these churches as the Most Ancient Church (Adamic Church), the Ancient Church (Church of Noah), the Jewish Church (the church established by Moses), the Christian Church (established by the Lord Jesus Christ), and the New Christian Church (based on the second coming of the Lord).

According to the writings, churches are instituted by God to provide humanity with the tools needed to understand God, his love for humanity, and his statutes, as well as how to live to achieve happiness in this world and eternal life. Each church has been given a revelation suitable to its character, although the universal principles of love to the Lord and charity to the neighbor never change. The integrity of each church was dependent upon its members remaining faithful to the universal principles of faith and charity. According to Swedenborg, the conjunction of faith and charity sustains a church, and their separation results in their fall.

Churches fall when the revelation given to them is perverted or "seen through." The love of self and the world are the sources of perversion. The people in these churches stopped relying on the Lord's revelation to know what to do and how to live, and chose to rely on their own natural wisdom instead. God's revelation seems inadequate and child-like to them, because "seeing through" shifts the terms or requirements by which an individual will see the truth.

Thus, each new revelation is accommodated to the new requirements of rationality demanded by humanity. The deeper the level of human self love, the greater is the requirement that revelation speaks to an individual's need to know, to understand, and to explain everything. Retrospectively, all previous accommodations or forms of revelation seem mysterious and incomplete. In Swedenborg's recounting of the history of the four previous churches, each one of them fell, and a judgment took place.

According to Swedenborg, the formulation of the doctrine of the Trinity at the Council of Nicea in 325 CE set the stage for the Last Judgment because it interrupted the unfolding of human spiritual perception that would have developed if Jesus Christ had been acknowledged as One with Jehovah. The formulation of a "trinity of divine persons from eternity" confounded reason and prevented the worship of the One God.

In addition to this fatal understanding of the trinity, an emphasis on miracles and the miraculous clouded people's understanding and perverted their freedom. People sought salvation in miracles, rather than seeking to understand God's Word and applying his eternal principles to life. The Protestant Reformation and the formulation of the "doctrine of faith alone" completely ruptured the already tenuous bond between charity and faith that existed in the Christian Church.

By the eighteenth century the "end of times" had come. According to Swedenborg, the description of the devastation associated with the Last Judgment in *Revelation* did not describe the end of the natural world as we know it, but was, in fact, a spiritual event that took place in 1757. The judgment was spiritual and not natural, because, as has been shown, the Word is essentially a document that focuses on spiritual matters.[37]

Swedenborg in his works made it clear that the Second Coming is now taking place. It does not refer to the physical coming of the Lord into the world a second time, but that the Lord is now fully revealed in the spiritual sense of the Word. The Second Coming is, therefore, an event that occurs in the minds and hearts of everyone who acknowledges the Lord Jesus Christ whose divine human is made fully visible within the New Christian Church.

THE NEW CHRISTIAN CHURCH

When Swedenborg died in 1772 no church organization dedicated to his revelation existed. Knowing Swedenborg's Swedish heritage, it would be natural to assume that some organization devoted to his religious vision might emerge there among his most intimate associates. The hostility of the Swedish Lutheran Church to religious innovation in general and to Swedenborgianism in particular made initial efforts to organize in Sweden futile.[38]

One interesting outcome of the suppression of Swedenborgianism in Sweden is that no one who personally knew Swedenborg was involved in the founding of a church based on his revelation. This is contrary to taken-for-granted expectations of church foundation, as well as to the general theoretic formulations on the subject. The church, when it was established, was founded by the *charisma of the book*.[39] This means that organizations were established by men and women who spontaneously found the power of the vision and the ideas in the books themselves so compelling that they decided to create organizations to preserve and sustain the message and to help them order their lives around it. This happened for the first time in London in 1787. It happened again in the Americas, Australia, and various European countries in the nineteenth century. In the twentieth century, it occurred in Ghana, Japan, Korea, Nigeria, Russia, South Africa, Sri Lanka, and the Ukraine. In the twenty-first century to date, additional organizations have been established in Kenya and the Philippines, and efforts are underway in China.

Starting groups based on common adherence to books takes more time than when a charismatic leader is involved. But clearly organizations have been and can be formed wherever the books happen to turn up. The circulation of books, although related to the movements of peoples, can also occur independently. Discovery of the books is, therefore, less dependent on religious structures and possible wherever books are found. However, it is important to observe that the growth of literacy and freedom is integral to a religion based upon the *charisma of the book*.

SWEDENBORGIAN CHURCHES

Swedenborgianism exists in three, well established, organizations in the world, all found in English speaking countries—one in Great Britain and two in the United States. Several less stable organizations also function, one is headquartered in the United States with strong ties to South Africa, and the other indigenous to South Africa. In addition, over the last 20 to 25 years, a number of new Swedenborgian organizations spontaneously arose in a variety of countries around the world.

THE GENERAL CONFERENCE

The establishment of the very first Swedenborgian or New Church organization took place in Great Britain in 1787. The organization is called The General Conference of the New Church. Two events mark the founding of this church: the baptism of five men into the Lord's New Church on July 31, 1787, and the ordination of two men into the priesthood of the New Church on June 1, 1788. These people were artists, artisans, merchants, and traders (farmers were conspicuously absent). Their religious backgrounds varied, but many were Methodists and other types of nonconformists. While these events sociologically mark establishment, almost 20 years passed before the organization was stable. Problems arose almost immediately after the initial acts of foundation due to deeply held differences among the founders about how the organization ought to be structured—whether hierarchical or congregational. Many nonconformists in England were congregational in form, but Methodism embraced hierarchy. As the newly founded Swedenborgian Church drew almost equally from nonconformists and Methodists, a struggle about what organizational form the church should take was almost inevitable. Swedenborg's writings themselves support a hierarchical church structure. Robert Hindmarsh (1759–1835), a printer in London and former Methodist, was a forceful advocate for this position. However, numerically the church was strongest in Lancashire, an area long noted for nonconformity. In 1815 a congregationally organization church was established at a conference held in Manchester, Lancashire. That organization still exists today.[40]

The high point of church membership for the Conference was in 1900, with a membership of 6,337 in 73 societies. Decline in the twentieth century was due to the general unchurching of Great Britain, but also to an insufficient number of trained ministers and the limited ability of congregational structures to deal with such broad societal change. One response was the decision in the late 1990s to ordain women. An even more radical departure from the past was the centralization of key functions of the Conference in 2000. Membership figures at that time show a total of 1,198 members in 30 congregations. In addition to centralizing, the Conference decided to deemphasize the Christian nature of Swedenborgianism and to take advantage of the Internet.

The challenges facing the Conference are all too clear; they must creatively respond to them or face failure and extinction. It is too early to assess the outcome of the changes they have made.

THE SWEDENBORGIAN CHURCH OF NORTH AMERICA

In 1817, only two years after the organizational structure of the General Conference was secured in Great Britain, the General Convention of the Church of the New Jerusalem was established in the United States. In that year, readers of Swedenborg's religious writings (first brought to the new nation in 1784) were scattered throughout the United States. They came together in Philadelphia to strengthen themselves through the creation of an organization. Although they were aware of the British Conference, and received encouragement, books, and pamphlets from them, they were always independently organized. They, too, adopted a congregational form of church government.

The individuals that were drawn to Swedenborgianism were artists, artisans, educators, entrepreneurs, merchants, and traders. They lived in old seaboard states and new states formed out of the Old Northwest Territory. Baltimore, Boston, New York, Philadelphia, and Cincinnati were cities with large Swedenborgian congregations. They came from a variety of religious backgrounds: Episcopalians, German Free-will Baptists, Congregationalists, Methodists, and Quakers, as well as others. Although initially Swedenborg's books came from England, the Philadelphia printer Francis Bailey (1744–1817) soon began to publish them himself, underwriting the expense by subscription. Benjamin Franklin, friend and neighbor to Bailey, was one of the subscribers. Convention prospered during the nineteenth century. At the high point of its membership in 1890, it had 154 societies, 119 ministers, and 7,095 members. A schism occurred in 1890 over the question of the authority of Swedenborg's writings and church government. Convention was not only congregationally organized, but decidedly anticlerical and open-minded. They read the writings for instruction, not for their "divine" authority.

The faction that broke away believed that Swedenborg's writings were divine, not just inspired by the Lord. Thus, the status of the writings was equal to the Old and New Testaments. They also believed that church government ought to be episcopal in nature, rather than congregational. They maintained that the writings themselves endorsed hierarchical church government. The open-mindedness of Convention led to the formation of a loosely organized structure of state associations. These associations were able to coexist, despite such fundamental differences, until the Pennsylvania Association under the leadership of General Pastor William Henry Benade (1816-1905) ordained a second bishop. This challenge to the rules of Convention pushed the two sides to the brink. Benade refused to back down, and three-quarters of the members of the Pennsylvania Association in support of him voted to withdraw from Convention. The schism affected membership not just because several hundred members withdrew, but now Convention was forced to compete for members with another Swedenborgian organization.

Changes in American culture also affected this organization. Swedenborg's teachings have a marked psychological element, which perhaps added to their attraction in the nineteenth century, particularly among cultural innovators. In the twentieth century, when psychology became a powerful secular movement, it was no longer necessary for cultural innovators to embrace religion in order to have access to psychology.

In addition, Swedenborgianism, in the nineteenth century, may have benefited by the broad public discussion of religion that existed prior to the Civil War. In postbellum America, religion quietly became a matter of personal faith, and other issues dominated public space.

In the nineteenth century, Swedenborgianism attracted people from all walks of life. John Chapman (1774–1844), better know as "Johnny Appleseed," distributed pages of Swedenborg's writings along with the seedlings he sold to Ohio's pioneers. He loved to share what he called "good news straight from heaven." In 1893 Swedenborgians were key organizers for the World Parliament of Religions held in Chicago in 1893. The idea of a Parliament in conjunction with the Chicago World's Fair originated with Charles Bonney (1831–1903), a Swedenborgian and a prominent attorney. Bonney joined the New Church as a teenager. Later he stated that it was his exposure to the teachings of the Swedenborgianism that "made a World's Parliament of Religions possible."[41] A teaching that possibly encouraged Bonney is an idea expressed in *Secrets of Heaven* that suggests a common religious culture may emerge despite a variety of doctrines, "if people acknowledge thoughtfulness toward others to be the essence of such a culture."[42] Bonney joined with other Swedenborgian and Christian leaders in Chicago in the organization of the Parliament. He delivered the opening and concluding addresses of the 17-day Parliament.

Today The General Convention is known as the Swedenborgian Church of North America. In 2000 Church total membership stood at 2,104 with 1,543 active members in approximately 40 congregations in the United States and Canada. The Swedenborgian Church of North America is known as the "liberal" branch of the New Church in North America. They have ordained women since 1970, and in 1997 they made the decision that sexual orientation should not be an impediment to ordination. Their vision of Swedenborgianism unites Swedenborg's emphasis on the importance of the beauty of variety and American individualism. They focus on Swedenborg's teachings about the marriage of good and truth within each individual and deemphasize his teaching on the institution of marriage.

In 2000 they relocated their theological school from the East to the West Coast. And from being a self-standing institution, they have become incorporated as the Swedenborg House of Studies at the Pacific School of Religion in Berkley, California, known as one of the most liberal theological schools in the United States. Obviously, the hope is that these changes will stimulate growth. Nonetheless, it is too early to assess the outcome.

THE GENERAL CHURCH OF THE NEW JERUSALEM

In 1897 a second American New Church organization was formed. Called the General Church of the New Jerusalem, it was founded by the group that broke with Convention in 1890. Differences with the autocratic style of the founder William H. Benade led to the incorporation of the church under the leadership of Bishop

Williams F. Pendleton (1845–1927) in 1897. The doctrinal positions remained the same. In addition, they were also strongly committed to developing a comprehensive educational system for the children of members. The emphasis on education also inspired the development of residential communities for members wherever possible. This inward turning pattern of development was similar to other late nineteenth century religious groups interested in protecting their heritage and providing for the future.

The ideational roots of its establishment attracted members from both the British Conference and Convention, creating an international organization from its inception. At the time of its incorporation, General Church congregations were established in Australia, Canada, and England, as well as in the United States. In 1900, three years after incorporation, the General Church had 560 members. The Pennsylvania community of Bryn Athyn became the Episcopal seat of the Church and the home of an academy that included a theological school, college, and high school.

Slow growth throughout the twentieth century increased membership to 4,585 in 2000. In 2005 that number stands just shy of 5,000 at 4,972 members. Although growth remains slow in most regions of the world, there are some notable exceptions, particularly in Africa, where church growth is much more rapid. Growth, nonetheless is a reality, and the total size of the international General Church community is 15,790 with over 70 congregations in over 16 countries in North America, Europe, South America, Africa, Asia, and Australia.

Several factors may account for the growth of the Church in Africa. The doctrine of one God, who is the Lord Jesus Christ, and the teachings about the nature of spiritual reality are particularly attractive to Africans. Another factor may be Swedenborg's teachings about the celestial genius of Africans. In the eighteenth century when many scientists, including Swedenborg's countryman, the botanist Carl von Linnaeus (1707–1778), believed that Africans were the link between Homo sapiens and the great apes, Swedenborg wrote that they had a higher spiritual genius than Europeans. Africans certainly would find this teaching a refreshing contrast to the unflattering bias about them held by many westerners.

Organizationally, the Church in Africa resembles the American model, but there are clearly cultural differences. As the Church grows, it is not unreasonable to assume that it will become more particularly African in its forms.

The General Church is more conservative than either of the other New Church organizations. Not only is it centralized and hierarchical, but it does not ordain women. This is a point of contention for some members of the Church. In 1988 an office of outreach was established, and the Church has strengthened this work since then. Currently, the director has established the goal of growth rate of 10 percent a year within ten years. Obviously, it is too early to make an assessment.

WORSHIP AND RITUALS

All three of these organizations have traditional patterns of worship and rituals that are Protestant in origin. Worship includes prayer, readings, singing, and a sermon. A copy of the Bible or the Word is placed on the altar, and it is opened at the beginning of the service. Lessons are read, and a sermon is preached. While the two congregational organizations may or may not use Swedenborg's writings in their services, the General Church always reads from the "writings" and refers to them in sermons. Often in small congregations, talks for children are included in the service, after which the children leave for Sunday school.

Recently, the two American organizations have developed participatory services, recognizing the importance of an involved laity for the life of the congregation.

Baptism and communion are celebrated as sacraments, and marriages, ordinations, and funerals are celebrated as rites. Funeral services are viewed by outsiders as uplifting, focusing, as they do, on the resurrection of the individual into spiritual life, not their death.

Because Swedenborgian doctrine focuses on the resurrection of the Lord Jesus Christ, and not the crucifixion, the cross is not a dominant symbol in New Church iconography.

OTHER ORGANIZATIONS AND DEVELOPMENTS

In addition to these groups, another internationally organized group was founded in 1937, called The Lord's New Church. It was established by former members of the General Church, who came from the United States, the Netherlands, and South Africa. In contrast to other Swedenborgian organizations, they believe that the writings of Swedenborg are not only divine, but they also have an internal or spiritual sense. As they interpret Swedenborg's writings, this sense becomes more and more apparent to an individual as he or she progresses in the process of regeneration. Until quite recently this group was organizationally unstable. Today it has about 1,000 members, primarily in Southern Africa, although the headquarters is in Pennsylvania.

The largest of the independently organized national New Church associations is the New Church of Southern Africa. Established in 1911, by a black South African, David Mooki (1876–1927), who had found a copy of *True Christianity* in a second-hand bookstore, it came under the umbrella of British Conference for almost 50 years. In 1970 it separated from Conference, and for 20 years was under the strong leadership of the founder's son, Obed S.D. Mooki (1919–1990). When he died in 1990, there were approximately 25,000 members. A schism occurred during the transition from a family dynasty to a more impersonal and democratic structure. Today the main group has approximately 15,000 members in 90 congregations, and the splinter group has approximately 5,000 members. Despite the problems this group suffered, they remain the largest single New Church organization in the world.

Four factors may account for the preeminence of the New Church of Southern Africa among Swedenborgian organizations: first, it is African; second, it was established almost 100 years ago by an indigenous African, with energy, vision, and an abiding commitment to the teaching of the New Church; third, at its inception it had a strong organization with a day school and its own theological school, a school that still exists; fourth, this organization had the good fortune to be the dominant partner in a merger with another religious body in South Africa, the Ethiopian Catholic Church in Zion in 1961. As a result of that merger a church with 5,000 adult members suddenly became a church with 25,000 members.

Independent Swedenborgian New Church organizations exist in the Czech Republic, Kenya, Korea, the Philippines, Russia, and Sri Lanka. The total affiliation of New Church organizations worldwide is approximately 50,000.

The relatively small size of this religion, when compared to other NRMs that survived their eighteenth century origins, may be attributed to the role played by the charisma of the book rather than charisma embodied in a person. Another factor may be the nondogmatic nature of the message. Swedenborg's teachings clearly argue that a person's salvation is not dependant upon the acceptance of his doctrines. This may affect both the zeal of the recruiter and the individuals being recruited. In any case, the number of people affected by his religious writings since 1749 and the publication of the first volume of *Secrets of Heaven* is incalculable.

THE SWEDENBORGIAN MOVEMENT'S CULTURAL IMPACT

The Swedenborgian Movement had a considerable impact on the world beyond the organizational context. The primary focus of this chapter has been an examination of the man, his message, and the institutional response to his work. But the noninstitutional response was considerable. The writers and artists who engaged Swedenborg's new spirituality were among the most creative and revolutionary makers of the modern era. Perhaps they were already pioneers; nonetheless, when they read Swedenborg, his appreciation of the spiritual either opened their eyes or opened them more widely, and they saw the world in a new and deeper way.

The English painter-poet William Blake (1757–1827) drew inspiration from Swedenborg's spiritual visions to create his own—from his *Songs of Innocence and Experience,* to his *Marriage of Heaven and Hell,* and *Jerusalem.* Blake was an artist who drew his audience inward to a world fashioned by mind and spirit. He crafted a world from the mind's eye, not from the natural world.[43] The American short story writer Edgar A. Poe (1809–1849) fashioned his famous tale "The Fall of the House of Usher" from a passage in Swedenborg's *Heaven and Hell,* number 528. In a discussion of the false idea that nurturing spirituality requires the renunciation of the world, Swedenborg writes, "This is because living an inner life and not an outer life at the same time is like living in a house without a foundation, that gradually either settles or develops gaping cracks or totters until it collapses."[44] Joseph Sheridan Le Fanu (1814–1873) the Irish sensational fiction writer did likewise in his work *Wylder's Hand* in which he used a discussion by Swedenborg concerning the fate of murderers in the afterlife to construct the plot.[45] The study of the religious works of Swedenborg was part of the intellectual development of the American poet Walt Whitman (1819–1892), the American landscape artist George Inness (1825–1894), the developer of European experimental psychology Gustav T. Fechner (1801–1887), and the father of American psychology William James (1842–1910).

All of these men used the spiritual insights and psychological truths found in Swedenborg's writings to present alternative views of the human mind and reality in their works. Their efforts and those of others transformed the understanding of history; external events were no longer believed to be as powerful in shaping human events as the world of motive and intention living within.

CONTROVERSIES AND ISSUES

Swedenborg's religious teachings challenge both traditional Christianity and radical empiricism. Therefore, it is not surprising that almost as soon as his works began to be published they became controversial. Many who read them were uncertain how to judge his experiences and his message. Some who read them found genuine truth and a vision of the Lord within, others were certain that these writings were the product of a deranged mind. Today, the same divergent responses occur. It is almost impossible to resolve such differences, because what is considered evidence from one perspective is dismissed from the other.

Swedenborg was clearly aware that such controversies would arise from his claims. He wrote in the first volume of *Secrets of Heavens:*

> Many will claim, I realize, that no one can talk to spirits and angels as long as bodily life continues, or that I am hallucinating, or that I circulate such stories in order to play on people's credulity, but none of this worries me, I have seen, I have heard, I have felt.[46]

The first world-historic figure to engage Swedenborg's vision was none other than the German philosopher Immanuel Kant (1724–1804). His published a response to his reading *Secrets of Heaven* in 1766, called *Dreams of a Spirit Seer.* Published anonymously, it directly challenged Swedenborg's claim to have seen, heard, and felt spiritual or metaphysical reality. Kant wrote that Swedenborg's complete works were "nonsense" and that he should be sent to a madhouse.[47] This accusation impacted Swedenborg's reputation for almost 240 years.

An article by John Johnson published in the *British Journal of Psychiatry* in 1994 reopened the discussion of Swedenborg's psychosis. Thus, it is clear that this issue is as alive today as it was 200 years ago. The problem is a question of what is accepted as evidence. The gulf between those who are willing to entertain Swedenborg's claims and those who are not is extremely broad. Huston Smith, a noted scholar of religion, attempted to narrow the divide in a 2001 Ingersoll Lecture at Harvard. Smith's lecture was titled "Intimations of Immortality."[48] Smith's acceptance of the reality of Swedenborg's clairvoyant experiences was an attempt to bolster Swedenborg's claims.

Interestingly enough, Swedenborg, himself, argued that the controversy was insoluble. His explanation is grounded on the necessity to preserve human freedom with regard to spiritual things. He writes in Divine Providence that "it is a law of divine providence that a person should act in freedom according to reason.... The Lord therefore guards human freedom as a person does the apple of his eye."[49]

Needless to say, today, human freedom is as suspect as the idea of immortality. Nonetheless, religion continues to thrive in the postmodern world of the third millennium.

THE FUTURE

There is no question about it, religion thrives in the world, but it does not thrive equally everywhere. The same is true for Swedenborgianism. While the focus of this chapter is on the history of the different long-standing New Church organizations, future growth of the New Church appears to be in developing nations around the world. Two Swedenborgian organizations, the General Church and The Lord's New Church, have expanded their efforts in this area. Both organizations are international in scope, and the General Church has demonstrated an overall pattern of slow growth since its founding. Recently the Lord's New Church had opportunities for growth in Eastern Europe, particularly in the Ukraine, while sustaining congregations in the United States and South Africa.

Over the past 20 years the General Church assisted the development of Swedenborgianism in Africa, Asia, Eastern Europe, and South America. Some of this work involved the expansion of activities in locations where the Church was already in existence. In other areas those who found Swedenborg's religious writings independently of one another made contact with the Church, and a relationship developed. As a result of this work, congregations developed in Brazil, Ghana, the Ivory Coast, Kenya, the Philippines, Togo, and Sri Lanka. Within the last year Swedenborgian organizations made contacts with individuals in China interested in developing Swedenborgianism there. The story of the development of the New Church in each of these localities has its own particularities. Nonetheless, each of them represents opportunities for church growth for the future.

CONCLUSION

Swedenborgianism did not begin like most founded religions with a charismatic leader; it began instead with the *charisma of the book,* offering human beings the opportunity to freely and rationally know a loving and visible God. Its foundation seems secure, but the process of growth has been slow. This is because the unfolding of a religion of the charisma of the book requires rational reflection. If after such reflection assent is given to the vision of the New Church, it has an enduring strength, because what is loved is sustained not by mysteries but by rationally understood truths. Such a faith is well suited to the needs of the modern world.

While Swedenborg's vision will not appeal to or persuade convinced naturalists or atheists, or those content with their faith, it does appeal to seekers, both in the West and in developing nations. Swedenborg himself did not have much hope for the development of the New Church in Europe, where scientific materialism, even in his day, had taken root. Today, it is even stronger. But he did have faith that the New Church would develop among what he called the Gentiles, or people who in his day were not part of the Christian world. In *Divine Providence,* number 322, Swedenborg writes, "I make these statements about Christians because non-Christians pay more attention to God than Christians do, because their religion is in their life." [50] It is not surprising, therefore, that when Swedenborg's religious writings are discovered by Christians or Gentiles who pay attention to God, their message is often welcomed and embraced.

Current demographic trends in the world seem to be favoring the growth of what Swedenborg called the Gentile nations, in contrast to the former Christian nations in Europe where populations are in decline. If birth rates are any indication, many European countries appear not to have faith in the future. Religious people, however, have a faith in the future, because they have a vision of eternal life. Swedenborg's religious writings offer a clear and detailed vision of eternal life, as well as a straightforward message about how to get there.

NOTES

1. Emanuel Swedenborg, *True Christianity* (West Chester, PA: Swedenborg Foundation, 1996), number 508. Note that all references in Swedenborg's works refer to paragraph numbers and not page numbers. Thus, they are the same in every edition.

2. Many Swedenborgians prefer to refer to their church and their religion as the New Church, because Swedenborg refers to the Church of the New Jerusalem, as mentioned in Revelation, as the symbolic embodiment of the New Christianity.

3. Listed in Jonathan S. Rose et al., eds., *Emanuel Swedenborg: Essays for the New Century Edition of His Life, Work, and Impact* (West Chester, PA: Swedenborg Foundation, 2005), 402–505.

4. Emanuel Swedenborg, *Arcana Coelestia* [New title: *Secrets of Heaven* forthcoming in Swedenborg Foundation's New Century Edition] (West Chester, PA: Swedenborg Foundation, 1997), number 68. Note all references in Swedenborg's works refer to paragraph numbers and not page numbers. Thus they are the same in every edition. Note that the Swedenborg Foundation has undertaken a New Century Edition with new translations, introductions, and some new titles. New titles will also be given in this chapter.)

5. Those interested could explore some of the following biographies: George Trobridge, *A Life of Emanuel Swedenborg: With a Popular Exposition of His Philosophical and Theological Teachings* (London: The Swedenborg Society, 1920); Signe Toksvig, *Emanuel Swedenborg: Scientist and Mystic* (New Haven: Yale University Press, 1948); Cyriel O. Sigstedt, *The Swedenborg Epic: The Life and Works of Emanuel Swedenborg* (New York: Bookman Associates, 1952); Ernst Benz, *Emanuel Swedenborg: Visionary Savant in the Age of Reason* (1948), trans. Nicolas Goodrick-Clarke (West Chester, PA: Swedenborg Foundation, 2002); Rose et al., eds., *Emanuel Swedenborg: Essays for the New Century;* Lars Bergquist, *Swedenborg's Secret,* (1999), trans. Kurt P. Nemitz (London: Swedenborg Society, 2005).

6. This was not at all unusual and was one of the primary means of publication in the eighteenth century. Another method was to gather funds from subscribers, who then received the published copies.

7. Included among his inventions were a submarine and an airplane.

8. In his outline Swedenborg indicated this was to be a 17-part work, but in the end he published studies of only four of the bodies' systems and studies of the organs of taste, smell, and touch. Studies of the remaining senses, the reproductive system, and discussions of "The Fiber," as well as something called "Rational Psychology," were left in manuscript form.

9. Emanuel Swedenborg, *Journal of Dreams,* trans. J.J. Garth Wilkinson (New York: Swedenborg Foundation, 1977), number 54.

10. Ibid., number 19.

11. Ibid., number 180.

12. Alfred Acton, *Introduction to the Word Explained* (Bryn Athyn, PA: Academy of the New Church, 1927), 126.

13. Swedenborg by this time was a well-known author in Sweden and in Europe. His works were reviewed in internationally respected journals. At the time of his retirement from the Board of Mines, he was one of very few intellectual Swedes with an international reputation.

14. The original note appears on the first page of Swedenborg's handwritten manuscript of his Bible index of Isaiah and Genesis. See Acton, *Introduction to the Word Explained,* 127, n. 3.

15. Ibid., 128. The fact that he began a new Bible index with the spiritual sense included is cited as evidence. An explanation of the spiritual sense will be taken up in the section on Doctrine.

16. Jonathan S. Rose, "Swedenborg's Garden of Theology," in *Emanuel Swedenborg: Essays,* 61, n. 20.

17. The relationship between Immanuel Kant and Emanuel Swedenborg is intriguing and complex. It would appear that Kant felt compelled to ridicule Swedenborg and his metaphysics, in order to ensure a place for his own philosophical enterprise. He wrote a book about Swedenborg and metaphysics in 1766 entitled *Dreams of a Spirit Seer.* See the attempt of Gregory Johnson to clarify it.

18. See the title page of *Delitiae Sapientiae de Amore Conjugiali* ... Amsterdam, 1768.

19. For details of these clairvoyant experiences see any of the biographies listed above. One involves Swedenborg seeing Stockholm while he was on the west coast of Sweden 400 miles away as discussed above. Another involves Swedenborg telling the Queen of Sweden something that only her deceased brother knew, and another describes how Swedenborg helped a widow find a receipt hidden by her husband. It was Frülein von Knobloch who asked Kant to comment on them. Although he gave a favorable account of Swedenborg to her, later he wrote a satire of Swedenborg entitled, *Dreams of a Spirit Seer.* A discussion of this small work is found in some biographies of Swedenborg and in Jane Williams-Hogan, "Emanuel Swedenborg," in *Dictionary of Gnosis and Western Esotericism,* ed. Wouter Hanegraaff et al. (Leiden, NL: Brill, 2005), 1096–1105.

20. See the title page of *Vera Christiana Religio* I & II (Amsterdam, 1771).

21. Sigstedt, *Swedenborg Epic,* 431, 432.

22. Emanuel Swedenborg, *Heaven and Hell* (West Chester, PA: Swedenborg Foundation, 2002), number 1.

23. Ibid., number 1.

24. Emanuel Swedenborg, *Divine Love and Wisdom* (West Chester, PA: Swedenborg Foundation, 2003), number 4.

25. Emanuel Swedenborg, *True Christian Religion* [*True Christianity*] (West Chester, PA: Swedenborg Foundation, 1996), number 163 (2).

26. Emanuel Swedenborg, *Other Planets,* in *Miscellaneous Theological Works* (West Chester, PA: Swedenborg Foundation, 1996). See this work for a discussion of the human inhabitants of other planets in this and other solar systems.

27. Swedenborg, *True Christian Religion* [*True Christianity*], number 71:2.

28. Swedenborg, *Divine Love and Wisdom,* number 1.

29. Swedenborg, *True Christian Religion* [*True Christianity*], number 247.

30. Emanuel Swedenborg, *Divine Providence* (West Chester, PA: Swedenborg Foundation, 2003), number 254.

31. Swedenborg, *Heaven and Hell*, number 304.

32. Ibid., number 445.

33. Emanuel Swedenborg, *Conjugial Love* [*Marriage Love*] (London: Swedenborg Society, 1989), number 457. The General Convention, which ordains homosexuals into their ministry, interprets Swedenborg's teachings on marriage to apply to the marriage of good and truth within an individual.

34. Ibid., number 68.

35. Rose, *Emanuel Swedenborg: Essays,* 66.

36. Swedenborg uses the term *ecclesiae* to refer to the different religions with their different revelations that have played a central role in the salvation history of humankind, even though the term as commonly used has a Christian connotation.

37. It should be pointed out that the judgments of all of the churches mentioned in the Word have been spiritual in nature.

38. Efforts to organize and publish his works were made by readers of Swedenborg's writings in Sweden during the 1770s and 1780s. They were harassed by officials and ridiculed by the press. The absence of religious freedom in Sweden led these efforts to go "underground" where they remained until 1874 when the State officially permitted Swedenborgians and other minority religions the right to organize. They did so immediately. Today there are two different Swedenborgian organizations in Sweden with four congregations.

39. This idea was first developed by the author in a 1997 paper presented at the American Academy of Religion Annual Meeting in San Francisco, CA, entitled: "Moving Beyond Weber: The Role of Written Texts in the Founding of the Swedenborgian Church."

40. Recent concerns about church growth have led the organization to implement the centralization of some church functions.

41. Quote taken from an article by Jane Williams-Hogan and David B. Eller, "Swedenborgian Churches and Related Institutions in Great Britain, the United States, and Canada," in *Emanuel Swedenborg: Essays,* ed. Rose et al., 304.

42. Quote taken from note 102 on page 304 in *Emanuel Swedenborg: Essays,* 205.

43. William Blake and his wife, Catherine, signed the roll at the First General Conference in London in 1789.

44. Swedenborg, *Heaven and Hell,* 528.

45. Ibid., 462:b[6].

46. Swedenborg, *Arcana Coelestia* [*Secrets of Heaven*], number 68.

47. Immanuel Kant, *Dreams of a Spirit Seer Illustrated by Dreams of Metaphysics,* trans. E. F. Goerwitz, ed. Frank Sewall (London: Swan Sonnenschein, 1900).

48. Huston Smith, "Intimations of Immortality: Three Case Studies" (*Harvard Divinity School Bulletin, The Ingersoll Lecture for 2001–02*: 12–16.

49. Swedenborg, *Divine Providence,* number 97.

50. Ibid., number 322.

FURTHER READING

Acton, Alfred. *Introduction to the Word Explained.* Bryn Athyn, PA: Academy of the New Church, 1927.

Benz, Ernst. *Emanuel Swedenborg: Visionary Savant in the Age of Reason* (1948). Translated by Nicolas Goodrick-Clarke. West Chester, PA: Swedenborg Foundation, 2002.

Bergquist, Lars. *Swedenborg's Secret* (1999). Translated by Kurt P. Nemitz. London: Swedenborg Society, 2005.

Kant, Immanuel. *Dreams of a Spirit Seer Illustrated by Dreams of Metaphysics.* Translated by E. F. Goerwitz. Edited by Frank Sewall. London: Swan Sonnenschein, 1900.

Rose, Jonathan S., et al., eds. *Emanuel Swedenborg: Essays for the New Century Edition of His Life, Work, and Impact.* West Chester, PA: Swedenborg Foundation, 2005.

Sigstedt, Cyriel O. *The Swedenborg Epic: The Life and Works of Emanuel Swedenborg.* New York: Bookman Associates, 1952.

Swedenborg, Emanuel. *True Christianity.* West Chester, PA: Swedenborg Foundation, 1996.

Swedenborg, Emanuel. *Arcana Coelestia.* [New title: *Secrets of Heaven,* forthcoming in Swedenborg Foundation's New Century Edition.] West Chester, PA: Swedenborg Foundation, 1997.

Swedenborg, Emanuel. *Heaven and Hell.* West Chester, PA: Swedenborg Foundation, 2002.

Toksvig, Signe. *Emanuel Swedenborg: Scientist and Mystic.* New Haven: Yale University Press, 1948.

Trobridge, George. *A Life of Emanuel Swedenborg: With a Popular Exposition of His Philosophical and Theological Teachings.* London: The Swedenborg Society, 1920.

Spiritualism

Robert S. Cox

In 1848, a new and quintessentially American system of beliefs began to spread from the heart of the Burned-Over District of New York State, the region that for a generation witnessed scorching religious revivals. At a time when the constant pressure of racial, class, and sectional strife, social and geographic flux, and the rise of industrialization left many Americans wondering whether the seams of their nation were coming unstitched, Modern Spiritualism offered a satisfying alternative to the evangelical settlement. While the revivals attracted millions and spawned innumerable groups devoted to social, political, and religious reform, many Americans were left in their wake dismayed, uncertain as to which way to turn, unable or unwilling to settle into any denominational conformity. "To join the Congregational Church," wrote one such man, "was saying, I am one of the 'elect.' To join the Universalists, was saying, God will take care of his offspring. Joining either of the others, was saying, we will try."[1] Exhausted by the "war of words" waged by competing revivalists, some turned inward to ask "who of all these parties are right, or, are they all wrong together?"[2]

For the writer and reformer William Denton, the answer was clear: "these churches of the living God, so called, are shams every one." Far from signifying the unification of the Christian body, the many churches were seen by individuals like Denton as signs of utter and irreparable rupture. Far from addressing the fraying of the union, evangelical competition and the "antagonism of sects and creeds" seemed signs of the sort of social division and moral decay that threatened to leave families, communities, and even entire nations, as the Tennessean Jesse B. Ferguson wrote, "severed in their aims, in devotion to false views of man's Spiritual interests," severed by the strivings of "men aiming professedly, at the same ends, while industriously engaged in each others injury or destruction."[3]

In the 1850s, Denton and Ferguson joined a growing number of Americans who rejected the sectarian impulse in favor of the more radical, Spiritualist approach to restoring unity in the spiritual body. Rooted in the belief that the dead had reestablished communication with the living, Spiritualism was a "perfectly democratic religion" for its believers, an "emphatically ... American religion" that reflected the progressive genius of the new nation.[4] Less hierarchical than Mormonism and Seventh-day Adventism, the other major religions to originate in the Burned-Over District, Spiritualism emphasized the authority of individual conscience, as opposed to the authority of the Bible and clergy, and it promised healing for the divisions tearing through the American body politic and hope that an age of harmony and unity had arrived. Balancing sensational performance against a penetrating philosophy, Spiritualism was like a pop-cultural amoeba, distilling a mixture of high culture and low, absorbing the language of scientific empiricism, occultism, and social reform in the course of emerging as the fastest growing religion in mid-nineteenth century America.

MULTIPLE ORIGINS

Placed into a magnetic trance by an itinerant phrenologist in December 1843, a young shoemaker's assistant from Poughkeepsie, New York, looked out over the audience before him and peered through their bodies as if they were sheets of glass. Inside, their organs shone in distinctive hues, every tissue glowing, every muscle, tendon, and vein illuminated. Their very thoughts were visible to his exalted vision, licking like flames at their heads, bright "like the breath of diamonds." This shoemaker, Andrew Jackson Davis, saw not only the anatomical structures of bodies, but "their indwelling essences and vitalic elements," their personalities, pathologies, and pasts. He saw disease and illness, and divined how to cure it, and, more importantly, he saw the anatomy of the soul as well as the body. In rapport with nature, Davis grasped the innermost secrets of life, the hidden virtues of plants, the physical structures of the earth buried beneath strata and time.[5]

The world that opened to Davis that day simultaneously marked the end of one era and the beginning of another. Davis's experiences and his newly discovered ability to cure the ill were a late instance in a century-long history of remarkable physical and mental manifestations associated with the sleeping body. In both the popular press and medical literature, somnambulists (sleepwalkers and mesmeric subjects) had frequently been noted for their preternatural abilities to diagnose and cure diseases by sight or touch, for their hypersensibility or insensibility, for their abilities to see through solid objects, read minds, travel mentally outside the body, and deliver fluent lectures on esoteric subjects, and, on rare occasions, for their capacity to see and converse with the dead. Davis's experiences as a magnetic subject would have been broadly familiar to Americans in the 1840s, but as he began not only to describe what he saw, but to write in his flowing prose about what his visions meant, Davis took the first tentative steps to creating what many would call a new era, the new dispensation of Modern Spiritualism. As a clairvoyant physician, mental explorer, and visionary, Davis learned that he too could see and converse with the invisible hosts of the dead and that behind our daily lives lay a deeper reality, a cosmic infrastructure uniting all creation.[6]

Four years later, while Davis was occupied in healing, writing, and lecturing on this new cosmology, the home of John D. Fox in Hydesville, New York, became the scene of equally startling revelations. Throughout the winter of 1847–1848, the spartan home had been afflicted by showers of disembodied raps sounding forth from the walls and floorboards and occasionally from thin air, often centered on Fox's teenaged daughters, Margaret and Kate. The nights were punctuated by unseen hands brushing past in the darkness and tables bustling about on their own, as mysterious in their intentions as the raps. Unable to determine the cause of these phenomena and unable to deter them, John and his wife slid gradually toward despair, praying that "if this thing was of the devil, that it might be removed from them."[7]

But Kate and Margaret remained unfazed, perhaps even amused by the noises and attention they attracted from their neighbors. Rather than recoil in fear or modesty, the girls delighted in the raps, until one night Kate took the bold step of addressing them directly. Following a particularly loud series of raps on March 31, 1848, she cried out "Here Mr. Split-foot," snapping her fingers, "do as I do!" and snap for snap, the thin air rapped back. Witnesses to this scene were stunned, surmising immediately that some intelligence must lay behind the knockings, an intelligence that could hear, understand, and respond to the spoken word. By posing a series of simple questions, responded to with an equally simple telegraphic code of raps signifying yes or no, the girls soon deduced that the source of the commotion was not some holy angel or fearful demon, but the spirit of a murdered man with an uncanny knack for clairvoyantly determining the number of Fox children (dead as well as living) and for revealing the names and dates of demise of their neighbors' relatives. Proof that the raps were from the dead came, as it would for years, through recitation of the drab details of family names and private histories, the spirit rapping out what could be known only to the most intimate or omniscient friends. It was as if a "spiritual telegraph line" had been strung between this world and the next, and under certain conditions "impossible for mortals yet to comprehend," the immortal spirits of the immaterial world had begun to use the "forces of spiritual and human magnetism, in chemical affinity" to commune with the living and divulge the secrets of the life beyond. In this bridge between natural and supernatural, material and immaterial, the barrier of death at last was breached.[8]

When Leah, the eldest Fox daughter, discovered that she too could elicit raps, the family followed the spirits' advice and moved to the nearest big city, Rochester, to take their spiritual demonstrations to the wider public. From almost the first rap, the Foxes met resistance from the orthodox and skeptical. Although the reality of spirits was widely accepted in popular culture, the claim of direct communication with them smacked of the sort of "enthusiasm" associated with religious charlatans and evoked fears of social and political disorder. In Rochester, a skeptical, even hostile crowd confronted the Foxes, and to prove themselves, the girls agreed to perform a public "test." In an exercise that was repeated often for public mediums (those who communed with spirits for members of the public, usually for pay), a committee of respectable citizens gathered at Corinthian Hall—the site of many antislavery and women's rights meetings—to determine once and for all if the young Foxes were telling the truth. Prodding, probing, scrutinizing the girls from all angles and in all positions, inspecting their clothing, "even their shoes, stockings, and under-gar-ments," forcing them to stand on insulating pillows in case some electrical means were employed to produce the raps, the committee (actually three successive com-mittees) finally pronounced themselves perplexed, unable to determine how the sounds were made. The Foxes were vindicated, at least for those who would believe.[9]

Like a chemical reaction in which a tiny seed introduced into a saturated solution triggers a rapid crystallization, Spiritualism took shape. In Rochester, where the fires of evangelical fervor had repeatedly flared, crowds thronged to the Foxes' demonstra-tions, coming for entertainment or enlightenment, out of curiosity, scorn, hope, or fear. Throughout the region where Davis first saw his visions and the Foxes first heard the raps, an intense interest in the afterlife materialized, shaped by theories of somnambulism, animal magnetism, phrenology, and clairvoyance, primed by the years of spiritual threshing and revival. As the Foxes toured cities such as Auburn, Buffalo, and New York City, they earned national attention, and their longer tour of the Midwest spread Spiritualist flames across the heartland.

Perhaps more importantly, as the Foxes toured and a nascent spiritual lecture cir-cuit began to spread word through a network of lecturers, people not only tested the spirits, they tested mediumship itself. New mediums sprang up spontaneously in many parts of the nation, and a corresponding spirit of innovation animated the search for more efficient, or more dramatic, means of communicating with the dead. The yes and no rapping code gave way to more expressive alphabetic codes, to table tilting, to automatic writing, to spirit drawing, to spirit music, to slate writing, to full body materialization, to direct impressions scratched onto the body, to photographs, and to a variety of ingenious mechanical devices for receiving spirit impressions, including the planchette and spiritoscope. At one end of the spectrum were mediums who could easily be confused with stage magicians, performing rope escapes for pay-ing audiences with "spirit" assistance, while other mediums were difficult to distin-guish from animal magnetists, clairvoyant physicians, or phrenologists were it not for their references to spirit communion. In a few cases, mediums like William Denton occasionally dispensed with references to the spirits altogether. The situation was further complicated by an unknown, but probably larger, number of private mediums, who communicated with spirits for friends and family and whose methods we still know very little about. While public mediums garnered attention on stage, it seems likely that as many or more individuals gained exposure to Spiritualist practice through the private séance, gathering around a medium in small "circles" to receive messages from the departed.

The proliferation in the technology of spirit communication is just one indication of how significant communication was for Spiritualists. The phenomenal growth of the movement, they noted, was attributable to the unique mixture of the philosoph-ical speculations of visionaries like Davis combined with the phenomena produced by mediums like the Foxes. Although admitting that their ranks included a few "enthusiasts, fanatics and impostors," Spiritualists insisted that theirs was a decidedly rational faith and that they took a radically empirical approach to spiritual knowledge.[10] While "mainstream" religions relied solely on faith in the written word of the Bible or church authority, spirit phenomena provided tangible evidence of all that was outlined in their philosophy. Simply put, they argued, "Spiritualism *works*."[11] Mediums could see disease directly and cure it. "Ours, too, is a generation seeking after signs," the New England Spiritualists Association claimed, "and we have them in the movements of tables and chairs by invisible power—in the music from pianoes, drums and trumpets, where no visible performer is near—in audible voices—in distinct vision of the departed, and in many other ways." The physical phenomena, in other words, were nothing less than "the foundation of the whole philosophy," and without such empirical proofs, the Association wrote, "we *sink* back on *faith alone,* deprived of a *tangible basis.*" Offering the surety that for many was lacking in the evangelical conversion experience, Spiritualists therefore urged the skeptical public to set aside their orthodox preconceptions and "come try" the spirits for themselves, to make their own decisions about the reality of what they heard and saw.[12]

And try they did. The Spiritualist movement grew, even though it had no formal structure, no agreed upon rituals, few leaders, and precious little agreement on whether it was a religious movement. By 1857, the former Universalist minister Uriah Clark estimated that there were nearly 1,000,000 Spiritualists in the United States—3,000,000 if one included inquirers—while other estimates, surely too optimistic, ran as high as 11,000,000. Within three years of the first raps at Hydesville, Spiritualism had spread to England and France, and within a decade, as far as Russia, Italy, and the Caribbean.[13]

SPIRITUALISM AND REFORM

Historians often explain the common threads running through an otherwise diverse religious and social movement by citing a deep and abiding predilection among the spirits (and Spiritualists) for social reform. Indeed, social reform and Spiritualism were often linked, and many of the most prominent white antislavery agitators were Spiritualists, including William Lloyd Garrison, Sarah and Angelina Grimke, and Gerrit Smith. The long-time abolitionists and feminists Isaac and Amy Post, for example, were among the earliest and most avid supporters of the Fox sisters, and Isaac Post soon experimented with his own mediumistic potential, publishing an important collection of spirit messages that bore a strident reformist stamp. In conversations with the spirits of public figures such as George Washington, Thomas Jefferson, Benjamin Franklin, and Elias Hicks, Post's reformist beliefs were confirmed by these great figures of American history, perched in their heavenly home. A repentant John C. Calhoun, for example, bitterly lamented his role in bolstering the slave power, while Washington regretted his militarism, and many others condemned sectarianism and the spirit of division that stalked the land. A small cadre of reform-minded ministers also took up mediumship, particularly Universalists, Quakers, and Unitarians, with a smattering of Presbyterians and Methodists, and antisectarian reformers like William Denton were also numerous.[14]

To explain why spirit communication and social reform might be linked, historians adapted the work of anthropologist I. M. Lewis, who theorized that spirit possession functions as an instrument for subordinate and oppressed members of society, particularly women, to challenge the normal relations of social power. Through possession, Lewis argued, women especially claim the attention and care of their husbands and other authority figures, and they sometimes can inflict financial damage, if nothing else, upon their oppressors. Furthermore, in receiving treatment for their illnesses, women forge a sense of community with fellow female members of healing cults, and such communities often survive for years, as exorcisms or healing rituals are repeated. Because the spirits speak through them, but are not of them, women give voice to views that would otherwise be socially forbidden. Spirit communication thus becomes a flexible instrument for resisting social oppression in a patriarchal society, an historically sensitive mode of "cultural resistance" that is "an embodied critique of colonial, national, or global hegemonies whose abrasions are deeply, but not exclusively felt by women."[15]

Building upon Lewis's insights, historian Ann Braude explored how the spirits spoke to gender relations in the nineteenth century United States. While noting the ties that Spiritualism had to antislavery, dietary and dress reform, temperance, and medical reforms, it was Braude's insight to call attention to the particularly strong relationship between Spiritualism and early feminism. Early in the Spiritualist movement, women played prominent roles as mediums, lecturers, and writers. Many of them confirmed that the dead believed heartily in gender equity for the living. Braude noted that not all feminists were Spiritualists, but she asserted that all Spiritualists were feminists, and like Lewis, she argued that this was because Spiritualism permitted the expression of radical critiques of gender inequality while adhering, at least on the surface, to Victorian gender norms.[16]

Victorian Americans typically imagined mediums as pious, highly sensitive, and highly strung—all traits then associated with women—and antebellum Spiritualists frequently stated that they waited passively for spirits to speak through them rather than actively calling them forth. At a time when it was controversial for women to address "promiscuous" (mixed sex) crowds, women outnumbered men in the ranks of trance lecturers. These lecturers typically claimed that they did not remember their lectures when they returned to their "normal" state, and sometimes they asserted that they disagreed with the sentiments expressed. In effect, female trance lecturers exploited existing ideologies of femininity (passivity, domesticity) and female capacity (piety, spirituality) to contest women's subordinate status and help shape a new, transformed vision of gender relations. In analogous fashion, Logie Barrow argued that the English working class used spirit communication to further workers' ends in subverting capitalist domination of their lives, while David Hess's studies of Spiritualism in modern Brazil suggest that possession and mediumship can subvert the ordinary relations of power within the patriarchy of the individual family. The spirits thus advocate for the weak, oppressed, and disadvantaged.[17]

However, the notion that mediumship was an instrument for resisting social oppression is complicated by the recognition that many Spiritualist feminists, such as the Grimke sisters, were public figures and controversialists long before they discovered Spiritualism. They confronted gender norms without help from beyond the grave. More subtly, as historian Alex Owen argues, whatever power or authority women gained through mediumship came in a highly circumscribed space—the séance room—and even at that, it was power only over that limited portion of the population who accepted the reality of spirit phenomena. For the rest, it was a source of contempt. As an instrument for advancing their cause, then, mediumship was unnecessary and unnecessarily limiting. Vieda Skultans has gone further, arguing that among Welsh Spiritualists in the 1960s, mediumship may have helped women feel better about their subordinate social position, but did not challenge it. Skultans's work echoes the suspicions of other researchers that a focus on the afterlife among Spiritualists might actually have diverted social action in this life.[18]

It should not be surprising that the range of political and social expression in Spiritualism was as broad as it was in American society at large. Though never as vocal or numerous as the social progressives represented by Post, Denton, or the Grimkes, a distinctively conservative vein can be found coursing through American Spiritualism, and this vein apparently grew in the years after the Civil War. Several antebellum southern Spiritualists, for example, claimed that the spirits supported slavery. Yet the northerner Robert Hare, a chemist and controversialist from Philadelphia, argued that a proper understanding of relations in the spirit world would support his reactionary political, economic, and social agendas. These voices were never as numerous as the progressive voices, but they were not isolated either, and we cannot dismiss them as mere aberrations.[19]

It is important to emphasize that the average Spiritualist seeker and average medium heard little or nothing about politics or social reform. Without wishing to dismiss the significance of reform in Spiritualism entirely, the content of spirit messages soon reveals just how exceptional figures like Post and Hare were. Spiritualists often voiced their suspicions about mediums who spouted the names of the famous or who transmitted messages that too conveniently aligned with their own perspectives, rejecting the messages along with the medium. The vast majority of messages transmitted by mediums were of a purely personal nature and appeared to most observers at the time—and since—as banal, insipid, or as the writer and reformer Lydia Maria Child suggested, "more disappointing than the golden key which unlocked *nothing;* for they are the merest mass of old rags, saw-dust, and clam-shells."[20] The content of the message, then, was evidently less important than the fact of communication.

SPIRITUALIST FAITH

Called at various times a movement, a philosophy, or a religion; Christian, non-Christian, or anti-Christian; reformist or conservative; occult, scientific, or antiscientific, Spiritualism was all of the above. Rather than defining their faith with respect to any prescribed set of ceremonies or specific creeds that "coerce or cramp the conscience," Uriah Clark suggested, Spiritualists followed "the doctrine of individual liberty and responsibility," living out the "right and duty of every man to seek all the light he needs as his guide, and settle for himself all matters between his own conscience and God."[21]

The "individual liberty" of conscience, of course, meant that Spiritualism would voice competing, confusing, and all too often contradictory claims about the nature of this world and the next. Neither spirits nor mediums were always reliable, as Spiritualists admitted, nor did they always agree, and at times it seemed that the "democratic" assertion that anyone was capable of mediumship meant only that every Spiritualist stuck to their own individual belief. Even prolific Spiritualist writers like Hudson Tuttle and James M. Peebles found it "exceedingly difficult" to characterize their faith. In its "narrowest sense," they concluded, Spiritualism entailed little more than a belief in the ability of the dead to communicate with the living and, by corollary, a belief in the "immortality" of the soul. "They who adopt this," they stated simply, "are Spiritualists." Beyond this basic precept, Spiritualism seemed easier to Tuttle and Peebles to identify by its aims and effects than its ideas, and, even at that, it had many sides. "Considered from its philosophical side," they wrote, Spiritualism "is rationalism; from its scientific side, naturalism; and from its religious side, the embodiment of love to God and man; inciting to purity of intention, holiness of heart, and the highest religious culture. It underlies all genuine reform movements, physiological, educational, social, philanthropic, religious; and, spanning all human interests with holy aim, it seeks to reconstruct society upon the principles of eternal justice,—the principles of equality, charity, and a universal brotherhood."[22]

To take Tuttle and Peebles at their word and discern how Spiritualism could be considered the source of all reform movements, we must move beyond seeing mediumship as an instrument to be wielded by the oppressed and examine in greater detail the points of faith upon which Spiritualists agreed. The multitude of divergent spirit voices still produced a degree of harmony. While no beliefs truly characterized all Spiritualists, most adherents agreed on a few fundamental principles, including the existence of a Divine Spirit, the "universal brotherhood" of mankind, the unceasing progression of the soul after death, and a belief that Hell was a condition of mind, rather than a physical place.[23] Fleshing out the implications of these concepts preoccupied Spiritualist writers and lecturers from the beginning, and these concerns were the subjects of dozens of thick descriptions of the afterlife in books, pamphlets, and articles, as well as the topic of endless discussions of the relationship between living and dead.

The pioneer of thick description was the visionary Andrew Jackson Davis. Based upon his psychic visions of the Summerland (heaven, the afterlife), Davis developed a "Harmonial philosophy" with which he contended that the "spiritual aspirations" of men and women would bring them "into harmonial relations with each other," and would result in the establishment of "one common brotherhood, where angelic wisdom and order can be freely unfolded." For Davis and many of his readers, this meant that they must reject sectarian Christianity as practiced by the established Protestant churches and also reject "every thing which is uselessly mysterious and supernatural." To replace all of this, Davis offered a vaguely Christian rationality that addressed "the cultivated heart through the expanded understanding" and that drew rhetorically upon modern natural science. While Davis argued that Jesus appealed to the "goodness" in civilized minds, he believed that in order to bring about an "era of Love," the modern "age of impulse" now demanded "an age of Reason" and "a 'Philosophy' which Jesus *did not* furnish ... a 'revelation' to the faculty of REASON, which the Bible *does not* contain." Reason and emotion, rationality and intuition were integral parts of Harmonialism, while blind faith and orthodoxy were not.[24]

The clearest expression of Harmonialism came in Spiritualist discussions of the progression of the soul after death and accounts of the geography of the Summerland. Recalling the visions of the Swedish mystic Emanuel Swedenborg, but differing in critical details, Davis described the Summerland as a series of concentric "spheres" within which numerous circles of spirits were drawn together by "affinity," or commonalty of interest, emotional connection, or moral condition. In the earliest Spiritualist accounts of the afterlife, the spheres were undifferentiated, populated by every deceased individual who shared a more or less equal level of spiritual development. Spiritualist visionaries differed on the number of spheres—few were permitted to glimpse them all—however, they agreed that the mortal world represented the lowest of these spheres and that death freed the soul to progress from this sphere to the next higher one. Rejecting Swedenborg's contention that mortals were the degraded remnants of a golden age, Harmonialists maintained that after the spirit was liberated from its body and its senses were unshackled, it embarked upon an irresistible upward progression, acquiring spiritual knowledge and wisdom. As they grew and perfected themselves, spirits ascended through the successive spheres to approach ever nearer to the Deity, spatially and spiritually.

In Harmonial philosophy (and again echoing Swedenborg), the mortal world was more than simply the lowest rung of spiritual development. It was a "type" of the spiritual, with every feature having "correspondence" with deeper realities in the eternal and spiritual spheres above. The "spirit land is but a counterpart of earth," a spirit in Baltimore informed the Presbyterian minister-turned-medium, Francis H. Smith, and "there is no condition natural, that there is not a corresponding spiritual and mental." Another spirit informed Abraham Pierce in Maine that the "physical body is but a fac-simile of the spiritual body, with all its senses and constituted parts... ordained and fitted to work in a physical or outward form." Nothing took place in the mortal world without ramifications beyond, and, conversely, events in the spirit spheres invariably echoed in the mortal, even in the individual body. Spirits from higher spheres communed with beings lower down, showering them with a steady influx of wisdom gained through their expanded spiritual sight. Several mediums reported that Benjamin Franklin and other great scientists of the past were actively engaged in devising new inventions and technologies to impart spiritual, and sometimes material, comfort to mortals. The afterlife was a dynamic and evolving place, and spirits engaged daily and hourly with the mortal world.[25]

There was, to be sure, continuity between the material and spiritual worlds. Despite their contempt for the physical body, Spiritualists did not reject mortal life. They insisted, in fact, that personal identity was maintained absolutely throughout the spheres, that personal tastes, memories, and attainments acquired in mortal life continued beyond the grave. Spirits were not (w)holy angelic presences so much as friends, neighbors, and relatives who had evolved incrementally in their spiritual consciousness.

In many ways, the spheres in which these liberated souls resided resembled nothing more than airy versions of Victorian American communities, reflecting middle-class tastes and ideals. Spirit homes and institutions were counterparts, and perhaps models, for those on earth. Spirits attended lyceums where they heard lectures from the better minds of the higher spheres, visited galleries to view the greatest works of art, attended concerts of the best musicians, took part in organizations for spiritual uplift and moral reform, and engaged in trades, not for wages as in life, but for the moral benefit that accrued from productive labor. Emphatically, Spiritualists insisted that the nuclear family would be reconstituted in the higher spheres, husband and wife, parent and child drawn together by their mutual "affinities" to live in homes that were counterparts of their tidy mortal homes, and, even more exciting, spirits would consort with those with whom they shared intellectual interests or other concerns while alive, regardless of parentage. Spiritualists even debated, vigorously, whether pets might be found in the afterlife, usually answering in the affirmative that this member of the family circle would also find its place at the heavenly hearth.

Affinity, so powerful a force in the afterlife, had a rich philosophical basis, drawing upon one of the key concepts of the early Spiritualist movement: sympathy. Since antiquity, sympathy had referred to the condition in which two or more individuals shared an emotional state or feeling, a complete sharing of pleasure or pain, but for the philosophers of the Scottish Enlightenment, the seemingly simple connection of feeling took on a new importance. More than just an emotional bond between two individuals, sympathy became the "universal bond of union." For these philosophers, sympathy suggested that the various parts of the world—natural, social, and divine—were enmeshed in reciprocal sets of causal relationships, ensuring that influences upon one part of the natural world would affect other parts, perhaps even all other parts.[26]

Just as Davis began his Spiritualist career by explaining disease and healing, so too did sympathy. Physicians were among the first to employ the concept of sympathy extensively, using it to explain the obscure physiological relationships that seemed to characterize the human body. Before modern theories of infection or nervous action, physicians invoked sympathy to explain how a cut on the hand produced a high fever and how an injury to one part of the body caused pain elsewhere. Although the head and stomach were only indirectly connected, for example, physicians noted that violent pains in the skull produced nausea in the stomach. They were not entirely sure how sympathies worked, but they were certain that sympathies were essential to understanding health and healing. Similarly, sympathy could explain the vexing problem of how an idea conceived in the brain could produce tears, pain, or pleasure. The same force explained how an animal magnetist influenced his subject, how medicines cured ailments, or how an injury sustained by one person could be felt by another: any time two bodies could be seen sharing the same state of feeling, sympathy was involved. Sympathy similarly explained attractions in the inanimate world, describing the relationship between two bodies such as the magnet and the loadstone, and it shaded easily into occult reasoning, providing a ready theoretical basis for astrologers to explain how the planets could influence the body or how lines in the palm could reflect a person's character.

In a key development for Spiritualists, Enlightenment philosophers speculated that sympathy extended beyond the world of physiology and the occult to society, in this world and the next. It was Adam Smith's trenchant analysis of the origins and limits of social bonds that stood as the most influential description of sympathy for antebellum Americans. In his *Theory of Moral Sentiments,* Smith constructed the philosophical scaffolding for a secure and stable social order, arguing that sympathy would be that scaffolding. To sympathize was a natural human tendency, he suggested: we tend naturally to share in the joys of others and to experience the pleasures of friends as if they were our own; when witnessing scenes of grief and distress, our emotions tend naturally to align with those of the sufferer, as when (in his most famous example) the crowd at an execution finds itself swaying to and fro while "gazing at a dancer on the slack rope."[27]

The problem, Smith argued, was that we do not experience sympathetic feelings with the same intensity as the person causing them, nor can we ever truly know another's motives or thoughts. At some level, other people remain inscrutable despite our sympathetic tendencies, and they often act in their own self-interest to the detriment of others, their behavior checked only by an inherent dread of social isolation should their actions be discovered. For sympathy to function in regulating moral behavior, Smith theorized that it required a conscious act to imagine the position of the other, or better yet, to imagine the position of an impartial spectator imaging both self and other. In this act of self-reflection, Smith argued that a lack of "immediate experience" with what others felt forced one to imagine "what we ourselves should feel in the like situation," but imagining what others felt involved turning scrutiny on one's own behavior: one imagined the feelings of others within the social context of oneself. The ultimate check on antisocial behavior was death or, as Smith called it, "the great poison to the happiness, but the great restraint upon the injustice of mankind, which, while it afflicts and mortifies the individual, guards and protects the society."[28]

Critical to Smith's moral sentiments was the concept of circulation. Financial circulation brought individuals together into networks of debts, obligation, and expectation. These networks blocked selfish behavior and forged reciprocal social bonds, while the circulation of sympathies and emotion ensured unity in the community. Yet sympathy had its limits. It was at its most powerful when linking people in close contact, such as families, but the more distant people were from one another, the less effective sympathy would be. Sympathy unified neighborhoods and communities, but the less frequently individuals encountered one another, the less likely they were to develop sympathetic ties. For Smith, the nation was the practical boundary of a sympathetic community, but other writers suggested very different boundaries. For all of these writers, however, the conclusion was straightforward: one must cultivate sympathy to permit society to exist at all.

For antebellum Spiritualists, sympathy held the same hope as it had for Smith, a means for uniting what seemed to be a fragmenting country, of overcoming what seemed to be a proliferation of social chasms between the races, creeds, genders, regions, and classes. While the language of sympathetic union was widespread in the United States, Spiritualists were particularly interested in it, and attempted to foster its circulation. "Oh, the power of sympathy!" one spirit exclaimed, "Mortals, you understand it not! When truly expressed, it flows toward the soul of its recipient in waves of light, which become tangible to the suffering one, and form a bridge over which he may pass to a condition of happiness and peace."[29] The spirits, who sounded utopian, assured mortal listeners that a new dispensation, a new era of happiness and peace would follow. But the surest evidence of the power of sympathy to bind and heal was found in the very visitations of spirits themselves: properly enacted, sympathy was so powerful that it overcame all barriers up to and including the greatest barrier of all, as Adam Smith insisted, the barrier of death.

Feeling keenly the separations of life, Spiritualists offered one means of reasserting the integrity of the body politic, of crafting a stable community in a shifting world. They articulated a theory of community predicated upon the social practice of sympathetic communion, a transcendent nexus of emotion that connected and coordinated all of life and death, but that required concerted effort. "Spiritualism," as one circle of radical Spiritualists determined, "is that which makes you feel that there are others in the great brotherhood of men, whose hearts beat in unison with your own"—that produces the emotion binding members of a community.[30] The spirits who assisted a person were those with whom he or she had powerful bonds in this life, usually family members, close relatives, and intimate friends. They were most tightly connected to the living, and the proof of an intimate connection became the surest test of a medium's authenticity: producing some innocuous sign such as a name or date of birth that verified the identity of the spirit was demonstration that the spirit belonged to the living sitter's sympathetic orbit.

If Spiritualists seemed to be reformers, it was because, like reformers, they felt the divisions and inequities of society and, like reformers, they felt compelled to address them. As a voluntary act, sympathy was something to be taken up, exploited, extended, and used to forge connections, and consequently a belief in the spirits propelled social engagement. Abolitionists, feminists, dress reformers, and temperance advocates found in Spiritualism a set of beliefs that was compelling because it offered a vision of society already in the process of being united.

This utopian formulation of Spiritualist sympathy provided a coherent structure to a stunning diversity of practice, however, but it did not persuade everyone, and it barely survived the Civil War. We do not know for certain why sympathetic reasoning declined—the half a million bodies lying dead on Civil War battlefields may have testified to its limitations as a social corrective—but it is noteworthy that with only a few exceptions, African Americans seldom became committed

Spiritualists. Sojourner Truth was a devoted believer and the quixotic Paschal Beverly Randolph ephemerally so, but they were exceptions. Far more typical was Frederick Douglass, who retained a respectful doubt in Spiritualism despite the fervor of so many of his white colleagues. The staunchest community of antebellum Spiritualists of color may have been the resilient circle of French-speaking residents of New Orleans. But in New Orleans the community was based in the free Creole (mixed race) population, a community that enjoyed a marginally higher status in antebellum New Orleans than the "pure African" population, and certainly higher than the most oppressed residents of the state, the enslaved.[31]

The reasons for the reticence of African Americans to take up Spiritualism are complex, but the brutality and corrosion of American race relations surely played a role. The prospect of universal sympathy may have seemed increasingly out of touch for whites after the war, but for African Americans, sympathetic union with whites seldom seemed possible in this life. The Creole spirit circle in New Orleans provides a gauge of what must have been a common experience among African American believers. When the postwar political order in the South was still being contested in the early years of Reconstruction, the circle received a number of optimistic messages from the spirits of their dead comrades, often veterans of "Colored" Civil War regiments, who announced that the day of sympathetic racial equality was dawning and that racial union might even be at hand. But as white counterresistance in the South and white northern indifference to African Americans became increasingly clear, the spirit messages turned away from change in this life to the prospect of recompense in the next. Harmony and equality would be postponed to a distant, spiritual future. Racial realities, in other words, trumped the hopes of spirit life.[32]

Therefore, in the years following the Civil War, the boundaries that Adam Smith foresaw as restrictive of sympathy became increasingly prevalent in American society. As relations between white and black deteriorated, and white Americans turned their attention to healing the scars of their divided white nation, white Spiritualists turned increasingly to refining the definition of their sympathetic community, imagining a new community based on the barriers of race. Beginning in the late 1850s, Spiritualist heaven became increasingly differentiated along racial lines, and race distinguished not only the body, but also the soul. The medium S. G. Horn insisted that "everywhere" in the afterlife, "the peculiarities of race still exist," with the races drawing together into their own racial zones, "the Hindoos and Turks each retaining their peculiar marks of character, colour, and development."[33] The Indian "Happy Hunting Ground" became an essential element of heaven, an utterly separate region in which Indians continued to live in their traditional ways, riding spirit horses and hunting spirit bison. The prominent Christian Spiritualist Eugene Crowell concluded that national distinctions and boundaries continued in the afterlife, just as personal identity did. In their own "divisions, or territories" in the afterlife, the "American, English, French, German, etc." continued to bear the distinctive "characteristics" they had on earth. From language to dress and decorum, "an American there is still an American," Crowell wrote, "an Englishman an Englishman, a German a German, an Indian an Indian, and a Negro is there still a Negro."[34] In psychic travels, the political radical and former abolitionist William Denton discovered that racial distinctions were on other planets, and there, too, darker races were inferior to lighter ones.[35] In redrawing the lines of the sympathetic community, Spiritualists mirrored trends in American society more generally, elevating race into an eternal and unchangeable marker of difference.

SPIRITUALISM SINCE THE 1880S

As the coordinating power of sympathy diminished, the Spiritualist movement lost the momentum and verve it enjoyed during its first quarter century. Sympathetic language continues to color Spiritualist discourse, and the tendency to view the world as an organic, interconnected whole remains common, but sympathy no longer plays the central conceptual role that it once did. As a result, with some notable exceptions, Spiritualist philosophy in the twentieth century usually lacked the reach and coherence of earlier years, and discussions of the phenomena tended to predominate. The spirits always had dramatic overtones, but the drama of mediumistic performances escalated between the 1870s and 1930s, with mediums materializing Indian spirits in full body form from dark cabinets to perform dances around the spirit circle, unseen hands whisking about the room, touching the communicants and moving objects through the air, unseen spirit musicians playing ethereal instruments, or the appearance of amorphous "ectoplasmic" projections that formed spirit hands or faces. Enlightenment and entertainment were intermixed.

The waning of Spiritualism during the last decades of the nineteenth century is usually attributed to the effects of personal scandals involving mediums and the widespread and recurrent evidence of fraud. That some Spiritualists espoused free love (finding one's spirit mate), divorce, and other radical political and social positions clearly hindered its popularity in "respectable" society, but the organized efforts to discredit Spiritualism had an even greater impact. The negative verdicts rendered by a series of high profile commissions to investigate Spiritualism were particularly significant, particularly the judgment of the commission convened at the University of Pennsylvania in 1886, funded by a bequest from the philanthropist Henry Seybert. Led by a group of socially prominent Philadelphians and noted scientists, the Seybert Commission stands out for the number and prominence of mediums it claimed to expose, as well as for the breadth of the methods of spirit communication it examined. Leaving few stones unturned in its devastating report, writing in a restrained style punctuated by a piercing wit, the Commissioners took apart some of America's best known public mediums, including Margaret Fox, James V. Mansfield, and the slate writer Henry Slade, leaving the impression of a tawdry and dishonest bunch, even when concrete proof of their misdeeds was not forthcoming. The debunking efforts of the magician Harry Houdini in the 1920s, and many other magicians in more recent years, were no less effective at swaying public opinion, casting mediumship into disrepute. Houdini's dramatic interventions during séances and his ability to identify the means by which mediumistic fraud was perpetrated played well in the popular press. Various combinations of academic respectability, celebrity, showmanship, and sensationalism, have kept debunking efforts and the fraud they uncover steadily in the public eye.[36]

More damaging than the external assaults upon the integrity of mediumship, however, were a spate of revelations from within the fold. Between the end of the Civil War and World War II, many mediums took to the lecture circuit to confess that they had cheated the gullible and bereaved. Typically their public lectures included demonstrations showing how they simulated spirit appearances. Margaret Fox herself became a publicly repentant medium in the 1880s, admitting that she produced the rapping sounds by cracking the joints of her toes and ankles, an allegation first made by a group of physicians in 1851. Although she later recanted her recantation, the admission by one of the movement's first and best known mediums had a significant impact on Spiritualism's reputation.[37]

Paradoxically, other critics leveled damaging allegations against Spiritualism from the opposite perspective. Members of "mainstream" denominations often complained that the problem with spirit phenomena was not that they were fraudulent, but that they were real, but diabolical in origin. More secular critics agreed that the phenomena were real, but insisted that they were of natural, not supernatural origin. Mediumistic deceit might still be involved, but the "electro-psychologist," John Bovee Dods concluded that the "involuntary powers and instincts" of the human mind were capable of producing all of the phenomena attributed to the spirits. Until late in the nineteenth century, the well known "facts" of clairvoyance, electricity, and animal magnetism were often invoked. Spiritualism, in other words, was natural and had no need of spirits at all.[38]

There was no single Spiritualist response to these critiques, but a number of different responses that resulted in a more fragmented "movement," if it could be called a movement at all. Some Spiritualists responded to the torrents of criticism by rejecting their critics out of hand, their will to believe prevailing over their critical concerns. All the commissions and investigations, Spiritualists claimed, were carried out under less than ideal conditions, were unfairly conducted, or were ill equipped to record spirit phenomena, but even more basic denials were not uncommon. When the French photographer Edouard Isidore Buguet admitted in court to using trickery to produce images of spirits, one of his clients blurted out that even if Buguet had faked some images, he had not faked his.[39] More sophisticated arguments suggested that both mediums and spirits were imperfect beings and were sometimes tempted to fake spirit phenomena to please the public, or, alternatively, they were sometimes mistaken in their understanding of the spirit world. After all, the spirits most likely to commune with the living were those who were closest to us sympathetically, lowest in the progression of spheres, and therefore least advanced in spiritual knowledge.

A longer lasting influence, however, was exerted by Spiritualists who wanted to purify their movement from within, distancing themselves from the supposed excesses of their peers and policing the boundaries of acceptable practice. Christian Spiritualists such as Eugene Crowell blended Spiritualism with liberal Christianity, arguing that their beliefs were fully consistent with scripture and properly understood, never conflicted. Christian Spiritualists, Crowell insisted, read the Bible as divinely inspired, but retained the right to use reason to judge what they read and reject whatever they found inconsistent with modern mores. Not only were Spiritualists good Christians, they were more like the primitive Christians of the early church than any of the modern sects.[40]

Other Spiritualists were more direct in their attempts to marginalize or silence alternative spiritual perspectives. Emma Hardinge Britten, an important medium and early historian of the movement, was a significant moderating figure, a sort of antiradical who attacked a broad range of free love advocates, communitarians, and infidels, whom, she complained, claimed direct divine inspiration and assumed "supreme and unquestionable authority in all matters, whether social, religious, temporal, eternal or financial."[41]

The net effect of such responses was that Spiritualist practice became increasingly circumscribed, homogenized, and less antagonistic to the established churches, or at least to the liberal wing of Protestantism. This trend was nursed by the separation of groups whose beliefs did not conform. Certainly, a hardy subculture of Spiritualism flourished among the lower classes, abjuring social respectability and maintaining tenuous connections to the likes of Crowell and Britten, but at least two New Religious Movements (NRMs) that emerged in the 1870s bore close relations with mainstream Spiritualism. Founded by Helena Petrovna Blavatsky and Henry Olcott in 1875, the Theosophical Society had broadly similar goals to mainstream Spiritualism—to promote universal brotherhood among humanity—but distinguished itself by emphasizing the esoteric and occult aspects of its knowledge and by blending in "eastern" beliefs in reincarnation and karma with spirit communion. Similarly Mary Baker Eddy elaborated upon Spiritualist and "mind cure" healing practices in establishing Christian Science in 1879, though she, like most Theosophists, was adamant that her beliefs were distinct from and superior to run-of-the-mill Spiritualism. In recent years, some trance channelers and psychics make similar claims to distinguish themselves from regular Spiritualist mediums, asserting that they communicate with higher and purer intelligences, not only with the spirits of deceased mortals.[42]

Shortly after the turn of the twentieth century, another offshoot of Spiritualism appeared in cities throughout the south and in major urban centers in the north, attracting a predominantly lower-class African American flock to services that drew syncretically on white Spiritualism, Catholicism, Hoodoo, and Voudon. Although their precise origins are unknown, these Black Spiritual Churches, according to the sociologist Hans Baer, represent one form of religious response to racism and social stratification, allowing believers to manipulate their own social position through magico-religious rituals and the acquisition of esoteric knowledge. Baer notes that the altars in many Black Spiritual Churches include statues not only of Jesus and the Holy Family, but of the Sauk Indian resistance leader, Black Hawk. As the central spirit in the pantheon of these churches, Black Hawk is both a symbol of, and encouragement to, resistance to white domination. Spiritualism also produced movements in the opposite political direction, becoming a focus during the 1930s for a fascist paramilitary organization led by William Dudley Pelley known as the Silver Shirts.[43]

Adaptable to a range of national and cultural contexts, Spiritualism was introduced into Brazil in the early twentieth century through the writings of the French theorist Alain Kardec. Spiritualism blended with a number of African and new world religious traditions and gained considerable popularity, with Spiritualists in Latin America far outnumbering Spiritualists in the United States. In Iceland it was instituted as a viable, formal option in the state church, the only place in the world where it enjoys state recognition.[44]

From the end of the Civil War to the end of the twentieth century, the evolution of mainstream Spiritualism was marked by a distinct tendency to organize and regularize practice, resulting in the formation of both a new field of scientific inquiry and the organization of the formal Spiritualist church. The affinity of Spiritualism with science and technology, of course, grew out of the rising authority of scientific reason and the optimistic and characteristically American fascination with the products of scientific research. For decades Spiritualists integrated new technologies into their descriptions of how spirits communicated, but not just any technology: they focused on those technologies that, like sympathy, promised to unite a distant and fractured nation. Telegraphy was one of the first metaphors for spirit communication, but spirits were equally attracted to the railroad, photography, telephone, and eventually television—any technology that allowed individuals to communicate with other individuals.

Beginning in the 1870s, Spiritualists built upon this rhetorical relationship with scientific methods and products to reemphasize the empirical character of their beliefs. Pioneered by figures such as the writer Epes Sargent, psychic scientists (not all of whom were Spiritualists) sought to use rigorous, objective methods to test theories of spirit action. The Society for Psychical Research in Great Britain, founded in 1882, and its counterpart in the United States founded three years later, helped define a field that attracted prominent members such as evolutionist Alfred Russel Wallace, physicists William Crookes and Oliver Lodge, physiologist Charles Richet, and psychologist William James. Psychical research earned a degree of academic respectability in the twentieth century, capped in 1935, by the establishment of a research institute at Duke University under the direction of J. B. Rhine.[45]

Other organizations nurtured the creation of a formal Spiritualist church. Early efforts to organize Spiritualists were often resisted by those who objected to anything that might "cramp the conscience." Several regional associations appeared in the 1850s, but generally disappeared within a few years, and while the first National Convention of Spiritualists was planned for August 1859, it was not actually held until 1864. Other conventions followed, but were generally unsuccessful in generating a national movement. Instead, borrowing a page from the evangelical sects, regional organizations like the New England Spiritualist Camp Meeting Association (founded in 1874) established a series of communities where Spiritualists could spend their summer holidays, communing with one another and the spirits. Lake Pleasant, Massachusetts (1876), Lily Dale, New York (1879), Camp Etna, Pennsylvania (1877), Cassadaga, Florida (1894), and Harmony Grove, California (1896) were among a score of such communities that became centers of Spiritualist practice.[46]

Spiritualist temples and Sunday Schools hastened the process, and by the 1880s, Christian Spiritualism emerged as the dominant paradigm within the Modern Spiritualist movement, blossoming in the formation of the first successful national organizations. Britten's National Federation of Spiritual Churches (now the Spiritualists' National Union) was founded in Great Britain in 1891, followed in 1893 by the National Spiritualist Association of Churches (NSAC), which remains the primary body in the United States for overseeing the ordination of ministers and certifying lecturers, mediums, and healers. In 1913, a somewhat smaller, but no less successful organization, the National Spiritual Alliance (TNSA), separated from the NSAC, primarily over the refusal of the former to accept the possibility of reincarnation. The NSAC is centered today at Lily Dale, and the TNSA at Lake Pleasant.

The churches associated with these organizations typically hold to some version of Britten's Seven Principles, a statement of the essentials of Christian Spiritualist faith familiar to the first generation of Spiritualist seekers: the fatherhood of God, the brotherhood of humanity, the communion of spirits and ministry of angels, the continuous existence of the human soul, personal responsibility, compensation or retribution in the afterlife for activities in this life, and the eternal progression of the soul. In practice, a Spiritualist service often resembles a generalized, noneucharistic Protestant service, including an opening hymn, usually with words rewritten to reflect Spiritualist beliefs, followed by a topical sermon. The sermon, however, may be delivered by the minister in trance, and messages from the spirits may be delivered. Healing is often singled out as a central function of Spiritualist ministries, providing physical, emotional, and spiritual aid to the afflicted.[47]

In this Christianized form, the Spiritualist movement enjoyed several periods of resurgence, when large numbers of individuals once again entered into conversation with the spirits. During the 1920s and 1930s, Spiritualism gained immense popularity on both sides of the Atlantic. Houdini, always the antagonist, attributed the rise of the movement to mediums taking advantage of widespread grief over the loss of life in the trenches during World War I, and to be sure, numerous books were published containing posthumous letters of soldiers killed in action. Spiritualism waxed again among the counterculture of the 1960s and New Age of the 1970s, tapping into a desire for the spiritually authentic and a turn away from mainstream churches. In this most recent formulation, Spiritualism often bears the traces of "Native American" religion, Goddess religion, Earth religion, and other NRMs. An "Indian" dream catcher is as common in a Spiritualist's window as the Seven Principles.[48]

At the dawn of the twenty-first century, Spiritualism and related beliefs are once again enjoying a surge of popularity, in part because of the dominant medium of the day, the television. Although estimates suggest that no more than about 115,000 people maintained formal membership in Spiritualist churches in 2001, the number of believers worldwide may approach 15,000,000, depending upon the definition of Spiritualism. Even as the formal Spiritualist churches remain small, however, variations on Spiritualist beliefs have spread throughout a vibrant popular culture that largely accepts the reality of the spirit world, appearing on television in the form of a variety of ghost whisperers and hunters and mediums such as John Edward. The spirits will continue to converse, it appears, and Spiritualism to progress.

NOTES

1. Thomas Richmond, *God Dealing with Slavery: God's Instrumentalities in Liberating the African Slave in America* (Chicago: Religio-Philosophical Publishing House, 1870), 41.

2. Donna Hill, *Joseph Smith: The First Mormon* (Garden City, NY: Doubleday, 1977), 34; Joseph Smith, *History of the Church of Jesus Christ of the Latter Day Saints,* vol. 1 (Salt Lake City: Deseret Book Co., 1963), 4.

3. William Denton, *Radical Discourses on Religious Subjects* (Boston: Denton, 1872), 176–77; J.B. Ferguson, *Spirit Communion: A Record of Communications from the Spirit-Spheres* (Nashville: Union & American Steam Press, 1854), 191.

4. Hudson Tuttle, *Arcana of Spiritualism: A Manual of Spiritual Science and Philosophy* (London: James Burns, 1876), 428.

5. Andrew Jackson Davis, *The Magic Staff, An Autobiography* (New York: J.S. Brown, 1857), 216, 217. Phrenology was the science of the study of the organs of the human mind, and in the United States during the 1840s, it frequently merged with the mind-influencing science of Mesmerism, a precursor to hypnotism.

6. "Modern Spiritualism" was the term used to distinguish the newly discovered means of communicating with spirits of the dead from historical and biblical accounts. Although Spiritualists argued that there was a continuity with ancient times, Modern Spiritualism was an historically specific emergence, tied to particular forms of spirit communication and, according to some believers, specific events in the spiritual world.

7. Emma Hardinge Britten, *Modern American Spiritualism: A Twenty Years' Record of the Communion Between Earth and the World of Spirits* (New York: the author, 1870), 556. See also Barbara Weisberg, *Talking to the Dead: Kate and Maggie Fox and the Rise of Spiritualism* (San Francisco: HarperSan Francisco, 2004); Nancy Rubin-Stuart, *The Reluctant Spiritualist: The Life of Maggie Fox* (Orlando, FL: Harcourt, 2004); David Chapin, *Exploring Other Worlds: Margaret Fox, Elisha Kent Kane, and the Antebellum Culture of Curiosity* (Amherst: University of Massachusetts, 2004).

8. Britten, *Modern American Spiritualism,* 39.

9. Ibid., 45.

10. Francis H. Smith, *My Experience, or Foot-Prints of a Presbyterian to Spiritualism* (Baltimore: the author, 1860), 39.

11. New England Spiritualists Association, *Constitution and By-Laws, List of Officers, and Address to the Public* (Boston: George K. Snow, 1854), 11.

12. G.A. Redman, *Mystic Hours, or, Spiritual Experiences* (New York: Charles Partridge, 1859), 106.

13. Britten, *Modern American Spiritualism,* 45; Eliab W. Capron, *Modern Spiritualism: Its Facts and Fantacisms, Its Consistencies and Contradictions* (Boston: Colby and Rich, 1855); Henry Spicer, *Sights and Sounds: The Mystery of the Day, Comprising an Entire History of the American "Spirit" Manifestations* (London: Thomas Bosworth, 1853); Uriah Clark, *The Spiritualist Register, With a Counting House and Speakers' Almanac Containing Facts and Statistics of Spiritualism* (Auburn, NY: U. Clark, 1857). Estimates on the number of Spiritualists are

inherently subjective since the only accurate criterion for calling oneself a Spiritualist is self-identification. Important studies of the early growth of the Spiritualist movement include Geoffrey K. Nelson, *Spiritualism and Society* (London: Routledge, 1969); Ann Braude, *Radical Spirits: Spiritualism and Women's Rights in Nineteenth-Century America* (Boston: Beacon, 1989); Frank Podmore, *Mediums of the Nineteenth Century* (New Hyde Park, NY: University Books, 1963).

14. Isaac Post, *Voices from the Spirit World, Being Communications from Many Spirits* (Rochester: Charles H. McDonnell, 1852). Key works on the connection between Spiritualism and reform include Nelson, *Spiritualism and Society;* Braude, *Radical Spirits;* Diana Basham, *The Trial of Woman: Feminism and the Occult Sciences in Victorian Literature and Society* (New York: New York University, 1992); and John Kucich, *Ghostly Communion: Cross-Cultural Spiritualism in Nineteenth-Century American Literature* (Hanover, NH: Dartmouth, 2004).

15. Janice Boddy, "Spirit Possession Revisited: Beyond Instrumentality," *Annual Review of Anthropology* 23 (1994); I.M. Lewis, *Religion in Context: Cults and Charisma* (Cambridge, UK: Cambridge University Press, 1986); I.M. Lewis, *Ecstatic Religion: A Study of Shamanism and Spirit Possession,* 2nd ed. (London: Routledge, 1989), 419.

16. Braude, *Radical Spirits.*

17. Logie Barrow, *Independent Spirits: Spiritualism and English Plebeians, 1850–1910* (London: Routledge and Kegan Paul, 1986); David J. Hess, *Samba in the Night: Spiritism in Brazil* (New York: Columbia University Press, 1994); David J. Hess, *Spirits and Scientists: Ideology, Spiritism, and Brazilian Culture* (University Park, PA: Penn State University, 1991).

18. Alex Owen, *The Darkened Room: Women, Power, and Spiritualism in Late Victorian England* (Philadelphia: University of Pennsylvania, 1990), 4; Vieda Skultans, *Intimacy and Ritual* (London: Routledge, 1974).

19. On Robert Hare, see Robert S. Cox, "Vox populi: George Washington's Post-Mortem Career," *Early American Studies* 1 (2003): 230–72; Robert Hare, *Experimental Investigation of the Spirit Manifestations, Demonstrating the Existence of Spirits and Their Communion with Mortals* (New York: Charles Partridge, 1855).

20. Lydia Maria Child to Parke Goodwin, January 20, 1856, *Lydia Maria Child Papers,* William L. Clements Library, University of Michigan.

21. Uriah Clark, *Plain Guide to Spiritualism: A Handbook for Skeptics, Inquirers, Clergymen, Believers, Lecturers, Mediums, Editors, and All Who Need a Thorough Guide to the Phenomena, Science, Philosophy, Religion and Reforms of Modern Spiritualism,* 3rd ed. (Boston: William White, 1863), 98, 102.

22. Hudson Tuttle and James M. Peebles, *Year-Book of Spiritualism for 1871* (Boston: William White, 1871), 15, 20–21.

23. A.B. Child, *Whatever Is, Is Right* (Boston: Berry, Colby and Co., 1860), 116; A.J. Davis, *The Present Age and Inner Life: A Sequel to Spiritual Intercourse* (Hartford: Charles Partridge, 1853).

24. Hudson Tuttle, *Arcana of Spiritualism: A Manual of Spiritual Science and Philosophy* (London: James Burns, 1876), 428; Britten, *Modern American Spiritualism,* 365; A.J. Davis, *The Approaching Crisis: Being a Review of Dr. Bushnell's Course of Lectures, on the Bible, Nature, Religion, Skepticism, and the Supernatural,* 2nd ed. (Boston: William White, 1870), 62; Davis, *Present Age and Inner Life,* 24.

25. Smith, *My Experience,* 213; Abraham Pierce, *Revelator, Being an Account of the Twenty-One Days' Entrancement of Abraham P. Pierce, Spirit-Medium,* 2nd ed. (Boston: Colby & Rich,

1870), 39; Josiah Brigham, *Twelve Spirit Messages from John Quincy Adams, Through Joseph D. Stiles, Medium* (Boston: Bela Marsh, 1859).

26. Christopher Lawrence, "The Nervous System and Society in the Scottish Enlightenment," in *Natural Order: Historical Studies of Scientific Change,* ed. Barry Barnes and Steven Shapin (Beverly Hills, CA: Sage Publications, 1979), 19–40; Norman S. Fiering, "Irresistible Compassion: An Aspect of Eighteenth-Century Sympathy and Humanitarianism," *Journal of the History of Ideas* 37 (1976): 195–218; James Rodgers, "Sensibility, Sympathy, Benevolence: Physiology and Moral Philosophy in *Tristram Shandy,*" in *Languages of Nature: Critical Essays on Science and Literature,* ed. L.J. Jordanova (New Brunswick, NJ: Rutgers University, 1986); Robert M. Young, *Mind, Brain and Adaptation in the Nineteenth Century* (Oxford: Oxford University Press, 1970); Graham Richards, *Mental Machinery: The Origins and Consequences of Psychological Ideas, 1600–1850* (Baltimore: Johns Hopkins, 1992); Stanley Finger, *Origins of Neuroscience* (Oxford: Oxford University Press, 1994); Robert S. Cox, *Body and Soul: A Sympathetic History of American Spiritualism* (Charlottesville: University of Virginia, 2003).

27. Adam Smith, *Theory of Moral Sentiments,* ed. D.D. Raphael and A.L. MacFie (Oxford: Clarendon Press, 1976), 10.

28. Ibid., 116, 13.

29. M.T. Shelhamer, *Life and Labor in the Spirit World* (Boston: Colby and Rich, 1887), 196.

30. W.W. Aber, *Rending the Vail* (Kansas City: Hudson-Kimberly Publishing, 1899), 289.

31. Nell Irvin Painter, *Sojourner Truth: A Life, A Symbol* (New York: Norton, 1996); John Patrick Deveny, *Paschal Beverly Randolph: A Nineteenth Century Black American Spiritualist, Rosicrucian, and Sex Magician* (Albany, NY: Syracuse University Press, 1997); Rene Grandjean Séance Registers, Special Collections Department, Earl K. Long Library, University of New Orleans.

32. Grandjean Séance Registers, UNO; Cox, *Body and Soul.*

33. S.G. Horn, *The Next World Interviewed* (Chicago: Progressive Thinker, 1896), 51.

34. Eugene Crowell, *The Spirit World: Its Inhabitants, Nature, and Philosophy,* 2nd ed. (Boston: Colby & Rich, 1880), 51, 55.

35. William Denton, *The Soul of Things,* 8th ed. (Wellesley, MA: Denton, 1888).

36. Seybert Commission, *Preliminary Report of the Commission Appointed by the University of Pennsylvania to Investigate Modern Spiritualism* (Philadelphia: Lippincott, 1887); A.B. Richmond, *What I Saw at Cassadaga Lake: 1888: An Addendum to a Review in 1887 of the Seybert Commissioners' Report* (Boston: Colby and Rich, 1889); Harry Houdini, *A Magician Among the Spirits* (New York: Harper, 1924).

37. Reuben Briggs Davenport, *The Death-Blow of Spiritualism: Being the True Story of the Fox Sisters, as Revealed by Authority of Margaret Fox Kane and Catherine Fox Jencken* (New York: G.W. Dillingham, 1888).

38. John Bovee Dods, *Spirit Manifestations Examined and Explained* (New York: Dewitt and Davenport, 1854).

39. Podmore, *Mediums of the Nineteenth Century.*

40. Eugene Crowell, *The Identity of Primitive Christianity and Modern Spiritualism,* 2nd ed. (New York: the author, 1875).

41. Britten, *Modern American Spiritualism,* 209.

42. Peter Washington, *Madame Blavatsky's Baboon: A History of the Mystics, Mediums, and Misfits Who Brought Spiritualism to America* (New York: Schocken, 1995); Antoine Faivre,

Theosophy, Tradition, Imagination: Studies in Western Esotericism (Albany: SUNY Press, 2000);
W. Michael Ashcraft, *The Dawn of a New Cycle: Point Loma Theosophists and American Culture*
(Knoxville: University of Tennessee, 2002); Gillian Gill, *Mary Baker Eddy* (Reading, MA: Perseus Books, 1998).

43. Hans A. Baer, *The Black Spiritual Movement: A Religious Response to Racism* (Knoxville:
University of Tennessee, 1984); Eckard V. Toy, "Silver Shirts in the Northwest: Politics,
Prophecies, and Personalities in the 1930s," *Pacific Northwest Quarterly* 80 (1989): 139–46;
Scott Beekman, *William Dudley Pelley: A Life in Right Wing Extremism and the Occult* (Syracuse: Syracuse University Press, 2005).

44. Hess, *Samba in the Night*; William H. Swatos and Loftur Reimar Gissurarson, *Icelandic
Spiritualism: Mediumship and Society* (New Brunswick, NJ: Transaction Publishers, 1996).

45. Janet Oppenheim, *The Other World: Spiritualism and Psychical Research in England,
1850–1914* (Cambridge: Cambridge University Press, 1995); R. Laurence Moore, *In Search
of White Crows: Spiritualism, Parapsychology, and American Culture* (New York: Oxford, 1977).

46. Britten, *Modern American Spiritualism; The New England Spiritualists' Camp Meeting
Association…* (Greenfield, MA: Field and Hall, 1886); Christine Wicker, *Lily Dale: The True
Story of the Town That Talks to the Dead* (San Francisco: HarperSan Francisco, 2003); Louise
Shattuck, *Spirit and Spa: A Portrait of the Body, Mind, and Soul of a 133-Year-Old Spiritualist
Community in Lake Pleasant, Massachusetts* (Greenfield, MA.: Delta House Press, 2003).

47. Emma Hardinge Britten, *The Lyceum Manual, A Compendium of Spiritual, Moral, and
Spiritual Exercises for Use in Progressive Lyceums Connected with the British Spiritualists' Churches
and Kindred Bodies* (Keighley, England: Wadsworth and Co., 1914).

48. See, e.g., Oliver Lodge's books, *Raymond, Or Life and Death* (New York: Doran, 1916)
and *Christopher, A Study in Human Personality* (New York: Doran, 1919).

The Theosophical Society

Robert Ellwood

INTRODUCTION

The Theosophical Society was founded in New York in 1875, principally by Helena P. Blavatsky (1831–1891) and Henry Steel Olcott (1832–1907). Their intention was to study the "ancient wisdom" believed still preserved within the symbolism and outer teachings of the world's religions and philosophies, and by various esoteric organizations, ranging from Freemasonry to the Druze of the Near East and the monasteries of Tibet. Theosophy's immediate ideological and experiential context was Spiritualism, in which both Blavatsky and Olcott had been active, eighteenth century occultism, including its popular expression in movements like Mesmerism and Freemasonry, and the nineteenth century occult revival associated with names like Eliphas Lévi and Edward Bulwer-Lytton. Although never large in numbers, Theosophy has had a significant role in disseminating Eastern religious concepts, such as karma and reincarnation, in the West, in the spiritual revitalization of then-oppressed nations like Ireland and India, and in modernist cultural movements such as nonrepresentational art.

BACKGROUND

Modern Theosophy must further be viewed not only in light of romanticism and the Victorian "war" between science and religion. In his inaugural speech as first president of the Society, Olcott portrayed science and religion as both locked into narrow dogmatisms, and also argued (in a manner that caused offence among Spiritualists) that the popular Spiritualism of the day was but a shallow, unreliable, and often fraudulent response to this crisis. Then, evoking the romantic appeal of the distant and the past, and the century's stunning advances in the recovery of ancient civilizations, he pointed to the possibility of a deeper and older wisdom that could transcend this split and form the foundation of a better human future:

If I rightly apprehend our work, it is to aid in freeing the public mind of theological superstition and a tame subservience to the arrogance of science.... Our society is, I may say, without precedent. From the days when the Neoplatonists and the last theurgists of Alexandria were scattered by the murderous hand of Christianity, until now, the revival of a study of Theosophy has not been attempted.[1]

Olcott added that such an attempt could not have been until conditions of "perfect political and religious liberty" were obtained, that is, in the United States of 1875. Thus the foundation of the Theosophical Society in America was of profound significance both for its own work and for its place in American history. Both temperamentally and ideologically, nineteenth and twentieth century Theosophists have tended to be social idealists, utopians, or reformers who fitted well into the mood of the "progressivist" era, favoring causes like labor reform, women's rights, animal welfare, and "progressive" education.

Olcott's idea that it was in the United States his new movement for the constructive recovery of ancient wisdom had to be first planted has a long lineage and large context, contributing to an image of the United States that Theosophy and its New Age progeny only enhanced. The New World as New Eden is a much reiterated theme, going back to Christopher Columbus's public relations efforts to picture the islands he had visited as paradises inhabited by innocent natives naked as Adam and Eve, despite his simultaneous labors of transporting, enslaving, and massacring those same primitives.

Calvinists and other serious believers, of course, could not overpraise the western paradise so long as its inhabitants, however noble in their savagery, were unbaptized. But Christian or visionary settlers seldom considered that if the America of the heathen was less than as idealized, here was a place where the European utopia could be built. Past history could be abolished, and humanity returned to the garden to start over again. We need only mention John Winthrop's "City Upon a Hill," or R. W. B. Lewis's classic study, *The American Adam*.[2] Lewis speaks of the "American myth" which "saw life and history as just beginning" on these virgin shores anew, "starting up again under fresh initiative, a divinely granted second chance for the human race, after the first chance had been so disastrously fumbled in the darkening Old World." This hope crested in the nineteenth century in such writers as Ralph Waldo Emerson, Walt Whitman, Oliver Wendell Holmes, and William Ellery Channing. It also found expression, according to Lewis, in the gnostic visions of Nathaniel Hawthorne and Herman Melville, though in a darker and more complex way that explored the perils as well as the splendors of American Adamic innocence.

Both visions came together in Theosophy, which managed to embrace progressivism and gnosticism alike, for it entered the late nineteenth century with an eye toward both the distant past and the future, hoping thereby to get beyond the schizophrenias of modernism. Evolution, extrapolated from Darwinism into vast cosmic-scale visions of spiritual as well as physical upward cycles, of whose movement one could now be an agent, was as much a part of its picture as the "ancient wisdom." So was attention to spiritual traditions both Eastern and Western; within them the ancient wisdom was believed to be housed, if often in camouflage. In general, the

Theosophical agenda sought the reconciliation of the modern world created by science and liberal political credos with global spiritual perspectives, and the ancient traditions underlying them. All this was an ambitious undertaking, almost too ambitious, for such a small and recently formed organization. Yet Theosophy found a niche in the world of the late nineteenth century and the twentieth century.

ROMANTICISM

In particular, Theosophy, like so many nineteenth century religious and spiritual movements, was a late heir of romanticism, though one very different from the feeling-tinged but theologically narrow romanticized evangelicalism or Catholicism of the era. Yet like those and other romantics, Theosophists tended to live in either an idealized past or a golden visionary future, but were bored or disillusioned with the present. That attitude of disillusionment focused on science as often as it made science the foundation of its radiant future. Not a few romantics shared Edger Allan Poe's deep disquiet (in his "Sonnet—To Science") as he addressed the scientific critic "Who alterest all things with thy peering eyes."

One way to revive romantic ethos was to return in spirit to the age when deity reigned in sacred grove and mysterious night sky. The intellectual nineteenth century was rich in classical learning, and not a few dreamers wished to get behind Swinburne's "pale Galilean," Jesus, and his joyless churchmen, or formal Christian traditions, to enter a time when divine wonder dwelt in rosy-fingered dawn and the wine-dark sea, something also animating that side of modern Theosophy, which has talked of clairvoyantly seeing the "devas" and "elementals" of nature. The Victorian age was also fascinated by the lost cities, even lost civilizations, its burgeoning archaeology had uncovered. They were not only in classical lands like Schliemann's Troy, but also in Asia, Africa, the New World, and the Pacific islands. Olcott tells us that, on an evening when a master (an advanced being) allegedly appeared to him as he was absorbed in reading, the book was Stephens's *Travels in Yucatan,* an early classic on Mayan ruins.[3]

Also in the Theosophical background was the romanticism-tinged nineteenth century occult revival, including such writers well known to Blavatsky and Olcott as Eliphas Lévi, pen-name of the French esotericist Benjamin Constant, and Edward Bulwer-Lytton. (The latter's occult novels, such as *Zanoni* and *The Coming Race,* had a discernible effect on Blavatsky's esoteric creativity, and by a strange coincidence or karmic connection, when she and Olcott made their journey to India in 1880, the Viceroy was none other than the novelist's son, the poet and romantic imperialist Lord Robert Lytton.) Even before their century lay the occultism of the eighteenth century, when persons like Cagliostro, Swedenborg, Mesmer, the half-legendary comte de Saint Germain, and the founders of modern Freemasonry created a sort of undertow to the Age of Reason that also advanced its agenda in significant ways.

Theosophy found ready resources for structuring itself in the two centuries' fascination with secret, initiatory degree lodges, Masonic or Rosicrucian, which characteristically laid claim to ancient confidential wisdom transmitted through its formulas to the worthy. Sometimes that assertion was not taken too seriously, and the lodges were more social than anything else, but the notion was nonetheless there that definite stages in the spiritual life existed, which could be mounted through a series of initiations, together with the particular training and knowledge imparted through each.

But Blavatsky insisted there was more: as Olcott put it, "the Spiritualism she was sent to America to profess and ultimately bring to replace the cruder Western mediumism, was Eastern Spiritualism, or Brahma Vidya."[4] Recognizing that most of the spirits evoked by the western mediums were tricksters or "shells," and laying hold of the ancient wisdom of the East as well as the West, Blavatsky and her circle harbored no doubt that Brahma Vidya was incomparably higher than the bumptious spirit faith of the New World.

THEOSOPHY AND THE SPIRITUAL EAST

That observation suggests a final source of Theosophy: the fresh discovery of the spiritual East by the West in the nineteenth century. The process had been cumulative in impact, a backwash from Europe and America's worldwide commercial enterprises, and in particular the colonial adventures of England in India. First came translations of the Upanishads and other Hindu sacred texts early in the century, those works of wisdom that so influenced sages like Emerson, Thoreau, and Schopenhauer, who in turn influenced Blavatsky. (It is interesting to note that, in *Isis Unveiled,* Blavatsky cites Schopenhauer with particular appreciation, while dismissing the metaphysical systems of Hegel and Schelling as "gigantic failures" unable to stem the rising tide of materialism.[5])

As for the Transcendentalists, Thoreau remarked that as he read the "stupendous and cosmogonal philosophy" of the Bhagavad-Gita (another great Hindu text), "the pure Walden water is mingled with the sacred water of the Ganges."[6] Walt Whitman's 1871 poem "Passage to India" seems virtually to encapsulate the spirit of the two Theosophical founders' migration to the subcontinent a few years later. The poet sang not only of "Passage O soul to India!" but also of "Passage to more than India!" The India then enjoying the high noon of the British Raj was not the India Theosophy sought: it was less India as a place than as an idea, a spiritual treasure-house of wonder and wisdom older and stronger than anything the West could offer, of Brahma Vidya rather than parlor-séance Spiritualism.

The Western discovery of Buddhism, and the sorting out of its various forms, was a longer process, but by the 1860s the scholarly foundations of modern Buddhist studies had been laid. Sir Edwin Arnold's immensely popular poem about the life of the Buddha, "The Light of Asia" (1879), did much to stimulate the religion's popular appeal. Indeed, the urbane Bostonian and Episcopal clergyman, Phillips Brooks, commented sardonically in 1883 that in the poem's wake "a large part of Boston prefers to consider itself Buddhist rather than Christian."[7] Olcott, in a role adjunct to his Theosophical labors, devoted much energy to the modernization of Buddhism in Asia and presented its case to the West, as a sort of "missionary in reverse."[8]

Theosophy both rode a rising wave of interest in oriental religion and enhanced its wide dissemination, especially on the popular level, along with the no less important Theosophical task of reviving the "ancient wisdom" of the West, storehoused among such as the Gnostics, Kabbalists, and Renaissance Platonists and Hermeticists.

BACKGROUND SUMMATION

The complex conditions for Theosophy's emergence as a spiritual movement and social force in the last quarter of the nineteenth century then included a new revival of the perennial "ancient wisdom" that had appeared before in the Renaissance, abetted by the Enlightenment's reason and science—and its occult underbelly—together with the Romantic's love of ancient mysteries and sense that the knowing power of imagination can exceed that of reason or science.

To this was added the ceremonial magician's feel for the reality of the transhuman spiritual realm, as represented by, say, the Masters or Secret Chiefs of Rosicrucianism, plus the Spiritualist's belief that these mysteries could be brought down to an almost everyday experiential level, and that the revealing of their arcana heralded not mere nostalgia for the past, but the beginning of a new era marked by radical progress and reform in all areas of human life.

Spiritualism, of course, was associated with such liberal causes as abolition of slavery, prison and educational reform, and the rights of women. Blavatsky, politically more European than American in orientation, was a passionate anticlerical in the Voltairean style and an admirer of such radicals of her day as the Italians Guiseppe Mazzini and Guiseppe Garibaldi. [She claimed to have fought and been wounded with the latter in the anti-Papal States battle of Mentana (1867), even though such sentiments somehow coexisted with warm feelings of loyalty toward the czar of Russia, and Eastern Orthodox Christians never shared her animus against Papists and Protestants.]

Freemasonry contributed the idea that one could inwardly prepare to receive the mystic light by a formal, degree-like system of initiations. Finally, Asia added its own versions of the primal lore, plus knowledge that both the ancient wisdom and the new movement were universal, not just Western. The new movement's nativity in the United States, land of religious and intellectual freedom, was, as we have seen, a necessary condition of its existence for Olcott and his associates.

THE FOUNDING AND THE FOUNDERS

The backgrounds and characters of the two principal founders of the Theosophical Society in 1875, Blavatsky and Olcott, were strikingly dissimilar. Blavatsky was born Helena de Hahn in czarist Russia to a family of high aristocratic connections. Her father was an officer in the army of the czar, and her mother a popular novelist whose stories inevitably involved women suffering at the hands of callous men. Even as a child Helena was willful and headstrong, though possessing great imagination, intelligence, and fascination for occult lore. At 18 she impulsively married N.V.

Blavatsky, a widower and provincial vice-governor more than twice her age. She soon left him, to spend most of the next 25 years wandering the world, by her account in search of esoteric wisdom, a quest culminating with mysterious initiations in Tibet in the late 1860s. In 1873 she came to New York, seeking, she said, to study Spiritualism in its homeland. There she encountered many Spiritualists, vehemently entered into their controversies, and also met Henry Steel Olcott.

Olcott, sprung from the solid American middle class, worked variously as an agricultural scientist, journalist, and lawyer. During the Civil War he served the Union as an investigator of fraudulent military suppliers, receiving the rank of colonel; he was also part of a team investigating the assassination of Lincoln. At the same time, Olcott had long had an interest in Spiritualism. In 1874 he was at the home of the Eddy brothers in Chittenden, Vermont, where nightly Spiritualist phenomena were reported. He was, in his reportorial capacity, preparing a series of newspaper articles on the otherworldly happenings.[9] By late 1874 Helena Blavatsky had also arrived at the mysterious farmstead. The convergence of the exotic immigrant and the Yankee journalist was an immediate success.

They kept in touch back in New York City, Olcott clearly fascinated by the unusual woman's volatile personality, remarkable psychic phenomena, and accented talk of faraway mysteries. Above all she spoke to him of the Masters of the Wisdom, adepts or mahatmas, who though still living in this world have attained high initiations. They inwardly governed the course of world affairs and were prepared to accept serious students. In time Olcott began his training under certain of them. Before long, for the further benefit of their esoteric studies, the two shared a series of apartments (though not, Olcott makes clear, the bedroom). The best known, dubbed the Lamasery, became a magnet for the city's coterie of seekers, esotericists, and bohemians, as well as Spiritualists. In his later reminiscences, *Old Diary Leaves,* Olcott well evoked the fascinating conversations, uproarious parties, and intriguing lectures for which the residence was famous.[10]

In 1875 the Lamasery crowd determined to form an organization for the study of the sort of borderline knowledge in which they were interested, which was so exceptionally manifested in Blavatsky and her lore. The group named itself the Theosophical Society; Olcott was elected first president, delivering the inaugural address already cited on November 17, 1875. The organization prospered in its original form for only a few months. During that time the group's members mostly listened to lectures on topics related to comparative religions, the occult, and western esotericism. Olcott and Blavatsky soon enough turned their attention to another project, the compilation of a massive book. This work, published by Blavatsky in 1877 as *Isis Unveiled,* was the first large-scale presentation of the wisdom she believed her long search had garnered.[11]

ISIS UNVEILED

This sprawling two-volume work may appear at first glance to be mainly a disorganized collage of accounts of travel to out-of-the-way places, including narrations of encounters with shamans and sorcerers, together with discourses on Masonic symbolism, Pythagoreanism, Neoplatonism, Gnosticism, and Eastern texts, interspersed with roundhouse assaults on conventional science and religion. But gradually certain overriding themes, emerge: nineteenth century science and religion alike were sterile and dogmatic, but if one paid attention to clues found in the "forbidden" lore to which the author pointed, to the experience of shamans and magicians, to the secrets of obscure initiatory orders and ancient texts, one would find hints of a primordial wisdom that could unify the worlds of science and religion.

This alternative world view showed life actually to be an initiatory journey, for those able to receive it as such, into the intricate splendor that lay behind the world as we ordinarily know it. Nature, including human nature, is a subtle and complex mixture of spirit and matter; the highest interaction of the two produces consciousness; masters or adepts exist here and there who can detach and direct potent energies of the spiritual side, roughly the "animal magnetism" of Mesmer, the *Vril* of Bulwer-Lytton, or the *prana* of yoga, to induce seemingly magical effects—though, of course, these are actually natural, but beyond our ordinary understanding of nature. Knowledge of this sort is the beginning, though far from the end, of the unveiled Ancient Wisdom.

THE JOURNEY TO THE EAST

After the successful publication of *Isis Unveiled,* the interests of Blavatsky and Olcott moved more and more in the direction of India, believed to be a mighty reservoir of those forgotten secrets. The inner turn toward India on the part of the founders appears to have commenced in an interest in Swami Dayananda Sarasvati and his Arya Samaj. The Arya Samaj was a Hindu movement advocating what appeared to be liberal religion, calling for simple worship and the elimination of elaborate and "superstitious" temple culti. It supported such progressive measures as modern education, abolition of caste based on birth, and the rights of women.

The relation with the Arya Samaj had begun in 1870, when Olcott had met Moolji Thackersey of Bombay on a ship to England. Corresponding with him again in 1878, the American invited the Indian to join the Theosophical Society. Thackersey, in turn, told Olcott in enthusiastic terms of the allegedly parallel work of the Arya Samaj. In 1878 the Society united at a distance with Swami Dayananda Sarasvati's organization, naming itself "The Theosophical Society of the Arya Samaj." Olcott felt at the time that the Arya Samaj's reconstructed Vedism was one with the spiritual universalism he identified with Theosophy. However, the Theosophists did not at first realize that Dayananda's positions were actually based on a sort of Hindu fundamentalism; he believed that the Vedas alone were revealed truth, and all later Hindu sources, not to mention all other scriptures, spurious. Vast was Olcott's disillusionment, confirmed later in India, when further information revealed that the Arya Samaj, for all its virtues, intended only conservative, integralist reforms within Hindu India, and so was of little interest to Western universalists.

Nonetheless, this relationship was an important factor in Blavatsky and Olcott's plan to journey to India in 1878–1879, a momentous move for the future of Theosophy. Blavatsky still felt that Dayananda was a master calling her. The subcontinent came more and more into their conversations, and the supernormal masters whom Madame Blavatsky was able to introduce to Olcott increasingly wore turbans.

Another reason for the Indian pilgrimage was the founding of the London branch of the Society that year, 1878, which the two wanted to visit en route. Moreover, the same year Blavatsky acquired U.S. citizenship; she was said to be the first Russian woman immigrant to do so. That would make travel in India somewhat easier, given the British Raj's almost paranoid suspicions of Russian designs on that land, even though the Yankee passport did not relieve her of a discreet police "tail" during some of her stay, and her adversaries often accused her, among other things, of being a spy for the czar. However, the mistrust of India's alien rulers made all the greater the enthusiasm of India's rising nationalists for the pair and for Theosophy.

Early in 1878 the "Theosophical Twins," as Olcott liked to call himself and Blavatsky, arrived in India, the land of their dreams. The two impressed some and aroused skepticism in others of the British community. But they were generally well received by Indians, being among the few Europeans in the heyday of imperialism to show much sympathy for Hindu religion and culture, or to stand, as Olcott did, with Hindus and Buddhists against aggressive missionaries and colonial overlords. Branches of the Theosophical Society were soon formed, and publications issued. An international headquarters was first established in Bombay, then moved in December 1882 to an estate at Adyar, near Madras (now Chennai) in south India.

Among the English converts was A.P. Sinnett (d. 1921), a newspaper editor. He was the recipient of the remarkable and controversial series of documents now called *The Mahatma Letters,* instructions from the masters, which often appeared in extraordinary ways. Their published collection is now one of the basic Theosophical texts.[12] These and later such letters, however, led to the Society's first and greatest crisis: the investigation by Richard Hodgson, of the Society for Psychical Research, into them and related alleged supernormal phenomena. The 1885 report, adverse to Blavatsky, did the nascent movement much harm, accusing the Theosophists of falsifying paranormal events to deceive the gullible.

At the same time, the relative success of Theosophy in India owes much to the movement's enthusiastic embrace of native culture and religion, and its implied critique of the Eurocentric mentality behind colonialism. Liberal-minded Europeans as well as Indians could appreciate this tack. Sometime Theosophists such as the British liberal Octavian Hume and Motilal Nehru, an important Indian nationalist in his own right as well as father of Jawaharlal Nehru, first prime minister of independent India, were among the founders of the Indian National Congress, with which Annie Besant (1847–1933) and M.K. Gandhi (also a sometime Theosophist) were later associated.

It is perhaps no accident that 1884, the year Theosophy was shaken by scandal concerning the alleged forging of letters from Mahatmas, was also the year India was riven by the Ilbert Bill crisis. This was an act proposed in the Viceroy's council that would have reformed India's judiciary in such a way that Europeans could in some cases be tried before native judges. It was violently opposed by most Europeans in India, and as strongly supported by Indians. In the wake of this upheaval between ruler and ruled, the scandal against Theosophy, known for its sympathy to "natives," was provoked by European investigators and missionaries, and in the upshot Blavatsky and other Theosophists were wildly cheered on the streets by Indian students.[13] Blavatsky returned to Europe in 1885, where despite failing health she completed her greatest work, *The Secret Doctrine,* published in 1888.[14]

THE SECRET DOCTRINE

This massive and remarkable tome is basically an account of the genesis of the solar system by emanation from the One, in accordance with tremendous cosmic cycles of divine activity and rest, and of the evolution of humanity through several worlds and races. Its first section, "Cosmogenesis," portrays the emergence of the differentiated cosmos from the stillness of pralaya, the rest between manifestations; the important theme is that, in those mysterious and remote workings, as in *Isis Unveiled,* consciousness and matter always coexist, though, of course, in very different ways in star and seed.

The second part, "Anthropogenesis," describes the human lineage on planet Earth. Fundamentally it is composed of a series of seven "root races," of which we are now in the fifth. These are regarded as overlapping and, though originally identified with various extant "races," may be thought of as much as stages in the evolution of consciousness as races in the biological sense. The concept has sometimes been labeled racist, but it should be recalled that in the nineteenth century the word "race" was often used where we might speak of nationality or even culture, and that the grand scheme relativized the whole matter by portraying the inevitable rise and fall of all races, nations, and empires—and for this Theosophists were also criticized by those who thought the British Empire, for example, ought to last forever.

The first two root races were primordial and "etheric" rather than fully physical. The third, the Lemurian, and the fourth, the Atlantean, have overtones of Paleolithic and Neolithic cultures, respectively. The book ends with an elaborate demonstration of the cryptic expression of this "ancient wisdom" in the arcane symbolism of numerous faiths and "mystery schools."

THE "SECOND GENERATION"

Blavatsky died in London in 1891. Although Olcott continued as president until his death in 1907, the Society was soon dominated by two "second generation" figures, Besant and Charles Webster Leadbeater (1854–1934). Leadbeater, a former Anglican priest, controversial because of alleged homosexuality and closely associated with Besant, represented the occult side of the "second generation." He produced a widely read series of books based on his "clairvoyant" investigations of the inner planes of reality, past and future lives, and the meaning of ritual.[15] Among the most representative of his works, largely based on lectures, are *The Astral Plane* (1895), *The Christian Creed* (1899), *The Devanchanic Plane* (1896), *The Hidden Side of Christian Festivals* (1920), *The Hidden Side of Things* (1913), *How Theosophy Came to Me* (1930), *Man Visible and Invisible* (1902), *The Masters and the Path* (1925), *The Other Side of Death* (1903), *An Outline of Theosophy* (1902), and *The Science of the Sacraments* (1920).

Two significant themes are evident from these and other titles. First, Leadbeater's fascination with aspects of reality concealed from ordinary sight, the "hidden side" of human nature and the life after death, led him, with the aid of clairvoyance, into vivid and detailed descriptions of those mysteries. Second, he was, like Annie Besant and others of his generation, profoundly concerned with reconciling Christianity with Theosophy, which for Leadbeater took the form of finding occult forces at work in such traditional Christian rites as baptism and the Eucharist. This quest eventually led to the formation of the Liberal Catholic Church in 1916, of which Leadbeater was a founding bishop. This small denomination uses ritual of the medieval Catholic sort, interpreting it in a Theosophical light.

In the first year of the new century, 1901, Leadbeater together with Annie Besant published a fascinating little book, still in print, called *Thought-Forms,* which seemed prophetic of the direction the avant-garde in the arts was headed in that brave new era. This book was full of illustrations and description, based on Leadbeater's clairvoyance, of colorful but abstract forms seen in the auras or over the heads of persons in various states of consciousness, from spiritual exaltation to anger and depression. Similar vibrant images were also associated with music of diverse sorts. Reportedly, this book and similar Theosophical works, including *The Secret Doctrine* and Leadbeater's richly illustrated *Man Visible and Invisible,* had a definite impact on the artistic development of several painters, most notably Piet Mondrian and Wassily Kandinsky, who were pioneers in cubism and other twentieth century forms of abstraction that sought to portray, by nonrealist means, the inner states of feeling and consciousness animating their subjects.[16]

ANNIE BESANT

Besant (International President of the Society after Olcott's death in 1907), tireless social reformer, activist in many causes, and freethinker (partly in reaction to her failed marriage to an Anglican clergyman), was converted to Theosophy after reviewing *The Secret Doctrine* and soon poured all her formidable energies into this movement.

Before becoming a Theosophist and student of Blavatsky just before the latter's death in 1891, Besant was an active and controversial socialist and union organizer, associated with the freethinking politician Charles Bradlaugh. She labored famously on behalf of birth control education, led a strike by the exploited girls who sold matches on street corners, and was a member of the London School Board. As the 1937 *Theosophical Year Book* put it,

In 1889 [when she joined the Theosophical Society], there was scarcely any modern reform for which she had not worked, written, spoken and suffered: women's suffrage and equal rights, better housing, school meals, abolition of sweated wages, penal reforms, Empire Federation, antivivisection ... reform of land laws, the right to freedom of thought and speech, a reformed system of electorates, the rights of subject peoples.[17]

Besant was a paragon of the 1890s progressivist spirit, and that spirit though redirected was scarcely dimmed by her transfer from free thought to Theosophy, and from England to India. As President she founded the Theosophical Order of Service, which has ever since actively supported causes in line with Theosophical principles. In India she established schools and labored on behalf of the abolition of child marriage and reform of the caste system, while her unabashed sympathy with Indian religions won her support from even the most orthodox brahmins, or upper caste Hindus.

Most significantly of all, her founding in 1916 of the Home Rule League, designed to make India a self-governing member of the British Commonwealth of Nations, put her in the center of India's political crucible, where nationalism and British resistance struggled against each other with increasing passion. Despite her insistence on nonviolence and constitutional procedure, she was interned by her own countrymen for three months in 1917, but then released to tumultuous enthusiasm. She was elected president of the Indian National Congress, the major indigenous independence organization, but soon lost support there to M. K. Gandhi, whose identification with the Indian masses she could not match and whose advocacy of complete separation from Britain and the West she did not share.

At the same time, Besant did not hesitate to support the British cause with all the passion of which she was capable in World War I, seeing it as a struggle between the forces of dharma (cosmic justice and order) and adharma, or even more broadly, between the Great Souls or Masters who labored on behalf of the Allied cause, the cause leading to human freedom, as over against the powers of darkness behind the other side, unholy powers who delighted in strife and slavery. (Her successor as International President, George Arundale, revived the same rhetoric in World War II.)

It was Besant more than any other single individual who made Theosophy a vehicle for what Catherine Wessinger has called "progressive messianism."[18] This viewpoint embraced, Wessinger believed, a millennialist belief in coming world perfection attained with superhuman help, in the persons of Masters and particularly the World Teacher, but achieved gradually rather than with apocalyptic suddenness. In Besant's vision, the messianic process would bring to fruition all the worthy causes for which she had labored with somewhat less hope, at least on the spiritual side, in her pre-Theosophical days.

It is worth noting how Theosophy attracted persons like Besant, or Blavatsky herself, intelligent and capable, painfully aware of injustice, given to idealism, and at the same time were what sociologists might call "status inconsistent"—because of gender, class, education, race, or other stigmata were unable to find a place equal to their abilities and dreams in the established churches or political world. They often drew fire from those worlds, yet gave as good as they got, and continued to present an alternative view of the world and its lines of authority.

Often these were examples of the so-called "New Woman" of the 1890s, the product of newly established colleges and graduate schools for women that were now producing an educated elite of women trying to enter the professional worlds of medicine, social work, and other fields. On another level, middle-class women were joining women's clubs where they were able to discuss intellectual topics and issues of the day—and Theosophical meetings could serve the same function—even as younger women engaged in bicycling, camping, and sports, all to the delight of some and the scandal of others. This expansion of female horizons clearly dovetailed with the progressivist political agenda. Numerous Theosophical women of the time, including Besant herself, fit the model well, as pioneer women lecturers and reformers; other Theosophical women were among the first physicians and college professors of their sex. It is easy to understand that a spiritual home in the Theosophical Society, with its evolutionary universe and tradition of gender equality, offered them—and men sympathetic to them—a way to deal with the "status inconsistency" they may still have felt against the male-dominated mainline ecclesiastical, educational, and political worlds.

KRISHNAMURTI AND THE ORDER OF THE STAR

The progressivist vision was greatly enhanced and popularized by the Krishnamurti enthusiasm of the 1910s and 1920s. In 1909, at Adyar in India, Leadbeater declared Jiddu Krishnamurti (1895–1986), the slight and unprepossessing son of a dedicated Theosophist and retired civil servant, to be the Vehicle of the Lord Maitreya (the future Buddha, also identified with Christ), or World Teacher, and said he must be trained for that purpose. To this end, Leadbeater and Besant undertook his education, first at Adyar, then in England, and finally in Ojai, California. Although the education results were mixed—Krishnamurti was unsuccessful in gaining admission to a British university—the once-unpromising youth grew into a handsome and pleasing man, who satisfied his mentors with simple yet cogent talks and writings on spiritual matters. Indeed, he attracted attention far beyond Theosophical circles. Mass media articles appeared with titles like "Messiah in Tennis Shoes," and none other than George Bernard Shaw once went so far as to call Krishnamurti "the most beautiful human being he ever saw."[19]

In 1911 the Order of the Star in the East was formed to prepare for the coming; this organization spread excitement through the Theosophical world by means of its publications and conventions that tingled with anticipation. The order produced a magazine, *The Herald of the Star*, a publishing house, Lotus Press, and a youth organization, the Servants of the Star.

The early twentieth century's extraordinary interest in Krishnamurti messianism seems to say something significant about those tumultuous times. Against a wildly erratic backdrop of progressivist optimism, the horror and despair of the Great War, and the giddy mix of futurist dreams and anxious sense of the world's foundations shaking of the 1920s, Krishnamurti and his cause projected a tangible eschatological hope, one that was truly universal, mingling East and West in the groundwork it was laying for a new age. For example, the Anglican clergyman and Krishnamurti devotee C. W. Scott-Moncrief, in an address, later published, entitled, "The Coming Christ and the Order of the Star of the East," made the program of the new messiah sound like no more than a natural extension of ultraliberal Christianity.

Christianity may triumph, he said, but in a new form to which all world religions will contribute. East and West are no longer watertight because races and religions interact. There is a new universalism: the priest cited such international activities as the labor movement, the women's movement, the Esperanto movement, "science itself," and groups like the Theosophical Society and Baha'i. The coming faith will, furthermore, be a "scientific religion," to which not only the natural sciences, but also such "sciences" as sociology, education, socialism, and eugenics will be reconciled. For all this, the mighty vision of a new world teacher, to appear in the East, will be requisite.[20] These are by and large causes with which, as we have seen, Theosophists of the progressive era were already involved.

However, in 1929, on the eve of the 1930s and of the Great Depression, when so many hopes were dashed and others born, the star suddenly set. At a camp of the Order of the Star in Ommen, Netherlands, before an audience of some 3,000, including Besant, Krishnamurti dramatically dissolved the Order and rejected for himself all organizations. In his famous speech, he proclaimed: "I maintain that truth is a pathless land, and you cannot approach it by any path whatsoever, by any religion, by any sect." Henceforth, until his death in 1986, the one-time "Vehicle" pursued an independent vocation as a distinguished lecturer and teacher of pathless truth and "choiceless awareness."[21] Many Theosophists, however, were devastated. Although the Theosophical Society carried on, doing useful work on perhaps a more stable and mature basis than in those halcyon years, it never again recovered the spirit, publicity, or numbers of its "golden age," the years roughly 1900–1930, when it was most closely associated with the progressivist spirit.

The major Theosophical organizations have continued, however, to present their teaching and life, mostly through lectures and publications, but increasingly through tapes and videos as well. By and large a liberalizing trend can be discerned, as Theosophists seem less concerned with the letter of the classic texts than with extracting major themes, such as the universal conjunction of consciousness and matter, and the ideas of evolution and cycles on all planes of reality, showing their compatibility with current science and philosophy.

OTHER THEOSOPHICAL GROUPS

Not all Theosophists were pleased by these developments. In the United States, the American section, under the presidency of William Q. Judge (1851–1896), an original founder of the Society, separated from Adyar as early as 1895. Judge, however, died only the next year, and was succeeded by Katherine Tingley (1847–1929), an American woman who, like Besant, had been a dynamic social reformer, and who was to lead her society into a remarkable communal venture. Hardly had she taken office when, in 1897, she closed almost all lodges of the American section and called the membership to take up residence in a utopian settlement she was establishing on some 350 acres at Point Loma, in San Diego.

That same year Besant launched a counteroffensive on behalf of the Adyar society, winning back to its allegiance most of the 50 lodges and 1,000 or so American Theosophists who did not feel led to move to Point Loma. For a time, however, all eyes were on that site by the blue Pacific. Initially enjoying generous financial support, the new planned community soon displayed two neoclassical buildings with aquamarine and amethyst glass domes illumined at night, residences, paradisal gardens and orchards, and the first open-air Greek theatre in America, where spectacular dramatic performances were enacted. A refectory served common meals to the citizens of "Lomaland" (some 500 at its height), and children were raised in a communal nursery and boarding school under an educational system called "Raja Yoga," said to develop young physical, mental, and spiritual faculties in perfect harmony. Lomaland took pride in remarkable achievements in several fields, including education, drama, art, and agriculture, including in the last the development of commercial avocado production.

Unfortunately, utopia could not last. After the death of Katherine Tingley in an automobile accident in 1929 and the onset of the Great Depression almost immediately after, the community fell into serious financial difficulties, and membership declined. Point Loma was finally closed in 1942 because of increased military activity in the area with the commencement of World War II. Initially, the dwindling and aging community moved to Covina, California, then, in 1950, transferred its headquarters to Pasadena, and later Altadena where, no longer a formal community, it maintains a Theosophical library and publication program.[22]

The third major Theosophical Society is the United Lodge of Theosophists (ULT), founded in 1909 by Robert Crosbie (1848–1919) as an "unsectarian" third force intended to reconcile the differences between the increasingly antagonistic Adyar and Point Loma groups. The ULT has become known as a conservative Theosophical presence, presenting only the "traditional teachings" of Blavatsky and Judge. It is also known for its policy of endeavoring to avoid "personality cults" by declining to announce or introduce speakers by name.

Also worthy of mention is the Temple of the People in Halcyon, California, founded in 1898 and moved to this site in 1904, as a community alternative to Point Loma, and with its own somewhat distinctive interpretation of Theosophy. Several other groups may be considered devolutions of Theosophy. Anthroposophy, founded by Rudolf Steiner, sometime leader of German Theosophists, separated from the international Society in 1912 as a result of Steiner's growing dissatisfaction with Besant, the Krishnamurti movement, and the "Eastern" tendencies of Adyar. This group, noted for the "eurhythmic" dance exercises and highly regarded Waldorf schools, and now spread worldwide, emphasizes Western and Christian mysticism. Groups following the books delivered through Alice Bailey, such as the Arcane School and the School for Esoteric Studies, and the "I Am" movement of the Saint

Germain Foundation, present later teachings believed to have been transmitted from Theosophical masters.

MAJOR THEOSOPHICAL IDEAS

A summary of major Theosophical ideas begins with the three "Declared Objects" of the Society. No formal affirmation is expected of Theosophists except one of sympathy with these objectives. They are, in brief and in current wording,

> To form a nucleus of the universal brotherhood of humanity;
> To encourage the comparative study of religion, philosophy, and science;
> To investigate unexplained laws of nature and the powers latent in humanity.

These offer a short summation of the essential foundations of a positive pluralism: acknowledgment of universal kinship; openness to learning and borrowing from all cultures; recognition that human nature and the universe bear many mysteries and hidden interconnections, which ought to keep one wary toward claims of final and exclusivist truth and able to rejoice in the presence of many perspectives.

The deeper, or at least more esoteric-seeming, concepts associated with Theosophy (though not regarded as mandatory dogmas) can be considered in light of these principles. *The Secret Doctrine* and other basic texts tell us, first, that the ultimate basis of brotherhood is one infinite and incomprehensible reality that underlies and unites all that is or can ever be. It expresses itself through both consciousness and matter, so that all phenomena represent the complex interaction of these two. Out of this oneness, many universes, solar systems, and worlds develop through immense cycles in accordance with the dynamics of the interaction of spirit and matter. The inhabitants of those spheres, called humans on earth, sometimes called the "pilgrims," move through these universes and worlds lifetime after lifetime in response to karma and the necessity of experiencing many modes of being, before returning to the Source, the One.

Finally, Theosophy affirms there is a reservoir of wisdom in our world, known to those well advanced on the path but accessible to all earnest seekers, that can help one to understand and grow in these truths. This is the wisdom first glimpsed in the study of comparative religion, philosophy, and science, the truth that is treasured by some esoteric orders and that is alive to those masters of the wisdom, also called elder brothers, mahatmas, or adepts, whose existence Theosophy has generally maintained. While they can occasionally be met in the midst of the modern city, by and large adepts dwell in quieter parts of the planet for the sake of their own spiritual peace, but by inner means they influence for good the evolution of earth, and teach those who are ready.

For Theosophy growth is not only a matter of intellectual learning. Progress also involves initiation or inward transformation—opening powers latent in humanity—and living in accordance with a spirit of openness toward unexplained laws of nature, and toward kinship with the divine in all life. For some Theosophists this entails living a relatively simple and natural life, vegetarian and free from the use of alcohol or tobacco, but these points are not mandated.

In general, in fact, the practice-oriented side of Theosophy is individualistic. The Society insists that it is not a religion or a church, Lodge meetings typically consist only of a lecture or discussion, and the only spiritual practice likely to be inculcated is meditation. There is a Theosophical group called the Esoteric School, composed of some though not all highly committed members, whose adherents promise to follow the above lifestyle rules and to study and meditate on a regular basis. Some Theosophists who desire spiritual or religious practice of a more ritualistic or public sort are also members of ritual groups traditionally associated with Theosophy, though institutionally separate, such as the Liberal Catholic Church, already mentioned, or the Co-Masonic Order, a Masonic group with many Theosophical initiates that admits both men and women. Others also belong to "mainline" churches. Lately many Theosophists have gravitated to Unitarian-Universalist churches.

CONCLUSION AND THE FUTURE OF THEOSOPHY

Theosophy entered the late nineteenth century with an eye toward both distant past and future, hoping to go beyond the wastelands of the day. Evolution, now read as vast cosmic-scale visions of spiritual as well as physical upward cycles, of whose movement one could now be an agent, was as much a part of its picture as the "ancient wisdom." The tensions between backward looking and forward moving were not entirely reconciled, but sometimes showed how ideological disequilibrium can be dynamic. Tension-based energy is, in fact, as Olcott intuited, a principle of America's novel historical role.

Catherine Albanese has spoken of the "kinetic revolution" behind the Transcendentalism of Emerson and Thoreau, certainly a background influence on Theosophy. The Concord sages' glorification of movement and change obviously reflected the era of the frontier and the clipper ships, but motion became for those New England thinkers a universal absolute. Emerson repeatedly spoke of rest as decay, of motion as a form of perfection, of challenges to leave the shore and plunge into the Unlimited and the Immensities. But if change is a universal perfection, then disequilibrium must be a good, for it is the "kinetic" inciter of change.[23]

Theosophy offers models for reconciling differences inherent in the universal kinetic through a kind of "triangulation" appeal to a higher, and older, common ground. Thus, Olcott sought to find the common ground of science and religion by appealing to ancient wisdom. The Theosophical spirit enables one to be both liberal and conservative, in the deepest philosophical meaning of these often-abused terms, on social and political issues. It likewise presents a model for constructive social change which, because of "triangulation," if the word may be used in this context, with large-scale patterns of evolution, including evolution of consciousness, comes closer to progressive eschatology than to revolutionary apocalyptic.

Has this outlook any social significance? Theosophy later influenced individuals of the New Deal era, like Vice President Henry Wallace (1836–1916), a sometime member of the Society, who combined deep-seated idealism with commitment to democratic political process in a pluralistic society. It was Wallace who persuaded

Franklin D. Roosevelt's Secretary of the Treasury, Henry Morganthau, to place the reverse of the Great Seal of the United States, with its arcane Masonic symbolism involving the topless pyramid, the eye in the triangle, and the words *Novus ordo seclorum,* on the dollar bill; he persuaded Morganthau that *Novus ordo* was Latin for New Deal.

Something of the Theosophical legacy in American life is suggested: the combining of occult wisdom from a distant past with pragmatic reform. That heritage carried its own legacy of the divinity and infinite potential of human life into present need. As Olcott understood, this could happen only on America's sacred ground, where the unity of diversity, *E pluribus unum,* for which Wallace and others yearned, could be realized, and the pluralism and the dynamic were also parts of Transcendentalist and Theosophical perfection in motion. Within the unlikely setting of Washington's corridors of power, Wallace was well known for his interest in "mysticism" and "occultism," particularly when they afforded a vision of the unity out of diversity for which he pined. Arthur Schlesinger, in *The Coming of the New Deal,* provides an insightful overview of this side of the New Deal Secretary of Agriculture and later Vice President. Schlesinger suggests that what particularly appealed to Wallace "was the hope that the vision of spiritual unity might enable him to join together the two halves of his own personality. For as both scientist and mystic, both politician and prophet, both opportunist and idealist, Wallace was split down the middle."[24]

Many other moderns were likewise divided, and for some of them, as for Wallace, the Theosophical vision was able, at least at times, to raise the split between inspiring past and evolutionary future to the level of creative tension or kinetic perfection, making the changes and chances of this world a progressive highway to a better world.

But in the early years of the twenty-first century, most Theosophical groups seem to be declining in membership. Perhaps, on the one hand, they have become hidebound, and, on the other, in some subtle way Theosophy's lore and particular style of spiritual energy is less attuned to the current generation than it was to the world of a century earlier. Or it may be a result of the "bowling alone" phenomenon: the tendency of postmoderns not to want to join organizations, and even less to go out to meetings. Increasingly, persons on the rolls of Theosophical organizations are members at large rather than attenders of lodge or study group meetings, finding the sustenance they require from books and the Internet rather than face to face. Yet to some the vision of Theosophy has never seemed more relevant to a troubled world.

NOTES

1. Henry Steel Olcott, "Inaugural Address," in *Applied Theosophy and Other Essays,* ed. H.S. Olcott (Adyar, Madras, India: Theosophical Publishing House, 1975), 34–35.

2. R.W.B. Lewis, *The American Adam* (Chicago: University of Chicago Press, 1955).

3. Henry Steel Olcott, *Old Diary Leaves, First Series, America 1874–78* (Adyar, Madras, India: Theosophical Publishing House, 1941), 377. The book is John Lloyd Stephens, *Incidents of Travel in Yucatan* (New York: Harper, 1843, and subsequent editions).

4. Olcott, *Old Diary Leaves, First Series,* 14–15.

5. H.P. Blavatsky, *Isis Unveiled,* 2 vols. (Wheaton, IL: Theosophical Publishing House, 1972; facsimile of first edition, New York: J. W. Bouton, 1877), 2:369.

6. Henry David Thoreau, *Walden* (New York: New American Library, 1942), 198–99.

7. Cited in Carl T. Jackson, *The Oriental Religions and American Thought: Nineteenth Century Explorations* (Westport, CT: Greenwood Press, 1981), 141.

8. See Stephen Prothero, *The White Buddhist: The Asian Odyssey of Henry Steel Olcott* (Bloomington: Indiana University Press, 1996).

9. Published as Henry S. Olcott, *People from the Other World* (Hartford, CT: American Publishing Co.,1875; reprint Rutland, VT: Charles E. Tuttle Co., 1972).

10. Henry S. Olcott, *Old Diary Leaves, Series I, 1878–83* (Adyar, Madras, India: Theosophical Publishing House, 1900, 1928, 1954).

11. Blavatsky, *Isis Unveiled.*

12. A.T. Barker, compiler, *The Mahatma Letters to A. P. Sinnett,* 3d rev. ed. (First pub. 1923; Adyar, Madras, India: Theosophical Publishing House, 1962). Vicente Hao Chin, Jr., ed., *The Mahatma Letters to A.P. Sinnett in Chronological Sequence* (Quezon City, Philippines: Theosophical Publishing House, 1993).

13. See Edwin Hirschmann, *'White Mutiny': The Ilbert Bill Crisis in India and the Genesis of the Indian National Congress* (Columbia, MO: South Asia Books, 1980). This useful volume does not mention Theosophy by name, however.

14. H.P. Blavatsky, *The Secret Doctrine,* 3 vols. (Adyar, Madras, India: Theosophical Publishing House, 1993; facsimile of 1888 edition)

15. See Gregory Tillett, *The Elder Brother: A Biography of Charles Webster Leadbeater* (London: Routledge & Kegan Paul, 1982).

16. Maurice Tuchman et al., *The Spiritual in Art: Abstract Painting 1890–1985* (Los Angeles County Museum of Art; and New York: Abbeville Press, 1986), especially 94–95, 134–39.

17. *The International Theosophical Year Book 1937* (Adyar, Madras, India: Theosophical Publishing House, 1936), 181.

18. Catherine Lowman Wessinger, *Annie Besant and Progressive Messianism (1847–1933)* (Lewiston, NY: Edwin Mellen Press, 1988.

19. Cited in Mary Lutyens, *Krishnamurti: The Years of Fulfillment* (New York: Farrar, Straus and Giroux, 1983), 27–28.

20. The Reverend C.W. Scott-Moncrief, "The Coming Christ and the Order of the Star in the East" (paper read in London November 27, 1911; published Auckland, New Zealand: Lotus Press, n.d.).

21. See Mary Lutyens, *Krishnamurti: The Years of Awakening* (New York: Farrar, Straus and Giroux, 1975); Mary Lutyens, *Krishnamurti: The Years of Fulfillment* (New York: Farrar, Straus and Giroux, 1983).

22. Bruce F. Campbell, *Ancient Wisdom Revived: A History of the Theosophical Movement* (Berkeley: University of California Press, 1980), 135–37. See also Emmett A. Greenwalt, *California Utopia: Point Loma, 1897–1942* (San Diego, CA: Point Loma Publication, 1978); W. Michael Ashcraft, *The Dawn of the New Cycle: Point Loma Theosophists and American Culture* (Knoxville: University of Tennessee Press, 2002).

23. Catherine L. Albanese, *Corresponding Motion: Transcendental Religion and the New America* (Philadelphia: Temple University Press, 1977).

24. Arthur Schlesinger, *The Coming of the New Deal* (Boston: Houghton Mifflin, 1919), 33.

FURTHER READING

Ashcraft, W. Michael. *The Dawn of the New Cycle: Point Loma Theosophists and American Culture.* Knoxville: University of Tennessee Press, 2002.

Besant, Annie. *An Autobiography.* London: Theosophical Publishing Society, 1894; 2nd ed. Benares, 1908; 3rd ed. Adyar, 1939).

Blavatsky, Helena Petrovna. *Isis Unveiled.* 2 vols. Wheaton, IL: Theosophical Publishing House, 1972; facsimile of first ed., New York: J. W. Bouton, 1877).

———. *The Secret Doctrine.* 3 vols. Adyar, Madras, India: Theosophical Publishing House, 1993; facsimile of 1888 ed..

Campbell, Bruce F. *Ancient Wisdom Revived: A History of the Theosophical Movement.* Berkeley: University of California Press, 1980.

Judge, William Q. *Ocean of Theosophy.* Covina: Theosophical University Press, 1948.

Lutyens, Mary. *Krishnamurti: The Years of Awakening.* New York: Farrar, Straus and Giroux, 1975.

———. *Krishnamurti: The Years of Fulfillment.* New York: Farrar, Straus and Giroux, 1983.

Olcott, Henry Steel. *Old Diary Leaves, First Series, America 1874–78.* Adyar, Madras, India: Theosophical Publishing House, 1941.

Prothero, Stephen. *The White Buddhist: The Asian Odyssey of Henry Steel Olcott.* Bloomington: Indiana University Press, 1996.

Tillett, Gregory. *The Elder Brother: A Biography of Charles Webster Leadbeater.* London: Routledge & Kegan Paul, 1982.

Tingley, Katherine. *The Gods Await.* Point Loma: Woman's International Theosophical League, 1926.

Wessinger, Catherine Lowman. *Annie Besant and Progressive Messianism (1847–1933).* Lewiston, NY: Edwin Mellen Press, 1988.

The American New Thought Movement

Dell deChant

New Thought is a global New Religious Movement (NRM) that began in the United States in the late nineteenth century as a popular religious expression of idealism, a philosophic tradition whose deep taproots can be traced to Plato (428–348 BCE). As a distinct religious tradition, New Thought and its early communities emerged out of Christian Science and the nineteenth century mental healing movement. In its earliest manifestation, it caught the attention of William James, who gave it considerable attention in *The Varieties of Religious Experience* (1902), referring to it as "the Mind-cure movement" and "the religion of healthy minded-ness."[1] The movement itself has its clearest origins in the writings, teachings, and organizational strategies of Emma Curtis Hopkins (1849–1925), an independent Christian Scientist and former student of the founder of Christian Science, or the Church of Christ, Scientist, Mary Baker Eddy (1821–1910). By the early twentieth century, New Thought was well established in the United States and a number of distinct subgroups emerged, most notably Unity and Divine Science. The movement grew steadily throughout the twentieth century, and today comprises several major denominations and many smaller groups, with representative communities in over 60 countries and perhaps as many as 500,000 members—making it the largest movement in what is called the "metaphysical" tradition.[2]

This essay is divided into four sections. The first section offers an overview and periodization of the history of the movement followed by a detailed study of its origins and early development. The second section focuses on the major New Thought denominations and significant figures in the movement's history. Section three outlines New Thought's primary beliefs and practices. The final section considers the future of the movement and the issues that confront it. The term "New Thought" refers to the movement as a whole, recognizing that in some cases individual denominations may differ from the characterization of the movement and other denominations.

ORIGINS AND EARLY DEVELOPMENT

New Thought's historical divisions vary, as do the choices and evaluations of major facts, key leaders, and significant dates. Relatively few academic studies of New Thought history exist, and no comprehensive critical histories. This is not the only area where scholarship on New Thought is underdeveloped, but it is an especially critical one. This essay offers a broad introductory sketch of New Thought for general readers as well as specialists. For purposes of this introduction, New Thought history can be divided into four major periods: (1) Prehistory (until 1888); (2) Early (1888–1927); (3) Classical (1927–1960); and (4) Modern (1954–present).

(1) Prehistory (until 1888): As noted earlier, the philosophical roots of New Thought go back through the Western Idealist tradition, originating with Plato. The line from Plato to the emergence of New Thought, however, follows a somewhat circuitous route. In its earliest manifestation, New Thought was a mental healing movement with clear affinities to Christian Science. From the many names of reference used before "New Thought" became standard in the 1890s,[3] "Mind Cure" (or Mind-cure) was probably the best known and most accurate. The year 1888 is cited as the end of New Thought's "prehistory" since it is the date traditionally accepted as the "mythic" founding of Divine Science, the first religious group in what would come to be called New Thought.[4]

(2) Early (1888–1927): New Thought's early period begins with the founding of Divine Science (1888) and concludes with the founding of the last major New Thought denomination of the early period, Religious Science (1927). The year after Divine Science began, New Thought's largest denomination, Unity, was founded. These three groups are notable because they are the only ones established in the early period of the movement that survived into the twenty-first century. Each of them was established by persons either directly taught by Emma Curtis Hopkins or indirectly influenced by her work. Unity was founded by the Fillmores, Myrtle (1845–1931) and Charles (1854–1948); Divine Science by Malinda Cramer (1844-1906) and Nona Brooks (1861-1945); and Religious Science by Ernest Holmes (1887–1960). The Fillmores and Holmes personally studied with Hopkins, and Brooks's affiliation was mediated by Hopkins's student, Kate Bingham. Only Cramer did not have an affiliation with Hopkins, although she began Divine Science in San Francisco a year after she attended Hopkins's class in that city.[5] It is of note that in this period the International New Thought Alliance (INTA) was founded (1914).

(3) Classical (1927–1960): New Thought's classical period begins with the founding of the youngest major New Thought group (Religious Science) and ends with the death of its founder, Holmes. During these years the three groups (now properly termed denominations) grew in size and influence, and numerous independent New Thought communities emerged. Among the three major groups, growth was constant, if not always rapid. In all of the groups, mental healing remained the focus. Periodicals, pamphlets, and books were published in abundance. Teachers and ministers spread the message of New Thought across the United States; churches (often called "societies" and "centers") were founded and congregations grew. As the

number of churches increased, the movements developed institutional structures to help promote growth, maintain continuity in teachings, and facilitate communication. The international scope of New Thought also became evident in this period as the denominations and independent groups established communities throughout the world—especially in English-speaking countries and in sub-Saharan Africa. A related movement, influenced by the teachings of Religious Science, Seicho-no-Ie ("Home of Infinite Life" or "House of Blessing"), was founded by Masaharu Taniguchi (1893-1985) in Japan in 1930.

(4) Modern (1954–present): By 1960, all of the major New Thought groups were led by persons other than their founders. New Thought's Modern period does not begin in 1960, however. It begins six years earlier, in 1954, when the first major internal division occurred within a New Thought group. In that year the Religious Science movement split into two groups, Religious Science International and the United Church of Religious Science. The division resulted in a significant expansion of the number of churches, members, and ministers committed to the teachings of Religious Science. During the Modern period, Unity and INTA also grew considerably. Divine Science, however, experienced slow and steady decline. Also during this period, the youngest major New Thought denomination was established: the Universal Foundation for Better Living, founded Chicago, Illinois, in 1974 by Johnnie Colemon (Johnnie May Colemon Nedd).

New Thought is a decidedly American NRM. A product of turn-of-the-century America (late 1800s, early 1900s), New Thought developed in the context of and was enriched by the secularization process. Although the roots of New Thought are in Christian Science and the earlier Mind Cure movement, from the outset New Thought offered believers an integrated world view and a comprehensive interpretation of individual existence and human life as a whole that distinguished it from both Christian Science and Mind Cure. This interpretation, which was based on a popularized version of philosophic idealism, was decidedly "optimistic," but it was an optimism grounded in the understanding that life's ultimate Truth is the omnipotence of good.

As New Thought grew out of the shadow of Christian Science and Mind Cure, mental healing continued to be a major component in the movement's teachings, but its implications expanded to include all areas of life. New Thought was comfortable with secularization, increasing urbanization, rapid industrialization, and commodity capitalism; and it brought a new gospel of happiness and prosperity to a young but developing American culture that was seeking both. In the period of New Thought's early development, American society was becoming increasingly secular; science, technology, personal wealth, and individual freedom were glamorized. During this era, and probably for the first time in world history, a large middle class, located on the socioeconomic scale between rich and poor, came into existence in the United States.

From this class New Thought drew (and has continued to draw) its greatest numbers of members. The three most important theoretical features in New Thought's successful evangelism of the middle class were originally (1) idealism, (2) optimism, and (3) scientific method. As America entered the twentieth century, many in its burgeoning middle class found themselves attracted to this new faith that proclaimed that God was wholly good, evil was only error, ultimate reality was mind, and one's life and world were predicated on one's thought. This was religious idealism designed for popular consumption by an optimistic, self-confident, self-made society in the making—a popular idealism for the masses.

New Thought was something more than popular philosophical idealism, however. It was also a pragmatic mysticism based on popular understandings of scientific method—a religious technology for the masses. In terms of its own rhetoric, this was a religion that persons could use, not a religion that used persons. In fact, as often as not, the early leaders of New Thought denied the religious character of their undertakings—choosing instead to refer to their organizations as schools, institutes, and societies.

From a practical standpoint, New Thought's early success is owed to four major factors: (1) the confidence of its leaders, (2) the professional empowerment of women, (3) the skillful use of mass media, and (4) criticism of existing religions. The first two factors are considered in detail here. Like zealous converts of any age, the confidence of the early New Thought leaders was total. They believed in their message with an intense conviction, and they taught with zeal, enthusiasm, and consummate commitment. Although seldom dogmatic (largely to avoid too close a connection with their perceived understanding of Christian Science), early leaders held to lofty ideals, articulated best by Hopkins, that a new era was dawning when the transformation of consciousness would herald a transformation of individuals and humanity as a whole.

New Thought was truly gender blind, and this proved to be a tremendous boon to the movement's evangelistic efforts. From the outset, with the ministry of Hopkins, New Thought ordained women, thus giving them professional status in an American society dominated by men. As a consequence, New Thought attracted talented women with professional aspirations. These women, who today might be attorneys, university educators, and public officials, became leaders in New Thought, since those other professions were closed to them. Women did not even receive the right to vote until 1920—more than 30 years after the first women were ordained by Hopkins. To this day, the majority of New Thought ministers are women, accounting for slightly over 60 percent of the nearly 1,600 ministers in the three largest New Thought groups: Unity, United Church of Religious Science, and Religious Science International.

Scholars and New Thought adherents alike debate the immediate background of New Thought: who should be cited as legitimate precursors, who is properly cited as its founder, and who should be cited among its early leaders. Although Hopkins seems most appropriately recognized as New Thought's founder, preinstitutional influences include nineteenth century Hegelianism, New England Transcendentalism, Swedenborgianism, Spiritualism, the mental healing practice and private instruction sessions of Phineas Parkhurst Quimby (1802–1866) and, of course, Christian Science and Eddy (herself a student of Quimby).

What is known as New Thought came into existence because of Hopkins's work. This understanding is relatively new, replacing the older position that recognized Quimby as the founder.[6] Quimby was a pioneer in mental healing. Originally attracted to mesmerism (hypnotism), he became an itinerant "mesmerist healer," using an assistant who in an hypnotic state would diagnose health challenges and prescribe material cures for clients. By 1847 (possibly earlier) he abandoned mesmerism and his assistant in favor of a new healing method. This method was a precursor to mental healing and Mind Cure, although it was based on a materialist premise, which was later rejected by both Christian Science and New Thought.

From 1847 to 1859, Quimby traveled alone, setting up temporary clinics where he would heal persons. His method was to sit down with people and "tell them their feelings and what they think is their disease." He would then correct their error in thinking, thus changing the "fluids of the system" and establishing "truth or health."[7] After 1859 Quimby settled in Portland, Maine, where he continued to practice his healing method. From 1859 until his death he instructed an inner circle of followers and outlined his method in writing. Selections from his work first appeared in 1921 in *The Quimby Manuscripts* and *The Complete Writings* in 1988.[8] Although Quimby's work laid the foundation for New Thought, he cannot be properly cited as its founder, mainly because of his rejection of religion and the materialist bent of his healing method.

Detailed study of the historical process through which Quimby-as-founder belief developed in New Thought is offered by J. Gordon Melton in "New Thought's Hidden History" and "The Case of Edward J. Arens and the Distortion of the History of New Thought."[9] A robust defense of the Quimby-as-founder belief can be found in two works by C. Alan Anderson, "Quimby As Founder of New Thought" and "Emma Curtis Hopkins: Organizational Founder and Metaphysical Confounder of New Thought."[10] The strongest versions of the argument against Quimby being cited as founder are those developed in support of Hopkins by Melton and Gail Harley.[11]

Aside from Quimby, the other major precursor of the movement is Eddy, whose contributions are usually depreciated in favor of Quimby's. This is unfortunate since Hopkins clearly understood her own work to be within the Christian Science tradition, and since she was certainly influenced by Eddy, with whom she studied. In this regard, Eddy's relationship to New Thought should be reconsidered.

Eddy experienced a healing as a result of Quimby's treatment in 1862. She studied informally with him for some time after the healing. In 1866, a few weeks after Quimby's death, Eddy had a serious accident—"pronounced fatal by physicians." Three days later, during a study of the Bible, she experienced a sudden healing predicated on the realization that: "Life is in and of Spirit; this Life being the sole reality of existence." In 1870 she offered her first class on mental healing, using a manuscript on which she had been working for some time. In 1875 the manuscript was published as *Science and Health*. More than all of Quimby's teachings and writings, this text helped lay the groundwork for the mental healing movement and its successor, New Thought.

In 1879, Eddy took another step that would prove to be of vast importance to the emergence of New Thought; she founded a religious institution. Chartered in Massachusetts, "The Church of Christ, Scientist" was the first religious group based on the principles of mental healing. The 1883 edition of *Science and Health* was revised; added to the text and the title was "*Key to the Scriptures.*" Eddy's addition of scriptural interpretation is the beginning of the modern allegorical (or "metaphysical") interpretation of the Bible. To maintain uniformity in teaching, in 1895, Eddy "ordained" the Bible and *Science and Health* as the only pastors in Christian Science, thus eliminating the possibility of individual sermons.

Eddy made notable contributions to the subsequent development of New Thought. She established a popular religion based on the principles of idealism. Significantly, she included the word "Christian" in the title of her movement—thus signaling its religious nature. She also created the first education program for persons desiring to serve as "mental healers," and the official institutional certification of these workers as "practitioners." She also published a serious and systematic exposition of her movement's teachings and utilized modern publication methods to propagate these teachings. But New Thought also differs from Christian Science. The most fundamental differences pertain to dogma, matter, and medicine. Unlike Christian Science, New Thought is nondogmatic. It does not see matter or the material world as an error or an illusion, and it is not opposed to the medical resolution of physical ills (the symptoms of mental error).

The distinction between Christian Science and New Thought and the birth of the younger movement both resulted from the work of Hopkins. She is properly credited as the founder of New Thought. In her lifetime she was called "Teacher of Teachers,"[12] meaning that she directly or indirectly taught and inspired the first generation of New Thought leaders.

Hopkins began her religious career as a Christian Scientist, becoming a student of Eddy in the early 1880s. She rose rapidly in the ranks and in 1884 was given the prestigious office of editor for the *Christian Science Journal.* For reasons still unclear, she was dismissed as editor in 1885. It is fair to believe that the dismissal was a result of the conflict between two extremely talented and religiously zealous individuals. The reason usually given is that Hopkins began to study spiritual teachings other than those of Eddy. Historian J. Gordon Melton suggests that the two may also have disagreed over Hopkins's remuneration.[13]

In 1886 Hopkins moved to Chicago, then a hotbed of independent forms of Christian Science. In Chicago, Hopkins and another Christian Science dissident, Mary Plunkett, began an independent Christian Science ministry and school. During her first years in Chicago, Hopkins cooperated closely with other Christian Scientists who had separated from Eddy. Also in 1886 she founded an educational institution, the Emma Hopkins College of Christian Science. The first class had at least 37 students, among them Katie Bingham, the practitioner who participated in the healing of Nona Brooks (a cofounder of Divine Science).[14] In a short time, students from around the country began traveling to study with Hopkins in Chicago, which led to the formation of the Hopkins Metaphysical Association in 1887 and

Hopkins's travels to San Francisco and New York City to teach classes. The Association claimed 21 member groups by the end of 1887, and a convention of the group in Boston, Massachusetts, attracted over 1,000 persons. The Association spanned the continent, with groups in San Francisco, Denver, Chicago, New York City, Boston, Maine, and other locations. Until her split with Hopkins, Plunkett served as president of the Association.

By late 1887, Plunkett left the organization, and in early 1888 she started her own organization in New York City. With her went the periodical for the emerging Hopkins Metaphysical Association, *Truth,* and, perhaps more importantly, its mailing list. In a short time, enrollment at the Seminary declined and groups began to leave the Association.

That the decline precipitated by Plunkett's departure lasted less than a year is yet another powerful testimony to Hopkins's leadership skills. To her remaining students, many of whom were outraged at Plunkett's actions, she declared:

> You are greater than disappointment.... Take the anger that shakes you like a reed in the wind. In the heat of your anger, treat some sluggish paralytic.... You soon forget the anger you felt at the friend in your strength of silent treatment.[15]

Hopkins quickly reorganized the Association, firmly establishing it as an ecclesiastical institution. As she affirmed: "[This] is not a business or a profession, it is a ministry."[16] In 1888 what had been the Emma Curtis Hopkins College of Christian Science became The Christian Science Theological Seminary, and in 1889 members of the first class of graduates were ordained—20 women and 2 men.[17] Hopkins's ordination of women marked the first time in American history (and possibly Western Christian history) that a woman ordained women. Although these new ministers were technically "Christian Science" ministers, they were functionally the first New Thought ministers. By 1893 Hopkins had ordained 111 persons and the Seminary had an enrollment of 350 students.[18]

The establishment of the seminary and the ordination of ministers confirmed the religious character of Hopkins's work while also giving greater cultural legitimacy to the work of the Association and its educational enterprise. No one else in the Mind Cure movement had gone this far—including Eddy.

Until this time, Mind Cure (both Christian Science and independent mental healing groups) was a lay movement. Although Eddy sanctioned teachers and practitioners, and ministers from other traditions were involved in the mental healing movement, Eddy's resistance to the ordination of ministers (except for the Bible and *Science and Health*) seems to have influenced the Mind Cure movement as a whole. With Hopkins's novel move, however, the developing New Thought movement suddenly ceased to be a lay movement of quasi-professional teachers and practitioners. Now it was a religious organization, ordaining ministers and sending them forth to preach and teach the new gospel of idealism, optimism, and self-improvement through mental healing.

As noted above, Hopkins, the "teacher of teachers," instructed and inspired nearly all of New Thought's early leaders. These include the Fillmores (cofounders of

Unity); Bingham, the teacher of Brooks (a founder of Divine Science); Annie Rix Militz (founder of Homes of Truth); Frances Lord (who established New Thought in England); H. Emilie Cady (author of Unity's most popular instructional text, *Lessons in Truth*); Ella Wheeler Wilcox (New Thought poet with wide cultural popularity); and Elizabeth Towne [publisher of the influential periodical, *Nautilus* (1898–1954)]. Near the end of her life, Hopkins tutored Ernest Holmes, founder of Religious Science.

Hopkins's students took her teachings to all parts of the United States. In the early years most churches were independent, and denominational structures were loose. Some of Hopkins's students opened their own training centers and sent forth their own ministers and teachers. This was the case with Unity and Divine Science. Hopkins's public ministry ended in 1895 when she closed the seminary and moved to New York City. Until her death in 1925 she continued to lecture, meet privately with students and clients, and write. Her two most notable books are *High Mysticism* (1920) and *Scientific Mental Practice* (n.d.).

Hopkins's impact cannot be overstated. Her major contributions were (1) the establishment of a seminary, ordination of ministers, and "sending" of ministers to all parts of the United States; (2) creation of a nationwide movement; (3) separation from Eddy's movement; (4) development of a primary organizational structure for others to follow; and (5) teaching nearly all the major first-generation leaders in New Thought.

MAJOR GROUPS AND SIGNIFICANT FIGURES

Even a modest historical survey of New Thought groups and leaders would be much too exhaustive for a survey of this kind. As a result, note will be made only of the major groups and certain important leaders. Charles Braden's *Spirits in Rebellion* gives additional details on major leaders of the movement from its formative period until the 1950s.

Hopkins Again

Until the emergence of Hopkins and her ministry, the independent (non-Eddy) Mind Cure movement was a loose association of healers, nearly all of whom understood themselves as private practitioners specializing in the use of mental healing techniques to cure the physical maladies of individual clients. The individualized dimension of mental healing is not absent in Hopkins, but in her work it becomes part of a far wider and deeper cultural enterprise. One cannot read Hopkins's work, review the history of her activities, and trace the careers of her students and not come to the conclusion that she sought a rather drastic transformation of the social order of her day. She couched the transformation in feminist and rather dramatic terms. "[A]ll things are becoming new," she wrote. "[S]ee how woman, the silent sufferer and meek yoke-bearer of the world is stepping quite out of her old character or role, and with a startling rebound from her long passivity is hurling herself against the age with such force and bold decision as to make even her friends stand aghast!"[19]

Hopkins's mission was not restricted to individual healing and counseling. These elements were not rejected, but her larger mission was the transformation of consciousness and culture. As she said to the 1891 graduates of her seminary:

> We ask the world, which is to be our church, to turn and listen to our preaching, for it is the quickening message from the Supreme of the universe announcing the second coming long expected, when every mountain of trouble shall be removed, every hill of difficulty obliterated.... [W]e thus set forth upon this ministry with the deliberate intention of converting the world to Christian Science.[20]

With this vision, New Thought was born, and Hopkins's students apparently accepted their teacher's direction. The most fertile ground for New Thought's early development was the regions of the Midwest and Far West. This is certainly due in part to Hopkins's evangelical tours of these regions but also to some degree a consequence of American westward expansion at the turn of the twentieth century and Christian Science's strength on the eastern seaboard. To this day, New Thought remains under developed in New England and on the East Coast as a whole—with the notable exceptions of New York City, Atlanta, Georgia, and Florida.

Early East Coast Developments

Perhaps the most significant East Coast figure was Warren Felt Evans (1817–1889), who is best understood as a precursor of New Thought. Evans was a Methodist minister, a devout Swedenborgian, and (like Eddy) a client of Quimby. Although largely forgotten by New Thought today, during his lifetime and shortly thereafter, Evans was a respected teacher, mental healer, and author. His most important contribution to later New Thought was his establishment of a philosophic basis in German Idealism for mental healing beliefs. For the bulk of his public life he resided in Boston, and, although his greatest influence was on the development of New Thought in the eastern United States, he is referred to in works by Hopkins and her students.[21]

Besides Evans, and more properly cited as New Thought leaders, early East Coast activists include Lord, whose *Christian Science Healing* (1887) was among the first works to introduce prosperity as a New Thought theme; Henry Wood (1834–1908), whose *The New Old Healing* (1908) and *The New Thought Simplified* (1908) helped introduce New Thought in East Coast intellectual circles; and Ralph Waldo Trine (1866–1958), the author of *In Tune with the Infinite* (1897), and many other books that popularized New Thought beliefs but had little official connection with the movement.[22]

Distinct religious communities with New Thought affinities also developed in the East. In 1894, Helen Van-Anderson established the Church of the Higher Life in Boston and in 1895 the Metaphysical Club of Boston was founded.[23] Other institutional expressions of New Thought in the East include the International Metaphysical League (1899), the New Thought Federation (1904), and the New Thought

Metaphysical Alliance (1906). Finally, Hopkins's work was continued, albeit in reduced form, by her sister Estelle Carpenter, Eleanor Mel, and others. Their community, Joy Farm, located in Connecticut, promoted Hopkins's teachings and its publishing arm, "The Ministry of the High Watch," published Hopkins's works after her death.[24]

Midwest and Far West

As important as these East Coast leaders and communities were to the prehistory and early development of New Thought, their impact on the movement was largely eclipsed by leaders and groups in the Middle and Far West. As New Thought grew, its greatest cultural impact was in the emerging urban centers of the American "frontier," cities like Chicago, San Francisco, Denver, Kansas City, Missouri, Seattle, Washington, and later Los Angeles, California. New Thought communities in these cities quickly became religious movements, as their leaders (following the Hopkins model) developed schools, publications, and organizations with loose institutional structures. Also, and again following Hopkins, they ordained ministers. To get an idea of how these movements emerged, it is helpful to review the development of the four groups that are the largest and oldest in New Thought. As a technical note, these groups are probably best termed "denominations" in the New Thought "family," as Methodism would be a "denomination" in the Protestant "family."

Divine Science

Although Divine Science recognizes two founders, Nona Brooks and Melinda Cramer, Brooks is of primary importance. Three other women can arguably be included as cofounders: Alethea Brooks Small (1848-1906), Fannie Brooks James (1854-1914), and Kate Bingham.

Each of the Brooks sisters played an important role in the emergence of the movement but the organizational impetus came from Cramer, who established a mental healing group in San Francisco in 1888. Cramer was a talented organizer, and, through communication with James, James was inspired to link her work in Denver with Cramer's group in San Francisco. Sometime later (and certainly by 1892), the Denver ministry adopted the name of Cramer's group, Divine Science.[25]

In 1896 Brooks quit teaching school and committed herself fully to the Divine Science ministry. Through her efforts and those of her sisters, the Denver ministry grew. In 1898 the Brooks' ministry was incorporated as the Divine Science College, and Nona was selected to be the minister. She was at first reluctant to accept the calling, but later relented, apparently due to the insistence of James. She was ordained by Cramer and conducted her first Sunday morning service on January 1, 1899.

Although Nona was apparently quite reserved, even timid, by nature, she served as the minister of the Denver church and the leader of the Divine Science movement for 30 years. She was the first female minister to perform a wedding in Denver. For this she was ridiculed in the Denver press. Although the Denver church grew and prospered during her tenure, and numerous students studied at the Divine Science College, Brooks was not strongly committed to institutional development, and the movement remained small.

Upon her resignation from leadership of the Denver church in 1929, Brooks spent time in Australia, accepted speaking invitations from numerous churches and INTA, and finally settled in Chicago where she concluded her ministerial career as leader of a small Divine Science church. In 1938 she returned to Denver to serve as president of the Divine Science College.

Besides Divine Science, Brooks had a major impact on the development of the greater New Thought movement. She served in leadership positions in the INTA, helped popularize New Thought in the Denver area and the West as a whole, and directly influenced Holmes, the great popularizer of New Thought, Emmet Fox, and numerous less significant leaders of the movement. Brooks never married, although she had a long-term relationship and profound friendship with Florence Hoyt.[26]

Divine Science is historically notable for its being the most loosely organized of all New Thought groups. Today Divine Science has less than 30 affiliated churches, most likely has "less than 5,000 members worldwide," and is represented by two small organizations, Divine Science Federation International (the older group) and United Divine Science Ministries (established in the 1990s).[27]

Unity

Unity began in Kansas City in 1889, when cofounders, Myrtle and Charles Fillmore, dedicated their lives to teaching and promoting what they termed "practical Christianity." Myrtle Fillmore's use of mental healing techniques to achieve a healing from tuberculosis was evidently the precipitating event. Traditionally Charles is given credit for organizing and managing the movement and Myrtle is presented as working behind the scenes to nurture and support Unity's followers.[28]

In its initial form, Unity was a publisher of periodicals and a prayer ministry— The Society for Silent Help, later renamed Silent Unity. Today Silent Unity is the largest and most well-known prayer ministry in the New Thought movement. By the early twentieth century, Unity functioned like a traditional Protestant denomination. The first step toward institutionalization occurred in 1903 with the incorporation of the Unity Society of Practical Christianity. Unity Society evolved into the Unity School of Christianity, which is today the Unity (and New Thought) organization most recognized by the general public. The development of affiliated ministries and its successful periodical outreach in the early twentieth century accelerated the movement's growth. This was enhanced by Unity's break with the INTA in 1922 and its initiation of annual conferences.

During the second half of the twentieth century, Unity gradually reduced its publication enterprise, with the pocket-sized, daily devotional magazine, *The Daily Word*, remaining its most representative periodical today. Notably, in the 1990s Unity discontinued *Wee Wisdom* (begun in 1893), which was the longest continually published children's magazine in the world. The movement remains committed to book publishing, with the works of Charles and Myrtle Fillmore among others continuing to be produced and distributed.

Unity's second major branch is the Association of Unity Churches (AUC), founded in 1966. The AUC is independent of Unity School and serves as the ecclesiastical arm of the movement. AUC ordains and supervises ministers, sanctions churches, and coordinates expansion activities. Members of the board of trustees are elected by representatives from member churches at annual conferences. Membership statistics are not available but an increase in the number of ministries in recent years suggests steady growth. As of 2001, there were 648 active ministers and 1023 licensed teachers serving in 936 ministries and 57 affiliated study groups in 64 countries. Outside of the United States, Unity's greatest concentration is in Africa, especially Nigeria, where there are 50 affiliated groups.[29]

In the 1990s two splinter groups formed, Unity-Progressive Council and the Federation of Independent Unity Churches, but neither have attracted a large following. The AUC is located near Unity Village in Lee's Summit, Missouri. Church membership statistics are not published but increases in the number of churches indicates steady growth over the past several decades. Total church membership is probably around 100,000, although the number of participants is probably considerably higher.

Unity is New Thought's largest denomination and is significant among New Thought groups for its strong Christian self-affirmation. The Bible is recognized as a primary text that "bears witness" to the word of God. Unity was once the trendsetter in the revitalization of the allegorical interpretation of the Bible, but has done little to advance this type of study since the 1960s. The allegorical method, called "metaphysical" interpretation in Christian Science and New Thought, treats the text as a symbolic document, with persons, places, and things standing for elements in consciousness. Charles Fillmore's *Metaphysical Bible Dictionary* (1931), is the fullest expression of this distinctive New Thought method of exegesis. In addition to the Bible, Unity's other primary religious text is Cady's *Lessons In Truth,* first published in 1894.

Like other nineteenth century New Thought groups, Unity emerged in the context of Christian Science, through the work of Hopkins. The Fillmores were students of Hopkins, receiving ordination from her in 1891, and Unity's theology reflects her influence. Mental healing (or "prayer treatment"), once a prominent feature of Unity, seems to be less of a focus in the movement today, with mainstream pastoral counseling and alternative healing methods having equal or greater popularity in many churches.

Religious Science

Religious Science recognizes Ernest Shurtleff Holmes as its founder. Before Religious Science was formally organized, Ernest was assisted by his brother, Fenwicke, a Congregationalist minister.

The turning point in Holmes's life came in 1907 when he read American Transcendentalist writer Ralph Waldo Emerson's *Essays*. After reading the work and accepting it as a guide for his own life, Holmes experienced healing of a throat ailment that had afflicted him for a long time. He also began attending the Christian Science "Mother Church" (Boston), and performed his first mental healings of others. Holmes did not take formal courses in Christian Science, although his healing system is similar to that used in Christian Science.

In 1915 Holmes gave his first lecture on mental healing. In 1916 the Holmes brothers started a mental healing periodical, *Uplift*, and Holmes immediately began to attract clients. He was ordained a Divine Science minister in 1917.

The brothers began Sunday morning lectures at the Strand Theater in Los Angeles in 1918 and, beginning in the early 1920s, they made lecture tours of East Coast cities. In 1924 Holmes studied privately with Hopkins in New York City. The brothers parted on friendly terms in 1925. Fenwicke returned to the East and enjoyed success as a lecturer and writer.

In 1926 Ernest's major work, *The Science of Mind*, was published. This book is probably the most thorough and comprehensive text on New Thought healing ever produced. In 1927 the Religious Science movement was born when Holmes founded the Institute of Religious Science and Philosophy and began a periodical, *Religious Science Monthly*, later renamed *Science of Mind* (1929). In 1929 he married Hazel Gillen.

Holmes began his movement and periodical after his studies with Hopkins. Like Brooks and the Fillmores, Holmes supposedly resisted establishing a religious institution, yet due to the influence of supporters, he relented and reluctantly did so.[30]

The Institute began ordaining ministers in 1939, and sometime in the early 1940s (the date is not certain) Carmelita Trowbridge founded the first Church of Religious Science in Alhambra, CA. Importantly, Trowbridge resisted efforts of the Institute to prevent her use of "church" in connection with Religious Science.

In 1949 the International Association of Religious Science Churches was established independent of the Institute. In 1953 the Institute established an ecclesiastical institution, The Church of Religious Science, to exercise control over the churches, and in 1954 nineteen churches affiliated with the International Association refused to join the new organization. Forty-six churches joined the Institute's Church. Since 1954 Religious Science has been represented by two different groups. Today these groups bear the names: United Church of Religious Science (successor of the Institute's organization), and Religious Science International (successor of the International Association).

Recent data indicate that today the United Church is the largest with 160 churches and 56 study groups, while Religious Science International has 107 religious churches and 27 "societies." Total membership for both groups is about 55,000.[31] Both groups developed representative democratic structures, ministerial education programs, and an international presence. A related movement, Seicho-no-Ie (noted earlier), was founded in Japan in 1930 by Msaharu Taniguchi, who was influenced in part by Holmes's writings.[32]

The International New Thought Alliance

The origin of the International New Thought Alliance (INTA) can be traced to 1914 and a New Thought conference in London, England. The Association's first annual congress was in 1915 in San Francisco. It was incorporated in 1917 in Washington, D.C. Precursors of INTA include the National New Thought Alliance (1907), the New Thought Federation (1904), and arguably the International Divine Science Association (1892). The general goal of these earlier groups was the unification of various individuals and organizations practicing mental healing, but none had any enduring success. Only with the establishment of INTA was this goal realized.

INTA has no single founder and its emergence as a distinct organization was the result of the efforts of a number of talented leaders, all of whom committed themselves, and in some cases their religious communities, to the INTA project. Early supporters included such notables as Militz, the Fillmores, Brooks, A.C. Grier, Thomas Troward, Horatio Dresser, Elizabeth Towne, and Ella Wheeler Wilcox. Although these influential leaders played a major role in publicizing and legitimating INTA as an umbrella organization, the person most responsible for the Alliance's success is James A. Edgerton (1869–1938). A lay person and former United States Post Office employee, Edgerton was the first president of the organization, holding that office from 1915 to 1923 and then again from 1934 to 1937.

Edgerton excelled at both diplomacy and organizational management, and the Alliance still follows the same basic organizational structures he established. Under his leadership, by 1920, the Alliance counted among its members New Thought's major denominations: Divine Science, the Homes of Truth, Unity, and the Church of Truth.

INTA's success as an umbrella organization for the New Thought movement is largely the result of the leadership of its presidents, the most important of whom were Raymond Charles Barker, Ervin Seal, Robert H. Bitzer, and the current president, Blaine C. Mays. Bitzer and Mays are notable for their success in expanding INTA internationally as well as within the United States. Together with Edgerton, they are the longest serving presidents of the Alliance, with Mays having served the longest of all: 1974–1996 and 1997–present.

Like other "big tent" organizations, INTA experienced its share of controversies, the two most notable ones occurring in 1922 and 1996. Both events apparently were caused by disagreements pertaining to leadership and mission. The 1922 event resulted in Unity School leaving the Alliance and the end of Edgerton's presidency the following year. The 1996 controversy led to the withdrawal of the leaders of a number of large churches and Mays' defeat in an election by Marguerite Goodall. Like Edgerton, Mays returned to the presidency, but in both cases the Alliance lost membership and support.

INTA is still recovering from the aftermath of the 1996 controversy and adapting to the continuing development of denominational forms of New Thought. Today, membership is increasing, with notable institutional members including the AUC,

United Church of Religious Science, Religious Science International, Divine Science Federation International, and United Divine Science Ministries, International.

PRIMARY BELIEFS AND PRACTICES

As noted previously, New Thought is a popular manifestation of religious idealism, a system whose most distant forebear was Plato. His philosophy in general and his idealism in particular had considerable influence on the development of Christian theology, especially through a religious system developed on the basis of his philosophy—Neoplatonism. By the later Middle Ages, this influence began to weaken, largely due to the rise of empirical methods of inquiry and analysis. After the Reformation in the sixteenth century, idealism entered a period of dormancy in Christianity and in Western thought as a whole.

Idealism refers to any system of thought that recognizes that the highest reality is mental. From among the numerous religious and philosophical figures who could be cited as distant precursors of New Thought, major thinkers include Origen (185–254), Augustine (354–430), John Scotus Erigena (810–877), and Anselm (1033–1109). In modern times, Rationalists like René Descartes (1596–1650) and Bendict de Spinoza (1632–1677) might be cited as philosophical forebears of New Thought. Finally, and just prior to the emergence of New Thought, the work of G. W. F. Hegel (1770–1831), stands as a major reaffirmation of the idealist tradition. In formal philosophy, Hegel's idealism was a brilliant but short-lived phenomenon. In terms of popular culture, however, it laid the groundwork for the Mind Cure movement, Christian Science, and shortly thereafter, New Thought.

As suggested by its origins, preinstitutional influences, and its relationship with Christian Science, New Thought's primary beliefs are idealistic in character, and its primary religious practices are informed by principles of mental healing. New Thought recognizes that its unique prayer technique is scientific in character.

New Thought's foundational world view and basis for its various ritual practices is the idealistic premise that a correlation exists between a person's consciousness (thoughts and mental states) and a person's physical-material experiences. Thus the root causes of physical-material limitations (for example, sickness, poverty, aging, death) are thoughts of limitation or a general state of consciousness that accepts the reality of such limitations. The source of these "error thoughts" or limited consciousness is "mortal mind." On the other hand, constructive and healthy thoughts, or a positive consciousness, establish positive conditions. The ultimate source of good thoughts or a positive consciousness is God, which is understood as Divine Mind. In short, mind is primary and causative; negative (mortal) thoughts create negative conditions and positive (spiritual) thoughts create positive conditions. The precise nature of this causative process is understood to be as exact as any natural law and mastery of the process a scientific undertaking.

Over time the various New Thought groups developed their own distinct teachings, religious terminology, and prayer or treatment rituals, but all maintain a primary focus on mental healing and the general principles described above. A simplified version of the basis for mental healing is the assertion that "Life is Consciousness," a concept popularized by Divine Scientist, Emmet Fox (1886–1951). This motto offers the best brief summary of New Thought's popular religious idealism and the principle upon which the movement bases its beliefs and practices—most centrally its prayer rituals.

By affirming that life is consciousness, New Thought declares that all material-physical phenomena result from one's mental states. The universe is mental, or, as most New Thoughters would say, God is Mind. God (Divine Mind) is also omnipresent and exists as both omnipotent good and absolute perfection: *good* in an Augustinian sense, in that evil has no actual existence, and *perfection* in a Platonic sense, in that it is the realm of pure incorruptible ideas (Platonic forms). Aside from God, common synonyms for Divine Mind are Truth, Principle, and Law. By "Truth" it is meant that Divine Mind is the Reality that eliminates all error (or "seeming evil") and frees one from material-physical limitations. In earlier times, Truth also functioned as a synonym for the New Thought religion; so one was a Truth student or attended a Truth center (church). "Principle" refers to the function of Divine Mind as the universal cause of all creation, specifically the plan or pattern through which Mind expresses itself. "Law" means that Divine Mind is characterized by a Divine Order that is as systematic and precise in its functioning as the laws of nature. Study and application of this Law by mental healers is just as scientific as the study and application of physical laws by empirical scientists. Familial terms, such as Father, Mother, Father-Mother, or Mother-Father, are also used in New Thought, but the primary understanding of God is decidedly nonanthropomorphic.

Humans are fundamentally spiritual in nature and linked to Divine Mind through their minds. The highest state of human consciousness is the point of contact between humans and divinity. When persons experience the reality of this connection, they participate in the perfection of Divine Mind and have access to Divine Ideas, and, as a consequence, the material-physical conditions in their lives reveal Divine Perfection. To the degree that people fall short of this realization, they likewise fall short of the manifestation of Perfection. This failure is an error in consciousness, "missing the mark," a mistake, a belief in "mortal mind" rather than Truth; but neither is a sin nor a manifestation of evil in the traditional Christian sense of those two terms. The result of such errors, nonetheless, is pain, illness, poverty, sickness, aging, and death.

Mental healing rituals such as prayer treatments, affirmations, decreeing, visualizations, and "treasure mapping," eliminate the mental errors and reestablish the right relationship with Divine Mind, the source of all good. When this is done, undesired conditions are eliminated and desired ones established. In New Thought, mental healing rituals are never conceived as changing or in any manner affecting God (Divine Mind). They are always an inner psychospiritual activity in the consciousness of the individual; her or his realization of the presence of God, which is Good and Perfect, Truth, Principle, and Law. In this realization lies the key to the effectiveness of all New Thought ritual practices.

In various ways, all New Thought rituals seek this realization, usually in the context of some specific healing exigency, typically called a "challenge." Once realized, the Divine Reality replaces the flawed condition, error is removed, Truth restored, and healing occurs. Classically, this is called a "demonstration."

In a certain sense, all rituals in New Thought are healing rituals, but the New Thought concept of healing extends to all areas of life, not simply to remedies for specific physical ailments. While ritual treatments for healing of specific physical ailments are still common in New Thought, the movement and its individual groups are always keenly aware that spiritual healing encompasses all areas of a person's life. As a result, New Thought rituals routinely focus on treatments for prosperity, peace of mind, harmonious relationships, love, joy, success, justice, and order. They can be as broad and general as treatments for world peace and harmony among nations or as specific as treatments for a new car and a passing grade on an exam.

Considerable differences (even disagreements) within the movement abound regarding mental healing techniques, technical terminology, distinctions between specific ritual activities (such as prayer, mental treatment, and meditation), and the degree of specificity in treatment rituals. Nonetheless, all consent to general agreement on the basic idealist principle (that life is consciousness), the fundamental belief that Divine Mind is Perfect and accessible by human beings, and that the properly administered mental healing treatment results in the realization of Divine Mind. This brings the reality of Divine Mind into physical-material expression, resulting in the elimination of the undesired condition and/or the manifestation of that which is desired—the demonstration. Believers engage in treatment rituals with a positive expectancy, typically recognizing that the desired outcome is already achieved and giving thanks in advance for the demonstration that they seek.

As noted above, ritual practice varies considerably in New Thought, with different groups using different techniques and terminology or emphasizing some concepts more than others: Unity's classical concept of the Silence and the process of Denial and Affirmation, Religious Science's emphasis on Law and Affirmative Prayer, and Divine Science's stress on Omnipresence. Broadly speaking, the rituals in the movement fall into three general categories: (a) public-congregational rituals, (b) private-personal rituals, and (c) professional rituals.

Public-congregational rituals in New Thought look and sound like congregational prayers in other religious traditions, with statements and requests being spoken aloud in religious environments by those attending services. A New Thought version of the Lord's Prayer is often part of the services in New Thought churches and frequently sung by the congregation. Churches may have standard opening prayers or affirmations, prayers in conjunction with offering collections, formal prayers for persons desiring healing, and closing benedictions. Specialized treatments may be offered at services for specific desires such as world peace, environmental healing, prosperity for the religious community, and harmonious weather conditions. In addition, most New Thought services also feature a period of meditation, which usually is directed by a speaker who affirms statements of religious significance to congregants and seeks to create a serene mental state. Meditations may involve group responses, visualizations, and gentle mental journeys to peaceful realms of thought. Public prayers, treatments, and meditations may be based on printed texts found in books, or periodicals published by the respective denominations.

In the category of private-personal ritual, New Thought communities show the same degree (and range) of dedication to prayer as other religious communities in which personal ritual practice is a vital part of life. New Thought is nondoctrinal and generally presents its teachings as conditional statements; for example: If one desires to live a full and meaningful life, then spiritual practices are necessary; if one seeks a healing, then a certain mental process should be followed; and so on. Thus, although ritual treatment is a central element in New Thought belief systems, the denominations themselves do not make this (or any other) religious practice obligatory; and in the absence of any survey data on the beliefs and practices of individuals in the movement, it is difficult to speak with assurance about how pervasive routine prayer activity is among members. Despite this qualification, those who are especially devout are most likely quite engaged with mental healing work on a routine basis, while those with less religious commitment are probably less engaged.

The personal rituals of the more dedicated members most likely featured at least one and possibly several daily treatment sessions. Depending on the particular group or personal background of the participant, such experiences might involve (or even be considered) meditations. Daily religious activities vary widely from person to person, although some common practices include a personal prayer or cycle of prayers spoken aloud or affirmed silently, reading of and reflection on a daily lesson and prayer or treatment found in a New Thought periodical, a systematic process involving different steps leading to a specific spiritual state (the Secret Place of the Most High, Oneness, the Christ Consciousness the Silence), visualization exercises, and a period of silence. These and other practices can be done individually or combined during a treatment session. The general aim of such sessions, however they are understood, is the recognition and affirmation of the reality of Divine Mind (Truth, Principle, Law) in the life of the participant.

In addition to daily rituals, from time to time most New Thoughters engage in personal treatment activities to resolve specific challenges or achieve specific desires. As noted above, rituals to eliminate physical ailments are common, but such ailments hardly exhaust the range of challenges dealt with through mental healing treatment. Others include financial limitation, inferior social or professional status, difficulties in relationships, aging, heartache, and guilt.

Increasingly in New Thought, rituals are focused on achieving personal goals or manifesting specific conditions or objects, even though their absence may not be particularly challenging. Thus, one may be quite successful at one's job, but greater success may be desired; one may have a nice home, but a better home is desired; a new car may be desired rather than an older one; and so on. In any of these situations, New Thought offers individuals mental healing exercises specific to the situation. Such exercises can be discovered through reading and study of texts dealing with prayer and treatment, courses taken at religious centers, or one-to-one work with a religious professional.

Typically, these exercises involve the following steps: realization of Divine Mind and affirmation of the reality of that which is desired in Divine Mind; recognition and affirmation of the individual's oneness with Divine Mind and the causative nature of consciousness; and thanksgiving (in advance) for the manifestation of that which is desired. In some instances, such as those in which an undesired condition must be eliminated, the reality of that condition (or the thought of it) is denied prior to the affirmation of the reality of the desired condition. Individuals practice these exercises until their demonstration occurs or they receive inner spiritual guidance otherwise. Regardless of the specific aim of prayer and treatment exercises and regardless of their outcomes, the mainstream of the movement asserts that the greater purpose of all such undertakings is a higher consciousness and a clearer realization of Divine Mind and the individual's oneness with It.

The category of professional rituals covers treatment work done by sanctioned religious professionals with or for another person. The office of the professional mental healer predates the New Thought movement itself and can be traced back to the Practitioner office in Christian Science and the independent mental healers of the nineteenth century. Today, professional mental healing treatment is done by ministers, practitioners (in some traditions), and, in the unique case of Unity School's Silent Unity ministry, individuals who have received special training.

In its purest form, professional prayer treatment is a psychospiritual exercise engaged in by a religious professional, within her or his consciousness. In this regard, religious professionals essentially treat themselves, following the same steps described earlier, seeking to realize Divine Mind in the context of the specific request brought to them by another. They are not really working on behalf of the person who contacted them; rather they are working for their own realization of the Truth in the context of that person's challenge or desire. To the degree that practitioners realize the Truth, and due to the Omnipresence of Divine Mind, their realization results in the elimination of the challenge or the manifestation of the desire about which they were contacted. As practitioners increase their own awareness, in so doing the improved awareness ultimately affects the well-being of the person who contacted them.

Without discounting this traditional form of professional treatment, most New Thought religious professionals have no difficulty with the rhetorical concept of praying for others, even though in practice they may follow the classical method of self-treatment. More notable is the fact that, in many New Thought communities today, prayers for others are offered by religious professionals, and from every indication (of language and tone) the prayers are actually being offered on behalf of the other person.

In summary, ritual practice in New Thought is as diverse as the movement itself. Different communities have different techniques and stress different concepts. Nonetheless, and despite the many differences in terminology and actual practice, the aim of prayer throughout the movement is essentially the same: to experience the reality of Divine Mind and bring that reality into manifestation, thus eliminating undesired conditions, manifesting desired ones, demonstrating or reestablishing Truth, and ultimately uplifting the world.

NEW THOUGHT'S FUTURE: ISSUES AND QUESTIONS

This final section examines some of the issues and questions that present themselves to New Thought and its denominations as the movement enters its second century. Topics surveyed here can be grouped into three general categories: Doctrine and Tradition, Education, and Cultural Communication. These serve as organizational headings for various secondary issues and questions related to the future of the movement.

The categories and their related issues and questions are linked at both the practical theoretical levels. As such, they are relevant to participants in New Thought and to scholars seeking to understand the movement. For the most part, New Thought has not given much attention to the topics covered here, and scholarship on the movement has largely ignored them.

Doctrine and Tradition

Broadly speaking, New Thought is a nondoctrinal movement that has been hesitant to articulate its teachings in a systematic manner. When formal statements have been made, they usually occur after the fact, as policy decisions made relative to teachings deemed contrary to those of the movement. These decisions often come about as the result of the appearance of new teachings or internal political tensions. Early in its history, New Thought wrestled with encroachment on its religious territory by Spiritualism, mesmerism, and various syncretistic teachings that blended Asian religious ideas with Theosophy and physical healing systems. This continues today with the presence of New Age teachings in the majority of New Thought churches. Without an established body of recognized teachings, nondoctrinal movements such as New Thought often have difficulty specifying their beliefs. While not necessarily a problem, this may lead to misunderstandings on the part of participants and outsiders trying to understand the movement.

In addition to its nondoctrinal character, New Thought has been oblivious to its own history and its place in the larger sweep of Western religious and cultural history. Most New Thought participants know little of the history of their own tradition and even less about its relationship to the religious and cultural history of the West. An example of this is the distorted history of the movement that venerates Quimby as the founder of New Thought and relegates the work of Hopkins to the margins of the tradition. Whether or not historical and cultural self-consciousness is necessary for a movement to succeed and thrive is not entirely clear; however, the lack of such an awareness on a wide scale seems relatively rare in movements well into their second century of existence.

Education

The primary category of "Education" introduces issues concerning how a religion teaches its lay participants and clerics. Clearly these issues have a direct relationship to issues found in the category of Doctrine and Tradition.

New Thought has always placed great value on the idea of education, and history reveals that the movement has seen education as one of its primary aims from Hopkins onward. From its earliest decades, New Thought has abounded with colleges, seminaries, and institutes. In name at least, the early New Thought groups understood themselves as institutions of religious education. Curiously, however, professional education in New Thought was something less than that suggested by the august titles of its schools.

This is not to say that New Thought failed in its educational aims, but the aims have not been fully realized. Beginning with Hopkins's College and her Seminary, New Thought endeavored to educate its participants and its leaders, and, for the most part, it has succeeded in doing so—up to a point. Within the context of its educational systems, New Thought has trained teachers, practitioners, and ministers, but that context has lacked certain elements commonly found in comprehensive religious educational systems, including: (1) systematic lay education programs, (2) accredited schools of higher learning, (3) support of scholarly endeavors and professional scholars within the movement, and (4) familiarity with theology in a general sense.

Perhaps the most important reasons that New Thought has not yet developed these elements are related to issues related to doctrine. In the absence of an accepted body of normative teachings, a movement finds it difficult to develop a comprehensive education program. In the absence of an historical awareness of the religious, intellectual, and cultural context of the movement, the movement does not possess a sensitivity to the necessity of a fully developed educational system, to say nothing about the development of a scholarly community and the theological enterprise as a whole. If a religion understands itself as ahistorical, it will have no reason to study its own history and the relationship of this history to the culture in which it and its members participate. It may even find such inquires threatening and move to trivialize them. This posture towards the study of history will be even more pronounced when the prospect of inquiry into a religion's teachings is presented, and the development of theological educational systems suggested.

As New Thought and its denominations enter their second century, issues related to formal education will doubtless grow. Unity and the Universal Foundation for Better Living are taking preliminary steps towards establishing schools based on norms of universally recognized accrediting institutions. These initiatives warrant attention by scholars, although important questions remain, given the movement's historical resistance to formal education.

Cultural Communication

The category of "Cultural Communication" introduces issues related to how a religion expresses itself in the public spaces of our common culture. This category is one in which New Thought has always been active.

Today, however, New Thought is confronted with important and pressing issues related to its communication with and within contemporary culture. For the most part, and again due to underdeveloped educational systems, New Thought is less than culturally sophisticated. It has sent forth ministers who are not conversant with the issues and demands of the culture in which they preach and teach. This, coupled with their less than complete theological and academic education, leads to the marginalization of their message.

Many New Thought leaders continue to reject the designation of their movement as a religion, yet they speak in churches and use religious language. Many who hold professional ecclesiastical titles have little understanding of religious history, theological specializations, or even the foundational teachings of the movement. Few can offer a systematic exposition of their faith or utilize a basic theological vocabulary. Some think that they are part of the New Age, and most place themselves in the ambiguous "metaphysical" movement even though the term has been appropriated by groups that are decidedly different from New Thought.

Most religions are not "normal" in the context of contemporary secular culture. The doctrines of most religions are at odds with the common sense beliefs of most people, even people who claim to be religious. Religions gain cultural normalcy not by becoming part of secular culture but by learning how to speak to its residents while managing to stand apart from the culture itself. Early New Thought leaders (Hopkins, Brooks, the Fillmores, and Holmes) were very good at this kind of speaking, yet subsequent generations of leaders have had difficulty articulating distinctly New Thought positions in the context of the larger culture.

All religions wrestle with the paradox of articulating a message that is seemingly denied by the culture that surrounds and sustains them. Theologians, perhaps beginning with liberal theology's Friedrich Schleiermacher (1768–1834), tried to resolve this paradox. It is a paradox that remains merely speculative and theoretical—until individual believers are faced with challenges to their faith. Then the paradox may prove problematic to the participant's faith, although not necessarily to the participant's involvement with the religion. And so the issue: How does a religion and its leaders assist in the cultivation of faith, a faith that is, at least in principle, predicated on idealist beliefs that are contrary to the cultural ideals of contemporary materialist culture? How is this done in the context of any religion? How is it done when many persons who are participants in a religion are heavily invested in a cultural system with a plausibility structure that is markedly different from, if not contrary to, their religious system? Moreover, how is this done in the context of a religion that is unsure of its own teachings, its own history, its very identity as a religion, to say nothing of its identity as an idealistic religion in the midst of a profoundly materialistic culture? Finally, how is this done in the context of a religion that puts such a high premium on individuality and the responsibility individuals have for both their challenges and their healings?

To consider the questions posed in the three categories of this last section, gives one a sense of the curious situation in which New Thought finds itself as it enters its second century. Whether or not New Thought is capable of engaging these questions remains to be seen. That it has not done so very well in the past and yet succeeded by any reasonable measure of success adds even greater curiosity to its current situation and the future of this, the American people's "only decidedly original contribution to the systematic philosophy of life."[33]

NOTES

1. See William James, *The Varieties of Religious Experience* (New York: New American Library, 1958), "Lectures IV and V."

2. For the use of "metaphysical" as a covering term for New Thought and various other nineteenth century new religions, see J. Stillson Judah, *The History and Philosophy of The Metaphysical Movements in America* (Philadelphia: Westminster Press, 1967), especially 11–19. Estimates on membership and global distribution from author and entries on New Thought groups in J. Gordon Melton and Martin Baumann, eds., *Religions of the World: A Comprehensive Encyclopedia of Beliefs and Practices* (Santa Barbara, CA: ABC CLIO, 2002).

3. See Judah, *History and Philosophy*, 172–173. He notes, "The name 'New Thought' designating the movement gradually displaced other terms during the 1890's."

4. See Robert Winterhalter, "Divine Science Federation/United Divine Science Ministries, International," in *Encyclopedia*, ed. Melton and Baumann, 400. This study follows the traditional, "mythic" history of Divine Science in its use of the 1888 date. Recent scholarship, however, has corrected the "oft-repeated statement in Divine Science literature" that Malinda Cramer (a founder of Divine Science) established the "Home College of Divine Science" in 1888. Cramer did establish a college in that year, but she called it the "Home College of Spiritual Science." See J. Gordon Melton, "How Divine Science Got to Denver," *Journal of the Society for the Study of Metaphysical Religion* 7, no. 2 (2001): 108–109. Only later is Cramer's work called Divine Science. Another reasonable date would be 1889, the founding of the Unity movement, although "Unity" was not used by the movement until sometime later.

5. Melton, "Divine Science," 107.

6. For support of Quimby as founder, see, for example, Charles S. Braden, *Spirits in Rebellion: The Rise and Development of New Thought* (Dallas: SMU Press, 1963), 47–88; C. Alan Anderson, "Quimby as Founder of New Thought," *Journal of the Society for the Study of Metaphysical Religion* 3, no. 1 (1997): 5–22. For Hopkins as founder, see, for example, Gail M. Harley, *Emma Curtis Hopkins: Forgotten Founder of New Thought* (Syracuse: SU Press, 2002), especially 48–55; J. Gordon Melton, "New Thought's Hidden History: Emma Curtis Hopkins, Forgotten Founder," *Journal of the Society for the Study of Metaphysical Religion* 1, no. 1 (1995): 5–39.

7. Phineas P. Quimby, "The Truth Is The Cure" (circular), as quoted in Braden, *Spirits in Rebellion*, 62.

8. See Horatio W. Dresser, ed., *The Quimby Manuscripts* (New York: Thomas Y. Crowell, 1921); Ervin Seale, ed., *Phineas Parkhurst Quimby: The Complete Writings* (Marina Del Rey, CA: DeVorss & Co., 1988).

9. J. Gordon Melton, "The Case of Edwards J. Arens and The Distortion of The History of New Thought," *Journal of the Society for the Study of Metaphysical Religion* 2, no. 1 (1996): 13–29. See n. 6 for "Hidden History."

10. For "Quimby As Founder of New Thought," see n. 6. For "Emma Curtis Hopkins: Organizational Founder and Metaphysical Confounder of New Thought," see *Journal of the Society for the Study of Metaphysical Religion* 8, no. 2 (2002): 107–119.

11. See Melton, "New Thought's Hidden History"; Harley, *Emma Curtis Hopkins: Forgotten Founder of New Thought*. See also J. Gordon Melton, *New Thought: A Reader* (Santa Barbara, CA: Institute for the Study of American Religion, 1990), 17.

12. For use of this title and its implications, see Harley, *Emma Curtis Hopkins: Forgotten Founder of New Thought,* 40. For a list of persons she taught, see Braden, *Spirits in Rebellion,* 143.

13. Melton, "New Thought's Hidden History," 11.

14. For other members of the class and further details on the College, see Harley, *Emma Curtis Hopkins: Forgotten Founder of New Thought,* 38–40.

15. Melton, "New Thought's Hidden History," 18.

16. Ibid.

17. Beryl Satter, *Each Mind a Kingdom: American Women, Sexual Purity, and the New Thought Movement, 1875–1920* (Berkeley, CA: University of California Press, 1999), 84.

18. See Braden, *Spirits in Rebellion,* 146.

19. *Christian Science* 1 (January, 1889): 111, as cited by Melton in *Journal of the Society for the Study of Metaphysical Religion* 1, no. 1 (1995): 24.

20. Emma Curtis Hopkins, "Baccalaureate Address [1891]," in Melton, *New Thought: A Reader,* 94.

21. The best study of Evans is in Braden, *Spirits in Rebellion,* chap. 4, 89–128. See also Judah, *History and Philosophy,* 160–168.

22. For additional details and a fuller treatment of these and other New Thought leaders in the East, see Braden, *Spirits in Rebellion,* 154–158, 164–169.

23. Ibid., 153.

24. Ibid., 147–149. See also Harley, *Emma Curtis Hopkins: Forgotten Founder of New Thought,* 130–131.

25. For an excellent critical history of the early years of Divine Science and its establishment in Denver, see J. Gordon Melton, "How Divine Science Got to Denver," *Journal of the Society for the Study of Metaphysical Religion* 7, no. 2 (2001): 103–122. Melton clarifies historical excesses in the movement's mythic history. See especially 108–109 for issues on the use of Divine Science by Cramer and the 1888 date of founding.

26. Hazel Deane, *Powerful is the Light* (Denver: Divine Science College, 1945), 124–126.

27. For membership and organization, see Winterhalter, "Divine Science Federation/United Divine Science Ministries, International," in *Encyclopedia,* ed. Melton and Baumann, 2:400–401.

28. As noted and further detailed by Dell deChant, "Myrtle Fillmore and Her Daughters," in *Women's Leadership in Marginal Religions,* ed. Catherine Wessinger (Urbana, IL: University of Illinois Press, 1993), 109–111.

29. Dell deChant, "Unity School of Christianity/Association of Unity Churches," in *Encyclopedia,* ed. Melton and Baumann, 4:1377.

30. Braden, *Spirits in Rebellion,* 294–295.

31. deChant, "Religious Science," in *Encyclopedia,* ed. Melton and Baumann, 3:1079. Data from 2001.

32. For a good brief study of Seicho-no-Ie and its affinities with New Thought, see Paul Alan Laughlin, "Seicho-no-Ie," in *Encyclopedia,* ed. Melton and Baumann, 4:1145–1146.

33. James, *Varieties,* 88–89.

FURTHER READING

Braden, Charles S. *Spirits in Rebellion: The Rise and Development of New Thought.* Dallas: SMU Press, 1963.

Harley, Gail M. *Emma Curtis Hopkins: Forgotten Founder of New Thought.* Syracuse: SU Press, 2002.

James, William. *The Varieties of Religious Experience.* New York: New American Library, 1958. Lectures IV and V.

Judah, J. Stillson. *The History and Philosophy of The Metaphysical Movements in America.* Philadelphia, Westminster Press, 1967.

Melton, J. Gordon. *New Thought: A Reader.* Santa Barbara, CA: Institute for the Study of American Religion, 1990, 17.

Satter, Beryl. *Each Mind a Kingdom: American Women, Sexual Purity, and the New Thought Movement, 1875–1920.* Berkeley, CA: University of California Press, 1999.

Seale, Ervin, ed. *Phineas Parkhurst Quimby: The Complete Writings.* Marina Del Rey, CA: DeVorss & Co., 1988.

North American Esotericism

Arthur Versluis

INTRODUCTION: WHAT IS ESOTERICISM?

The word "esoteric" refers to knowledge reserved for a few; it derives from the Greek word *esotero,* meaning "within," or "inner." Here, the word "esoteric" implies inner or spiritual knowledge held by a limited circle, rather than "exoteric," publicly known or "outer" knowledge. The term "Western esotericism" refers to inner or hidden spiritual knowledge transmitted through Western European historical currents that in turn feed into North American and other non-European settings. Esoteric knowledge ran throughout Western history from antiquity to the present, ranging from the mysteries of ancient Greece and Rome to Gnostics to hermetic and alchemical practitioners, all the way to modern esoteric groups.[1] Specific currents under the category of Western esotericism include alchemy, astrology, Gnosticism, Hermeticism, Kabbalah, magic, mysticism, and various secret or semisecret societies.

One definitive characteristic of esotericism is "gnosis" (from the Greek for "knowledge") or direct spiritual insight. This characteristic has the advantage of being broad enough to include the full range of esoteric traditions, but narrow enough to exclude exoteric figures or movements. Gnosis typically refers to two broad types of knowledge: cosmological and metaphysical. Cosmological traditions or currents include alchemists, who search for direct spiritual insight into nature and seek to alter certain substances thereby; astrologers, who seek direct insight into the cosmos and use it to analyze events; and magicians, who seek direct insight into the cosmos and attempt to use it to affect the course of events. Metaphysical currents include mystics or theosophers, who seek transcendent insight into the divine. Broadly speaking, in Western esotericism seekers want direct spiritual insight into the hidden nature of the cosmos and of themselves—they strive for gnosis, either cosmological or wholly transcendent. While these categories may seem mutually exclusive, in practice, they blur together.

In other words, Western esoteric traditions contain secret or semisecret knowledge about humanity, the cosmos, and the divine. While North American currents tend more toward pragmatism and practice than speculation, American esotericisms includes the full range of these currents.

EUROPE AND EARLY AMERICA

European and North American currents are complex and deeply intermingled. To study North American forms of esotericism, one must also study not only their European origins or antecedents, but also their complicated trans-Atlantic relationships and successors. This complexity is evident almost from the onset of English and European colonization of North America, in the export of folk magic, astrology, and alchemy, in the founding of the American republic (for instance, with the prevalence of Masonry among the Founding Fathers), and in so many subsequent important figures and movements, from Ralph Waldo Emerson to Paschal Beverly Randolph to the Blavatskyan Theosophical Society.

In eighteenth century Europe, the cultural landscape was filled with esoteric secret or semisecret societies. For example, Rosicrucianism evolved from a series of enigmatic treatises published at the beginning of the seventeenth century to a wide array of actual initiatory organizations. By the late eighteenth century and the founding of the United States, many European initiatory groups took the name Rosicrucian, or a similar one, like the Gold-und Rosenkreutz (Gold and Rosy-Cross) Order that emerged during the 1770s in Germany, as well as numerous lodges under the name "Golden Rosy-Cross of the Ancient System" in 1777.[2] Rosicrucian groups or individuals in general embraced an alchemical view of the cosmos as a system of correspondences to be decoded and believed in social development toward a harmonious and fraternal future that joined together elements of what we would today term religion and science.

Speculative Freemasonry emerged from a Rosicrucian environment in the early eighteenth century. Like Rosicrucianism, Freemasonry is an ethical tradition that conveys cosmological knowledge, evidenced by its emphasis on building and architecture. Originally, masonry was "operative," meaning that it belonged among the medieval trade guilds, but in the early eighteenth century in England, "speculative" Freemasonry emerged, and this type of Freemasonry quickly permeated the American colonies.

As is well known, many signers of the Declaration of Independence were Masons. George Washington became a Mason on November 4, 1752, and strongly encouraged his generals, officers, and soldiers in the Continental Army to join Masonry. Washington even appeared in full Masonic regalia before the troops while celebrating the retaking of Philadelphia in 1778.[3] Boston's St. Andrew Lodge was led by Dr. Joseph Warren and included among its members Paul Revere, who was later to become Grand Master of Massachusetts.[4] This lodge met at "The Green Dragon, or the Arms of Freemasonry," a Mason-owned tavern near the Boston Harbor, the site of the Boston Tea Party of 1773. In part, out of these origins emerged the American Declaration of Independence in 1776.

By the early nineteenth century, Masonry was so widespread in the United States that it was regarded by many evangelical Christians as well as many non-Mason citizens as dangerous to civic well-being. Popular resentment of the Masons' purported political and social power via their Masonic connections emerged after the notorious disappearance of William Morgan on September 14, 1826. Morgan was a stonemason living in western New York state who intended to publish a book in which he unveiled the secrets of Masonry. A group of Masons set fire to the printer's shop where the book was being printed, and when the fire was subsequently put out, the Masons had Morgan and his printer, David Miller, arrested. When Mrs. Morgan went to the jail to find her husband, he was gone and was never seen again. Out of people's anger at the presumed kidnapping and murder of Morgan emerged the Antimasonic party, the first third party in American history. In New England, the Antimasonic party[5] rivalled and in some instances surpassed mainstream political parties in votes.[6]

Opposition to Masons in the United States did not end with creation of a political party, the Antimasonic Party—there was also violence. In March 1830, Antimasons forced their way into a Boston lodge, expecting to find an arsenal, but instead discovered 43 ritual swords and some spittoons. Masonic buildings were defaced. Angry Masons in turn shouted down and drove away Antimasonic speakers. Although Masonry did recover from this period of attack in the early nineteenth century, the hostility toward Masonry did not vanish, but remained an undercurrent in American society, as well as a spur toward the creation of competing quasi-Masonic fellowships like the Grange association for farmers, the Odd Fellows, the Elks, and other lodges. Widespread fear of Masonry as a secret organization with hidden political power helps explain why, although Masonry was immensely important in the founding of the United States and its ideals were influential in the writings of many of the first great American literary-political figures, Masonry never regained its earlier sociopolitical authority.

FOLK MAGIC AND COSMOLOGICAL CURRENTS

Many European esoteric cosmological traditions came to the New World through popular or folk currents by the nineteenth century. Elsewhere I categorize these currents, roughly, as (1) astrology; (2) sympathetic magic; (3) dowsing; (4) spiritualism; and (5) mesmerism. These five primary currents were widespread in American popular culture during this period and, as John Richards shows, were still represented in Appalachian culture of the early twenty-first century.[7]

Whereas in the eighteenth century, astrological manuals and almanacs were fairly widely distributed, a significant portion of the astrological material published in the United States during the nineteenth century was in the native languages of specific ethnic groups rather than in English for a mainstream audience—in particular, one finds a number of books published in German in Pennsylvania. A more widely distributed book, published in Boston by the author in 1854, was Dr. C. W. Roback's *The Mysteries of Astrology and the Wonders of Magic, including A History of the Rise and Progress of Astrology and the Various Branches of Necromancy. The Mysteries of Astrology* is an astrological primer and, like the farmer's almanacs and lunar planting schedules that continued through the entire period, helps demonstrate the underground continuity of astrology.

During the nineteenth century, herbals were popular. They classified plants on the basis of their astrological characteristics. Some plants are solar, some lunar, some Venusian, some Martial, and so forth. By applying the proper balance of herbs to the patient, a healer could adjust astrological imbalances in the patient and cure the illness—this is the theory behind a tradition of astrological or sympathetic medicine seen in books from around the time of Shakespeare onward, like Nicholas Culpeper's famous herbal.[8] These traditions of sympathetic magic or astrological medicine continued as mostly hidden currents throughout the nineteenth century and into the twentieth.

Three folk traditions are particularly important: Native American herbal traditions; slave and ex-slave magical traditions; and Pennsylvania German traditions of *hexenmedizin* or "powwow."[9] In North America folk magical traditions from Africa, England, Ireland, Scotland, and Germany often combined with local or regional Native American traditions to form modified or hybrid folk magical traditions. Jon Butler's observation remains valid—that we have insufficient research on the nature of these magical traditions during this period.[10] But these three, sometimes overlapping groups or communities, represent only the most visible forms of what remained often largely invisible and unexamined in communities across the United States right into the twentieth century.

For example, dowsing was a practical American skill throughout the nineteenth and twentieth centuries. The dowser walks over the land holding a forked wooden or metal divining rod that dips downward over the place where water is found. Broadly speaking, dowsing (and sometimes other forms of divination too) is not generally frowned upon in the way that other forms of magic often are, and it remains a widespread phenomenon in the American hinterlands to this day.

Better documented is the phenomenon of Spiritualism. Conventionally, most historians maintain that Spiritualism began in the United States with the Fox sisters in 1848. However, such phenomena have a long history in both Europe and North America. English author John Aubrey published his *Miscellanies* in 1696, and it included sections on apparitions, voices, impulses, omens, knockings, and invisible blows. And after all, Heinrich Cornelius Agrippa's influential *Three Books of Occult Philosophy* included sections on how spirits may be called up, on prophetic dreams, and so forth.[11] Throughout early modern history, many examples exist showing that people believed in connections between the invisible or spiritual and visible worlds.

Still, earlier esoteric forms of Spiritualism or necromancy differ from the form that swept the United States in the nineteenth century because European precedents tended to belong to secretive groups or individuals. In the United States, spirit rapping and similar "occult" phenomena assured people that invisible beings were real and that personalities survived death, something that was important in the wake of the American Civil War. Spiritualism became a widespread phenomenon, involving even promoters like P. T. Barnum. Although Spiritualism had predecessors in European esoteric lodges, in the United States it was not very esoteric at all.

"Animal magnetism," or Mesmerism, was also important. This phenomenon is now known chiefly as hypnotism, although Mesmerism included other dimensions than hypnotism, including hidden energy currents in the body. Friedrich Mesmer (1734–1815), an Austrian physician and astrologer, became well known in Paris for the miraculous healings and weird psychic phenomena that accompanied his stage shows. With the infallible instinct of the showman, Mesmer turned animal magnetism or hypnosis into a stage event. Animal magnetism was supposedly a universal fluid that could be manipulated by a practitioner to effect healing.

Mesmerism spread quite widely when in the American colonies it linked with the "New Church" of the followers of Emanuel Swedenborg (1688–1772). Andrew Jackson Davis (1826–1910) was also important in the history of American Mesmerism. He was known as the "seer from Poughkeepsie, New York." Davis believed that he was not indebted to any other writer, but one finds in Davis's work an unmistakable indebtedness to the socialism of Charles Fourier, to European folk medicine, to Mesmerism, and to Swedenborg. Davis and most of the Spiritualists rejected conventional forms of Christianity, but they often called themselves Christian, widening their audience and thus, in a characteristically American way, making what was esoteric, exoteric.

ESOTERIC SEXUALITY AND AMERICAN UTOPIANISM

The United States has been the site of a number of fairly successful utopian communities, among them such groups as Ephrata, which flourished not far from Philadelphia in the eighteenth century, the Harmony Society of Johann Georg Rapp (1757–1847) and his adopted son, Frederick Rapp (1775–1834), the ill-fated Fruitlands community founded by Amos Bronson Alcott (1799–1888), the Oneida community of John Humphrey Noyes (1811–1886), and the Brethren of the New Life, founded by Thomas Lake Harris (1823–1906). All of these utopian groups derive their philosophy either directly or indirectly from Christian theosophic mysticism in the tradition of Jacob Böhme (1575–1624). Those communities that developed esoteric sexual theories and practices (notably Noyes and Harris) were drawing in part on a preexisting tradition of the androgynous angelic spiritual unity that is found in the works of Emanuel Swedenborg as well as in earlier alchemical works. John Humphrey Noyes, founder of the well known Oneida community in western New York state, was from a merchant family and graduated from Dartmouth College. Noyes was converted in the great revival of 1831 and went to divinity school at Yale, where he supported radical causes. Noyes opposed the institution of marriage as commonly understood, and after he gathered a perfectionist community in Putney, Vermont, he began to publish his views, which scandalized his neighbors and ultimately caused his community to flee to Oneida in 1848.

The Oneida community pursued an interesting and relatively well-organized kind of socialism in which matters of procreation and sexual intercourse as well as most other decisions were subject to community judgment. Oneida, which by 1851 numbered 205 members, was controversial for its sexual views, but, in fact, was fairly conservative in many respects. The community was industrious and, in addition to farming and logging, saw to the production of dinner silverware. Indeed, when the community disbanded in 1881, it did so by forming the Oneida Corporation, which today still is responsible for manufacturing Oneida silverware.

Noyes's particular version of male continence was the centerpiece of Oneida's unique sexuality. As practiced at Oneida, it consisted of sexual intercourse without male ejaculation, which Noyes believed transformed intercourse from an animalistic rutting into, at least potentially, a vehicle of spiritual experience. This view has parallels in both Hindu and Buddhist Tantrism, but Noyes almost certainly did not get his approach to sexuality from Asian traditions. Instead, there are European precedents for such a view, both medieval, as in the Cathars, and more modern, in particular among the Christian theosophers.[12] It is entirely possible that at Yale, Noyes read works that inspired his later views of sexuality and religion, but precisely which works remains uncertain.

Thomas Lake Harris was born in England, and came to the United States in 1828. In 1845, he became a Universalist minister, a career that served him for less than two years, for in 1847 he joined Andrew Jackson Davis and the Spiritualists. Harris soon left Davis's group, eventually announcing his own esoteric millennialist group called the "Brotherhood of the New Life," which was intended for the "reorganization of the industrial world."[13] Harris established his group at Brocton, Salem-on-Erie, New York, and finally in California. He taught a complex mysticism with some sexual dimensions, the underlying idea being that through spiritual practices it is possible to restore human beings and nature to an original paradisal state.

Harris was a prolific author and also wrote and published a number of hymns and songs. Among his many books are *Arcana of Christianity: An Unfolding of the Celestial Sense of the Divine Word* (1858–1867), *The Millennial Age: Twelve Discourses on the Spiritual and Social Aspects of the Times* (1860), *The Breath of God with Man* (1867), and *The Golden Child* (1878), the daily chronicle of life in the California community Harris founded. In essence, Harris joined together Christian millennialism with Swedenborgian thought, but also drew on a range of other esoteric traditions.[14] Harris's esotericism was thoroughly European in origin, emerging almost totally out of Swedenborgianism, and it was quite sophisticated.[15]

While Noyes and Harris were more widely influential—both because of their writings and because of the utopian communities that each led, yet a third figure was influential in this American esoteric pragmatism: the remarkable Alice Bunker Stockham (1833–1912). Stockham founded no utopian community and, like Harris, was overlooked by scholars, but she was a significant author whose work continues and develops the Noyesian tradition of *coitus reservatus* (or males not ejaculating during sexual intercourse) in marriage. One of the first female M.D.s in the United States, trained as an obstetrician/gynecologist whose practice was based in Chicago,

Stockham's work reflects her medical training and perspective. In it, Swedenborgian or Böhmean mysticism is missing, but she advocated what we might call a more secular sexual mysticism of human creativity.

Stockham's work is unique, particularly her book *Karezza.* Harris's teachings were truly esoteric, and even Noyes's teachings were primarily for the benefits of his followers, but Stockham disseminated the idea of *coitus reservatus* as widely as possible. Her books, especially *Karezza,* are filled with the spirit of proselytization for what she clearly saw as a possible, indeed, a necessary sociosexual revolution. The relations between the sexes could be entirely transformed, if only husband and wife would begin to practice the ascetic discipline of occasional intercourse without ejaculation.

Yet she went further, arguing that just as ordinary sexual intercourse led to procreation, so spiritual intercourse conducted without ejaculation would lead to what she calls "procreation of thought," and to a higher union of male and female. While Stockham is exoteric in her desire to convey her sexual theory as widely as possible, she relied on a long and rich Western esoteric tradition, as, for example, when she said that "in every soul there is a duality, the male and female principle," and that "though but one in spirit, in spiritual expression soul in every person is twofold, a blended male and female."[16] Thus, she continues, "as sex is in the soul[,] it is not impossible, as spiritual unity is developed, that a procreation of thought may be accomplished—that is, a procreation on the spiritual plane, not of individuals, but of principles and theories that can be practically developed for the good of the world."[17] Hence, even the more classically esoteric dimensions of Stockham's thought—like the aspiration to nonduality or androgyny—ultimately is legitimated for her only by its practical exoteric consequences "practically developed for the good of the world."

Stockham's work stands in the long American tradition of universalism and pragmatism whose greatest representative is Ralph Waldo Emerson, a tradition with no lack of representatives proceeding into the twentieth century with figures like Alan Watts, as well as groups like the human potential movements, and philosophies and ideologies like East-West syncretism. New Age figures and sects should also be included in this heritage. Nearly every one of the utopian figures and groups mentioned here were exemplars in the long tradition of American pragmatist esotericism, or esoteric pragmatism.

LITERARY "OCCULTISM" IN THE AMERICAN RENAISSANCE

The emergence of an industrial American society in the nineteenth century meant that, at least for a time, alchemy, astrology, and other esoteric traditions of intellectuals or the upper class were by and large not only discarded, but also denigrated because they were not conducive to industrialization. The same was true for the folk magic traditions from Native American, African American, Pennsylvania German, and utopian origins. But at least some of the early industrial processes, chiefly concerned with soap, wax, metallurgy, and medicine, emerged from the efforts of alchemists. The American alchemist George Starkey was still widely known some time after his death because of the continuing sale of what had become known as "Starkey's Pill."[18] However, these innovations occurred during the period of transition to modern scientific industrialism during the early to mid-nineteenth century. In general, modern scientific rationalism and earlier Western esoteric traditions appeared incompatible with one another, and during the nineteenth century, scientific rationalism won what seemed a convincing victory, suppressing or marginalizing esoteric traditions.

But this suppression was not nearly as complete as it might initially seem. Certainly, if we look at the decline in publication of many astrological almanacs or the decline in the number of practicing alchemists, "occultism" or esotericism seems to have significantly diminished in American society by the mid-nineteenth century. But esoteric themes were used by major American authors of the American Renaissance during the mid-nineteenth century in New England. Indeed, these authors worked with esoteric themes and traditions that had preoccupied many of their ancestors, so that the American Renaissance may well be seen from this angle as the transference of esoteric traditions into literary consciousness.

The presence of esotericism in the works of most of the major American authors of this era, from Edgar Allan Poe, Nathaniel Hawthorne, and Herman Melville to Emerson, Emily Dickinson, Amos Bronson Alcott, and Margaret Fuller, is undeniable. These authors relied on different currents, but the importance of prior esoteric traditions for the American Renaissance is undeniable. By drawing upon alchemy, astrology, theosophy, Swedenborgianism, Mesmerism, Rosicrucianism, Freemasonry, and many other esoteric movements and ideas, these authors expressed in their published work basic themes that had enormous resonance in the popular mind and remained as living forces in the American imagination.

Perhaps surprisingly, it is in the poetry of the time that we find the most traces of intellectualized esotericism. Melville voiced views in his poetry that he did not express quite as openly in his fiction. We see this in poems like his "Fragments of a Lost Gnostic Poem," "The New Rosicrucians," or "Clarel." "Fragments of a Lost Gnostic Poem" ends this way:

> Indolence is heaven's ally here,
> And energy the child of hell:
> The Good Man pouring from his pitcher clear,
> But brims the poisoned well.

It is not surprising that some of Melville's many voices are decidedly esoteric in nature, even if his own views were probably most clearly set forth in that sardonic riddle of a book, *The Confidence Man*. Fuller also wrote poems that are indisputably esoteric, perhaps most notably "Winged Sphynx," "My Seal Ring," "Sub Rosa-Crux," and above all "Double Triangle," probably the best of her poems, whose accompaniment is the esoteric illustration that originally appeared at the beginning of *Woman in the Nineteenth Century*. Here are a few lines from the poem:

When the perfect two embrace,
Male and Female, black & white,
　　Soul is justified in space,
Dark made fruitful by the light;
　　And, centred in the diamond Sun,
　　　　Time & Eternity are one.[19]

Some of the most experiential esoteric poems were written by Dickinson, who like Melville was very much influenced by that entertaining author on all manner of esoteric lore, Sir Thomas Browne. Dickinson was not inclined toward scholarly inquiry into hermeticism or theosophy, but she was interested in such topics as witchcraft and posthumous existence, and if her life was outwardly stationary, inwardly she journeyed on a spiritual and psychological path that resembles at times a kind of Christian shamanism.[20]

MAGICAL CURRENTS

The end of the nineteenth century represents a burgeoning of various Western magical groups as well as of syncretic movements like the Theosophical Society of Helena Blavatsky (1831–1891) or the Anthroposophical Society of Rudolf Steiner (1861–1925), both of which themselves included magical elements and even, in the case of the Theosophical Society, a special magical wing called the "Esoteric Section" and headed by William Q. Judge (1851–1896) and later his successors. This semisecret magical group within the Theosophical Society undoubtedly arose as a reaction to the growing recruitment power of the Order of the Golden Dawn, founded in 1888 by William Wynn Westcott (1848-1925) and Samuel Liddle MacGregor Mathers (1854–1918), both already members of the Societas Rosicruciana in Anglia, a secret Rosicrucian group. The Order of the Golden Dawn supposedly began when a hidden and encoded manuscript bearing the keys to the work of the Abbott Trithemius was found; but the Golden Dawn practiced ceremonial magic with a pronounced Masonic ritual flavor, drawing also upon Christian Kabbalah and a number of preexisting magical or "occultist" traditions.[21] Arguably the most important contribution of the Golden Dawn was its systematization of magic in a series of Masonic grades. All of these groups represent very complicated interrelationships between American, English, and European figures, and all had American dimensions.

Thus, the Golden Dawn's systematization of ritual magic owed at least something to its predecessors, among these the African American magician Paschal Beverly Randolph (1825–1875) and the Hermetic Brotherhood of Luxor. Randolph was born in New York and learned various occupations before, in the early 1850s, taking up a Spiritualist vocation, eventually serving as an on-stage trance medium and then as a psychic and healer. Randolph's various books and treatises—in which he also claimed himself as heir to the secrets of Rosicrucianism while later acknowledging that his Rosicrucianism came out of his own head—were chiefly about sexuality. In such works as *The Ansairetic Mystery, Eulis,* and *The Golden Secret,* Randolph outlined his perspective on the mysteries of sexuality, which included sexual magic. Randolph insisted on the importance of women's sexual satisfaction and included in some of his works directions for sexual magical practices that attracted the attention of local New England legal authorities at least once. Randolph was an advisor to and laborer for Abraham Lincoln, and after the Civil War was for a short time the principal of Lloyd Garrison Grammar School in New Orleans. Within the history of American esotericism, he is most important for establishing the general outlines of sexual magical practices to be followed and developed by subsequent groups both European and American.

One of the most complicated avenues of Randolph's influences has been to a considerable degree unraveled by Joscelyn Godwin, Christian Chanel, and John Deveney in their collection of documents entitled *The Hermetic Brotherhood of Luxor* (1995). In this work, the authors show how Randolph's cosmological and sexual teachings made their way to England, to a small group of occultists who drew upon them and even plagiarized them in creating their own system of magical practice and an esoteric order. It is by no means clear when Randolph conceived his own cosmology regarding the individual "monad's" evolution toward immortality—he claimed that he learned it during his travels in the Mideast in 1861.[22] The Hermetic Brotherhood of Luxor disseminated Randolph's ideas much more widely in Europe and North America.[23]

In his turn, Aleister Crowley (1875–1947)—who joined the Order of the Golden Dawn in 1898, and who went on to found his own order, the Astrum Argentinum [incorporated into the Ordo Templi Orientis (OTO), founded by Carl Kellner (1850–1905) and Theodor Reuss (1855–1923)]—continued the emphasis on sexuality in magical ritual. Crowley's OTO developed a luciferian tendency that manifested not only in his writings, but also in the incorporation of rituals like the Gnostic Mass, the ritual consumption of wafers consisting in part of semen and menstrual fluid. Crowley enjoyed negative publicity, calling himself "the Great Beast," and was a favorite subject for tabloid journalism. But his voluminous writings remain an important part of the history of twentieth century magical esotericism, and the OTO continues to the present day.

The late twentieth century saw the emergence of various other neo-Gnostic groups not to mention the development in the late twentieth century of Wicca or witchcraft, neopaganism, and various magical groups, all of which draw on sexuality as a primary basis for magical power. Many of these groups share certain tendencies: (1) to assert their superiority over conventional forms of morality; (2) to hold sexual rites for purposes of magical power; and (3) to react explicitly against conventional forms of organized Christianity, even if insisting upon the necessity of attaining some kind of gnosis. One also can discern an increasing tendency away from the eighteenth century Masonically inspired hierarchic orders that persisted throughout the twentieth century, and toward an eclectic individualism. Perhaps nowhere is that individualism more apparent than in Chaos magic.

Just as the turn of the nineteenth century saw dramatic growth of various magical orders that were both innovative and dependent on earlier tradition, so the turn of the twentieth century once again saw the emergence of a bewildering variety of new groups and orders. One of the most important was Chaos magic, which spawned several orders, among them the order of the Illuminates of Thanateros. In the introduction to his book *Liber Null and Psychonaut,* one of the defining works of this movement, Peter Carroll writes that "The Illuminates of Thanateros are the magical heirs to the Zos Kia Cultus [of Austin Osman Spare] and the A.'. A.'..."[24] But whereas the Golden Dawn drew upon Renaissance white magic and Jewish Kabbalism, Chaos magic reflects a distinctly darker nature, sometimes referring to itself as "grey magic."

Perhaps the most significant aspect of Chaos magic is its approach to initiations, central to Western esoteric traditions like Freemasonry or Masonically influenced ceremonial magical orders. Whereas some in magical orders, like the Golden Dawn, integrated magical practices with, for instance, Roman Catholicism, the Chaos magicians of the early twenty-first century scorned traditional religions. Individualism is the hallmark of Chaos magic. In this movement, the term "initiation" takes on the neoshamanic meaning of a period of trial and growth rather than an institutionalized series of hierarchic degrees. Chaos magic represents an anarchic and radical individualist movement that is by self-definition antitraditional.[25]

LITERARY ESOTERICISM IN THE TWENTIETH CENTURY

In twentieth century American literature, among the important and indicative figures are the modernist poet H.D. (1886–1961), the Beat novelist William S. Burroughs (1914–1997), and the science fiction writer Philip K. Dick (1928–1982). H.D.'s work contains many traditional Western esoteric currents, including alchemy, astrology, and sexual mysticism, while Burroughs's later work contains more contemporary magical currents, and Dick's work has modernized projected Gnosticism.

Of these three, the most thoroughly permeated with Western esoteric currents was H.D. That H.D.—born Hilda Doolittle—was fascinated with esoterica is well known. Susan Friedman outlines the intertwining of H.D.'s biography and her fascination with mysticism, the Tarot, numerology, astrology, magic, psychic insights or visions, various heresies of antiquity including the Ophites and other Gnostic groups, Rosicrucianism, and the Christian theosophy of Count Nikolaus von Zinzendorf (1700–1760) and the Moravians.[26] H.D. is a twentieth century representative of an American feminine literary lineage that harks back to nineteenth century American Renaissance authors Emily Dickinson and Margaret Fuller. Fuller, like H.D., was fascinated with numerology, astrology, and what we might term esoteric correspondences or patterns in life. She created a hermetic emblem for herself and was very interested in doctrines of occult or hidden sympathies between humanity and nature. Likewise, H.D. was fascinated by esoteric correspondences in her life, was a reasonably accomplished astrological interpreter, and by 1911 saw the emblem of the thistle and serpent as her own. Works by H.D. that give evidence of esotericism include her poems in *Trilogy* and *Vale Ave* as well as her novel *The Gift*, but the much earlier work *Notes on Thought and Vision* help to make clear H.D.'s gnostic perspective in relation to literature. *Notes* is a very unusual work; written in July 1919 in the Scilly Islands, it argues for the characteristically Emersonian idea of an "overmind" as a model of higher consciousness.

During the London blitz in World War II, H.D. wrote the collection of three long poems later published as *Trilogy*. These three poems were "The Walls Do Not Fall," "Tribute to the Angels," and "The Flowering of the Rod." In "The Walls Do Not Fall," H.D. develops many of the themes that were initially sketched in *Notes on Thought and Vision*. These themes are clearly esoteric: she writes of her experience of "nameless initiates" as her "companions," of the "alchemist's secret," of "the most profound philosophy," of the stars as beings who can be invoked by spells, and much else. It is obvious from "The Walls Do Not Fall" that although H.D.'s outward circumstances were the terrors of war, the poem is at heart profoundly esoteric in its unified vision of reality amid the shards of bomb-shattered modernity.

The most important of her esoteric works was the novel *The Gift*, which was not published in a full version that included H.D.'s complex mysticism drawn from her family's Moravian tradition. H.D. was herself a baptized Moravian, but the Moravian Church of the twentieth century was vastly different from the Herrnhuters of Count von Zinzendorf who settled in Bethlehem, Pennsylvania, in the middle of the eighteenth century. Zinzendorf and his group were far more esoteric in their interests than those who followed them. Rimius's works, cited by H.D. in her notes, make clear this distinction. Rimius, Zinzendorf's most effective detractor, accused the early Moravians of "gross and scandalous ... Mysticism," of the "*Arcana,* or Secret Counsels of their Leaders," as well as of "Secrets probably known by the adepts alone."[27] H.D. avidly read the works of Rimius and much else in order to fashion an extraordinary novel that embodies many currents of Western esotericism, most notably those of Christian theosophic mysticism. In H.D.'s work, we see nearly all the major currents of Western esotericism.

By contrast, the later works of Burroughs show that the author incorporating magical and alchemical elements, as well as some aspects of Egyptian religious tradition. He is best known for his earlier writing, like his novel *Naked Lunch*. But in *The Western Lands* (1987) and *The Place of Dead Roads* (1984) Burroughs explores a surreal, nightmarish world populated by demons, a world he describes in part by way of a magical interpretation of ancient Egyptian religion. There is, of course, a long-standing Western esoteric tradition based on Egyptian religion and magic, of which Burroughs is only one exemplar. His work was popularized not only through film versions of his novels, but also through his spoken word appearances on musical works. Bill Laswell's band *Material* produced an album featuring as lyrics Burroughs reading from *The Western Lands,* all of which served to disseminate his more occult works.

As for Dick, a science fiction writer, his primary connection to Western esotericism also becomes most evident in his later work, which he saw not as science fiction, but as secret Gnostic truth. He believed that he was like a Gnostic in the period of the Roman Empire millennia before. Dick claimed that he encountered the Vast Active Living Intelligence System, or VALIS, about which encounters and insights he wrote at great length not only in such published works as *Valis* (1981), but also in voluminous journals. Dick inspired a kind of posthumous cult following whose interest turns especially on the Gnostic themes of his later works.[28]

SYNCRETISM AND UNIVERSALISM

One of the more noteworthy aspects of modern intellectual history is the tendency toward syncretism and universalism as manifested in movements as diverse as the New Age movement and perennialism or Traditionalism. Traditionalism as a movement appeared with the singular voice of the French author René Guénon (1886–1951), whose books and articles all bear the stamp of a man utterly convinced that his work was absolutely true. Guénon was highly critical of the modern industrialized world, which he saw as emerging from the destruction of the orthodox world religious traditions and traditional cultures of the past. The intellectual esotericism that Guénon initiated was espoused by Frithjof Schuon (1907–1998), whose severe and abstract works are seen by some Traditionalists as the culmination of the movement.

Schuon was born in Basle, Switzerland, and trained as a textile designer. He worked in Paris, where he corresponded with Guénon, and later met Guénon in Egypt. He evidently had some contact with Sufis or Muslim mystics, and his many books are infused with an abstractness that owes a great deal to the aniconic Islamic tradition. Among his books are *Understanding Islam* (1963), *Islam and the Perennial Philosophy* (1976), *Christianity/Islam: Essays on Ecumenic Esotericism* (1985), as well as *In the Tracks of Buddhism* (1969), *The Feathered Sun: Plains Indians in Art and Philosophy* (1990), and *Light on the Ancient Worlds* (1966). Only in the early 1990s, late in his life, did the public learn that Schuon was the center of a *tariqah,* or esoteric group based in Bloomington, Indiana. Schuon wrote from a universalist or transcendent position, as more or less pure intellect removed from the modern world, and he lived much of his life in reclusion as the leader of a Sufi or quasi-Sufi universalist initiatic group. Schuon and a number of other European and British Traditionalists who chose to live in North America reveal just how complexly intermingled are Western esoteric currents across continents in the modern era.[29]

NEW AGE UNIVERSALISM

Another instance of globalist universalism is the New Age movement. Wouter Hanegraaff surveys the entire New Age movement in detail, and comes to the general conclusion that

> All New Age religion is characterized by the fact that it expresses its criticism of modern western culture by presenting alternatives derived from a secularized esotericism. It

adopts from traditional esotericism an emphasis on the primacy of personal religious experience and on this-worldly types of holism ... but generally reinterprets esoteric tenets from secularized perspectives. Since the new elements of "causality," the study of religions, evolutionism, and psychology are fundamental components, New Age religion cannot be characterized as a return to pre-Enlightenment worldviews, but is to be seen as a qualitatively new syncretism of esoteric and secular elements. Paradoxically, New Age criticism of modern western culture is expressed to a considerable extent on the premises of that same culture.[30]

In sum, writes Hanegraaff, "The New Age movement is characterized by a popular western culture criticism expressed in terms of a secularized esotericism." If Hanegraaff is right in his conclusions, then the New Age movement is a secularizing current of thought that nonetheless shares common origins with Traditionalism itself.

Both Traditionalism and the New Age movement have common antecedents in the nineteenth century. Probably the most important antecedents are in German *Naturphilosophie* and European Romanticism, in the late nineteenth century "New Thought" movement, in the various syncretizing "occult" or esoteric figures and lodges of the late nineteenth and early twentieth centuries, as well as in pivotal figures like Swedenborg, William Blake, and above all, Emerson. All of these various currents of thought elevate individual syncretism and synthesis, joining together apparently disparate perspectives in a more general overview that takes on a universalist flavor. This syncretic universalism emerges throughout the nineteenth and twentieth centuries in figures as diverse as Steiner, Schuon, and Ken Wilber (b. 1949), each of whom presented himself as a surveyor of the entire human religiocultural inheritance. They differ from one another chiefly in their degree of incorporation or rejection of scientific-evolutionist premises.

The New Thought movement, with its pastiche of influences from Spiritualism, Mesmeric healing, Western esoteric traditions like Hermeticism and Böhmean theosophy, Asian religious traditions, and evolutionist science, represents the late nineteenth century predecessor and counterpart to the late twentieth century's "New Age" movement. Many of the themes of both movements go directly back to Emerson, including (1) That direct spiritual experience of the individual is more important than adherence to organized religious traditions. (2) That behind or within all traditions is a "perennial philosophy" or esoteric center, which the individual can realize for him or herself. (3) That we are moving toward a new era in human understanding, an era that unites science and spirituality. (4) That suffering does not have any ultimate reality and that we can choose to overcome or transcend it. (5) That we can derive from Asian religious traditions such concepts as *karma* or enlightenment and place them in an individualistic modern context. These are only a handful of such themes, but they show what constitutes, as Harold Bloom has argued, an "American religion."[31]

Numerous such strands link earlier esoteric traditions, the nineteenth century American New Thought movement, and the late twentieth century American New Age movement. Hanegraaff suggests links between such figures as Friederike

Hauffe (1801–1829)—known as the "Seeress of Prevorst," who was a medium and "channel" for "higher beings" after she was magnetized by the German doctor and poet Justinius Kerner—and much later figures like Jane Roberts (1929–1984), who became well-known as the channel for the "spiritual teachings" of a discarnate spirit named "Seth."[32] Between these two figures stands the nineteenth century work and life of Andrew Jackson Davis, also a medium or channel who became a widely known author and public figure of his time, and who claimed to have spoken with none other than Swedenborg himself in the afterlife. Clearly there is a series of linked figures who represent common tendencies, not just through their identities as famous "spirit mediums" or "channels," but through their works as emerging from and reflecting the fundamental premise that the individual, without the intermediary of the church, can contact higher beings and reveal spiritual truths.

The New Age movement is noteworthy for its syncretism, perennialism, radical spiritual individualism, and above all, its cosmic optimism, as well as its grafting of various elements of Asian religious traditions (using concepts like karma or reincarnation, for instance) into what remains a fundamentally Western millennialist outlook. This millennialism is basic to the writing of authors like David Spangler, who wrote that "The New Age is a concept that proclaims a new opportunity, a new level of growth attained, a new power released and at work in human affairs, a new manifestation of that evolutionary tide of events which, taken at the flood, does indeed lead on to greater things, in this case to a new heaven, a new earth and a new humanity."[33] And one sees a similar if perhaps less extreme millennialism in such various late-twentieth century New Age authors as Shakti Gawain, Shirley MacLaine, and George Trevelyan.

But as Christoph Bochinger argues, the term New Age is actually at least as much a marketing category as it is a school of thought.[34] He is certainly correct that the term New Age did become a category for a whole potpourri of merchandising possibilities. The river of this merchandise might look fairly wide. It carries along in its current crystals and scented candles, quasi-scientific tomes by figures like Fritjof Capra, various forms of Chinese herbalism or acupuncture, "channeled" books dictated by various discarnate entities claiming great antiquity and wisdom, and cultish Western figures claiming themselves to be representatives of Hindu or Native American or other traditions. But this river is also fairly shallow. It has been harnessed more than once as a means of making money, and sometimes observers wonder if that is not, in the end, its primary function.

For this reason, it is unjust to place too much emphasis on the origins of the New Age movement in the thought of an Emerson or, for that matter, in Western esotericism as a whole. There is a naiveté, a crassness, and a superficiality in the New Age movement missing in earlier Western esoteric traditions or in the works of Emerson. Hanegraaff is correct that the New Age movement owes much to earlier Western esotericism. But he is also convincing in arguing that the New Age movement is fundamentally a secularization of preexisting Western esoteric currents.

INDEPENDENT SPIRITS

If the most visible twentieth century religious phenomena from a sociological perspective are the New Age movement on the one hand and the emergence of fundamentalist religious movements on the other, other figures remain stubbornly independent from these various social movements and follow their own paths toward transcendence. Some of these esoteric authors or figures emphasize cosmological mysteries, while others represent what is often called the via negativa (or "negative way") of transcendent mysticism that goes beyond all images or forms and that has exemplars in the past like the great medieval Christian mystic Meister Eckhart. This, too, is an esoteric tradition, perhaps the most esoteric of all.

In his *The Book of Enlightened Masters: Western Teachers in Eastern Traditions* (1997), Andrew Rawlinson includes entries on hundreds of Westerners who assumed the role of spiritual teacher, often within various Asian religious traditions. Many independent spiritual teachers in the West were strongly influenced by Asian religious traditions, but they remain largely or totally independent of formal affiliation, and often these independent spirits are more accurately identified as part of a larger Western esoteric current.

A good example is G. Ivanovich Gurdjieff (1866–1949), a controversial figure who may have spent several years (perhaps 1905–1907) studying in a Sufi monastery or, by another account, with a secret group called the Sarmoun[g] Brotherhood somewhere in central Asia.[35] Whatever the truth about his contacts with hidden Asian spiritual traditions, Gurdjieff came to live in Western Europe and established there a center for spiritual training. He also wrote a number of long and, for the most part, seemingly impenetrable books, which attracted a number of prominent disciples. These included J. G. Bennett (1897–1974), Jeanne de Salzmann (1889–1990), and P. D. Ouspensky (1878–1947), each of whom established his or her own spiritual centers and traditions. Gurdjieff and his main disciples tended to focus their works on what we might term cosmological mysteries as well as on the hidden dimensions of human potential.

It is rather difficult to outline Gurdjieff's teachings, because he himself was not exactly systematic as a teacher, and he was also a trickster and raconteur. Yet central to his teaching is the idea, common to many esoteric traditions, that humanity is "asleep" and needs to be awakened. This awakening is best accomplished by someone who is himself "awake," and Gurdjieff and his disciples certainly saw him as awake. He was notorious for his confrontational style, for ordering his disciples to do humiliating or painful work, and for his erratic behavior—in short, for playing the role of the peremptory and all-knowing guru. He left a real legacy in the West, one with a powerful impact on the arts, not only in the dances supervised by de Salzmann, his official successor, but also in popular music and the other fine arts. Yet Gurdjieff's influence often remains hidden, because the groups that he inspired do not operate publicly—they remain, in the strictest sense of the word, "esoteric."

If Gurdjieff represents one extreme among this group of independent spirits, that of independent guru figures with an enduring social and cultural influence, at the other extreme are figures represented by Franklin Merrell-Wolff (1887–1985)—an American who, although he chronicled his own awakening experience at great length, never established any school or sociocultural forms at all—and Bernadette Roberts (b. 1931), a surprisingly little-known American Christian gnostic. Merrell-Wolff and Roberts each underwent profound spiritual awakenings. They represent the austere and individual path toward spiritual awakening or transcendence, a path without flamboyant teachers like Gurdjieff, without institutional support of any kind, a straight and steep path toward sheer self-transcendence.

Merrell-Wolff's primary account of his spiritual awakening is in his book *Pathways Through to Space,* which he describes as "a record of transformation in consciousness written down during the actual process itself."[36] Merrell-Wolff had been reading Paul Deussen's *The System of the Vedanta,* an exposition of Shankaracarya's metaphysics, while prospecting for gold in California. Then, sitting on a porch swing, he had what he called a "Recognition," after which, he wrote, "I have been repeatedly in the Current of Ambrosia. Often I turn to It with the ease of a subtle movement of thought. Sometimes it breaks out spontaneously."[37] He discovered subsequently that his wife and other people perceived this "Current." The essence of the Current was the realization of transcendence of self, and Merrell-Wolff describes it in traditional alchemical terms: "Emptiness is thus the real Philosopher's Stone which transfers all things to new richnesses; It is the Alkahest that transmutes the base metal of inferior consciousness into the Gold of Higher Consciousness."[38]

Merrell-Wolff's work is esoteric in the strict sense of the word, although he is a somewhat accessible author. Merrell-Wolff relied upon the language and symbolism of alchemy, but he also represents the influx of Asian religious thought into American intellectual life in the twentieth century. His writing conjoins the American philosophical current of William James with Buddhist and Hindu perspectives. In sum, Merrell-Wolff is an extension of the Emersonian tradition of the independent sage, one who does not seek to ascend by degrees, but who leaps at once into the throne, as Emerson put it in his first book, *Nature.*

Quite a different character is Bernadette Roberts, a Christian contemplative in the lineage of Dionysius the Areopagite, Meister Eckhart, and the author of *Cloud of Unknowing.* She does not see herself as having these direct antecedents. She describes herself as "outside the traditional frame of reference—or the beaten path of mystical theology so well travelled by Christian contemplatives."[39] And a close examination of her work shows that its central theme is realizing the absence of any substantive self, which is Buddhist, and, indeed, she spent at least a week with Zen Buddhist contemplatives.[40] But unlike Merrell-Wolff, she insists that Buddhism and Vedanta are not central influences for her; she is a Christian contemplative. What she does not acknowledge as readily is that her antecedents in the Christian tradition are figures like Dionysius, Eckhart, and the author of the *Cloud,* or that she belongs to the long-standing tradition of the *via negativa.* She even writes early in her career that "In the Christian tradition, the falling away of self (not the ego) has never been addressed!"[41] Still, late in her book *The Experience of No-Self,* she recognizes her deep affinity with Eckhart as "one who has made the journey [to no-self] and crossed over," and it is to his tradition that she certainly belongs.[42]

The heart of Roberts's work lies in her journey to and progressive realization of what she calls no-self. She outlines this journey in her book *The Experience of No-Self,* and its culmination in her subsequent book *The Path to No-Self.* No personal self, no personal God—by the strictest definition, Roberts's work belongs to the via negativa. In both the writings of Dionysius the Areopagite and of Roberts there is sheer transcendence. The difference is that Roberts's work is strikingly autobiographical in nature; she takes us along with her on her journey to no-self. And this, too, she shares with Merrell-Wolff, who also offers us the kind of contemplation he undertakes and a detailed account of his experiences along the way. Roberts is not interested in her antecedents and even says that to read the works of prior mystics is misguided, whereas Merrell-Wolff was exceedingly interested in them.

But both Roberts and Merrell-Wolff offer extended, multivolume commentaries on their spiritual experiences, and both of them see themselves as pioneers and their books as chronicles of their inner experiences. It is, I think, no accident that both are American and both lived in California. They represent very American tendencies—above all, the willingness to strike out on one's own, the refusal to accept received ways of thinking, and the insistence on one's own direct experience as the arbiter of what is true. All of these are Emersonian characteristics that remain deeply ingrained in the American character. And both figures represent the very American notion of an individualized esotericism.

CONCLUSION

Until relatively recently, the field of "esotericism" or "esoteric studies" remained more or less ignored in academia. Francis Yates and Antoine Faivre were exceptions among scholars interested in this field. But throughout most of the nineteenth and twentieth centuries, few scholars admitted that esotericism or "Western esoteric traditions" were worthwhile areas of study, or that such diverse traditions or movements as alchemy, astrology, magic, Rosicrucianism, and theosophy all bear certain defining elements in common. This situation, however, most emphatically has changed, and by the early twenty-first century, there were many new publications and scholarly organizations devoted to the study of Western esotericism.

With the wild success of potboiler novels like *The Da Vinci Code* by Dan Brown, with "New Age" distribution networks and stores across the United States, with the unprecedented availability of esoteric source works in alchemy, astrology, and magic, with the proliferation of magical groups and other esoteric movements too numerous and complexly related to detail here—not to mention the development of Western esotericism as a widely recognized area of academic study—it becomes clear that the late twentieth and early twenty-first centuries represent one of those relatively rare interludes in history like the Silver Age in early twentieth century Russia or second century Alexandria, Egypt, when what previously was esoteric becomes more widely accessible. It is perhaps too early to definitively outline every aspect of

American esotericism, but there can be no doubt that here is found one of the most vital areas of contemporary American alternative religious life.

NOTES

1. See Arthur Versluis, *Magic and Mysticism: An Introduction to Western Esotericism* (Lanham: Rowman Littlefield, forthcoming), Introduction. The group of scholars who founded the North American-based Association for the Study of Esotericism (ASE) defined the terms "esoteric" and "esotericism" in the following way:

> The word "esoteric" derives from the Greek *esoterikos*, and is a comparative form of *eso*, meaning "within." Its first known mention in Greek is in Lucian's ascription to Aristotle of having "esoteric" [inner] and "exoteric" [outer] teachings. The word later came to designate the secret doctrines said to have been taught by Pythagoras to a select group of disciples, and, in general, to any teachings designed for or appropriate to an inner circle of disciples or initiates. In this sense, the word was brought into English in 1655 by Stanley in his *History of Philosophy*. Esotericism, as an academic field, refers to the study of alternative, marginalized, or dissident religious movements or philosophies whose proponents in general distinguish their own beliefs, practices, and experiences from public, institutionalized religious traditions. Among areas of investigation included in the field of esotericism are alchemy, astrology, Gnosticism, Hermeticism, Kabbalah, magic, mysticism, Neoplatonism, new religious movements connected with these currents, nineteenth, twentieth, and twenty-first century occult movements, Rosicrucianism, secret societies, and theosophy.

See the Association for the Study of Esotericism Web site, http://www.aseweb.org.

2. Antoine Faivre, *Access to Western Esotericism* (Albany: SUNY Press, 1994), 79.

3. See Bobby Demott, *Freemasonry in American Culture and Society* (Lanham: University Press of America, 1986), 17.

4. Ibid., 238*ff.*

5. See Paul Goodman, *Towards a Christian Republic: Antimasonry and the Great Transition in New England, 1826–1836* (New York: Oxford University Press, 1988), 3*ff.*

6. See Arthur Versluis, "The Occult in Nineteenth-Century America," in *The Occult in Nineteenth-Century America,* ed. Cathy Gutierrez (Denver: Davis, 2005). Paul Goodman, *Towards a Christian Republic,* 3*ff.*

7. See John Richards, "Folk Magic and Protestant Christianity in Appalachia," *Esoterica* VIII (2006), www.esoteric.msu.edu.

8. Culpeper's herbal was reprinted and available in the nineteenth century both in England and in the United States. See, for an American herbal of the period, Samuel Stearns, *The American Herbal, or Materia Medica* (Walpole, NH: D. Carlisle, 1801); Samuel Henry, *A New and Complete American Medical Family Herbal* (New York: Samuel Henry, 1814).

9. See, in this regard, David Kriebel, "Powwowing: A Consistent American Esoteric Tradition," *Esoterica* IV (2002): 16–28.

10. See Jon Butler, "The Dark Ages of American Occultism," in *The Occult in America: New Historical Perspectives,* ed. H. Kerr and C. Crow (Urbana: University of Illinois Press, 1983).

11. John Aubrey, *Miscellanies upon the Following Subjects* (London: E. Castle, 1696); H.C. Agrippa, *Three Books of Occult Philosophy,* trans. James Freake (London: Gregory Moule, 1651).

12. See Arthur Versluis, *The Mysteries of Love. Eros and Spirituality* (St. Paul: Grail, 1996), 115*ff.*

13. James Webb, *The Occult Underground* (LaSalle: Open Court, 1974), 125.

14. See Hannah Whitall Smith, *Religious Fanaticism* (London: Faber, 1928).

15. See Thomas Lake Harris, *The Arcana of Christianity*, 2 vols. (New York: Brotherhood of the New Life, 1867); Thomas Lake Harris, *The Breath of God With Man* (New York: Brotherhood, 1867).

16. Alice B. Stockham, *Karezza* (Chicago: Stockham, 1896), 94.

17. Ibid., 95.

18. See William R. Newman, *Gehennical Fire: The Lives of George Starkey, an American Alchemist in the Scientific Revolution* (Cambridge: Harvard University Press, 1994).

19. Ibid., 233.

20. The esoteric aspects of all these authors' works (and a number of others' are discussed in Versluis's *The Esoteric Origins of the American Renaissance* (New York: Oxford University Press, 2001). Dickinson's autobiographical record in her poems is comparable to the spiritual autobiographies of women like the seventeenth century Ann Bathurst, part of whose spiritual diary is to be found in Arthur Versluis, ed., *Wisdom's Book: The Sophia Anthology* (St. Paul: Paragon House, 2000).

21. See, for some background on the tangled skein of the Golden Dawn's contemporary and predecessor groups, Joscelyn Godwin, *The Theosophical Enlightenment* (Albany: SUNY, 1994), especially Chap. 11: "From the Orphic Circle to the Golden Dawn."

22. See J. Godwin, C. Chanel, and P. Deveney, eds., "The Practical Magic of the H.B. of L.," *The Hermetic Brotherhood of Luxor* (York Beach: Weiser, 1995), 68–77, chiefly based on sexuality and including the development of clairvoyance.

23. A major subsequent figure in the Hermetic Brotherhood of Luxor was none other than Thomas Johnson (1851–1919), the American Platonist, who was, in fact, president of the American Central Council of the H.B. of L. See on this point for documentation, Godwin, Chanel, and Deveney, eds., *The Hermetic Brotherhood of Luxor*, 380.

24. Peter J. Carroll, *Liber Null and Psychonaut* (York Beach: Weiser, 1987), 7.

25. See, for instance, Carroll, *Liber Null and Psychonaut;* also Phil Hine, *Condensed Chaos: An Introduction to Chaos Magic* (Tempe: New Falcon, 1995).

26. Susan Friedman, *Psyche Reborn* (Bloomington: Indiana University Press, 1981), 157–206.

27. Rimius, *A Candid Narrative* (London: A. Linde, 1753), 70, 9, 19.

28. See Lawrence Sutin, *Divine Invasions: A Life of Philip K. Dick* (New York: Carroll & Graf, 2005), as well as various Web sites. Good collections of links can be found via the "Scriptorium" on www.modernword.com or via www.philipkdick.com.

29. For contrasting views of the history of Traditionalism, see Mark Sedgwick, *Against the Modern World: Traditionalism and the Secret Intellectual History of the Twentieth Century* (New York: Oxford University Press, 2004); and Kenneth Oldmeadow, *Traditionalism: Religion in the Light of the Perennial Philosophy* (Colombo: Sri Lanka Institute of Traditional Studies, 2000).

30. Wouter Hanegraaff, *New Age Religion and Western Culture: Esotericism in the Mirror of Secular Thought* (Leiden: Brill, 1996; Albany: SUNY, 1998), 521.

31. See Harold Bloom, *The American Religion* (New York: Simon & Schuster, 1992).

32. Hanegraaff, *New Age Religion*, 437.

33. See David Spangler, *Revelation: The Birth of a New Age* (Findhorn, Scotland: Findhorn, 1977), 91.

34. Christoph Bochinger, *"New Age" und moderne Religion: Religionwissenschaftliche Untersuchungen* (Gütersloh: Chr. Kaiser, 1994).

35. See G. Ivanovich Gurdjieff, *Meetings With Remarkable Men* (New York: Dutton, 1963), 161; G. Ivanovich Gurdjieff, *Herald of Coming Good* (Paris: La Société Anonyme, 1933), 19; Andrew Rawlinson, *The Book of Enlightened Masters* (Chicago: Open Court, 1997), 282–291.

36. Franklin Merrell-Wolff, *Experience and Philosophy* (Albany: SUNY, 1994), x.

37. Ibid., 7.

38. Ibid., 15.

39. See Bernadette Roberts, *The Experience of No-Self: A Contemplative Journey* (Boston: Shambhala, 1982), 114.

40. Ibid., 108.

41. Bernadette Roberts, *The Path to No-Self: Life at the Center* (Albany: SUNY, 1991), xv.

42. Ibid., 199.

FURTHER READING

Bloom, Harold. *The American Religion.* New York: Simon & Schuster, 1992.

Esoterica. http://www.esoteric.msu.edu.

Faivre, Antoine. *Access to Western Esotericism.* Albany: SUNY, 1994.

Faivre, Antoine, and Jacob Needleman, eds. *Modern Esoteric Spirituality.* New York: Crossroad, 1992.

Godwin, Joscelyn. *The Theosophical Enlightenment.* Albany: SUNY, 1995.

Gutierrez, Cathy, ed. *The Occult in Nineteenth-century America.* Denver: Davis, 2005.

Hanegraaff, Wouter. *New Age Religion and Western Culture: Esotericism in the Mirror of Secular Thought.* Leiden: Brill, 1996/ Albany: SUNY, 1998.

Kerr, Howard, and Catherine Crow, eds. *The Occult in America: New Historical Perspectives.* Urbana: University of Illinois Press, 1983.

North American Association for the Study of Esotericism, www.aseweb.org.

Rawlinson, Andrew. *The Book of Enlightened Masters.* Chicago: Open Court, 1997.

van den Broek, Roelof, and Wouter Hanegraaff, eds. *Gnosis and Hermeticism* New York: SUNY, 1997.

Versluis, Arthur. *The Esoteric Origins of the American Renaissance.* New York: Oxford University Press, 2001.

———. *Magic and Mysticism: An Introduction to Western Esoteric Traditions.* Lanham: Rowman Littlefield, forthcoming.

———. *Wisdom's Children: A Christian Esoteric Tradition.* Albany: SUNY, 1999.

———. *Wisdom's Book: The Sophia Anthology.* St. Paul: Paragon, 2000.

Eckankar

David Christopher Lane

One of the great difficulties in understanding the origins of ancient religions is the lack of information. Imagine going back in time some 2000 years and being able to witness the evolution of Christianity from its founder's ministry and death to the rise of Paul's missionary work. It would, unquestionably, radically alter the histories we have today of what happened then. The study of New Religious Movements (NRMs), especially those founded during our lifetime, offers unique and valuable insights into how religions in the past formed. Indeed, one can argue that putting a microscope to today's emerging religions offers us a refined telescope into the birth pangs of ancient traditions.

Eckankar, as founded by Paul Twitchell (d. 1971) in the mid-1960s is a remarkably rich example of how a new religion evolves in much quicker spurts than might be imagined. Yet, because Eckankar is still in its infancy, we can actually delineate varying stages of its growth with documented detail that is sorely lacking in studies of religions hundreds or thousands of years old. What this suggests, of course, is that an understanding of what occurs in religion today may provide us with a window to better appreciate what might have transpired in faiths eons ago.

THE FOUNDING OF ECKANKAR

The very first issue that confronts both the believer and the outsider is pinpointing the exact date when Eckankar was founded. If we merely rely on Eckankar's official literature, supplied originally by Twitchell and his eventual successors, Darwin Gross (b. 1928) and Harold Klemp (b. 1942), the date is unambiguous: October 22, 1965. Klemp, the current leader of Eckankar, points out that on this date Twitchell received "the Mahantaship," one of the key features in God-Realization that distinguishes Eckankar from other teachings. As Klemp explains in *A Cosmic Sea of Words: The Eckankar Lexicon* (1988): "Mahanta, mah-HAHN-tah The INITIATE of the Fourteenth Circle; the Mahanta, the Living ECK Master; the full force of the Rod of ECK Power and the Mantle of the Mahanta are embodied directly in him; all those who come to him in the present age have been with him since their advent into the world; the body of the Mahanta is the ECK, which is the ESSENCE of God flowing out from the OCEAN OF LOVE AND MERCY, sustaining all life and tying together all life forms; an expression of the Spirit of God that is always with you; the LIVING WORD; the VI-GURU, the LIGHT GIVER; a state of GOD CONSCIOUSNESS which is beyond the titles given in religions which designate states of CONSCIOUSNESS; the sublime ECK in expression at the highest level. This special incarnation of the SUGMAD makes an appearance but once every five to a thousand or more years, depending upon the part he is to play in a major uplift-ment of consciousness on every plane."[1]

It may be more than just an interesting coincidence that October 22 also happens to be Twitchell's birthday, since scholars such as the late John Sutphin argue that Eck-ankar was more or less created by Twitchell and reflects many aspects of his own biography, real and fictional.[2] Along these lines, considerable evidence suggests that Eckankar was formed several years before the fall of 1965. Indeed, "Paul Twitchell, Man of Parts," an interview by Jack Jarvis of the *Seattle Post Intelligencer,* appears to be the first article written about Twitchell and his new group, Eckankar. The inter-view was conducted on July 9, 1963. Twitchell's later article, "The Square Peg," was written in response to Jarvis's interview. Twitchell claimed that he was besieged with telephone calls and mail asking, "What in heaven's name is a Cliff-Hanger?" In the "Square Peg," Twitchell responded: "The Cliff-Hanger is a one-man cult. I am the original Cliff-Hanger and its sole disciple. This zany character is called the vanguard of a new religion, entitled 'Eckankar,' a Hindu word meaning union with God. This unorthodox philosophy received a wide welcome among the European intellectuals and college circles following the publishing of my works in European Magazines. The Cliff-Hanger seeks solace in meditation and bi-location experiences common in the lives of the Old Christian Savants."[3]

"Eckankar, The Bilocation Philosophy," published by *Orion Magazine* in January 1964, seems to be Twitchell's first public article entirely devoted to his new move-ment. In it Twitchell writes: "Eckankar, the philosophy of out of body experience, is that understanding which I have gained from bi-location excursions similar to those in the lives of saints of all faiths. Eckankar is the study of bi-location experi-ence." In the same article, Twitchell explains the difference between Eckankar and the various Eastern philosophies: "The orthodox Eastern Philosophies teach that man must become one with God, but I cannot hold to this concept. The individual self of man becomes a coworker of God, not a part of the unity of Him, in the sense of being one with the divine source, anyways, for we are dwelling in the body of God..."[4]

Although Eckankar, according to Twitchell, was not "officially" founded until October 22, 1965, it did, nevertheless, have several years of preparation behind it. The *Psychic Observer* published several of Twitchell's articles prior to 1965. "The Cliff-Hanger," printed in July 1964, expounds Twitchell's definition of the "enig-matic one" and of the Cliff-Hanger's philosophy—Eckankar: "Eckankar, which I formed out of my own experience, is the term used for the philosophy I have developed for the Cliff Hanger. It is based on Shabd yoga, a way out form of yoga. The word is the Hindu locution for the cosmic sound current which is known in our vernacular as the cosmic river of God."[5]

In a later article, "The God Eaters," dated November 1964, for *Psychic Observer,* Twitchell elaborates on the impetus behind Eckankar: "Eckankar is the philosophy of phardar pax Latehue walae, or what you know as the Cliff Hangers. This grew out of my visits to Agam Des, the land of the God Eaters. The basic axiom of this philosophy is: Power is the only force generated by Occult knowledge."[6]

It was thus by a series of articles on the philosophy of Eckankar and on the eccentric personality of the "Cliff Hanger" that Twitchell laid down the public groundwork for Eckankar. Brad Steiger, in his biography of Twitchell, *In My Soul I Am Free,* asked Twitchell when he really began to formulate how to spread the message of Eckankar. Twitchell replied, "probably when my sister Kay Dee died in 1959." In response to Steiger's question on when he changed from being a "Cliff-Hanger" to a spiritual adept, Twitchell replied: "The switchover from the Cliff Hanger to Eck began taking place after I met my present wife, Gail. She insisted that I do something with my knowledge and abilities."[7]

As for the reasons why Twitchell founded Eckankar, the conventional view is that he felt prompted by his previous spiritual masters to reintroduce the ancient path that was introduced to him by such luminaries as Sudar Singh and Rebazar Tarzs, both of whom he claims to have met while traveling in the East. This lineage, known as the Vairagi masters in Eckankar, allegedly traces its genealogy back through some 970 Living Eck Masters to Rama, an avatar of Vishnu in Hinduism. In other versions, the teachings go even further back to Gakko, a spiritual essence that traveled from the city of Retz on the planet Venus to Earth six million years ago. A closer review of Twitchell's actual biography reveals some startling discrepancies, not the least of which is that Twitchell apparently never visited India or Tibet when he claimed. In addition, Sudar Singh and Rebazar Tarzs are not genuine historical personages but literary inventions developed by Twitchell to conceal his past associations. What we do know from historical records and documentation is that Twitchell's spiritual biography is quite different than the mythologized versions he later tried to pass off as factual. This is especially interesting for scholars of religion, ancient or new, because it shows that hagiography can happen even *during* the lifetime of a religious leader and does not necessarily have to wait for his or her death. And such hagiography does not have to be due to the overzealousness of a guru's followers, but can instead originate fully blown from the leader himself.[8]

Twitchell apparently had a long history of embellishing his resume. Even the current head of Eckankar, Klemp, called Twitchell a "yarn" teller who was not shy in padding a story to promote his career or his ideas.[9] How much of a yarn Twitchell weaved in developing Eckankar is the subject of wide debate among current and former followers. The debate begins, appropriately enough, with Twitchell's birth date. Five contrasting accounts exist of the birth date of John Paul, the second and last son of Jacob and Dorothy (Effie) Troutman Twitchell: 1908, 1909, 1910, 1912, and 1922. The date now most widely accepted is 1909, primarily because it is listed in the Thirteenth Census of the United States, done in 1910, where Paul is cited as being six months old at the time. This date is also supported by the published volume, *Genealogy of the Twitchell Family: Record of the Descendants of the Puritan— Benjamin* which was privately published by Herbert K. Twitchell in 1929. The two most questionable dates are 1912 and 1922, which appear, respectively, on Twitchell's first and second marriage certificates. The 1922 date is also listed by Twitchell's widow, Gail Atkinson, on his death certificate in 1971. Why Twitchell apparently shaved some 13 years off his age is open to speculation, but it should be noted that Paul met his second wife in Seattle, Washington, in the early 1960s when she was barely twenty years old and when he was (according to the 1909 birth date) in his early fifties. Twitchell's birth place is less controversial, even if his official biographer claimed it was China Point, it is generally agreed even in Eckankar circles that Paul was born in Paducah, Kentucky.[10]

While Twitchell's biography gives us a clue into some of the formative influences on his thinking and his eventual movement, it is also important to note that Twitchell himself acknowledges Gail as instrumental in encouraging him to do something with his talents, and that the switchover from his more bohemian days to Eckankar were attributable, at least in part, to her. It is also worth noting that in this interim period between 1962 and 1965, Paul was financially strapped and temporarily borrowed several hundred dollars from Gail. This prompts a larger, perhaps unanswerable question, of whether or not economic conditions can be a motivating factor for some spiritually inclined individuals to test out their wares in the religious marketplace. And if so, to what extent do these financial considerations impact on the varying products that eventually get produced? This is clearly a debatable issue and is often viewed by devotees as a cheap form of reductionism. However, clearly Twitchell's own pen indicates that he created Eckankar to make a profit. As he himself said in response to a question placed by Steiger, "I do not run Eckankar as a non-profit organization. Most people in this line of work do indeed use the religious non-profit organization provision as an escape clause on their taxes. Eckankar is licensed in the state of Nevada as a business organization."[11]

Twitchell's first wife, Camille Ballowe, recalled that he was always a religious seeker and that he searched out gurus, mystics, and spiritual paths throughout their time together. Of the spiritual groups and masters Twitchell encountered, four had a definable impact on him and his teachings: the Self-Realization Fellowship (particularly the Self Revelation Church of Absolute Monism), Theosophy, Scientology, and Sant Mat (specifically through the Ruhani Satsang branch). These four groups, along with Twitchell's wide reading and varied involvements, contributed to his unique religious vision.[12]

How much these prior associations contributed to Eckankar is disputed, since many of Twitchell's ideas seem to be directly lifted, sometimes verbatim, from several key books published by Radha Soami Satsang Beas. We know that Twitchell was personally associated with three spiritual teachers in the 1950s, Swami Premananda (1903–1995) of the Self-Revelation Church of Absolute Monism, Kirpal Singh (1894–1974) of Ruhani Satsang, and L. Ron Hubbard (1911–1986) of Scientology.

Twitchell and his first wife joined the Self-Revelation Church of Absolute Monism around 1950. Swami Premananda, the founder of the Church, was closely associated with Paramahansa Yogananda (1893–1952) of the Self-Realization Fellowship (known as Yogoda Satsanga Society in India). It was from Swami Premananda that Twitchell learned Kriya yoga, a psychophysical discipline for mastering the pranic life current. In 1950, Twitchell and Camille moved to the Church compounds in California. During much of this time he edited the Church publication, *The Mystic Cross.* In 1955, Swami Premananda asked Twitchell to leave the Church for personal misconduct. In that same year, Twitchell and Camille were separated. Five years later, Camille sued him for divorce on grounds of desertion.[13]

After leaving the Self-Revelation Church in Washington, D.C., Twitchell met Kirpal Singh, the founder of Ruhani Satsang. It was Kirpal Singh who, arguably, had the greatest impact on Twitchell and the theology behind Eckankar. Kirpal Singh was a disciple of the Radha Soami Satsang Beas master, Sawan Singh (1858–1948). He was initiated in 1924 and served his guru for over 24 years. In 1948, after Sawan Singh died and bequeathed his spiritual ministry to Jagat Singh, Kirpal Singh claimed that he was the true heir to his guru's mission. Subsequently, he founded a new movement named Ruhani Satsang, which was a center "for imparting purely spiritual teachings and training for mankind, irrespective of class barriers, such as caste, colour, creed, sect, age, education or advocation."[14]

In 1955 Kirpal Singh made his first tour of the United States. In that same year, Twitchell was initiated and became a follower of Kirpal Singh and his Satsang. Around this time (1956–1957) Twitchell told Betty Shifflet and Wave Sanderson (both initiates of Kirpal Singh) that Kirpal Singh appeared in his Nuri Sarup (light body) over the weekend and dictated some of a book to him. In this regard, Kirpal Singh comments: "Paul Twitchell used to write to me every week, 'Master came and sat down on the chair and dictated his teachings to me. He published them in the Tiger's Fang.'" Writes Twitchell: "I have talked with and taken down the words of Kirpal Singh who appeared in my apartment in Nauri-raup [sic], his light body, although his physical body was six-thousand miles away in India."[15]

These two quotations are significant because years later, after Eckankar was founded, Twitchell, in his book, *The Tiger's Fang,* changed Kirpal Singh's name, depending on the context, to Sudar Singh and Rebazar Tarzs. Apparently, there was a split of some sort between Twitchell and Kirpal Singh in the mid-1960s. Why this was so has been the basis of an ongoing controversy among critics of Eckankar. Reno H. Sirrine in a personal letter to the author, dated February 22, 1977, says: "Master Kirpal Singh told me that he did not return the manuscript, The Tiger's Fang, because many of the inner experiences he described were not complete or accurate."[16]

About this episode, Kirpal Singh comments: "I tell you one American was initiated by me—I've got the initiation report in his own handwriting. Then he wrote to me, 'The Master's Form appears to me inside.' That form used to speak to him, dictate to him, inside. And all that dictation was put into a book and the manuscript was sent to me in 1963. Later he sent me another letter, "Return my book, The Tiger's Fang." I returned his book. That was dictated by me on the inner planes, and that's all right. He changed that book before printing; where he mentioned my name, he changed it to another guru's name...."[17]

Eckankar, however, had a series of different reactions to Kirpal Singh's allegations. On one extreme, they denied that Twitchell was ever associated with Kirpal Singh. Indeed, Twitchell himself intimated as much in a personal letter to Kirpal Singh where he threatened his "former" master with a lawsuit for defamation. Twitchell writes, "I have never recognized you as a master, or that you give initiations, and that your work is not in the best interest of spirituality. Your teachings are orthodox, and as a preacher you are not capable of assisting anyone spiritually."[18]

Later after Twitchell's death, Gross, his successor and eventual husband of Twitchell's widow, Gail, argued vehemently that Twitchell was never initiated by Kirpal Singh. Writes Gross, "I know for my own self, the corporation used to have a letter that Paul wrote to Kirpal Singh: (a) telling him to leave him alone; (b) that he never was initiated by Kirpal Singh; and (c) he was never a student."[19]

Darwin's former secretary when he was head of Eckankar elaborates, "Sri Darwin Gross, the Living Eck Master of Eckankar has stated that he knows for a fact that Paul Twitchell only had two Eck Masters during his earthly stay here; the Tibetan Rebazar Tarzs and Sudar Singh, and no one else. They were the only Masters to initiate Paul Twitchell Kirpal Singh and the Radha Swoami [sic] tried to 'claim' Paul Twitchell and use him for their own purposes, as have other groups from the East and West. Paul mentioned this several times and at one point wrote a letter to Kirpal Singh and his associates stating that he, Paul, would take Singh and his associates to court if necessary. Due to the threats and harassment and material Kirpal Singh and Mr. Khanna tried to use against Paul Twitchell by faking Paul's signature on many papers. Paul wrote that letter that his widow, Gail Twitchell, gave me permission to read...."[20]

This is an important controversy because many of Eckankar's ideas stem from Kirpal Singh's teachings, directly and indirectly. Why Twitchell would go to such lengths to deny what he himself already admitted in print prior to Eckankar's founding is not so much troublesome as revealing. More precisely, why would Twitchell change the names of genuine historical characters in his books and replace them with mythological figures that have apparently no historical basis?

One argument has it that the key to understanding Eckankar's early evolution hinges on understanding why Twitchell chose to change significant features of his autobiography for public consumption. In other words, what Twitchell chose to edit out of his life story is just as illuminating as what he left in. Twitchell's editing of names reached a pinnacle when he decided to publish in book form *The Flute of God.* The work was originally printed in installments in *Orion Magazine,* from 1965 to 1967. The first six chapters of the text profusely mention the names of Kirpal Singh, Sawan Singh, and Jesus Christ. When Twitchell had the book republished, however, he redacted every single mention of Kirpal Singh, Sawan Singh, and Swami Premananda. In some cases, he even edited out the name Jesus and replaced it with "Gopal Das" or other Eckankar Masters. And, although he quotes from the Bible, he even changes the name of his source (to that of the *Shar-iyat-Ki-Sugmad*) while retaining the same biblical quotation. Below is a comparison study of the two versions. Remember that the *Orion* version is the earliest and that Twitchell's editing is primarily "name replacements."

The Flute Of God by Paul Twitchell as it appeared in installments in *Orion Magazine*. Chapter I—"In The Beginning" (March–April, 1966): Par. 3: "I remember very well when Swami Premananda, of India, who has a Yoga church in Washington, D.C., said, 'When someone asked Bertrand Russell what his philosophy of Life was, he wrote several volumes of books on the subject.'"

The Flute Of God by Paul Twitchell as published by Illuminated Way Press (1970). Chapter I—"In The Beginning": Par. 3: "I remember very well when Sudar Singh, the great Eck Master said, 'When someone asked Bertrand Russell what his philoso-phy of Life was, he wrote several volumes of books on the subject.'"

The Flute Of God by Paul Twitchell as it appeared in installments in Orion Mag-azine. Chapter I—"In The Beginning" (March–April, 1966): Par. 15: "I have studied under many teacher [sic], and may yet have to study under more. Like Meher Baba, the Indian saint, who was said to have 19 teachers to help him gain his place in the universe, I have so far had seven, some outstanding ones, including Sri Kirpal Singh, of Delhi, India."

The Flute Of God by Paul Twitchell as published by Illuminated Way Press (1970). Chapter I—"In The Beginning": Par. 16: "I have studied under many ECK Masters only they have led me to the highest truth. Like Fubbi Quantz, the ECK saint, who was said to have nineteen teachers to help him gain his place in the universe, I have also had several, each outstanding, one being Sudar Singh of India."

The Flute Of God by Paul Twitchell as it appeared in installments in *Orion Magazine*. Chapter I - "In The Beginning" (March-April, 1966): Par. 16: "Each has had a place in my growth toward the spiritual goal; each are equally great in their work for mankind. However, I have felt a closer kinship and friendliness to Kirpal Singh, who has shown me a lot of the other work during my first year or so under him. Since we have parted he keeps an impartial view toward me and my research. Therefore, if I quote him in these pages it is because I feel that he is sympathetic and interested in my work."

The Flute Of God by Paul Twitchell as published by Illuminated Way Press (1970). Chapter I—"In The Beginning": Par. 17: "Each has had a place in my growth toward the spiritual goal; each is equally great in his work for mankind. However, I have felt a closer kinship and friendliness to Sudar Singh, who showed me a lot of the other work, during my first year or so under him. Since we have parted he has retained an impartial view toward me and my research. If I quote him in these pages it is because I feel that he is sympathetic and interested in my work and led me to Rebazar Tarzs."

The Flute Of God by Paul Twitchell as it appeared in installments in *Orion Magazine.* Chapter I—"In The Beginning" (March–April, 1966): Par. 32: "Life fascinates me. Certain details of life to be worked out are strange. Lying on the bed late at night I watch the pattern of shadows weaving about the room. In the presence of familiar night visitors like Kirpal Singh, or Rebazar Tarzs, a Tibetan Lama, who come often in their Nuri-Sarup, or others, some strangers, some friends, I wonder about life."

The Flute Of God by Paul Twitchell as published by Illuminated Way Press (1970). Chapter I—"In The Beginning": Par. 34: "Life fascinates me. Certain details of life that have to be worked out are strange. Lying on the bed late at night I watch the pattern of shadows weaving about the room. In the presence of familiar night visitors like Sudar Singh, or Rebazar Tarzs, the ECK Masters who come often in their Nuri-Sarup bodies, or others, some strangers, some friends, I wonder about life."

What all these comparative redactions show is that Twitchell replaced historical figures (even ones that he had direct associations with in his past) with a bevy of Eck Masters, a large number of whom have names and lives that cannot be historically documented. To skeptics, this demonstrates that much of Eckankar's history is made up by its founder in order to conceal his genuine spiritual roots. A number of competing theories advocate why Twitchell wanted to do this, ranging from the purely economic (Kirpal Singh's group did not charge money, whereas Twitchell's group does) to the benevolent (Twitchell respected that his former teachers may not have wanted to be associated with his newly minted spiritual path).

Doug Marman, a respected apologist for early Eckankar history, contends that Twitchell's redaction stems from a pivotal incident when Kirpal Singh did not approve Twitchell's written work, particularly his book *The Tiger's Fang.* Writes Marman: "In other words, this incident must have made it abundantly clear to Paul that the teachings of ECKANKAR should not be based on an association with other teachings from Paul's past. Using the names of these teachers, if they were not sympathetic to his teachings, was not fair, and more importantly, referring to them was distracting from the vision of the ECK teachings that Paul was bringing out. While Paul started out talking openly about his previous teachers, he suddenly realized that although they had contributed to his education—they were not to be a part of the real lineage of the spiritual teachings that Paul was trying to teach." [21]

Of course, Kirpal Singh's followers have a different interpretation. Writes Stuart Judd, "One of His oldest Western disciples [Paul Twitchell] had published a series of books, without getting Master's permission, in which he recounted his inner experiences in great detail. According to the books, he had in fact reached Sach Khand. These books, with accompanying letters, arrived in India one by one while I was there, and Master spoke about them at great length to a few of us. In fact, He spoke with us for five successive days for an hour at a time (sometimes I was alone with Him, but usually one or two others were also present) and made it plain that He was thoroughly displeased with the books and also the correspondence. It was evident that the disciple was maintaining that he had permission from the Master within to publish the books, and that (according to him) the Master within had withstood the repetition of the five charged names. But Master made it very clear that there was some deep and serious error here: not only had He not given permission for the books to be published, but the disciple was most decidedly not in Sach Khand. This was puzzling to us. We asked Him how it could be. He said, "I quite fully admit that the Master did take him in His lap and showed him some of the inner treasures, that's right; but he misused what he had been given, and it turned sour." Then one of us asked why the Master would show some of the inner treasures to someone who would misuse them. Master leaned forward, His eyes blazing: "Look here! Who crucified Christ? Tell me that! Who crucified Him? Was it not Judas? One of His own!" And then He spoke about Paul Twitchell ... we saw that Masters give to disciples out of their love for them; that the disciples may use or misuse what they are given."[22]

I think this is a very significant chapter in the ongoing evolution in Eckankar because it reveals in a nutshell how two completely divergent interpretations can arise from one incident, and how, in turn, each side can reinterpret the opposing camp along theological lines. One thing is certain in this episode between Kirpal Singh and Twitchell (besides the acrimony): Twitchell genealogically dissociated himself and his group from key anchors in his past and in so doing assured that Eckankar would be autonomous. If he had not severed his ties to his former teachers, Twitchell might be viewed as merely an offshoot (of which there are many) from more ortho-dox Sant Mat lineages. As it stands, most Eckists do not know about Twitchell's for-mer spiritual teachers, and Eckankar literature purged most of their names from the official records as well.

Twitchell joined Scientology around 1958. Apparently he was a staff member of the group and attained the much sought after status of "Clear." Twitchell was highly influenced by Hubbard and Scientology. Recently, a number of important docu-ments surfaced that shed more light on Twitchell's involvement with the group. A former Scientologist and friend of Twitchell in the 1950s recalls: "Paul Twitchell was a writer hired by L. Ron Hubbard to be in charge of selecting articles on Scien-tology submitted by parishioners to be published in either Scientology publications or elsewhere as a testimony to the worth of Scientology. When Paul Twitchell found out about the inner workings of Scientology, I remember him saying, "Boy, there is a lot of money in religion."[23]

Twitchell regularly wrote for a Scientologist magazine entitled *Ability*. For instance, Twitchell wrote two articles, "The Psychology of Slavery" and "Outsight." In both he speaks very highly of Hubbard. Below are two pertinent excerpts that exemplify Twitchell's keen regard for the founder of Scientology. The first puts Hubbard in the vanguard of contemporary teachers: "To build an attitude of defeat into the minds of the enemy is the constant goal of the dictators. Fortunately for the human race there are capable individuals who, like L. Ron Hubbard, founder of Scientology, leader of one of the many groups, are working to help man free him-self from such ruthless control. Freedom from artificial conditioning of ingrained reflexes against enslavement of the reactive mind makes such individuals dangerous to the totalitarians. Scientology can undo, fortunately, the poison of psychology the mass-mind has been fed."[24]

The second passage praises Hubbard's teaching about self-reliance: "Some religious teachings, especially the Hindu practices, affirm that one needs a Guru, or Teacher, for guidance even though the pupil can exteriorize at will. The difference between Scientology and these religious practices is that Ron Hubbard shows us what to do before and after exteriorization. Then following exteriorization we can have use of this ability of OUTSIGHT at its maximum level. In other words, Ron teaches us to stand upon our own feet as thetans and not depend upon a Guru to be at our side at all moments instructing us what to do, as the Hindus teach. However, a thetan must be granted beingness in order to gain experience in the handling of his capabilities, and without interference from another. That is why Ron never dictates or interferes with our beingness or personal lives, for he realizes that as long as a Scientologist depends upon another to help him he is still effect, not working from cause point, and his self-determinism is low."[25]

What is most controversial about Twitchell's involvement with Scientology, though, is the allegation that he appropriated verbatim excerpts from Hubbard's works. A classic example of this comes from *Letters to Gail* where Twitchell copies Hubbard's "The Axioms of Scientology" without mentioning his source. The implication is that Twitchell invented the axioms. The following is a comparison study of Paul Twitchell's plagiarism:

THE AXIOMS OF SCIENTOLOGY
By L. Ron Hubbard

Axiom 1. LIFE IS BASICALLY STATIC. Definition: a Life Static has no mass, no motion, no wave-length, no location in space or in time. It has the ability to postulate and to perceive.
Axiom 2. THE STATIC IS CAPABLE OF CONSIDERATIONS, POSTULATES, AND OPINIONS.
Axiom 3. SPACE, ENERGY, OBJECTS, FORM, AND TIME ARE THE RESULT OF CONSIDERATIONS MADE AND/OR AGREED UPON OR NOT BY THE STATIC, AND ARE PERCEIVED SOLELY BECAUSE THE STATIC CONSIDERS THAT IT CAN PERCEIVE THEM.
Axiom 4. SPACE IS A VIEWPOINT OF DIMENSION.
Axiom 5. ENERGY CONSISTS OF POSTULATED PARTICLES AND SOLIDS.
Axiom 6. OBJECTS CONSIST OF GROUPED PARTICLES AND SOLIDS.
Axiom 7. TIME IS BASICALLY A POSTULATE THAT SPACE AND PARTICLES WILL PERSIST.
Axiom 8. THE APPARENCY OF TIME IS THE CHANGE OF POSITION OF PARTICLES IN SPACE.
Axiom 9. CHANGE IS THE PRIMARY MANIFESTATION OF TIME.

Axiom 10. THE HIGHEST PURPOSE IN THIS UNIVERSE IS THE CREATION OF AN EFFECT.

LETTERS TO GAIL [FEBRUARY 22, 1963]
By Paul Twitchell

1] Life is basically a divine spark. Therefore, this life spark has no mass, no motion, no wavelength, no location in space or in time. It has the ability to postulate and to perceive.

2] ...It is capable of postulates and powers.

3] ...Space, energy, objects, form, and time are the results of the powers or agreements by the Soul, they are perceived solely because Soul realizes that It can perceive them.

4] SPACE is a viewpoint of dimension.

5] ENERGY consists of postulated particles in spaces.

6] OBJECTS consist of grouped particles.

7] TIME is basically a postulate that space and particles will persist.

8] The APPARENCY OF TIME is the change of position of particles in space.

9] CHANGE is the primary manifestation of time.

10] ...That the highest purpose in the universe is the creation of an effect.

The issue of plagiarism haunted Twitchell from the latter part of the 1960s. In many of his books he apparently borrowed passages without proper attribution from several occult and mystical works. Most striking, however, is Twitchell's use of hundreds, if not thousands, of passages from the writings of Julian Johnson, a former surgeon and an initiate of Kirpal Singh's guru, Sawan Singh. Johnson, a native Kentuckian, was initiated into Radha Soami on March 1, 1931. The next year Johnson left his medical practice in California and traveled to Beas, India, in order to serve his guru, Sawan Singh. From 1933 to 1939, Johnson devoted much of his time to writing about his master and his experiences in the Radha Soami path.[26]

He first helped Sewa Singh in translating the Hindi book *Sar Bachan* (authored by the founder of Radha Soami, Shiv Dayal Singh, and regarded as the central text to the group's theology) into English. Later, he authored four of his own books on Radha Soami. Johnson's first work, *With a Great Master in India,* was a compilation of letters he wrote to Americans about his first 18 months in India studying under the master. His next two books, *Call of the East* and *The Unquenchable Flame* were semi-autobiographical accounts of himself and his future wife, Elizabeth Bruce. Yet, it was not until 1939 that Johnson's most famous work, *The Path of the Masters,* was published. The English book was the first of its kind; it described in detail the history and practice of Santon-Ki-Shiska (Sant Mat).

By 1955, the year Twitchell received initiation from Kirpal Singh, several books had been published in English about Sant Mat and Radha Soami. However, it was Johnson's climatic text, *The Path of the Masters*, which remained the most popular explication. This book served as a beacon for attracting seekers to either Charan Singh of Radha Soami Satsang Beas (who was Jagat Singh's successor) or Kirpal Singh of Ruhani Satsang. Twitchell, arguably, first came into contact with the work in the mid-1950s, if not earlier. Although Twitchell does not cite *The Path of the Masters* by name or refer to Johnson in his writings, he has, nevertheless, cited another key Radha Soami text—*Sar Bachan*—which Johnson edited.[27]

The overall influence that Johnson's books—*The Path of the Masters* and *With a Great Master in India,* in particular—had on Twitchell's own spiritual writings is truly remarkable. Twitchell not only borrowed and learned from the book, he also copied it … word for word.

The striking similarities between Twitchell's work and Johnson's earlier writings are astounding. Three of Twitchell's books, *The Tiger's Fang, Letters to Gail* (both volumes), and *Shariyat-Ki-Sugmad,* appear to contain almost verbatim excerpts from Johnson's 1939 work, *The Path of the Masters.*

Yet, it is Twitchell's 1966 book, *The Far Country,* that raises the serious question of his originality. This work contains well over 400 paragraphs from Johnson's two books, *The Path of the Masters* and *With a Great Master in India,* without so much as a single reference to them. Realizing that Twitchell was intimately acquainted with Johnson's books (even Eckankar's former President, Dr. Louis Bluth, admits that he loaned his Radha Soami books to Paul Twitchell), the real question that arises is, "Did Twitchell knowingly plagiarize from them?" Although there are two contrasting viewpoints on this question, the inevitable answer is, "Yes, he did—unmistakably so." However, Eckankar strongly disclaims that their founder plagiarized from anybody. In a personal letter to the author, dated July 5, 1977, Eckankar's attorney, Alan H. Nichols, elaborates: "With a wide background of study you will find many similarities both approximate and exact in many religious statements, history, and mythology. Whether one is a student of Zoroaster, Mohammed, Buddha, Jesus, or Tao, many of the same things are said and (when translated) in the same way.… How did you know Johnson didn't obtain his information from Twitchell or Rebazar Tarzs [sic] or some other common source? Don't be surprised that many people find the same truths and even in the same words, commandments, etc., whether they are concepts, stories of events, or levels of God Worlds or consciousness."[28]

Johnson had a unique style of writing, as can easily be noticed by reading his books. Indeed, this very point has caused some criticism of him. Thus, when one notices the coincidences between Johnson's and Twitchell's writings, it is not a question of "truth" being expressed but of style being copied.

To understand Twitchell's literary indebtedness to Johnson better, consider the following facts: (1) Johnson wrote all of his books on Radha Soami in India during the 1930s. Twitchell authored all of his works on Eckankar in the United States during the 1960s and the early 1970s. (2) Twitchell stated in at least two published pieces that he considers *Sar Bachan* to be his "Bible." The book was edited by Johnson in the early 1930s.

Perhaps Twitchell's most revealing plagiarism, and one that cuts at the very root of Eckankar's claim for originality, occurs in *The Far Country.* Not only does Twitchell appropriate Johnson's words in *The Path of the Masters,* but he also plagiarizes Johnson's quotation of Swami Vivekananda—forgetting in the process that two different people are speaking. The following is a comparison of Johnson's 1939 writing and Twitchell's 1966 writing.

Julian P. Johnson, *The Path of the Masters* [1939] [Johnson is quoting Swami Vivekananda in the following passage; Johnson, by the way, properly references his quotation.]

> Something behind this world of sense, world of eternal eating and drinking and talking nonsense, this world of false shadows and selfishness, there is that beyond all books, beyond all creeds, beyond the vanities of this world—and that is the realization of God within oneself. A man may believe in all the churches in the world; he may carry on his head all the sacred books ever written; he may baptize himself in all the rivers of earth—still if he has no perception of God, I would class him with the rankest atheist. And a man may have never entered a Church or a mosque, nor performed any ceremony; but if he realizes God within himself, and is thereby lifted above the vanities of the world, that man is a holy man, a saint, call him what you will.

[The following passage is directly from Julian Johnson.]

> First of all, it is not a feeling. Secondly it is not a metaphysical speculation nor a logical syllogism. It is neither a conclusion based upon reasoning nor upon the evidence of books or persons. The basic idea is that God must become real to the individual, not a mental concept, but a living reality. And that can never be so until the individual sees Him. Personal sight and hearing are necessary before anything or anybody becomes real to us....
>
> Paul Twitchell
> *The Far Country* [1966]

> Sugmad is beyond this world of senses, this world of eternal eating and drinking and talking nonsense, this world of false shadows and selfishness. It is beyond all books, beyond all creeds, beyond the vanities of the world. It is the realization of the Sugmad within oneself.... A man may believe in all the churches in the world; he may carry in his head all the sacred books ever written; he may baptize himself in all the rivers of the earth—still if he has not perception of the Sugmad, I would class him with the rankest atheist. And a man may never enter a church or a mosque, nor perform any ceremony; but if he realizes the Sugmad within himself, and is thereby lifted above the vanities of the world, that man is a holy man, saint; call him what you will.
>
> First of all, it is not a feeling. Secondly, it is not a metaphysical speculation, nor a logical syllogism. It is not a conclusion based upon reasoning, nor upon the evidence of books or persons. The basic idea is that the Sugmad must become real to the...

The preceding comparisons reveal two things: (1) Twitchell incorporated Johnson's quotations (in this case, Swami Vivekananda's elucidation) without giving any reference note to him or the Swami. Instead, Twitchell claims that the Eck Master, Rebazar Tarzs, was speaking directly to him. And (2) in *The Far Country,* Twitchell not only exposes his outright plagiarism of *The Path of the Masters* but reveals that almost all of Rebazar Tarzs' dialogue is taken surreptitiously from Johnson's writings. Naturally, the authenticity of Twitchell's account of Rebazar Tarzs raises some serious questions about the historicity of the Tibetan master.

However, though there are many instances of Twitchell's almost verbatim copying of previously published words that were not his own, he placed them in differing contexts and occasionally altered their meanings. Thus, it would be inaccurate to merely say that Eckankar is a plagiarized version of Radha Soami or Scientology. No, Eckankar is a unique reworking of these influences into a mosaic that distinguishes itself from other like-minded groups.

Thus, Eckankar is nothing more than the sum total of Twitchell's experiences, or, if not entirely his own "personal" observations, at least his own unique choice of differing spiritual and occult teachings. As Twitchell himself wrote, "Eckankar, which I formed out of my own experience is the term used for the philosophy I have developed for the Cliff Hanger."[29]

Some of what Twitchell teaches is garnered from Ruhani Satsang. The differences, however, between the two movements are not only distinctive but fundamental. The variances, which in part can be traced to Twitchell's inclusion of alternative spiritual concepts (from "Tone Scales" to "Golden Temples"), reveal some crucial points of departure for Eckankar from the ethical and practical foundation of Ruhani Satsang.

One significant change that Twitchell brought about in Eckankar was his restructuring of the traditional Sant Mat "eight plane" cosmology. Twitchell did this, though, only after having used the original Sant Mat cosmology in several of his earlier books—most notably in *The Tiger's Fang* and *The Far Country.* The intriguing aspect is that Twitchell's revised and copyrighted "twelve plane" cosmology (which is given in the *Spiritual Notebook* and was standard in Eckankar by 1971) contradicts his previous "eight plane" one. The following is a comparison chart of the two cosmologies.

Original (based upon the Sant tradition; depicted in Twitchell's first books on Eckankar):

1. Sahasra dal Kanwal; sounds—bell and conch
2. Brahm Lok (Trikuti); sounds—big drum (thunder)
3. Daswan Dwar; sounds—violins (sarangi)
4. Bhanwar Gupha; sounds—flute
5. Sach Khand; sounds—vina (bagpipe)
6. Alakh Lok*

7. Agam Lok*

8. Anami Lok (Sugmad)*

Revised (as given in the *Spiritual Notebook* and standard by 1970):

1. Elam (Physical); sounds—thunder

2. Sat Kanwal Anda (Astral); sounds—roar of the sea

3. Maha-Kal/Par Brahm (Causal); sounds—tinkle of bells

4. Brahmanda Brahm (Mental); sounds—running water

5. Sat Nam (Soul); sounds—single note of flute

6. Alakh Lok; sounds—heavy wind

7. Alaya Lok; sounds—deep humming

8. Hukikat Lok; sounds—thousand violins

9. Agam Lok; sounds—music of woodwinds

10. Anami Lok; sounds—whirlpool

11. Sugmad Lok; sounds—music of universe

12. Sugmad/Living Reality; sounds—music of God

The most noticeable difference in the two cosmologies is in the location of the various sounds (known in Radha Soami as shabd dhuns). Note that in the first "eight plane" cosmology the sound of the flute is heard on the "fourth" plane (Bhanwar gupha), one region below Sach Khand (the eternal "soul" realm), whereas in the "twelve plane" chart, the sound of the flute is now heard on the "fifth" plane (Sat Nam; the "soul" region). This contradiction, while perhaps not noteworthy in any other spiritual tradition, is crucial in Shabd yoga, where the whole essence of the path is based upon the internal hearing of the "sound current" or "audible life stream." The knowledge of which sounds to listen to and which to discard is an extremely important part of the teachings. Other variances in the cosmologies include: (1) The sound of the thunder that was heard in Trikuti (causal realm) in the original Sant Mat cosmology is now according to the "twelve plane" chart heard in the physical region (Elam). (2) The tinkle of bells that was originally heard up to and through the first plane (Sahasra dal Kanwal) is now heard in the third region (MahaKal-Par-Brahm). (3) Par Brahm that used to be in Daswan Dwar (i.e., beyond mind and matter) is now in the causal realm—a region that was previously in Trikuti (the home of the mind).

The preceding comparisons are important in understanding that, although Twitchell employed basic Sant Mat concepts in the beginning of his group, the teachings themselves have undergone an evolution in Eckankar. This not only signals Twitchell breaking off from Ruhani Satsang doctrines but also indicates an evolving (and not a stationary) superstructure within Eckankar. More precisely, what

Twitchell may have taught in Eckankar in 1965 and 1966 may not have been disseminated near the end of his life.

DARWIN GROSS AND HAROLD KLEMP

When Gross appointed Klemp as the "Living Eck Master" in 1981 he had no idea that two years later his successor would excommunicate him from Eckankar, ban his books from sale, and instigate a lawsuit against him for business impropriety and copyright infringement. But that is exactly what happened. In a "Personal and Confidential" letter dated January 4, 1984, Klemp informed Gross of his removal from Eckankar:

> Dear Darwin:
> The Order of the Vairagi ECK Masters no longer recognizes you as an ECK Master. As the agent of the ECK, I have removed all of your initiations in ECK as well as terminated your membership in ECKANKAR. You are not capable or authorized to act or speak for or about the Vairagi ECK Masters, ECKANKAR or the ECK teachings, nor are you to hold yourself out as an ECK Master or ECK member. Do not directly or indirectly associate yourself or your activities with the sacred teachings of ECK or ECKANKAR in any way.

Naturally, Gross did not accept Klemp's excommunication, since it was Gross himself who appointed Klemp as the Living Eck Master. In a letter, dated February 1984, and widely distributed amongst interested Eck chelas, Gross presented his own version of the breach between Klemp and himself.

> Dear One:
> Many individuals who are spiritually awake are concerned about the misguided information coming out of Menlo Park. The Vairagi Masters do recognize me as a Vairagi Master. My initiations cannot be removed by Harold or anyone else. Harold Klemp does not have that authority. He was given a spiritual responsibility, which he has lost. He no longer holds the Rod of Eck Power.
> It is my duty and responsibility as a Vairagi Master to inform you that there have been many severe charges and false accusations made against me by ECKANKAR, the Corporation, Harold Klemp and others, at the World Wide of Eck, 1983, and on the tape of the 1983 World Higher Initiates Meeting. I was removed from the World Wide program, for it would have upset their plans. The schism that has come out of ECKANKAR was started by the ECKANKAR board, for I did not start this rift in ECKANKAR.

According to court documents filed in the United States District Court for the District of Oregon by Eckankar's attorneys Esler & Schneider, Gross breached his contract as President of Eckankar (and his lifetime employment agreement which gave him $65,000 a year for the rest of his life) by the following "material" respects:

A. Diverting corporate opportunities to his own private benefit and profit;

B. Using corporate assets for his own private benefit without any legitimate or reasonable benefit to defendant [Eckankar] or its corporate purposes;

C. Regularly and habitually failing to perform his duties as an officer of defendant [Eckankar];

D. Failing to live up to the high moral image expected of an officer and Trustee of a religious corporation;

E. Failing to support and assist the Living ECK Master [Harold Klemp] in spreading the message of ECKANKAR;

F. Failing to show reasonable respect and courtesy to the Living ECK Master [Harold Klemp];

G. Converting and attempting to convert property of ECKANKAR to plaintiff's [Darwin Gross's] advantage;

H. Transferring and attempting to transfer property of and rights outside the direct control of defendant in contravention of the direct instructions of the Living ECK Master and defendant's Board of Trustees;

I. Teaching and spreading doctrines which, in the opinion of the Living ECK Master, are not consistent with the teachings of ECKANKAR;

J. Failing to retire when requested to do so; and

K. Failing to retire from public activities upon his termination as defendant's president and when requested to do so by the Living ECK Master.[30]

Gross's followers do not see any impropriety in their teacher's actions. Rather, they see him in a dual function where his spiritual power is not stripped or questioned by his human wants and desires. Most of Gross's work, these chelas contend, is done on the inner planes in his "other," higher spiritual bodies. What Gross presents on the outer is not what he is on the inner.

One of the major disputes between Eckankar and Gross was over the latter's life-time contract. Before Gross resigned as "Living Eck Master" in 1981 he signed an agreement with Eckankar, which would pay him $65,000 for life, plus other perks such as use of a company automobile (and insurance), complete medical and dental coverage, entertainment expenses, and other assorted business expenses. Unquestionably, the contract is a lucrative one that is beneficial to Gross both before and after retirement. In August 1983, however, Gross's contract with Eckankar was terminated. Today, Gross has no official connection with the movement he once led for ten years.[31]

Under Klemp's leadership, Eckankar expanded its core audience worldwide with an estimated paid membership of between 40,000 to 100,000 members yearly. (Eckankar does not provide exact numbers of their membership.) Klemp also produced a wide ranging series of books and discourses and moved Eckankar's former center of operation from Menlo Park, California, to Chanhassen, Minnesota (a suburb of Minneapolis) where he established "The Temple of Eck." According to their own accounting, Eckankar has members from over 100 countries around the world.

During Klemp's tenure, Eckankar also systematized its teaching and made it more accessible to the general reading public by lessening its emphasis on Twitchell's extensive use of Indian (particularly Hindi/Punjabi) influenced terminology. Eckankar's official Web site presents a codified version of its belief system: "Soul is eternal and is the individual's true identity. Soul exists because God loves it. Soul is on a journey to Self- and God-Realization. Spiritual unfoldment can be accelerated through conscious contact with the ECK, Divine Spirit. This contact can be made via the Spiritual Exercises of ECK and the guidance of the Living ECK Master. The Mahanta, the Living ECK Master is the spiritual leader of Eckankar. Spiritual experience and liberation in this lifetime are available to all. You can actively explore the spiritual worlds through Soul Travel, dreams, and other spiritual techniques."[32]

While Eckankar was directly influenced by Sant Mat and other religions, it has, in turn, influenced a number of NRM offshoots, including the Movement of Spiritual Inner Awareness (MSIA), founded by John-Roger Hinkins; Masterpath, founded by Gary Olsen; The Ancient Teachings of the Masters (ATOM), founded by Darwin Gross; The Divine Science of Light and Sound, founded by Jerry Mulvin; the Sonic Spectrum founded by Michael Turner; and the recently formed Higher Consciousness Society, founded by Ford Johnson. Each of the founders of these groups was at one time a member of Eckankar, and they have incorporated many of the Eck terms and ideas into their respective organizations.[33]

NOTES

1. Harold Klemp, *A Cosmic Sea of Words: The Eckankar Lexicon* (Chanhassen, MN: Eckankar Organization, 1988). See "Mahanta" under the letter "M" in the dictionary.

2. See http://elearn.mtsac.edu/dlane/ekdocuments.html, which has Sutphin's letters on this subject.

3. See David Christopher Lane, *The Making of a Spiritual Movement: the Untold Story of Paul Twitchell and Eckankar* (Del Mar: Del Mar Press, 1983), Chap. 3.

4. Paul Twitchell, "Eckankar: The Bilocation Philosophy," *Orion Magazine* (January 1964).

5. Paul Twitchell, "The Cliff Hanger," *Psychic Observer* (July 1964).

6. Paul Twitchell, "The God Eaters," *Psychic Observer* (November 1964).

7. Brad Steiger, *In My Soul I Am Free* (San Diego: Illuminated Way Press, 1974), 64.

8. See David C. Lane, *Radhasoami Tradition: A Critical History of Guru Succession* (New York: Garland Publishers, 1992).

9. See Eckankar's official Web site, http://www.eckankar.org/Masters/Peddar/hisStory.html.

10. See Doug Marman, *Dialogue in an Age of Criticism,* http://www.littleknownpubs.com/Dialog_Coins.htm.

11. Steiger, *In My Soul I Am Free,* 69.

12. See Lane, *The Making of a Spiritual Movement.*

13. See Ford Johnson, *Confessions of a God Seeker* (Silver Spring, MD: One Publishing Inc., 2004).

14. Kirpal Singh, *Ruhani Satsang: Science of Spirituality* (Delhi: Ruhani Satsang, 1970), 1.

15. Paul Twitchell, "Eckankar: The Bilocation Philosophy," *Orion Magazine* (January 1964).

16. Reno H. Sirrine in a personal letter to the author, dated February 22, 1977.

17. Kirpal Singh, *Heart to Heart Talks, Volume One* (Delhi: Ruhani Satsang, 1975), 53.

18. Dorothe Ross, "All That Glistens is Not Gold," *Leadership in Eck* (July-August-September, 1976).

19. Internet transcription published on alt.religion.eckankar (accessed November 20, 2005).

20. Bernadine Burlin, personal letter to the author, dated April 5, 1977.

21. Doug Marman, online book, *Dialogue in an Age of Criticism,* http:// www.littleknownpubs.com/Dialogue_TOC.htm.

22. Internet transcription published on alt.religion.eckankar (accessed November 20, 2005).

23. Ex-Scientologist member, personal letter, June 23, 1987. See also Lane, *The Making of a Spiritual Movement,* Appendix Two.

24. Paul Twitchell, "The Psychology of Slavery," *Ability* 61 (1957): 6.

25. Paul Twitchell, "Outsight," *Ability* 70 (1958): 9.

26. Julian Johnson, *With a Great Master In India,* 5th ed. (Beas, India: Radha Swami Satsang, 1971, originally 1934); Julian Johnson, *Path of the Masters* (Beas, India: Radha Swami Satsang, 1985, originally 1939).

27. Paul Twitchell, *Letters to Gail, Volumes One and Two* (San Diego: Illuminated Way Press, 1977).

28. Personal letter to the author, dated July 5, 1977.

29. Paul Twitchell, "The Cliff Hanger," *Psychic Observer* (July 1964).

30. See Lane, *The Making of a Spiritual Movement,* Chap. 9.

31. Ibid.

32. See Eckankar's official Web site, http://www.eckankar.org.

33. See Andrea Grace Diem, *The Guru in America: The Influence of Radhasoami on New Religions,* http://members.tripod.com/~andrea65/gurutitle.html.

FURTHER READING

Johnson, Ford. *Confessions of a God Seeker.* Silver Spring, MD: One Publishing, Inc., 2004.

Klemp, Harold. *A Cosmic Sea of Words: The Eckankar Lexicon.* Chanhassen, MN: Eckankar Organization, 1988.

Lane, David Christopher. *The Making of a Spiritual Movement: the Untold Story of Paul Twitchell and Eckankar.* Del Mar: Del Mar Press, 1993.

Steiger, Brad. *In My Soul I Am Free.* San Diego: Illuminated Way Press, 1974.

Twitchell, Paul. "Eckankar: The Bilocation Philosophy," *Orion Magazine* (January 1964).

Twitchell, Paul. "The Cliff Hanger," *Psychic Observer* (July 1964).

Twitchell, Paul. "The God Eaters," *Psychic Observer* (November 1964).

The New Age: A Twentieth Century Movement

Susan Love Brown

INTRODUCTION

The New Age movement began in the United States in response to the cultural revolution that took place in the 1960s and coincided with the coming of age of the Baby Boomer generation. It began as a spiritual movement that embraced ideas and rituals from the East, such as Zen Buddhism and yoga, and combined them with western religious ideas and rituals, scientific language, and magical and mystical world views. In time, the New Age movement embraced many other nonwestern religious traditions, such as shamanism, Native American religions, and even witchcraft. It is distinguishable from more conventional religious groups and movements in that it is not necessarily attached to any formal institutions, has no single leader, can be practiced largely by individuals separately and together, and provides maximum freedom of interpretation.

The term "New Age" is most closely correlated with the astrological idea that we are about to enter a new age, the Age of Aquarius, which will arrive around 2012,[1] or has already arrived according to some. Each new age, arriving in 2100 year cycles, brings with it a new consciousness and, consequently, the opportunity to refine and renew values. The values being challenged are notions of progress, material wealth, unbridled technology, and the uncritical use of the environment without consideration for the negative consequences. The Age of Aquarius also brings with it the rediscovery of important old values and the wisdom of previous cultures, spiritual practices, and ways of living that complement the new consciousness. According to Wouter J. Hanegraaff, "…the 'New Age' under the sign of Aquarius will presumably exemplify everything which has been neglected or missing during the Piscean Age. The New Age emerges as the positive mirror image of the Old Age."[2] Paul Heelas, speaking primarily about the British manifestation of the New Age, refers to it as "self-spirituality," a term that clearly distinguishes it from the mainstream religions with which it competes.[3]

According to J. Gordon Melton, "The New Age movement ... is a revivalist movement more analogous in form to the post-World War II healing movement in the Pentecostal churches, the Ecumenical movement among liberal Protestants in the 1960s, or the Jesus People Movement of the 1970s. Each assumed the existence of stable religious (denominational) structures from which they drew their basic ideas."[4]

Because the New Age movement is so diverse and has no single leader or manifestation, it may seem at first to lack coherence. But there are certain principles that tie together the various facets of the New Age.[5] First of all, there is the emphasis on transformation of self, society, and environment for the purpose of improvement. This element of transformation has been identified as the truly distinctive element of the New Age. In *The Aquarian Conspiracy,* Marilyn Ferguson emphasizes this transformation of self and environment as a key property of the New Age.

Second, New Age advocates emphasize experience as the source of knowledge, experience that can be repeated and verified by others. This experience is achieved through movement, ritual, and feeling as opposed to dogma and doctrine.[6] For many, this emphasis on experience as opposed to dogma represented a shift from a faith-based approach to a scientific approach.

Third is the holistic nature of the New Age, emphasizing the unity not only of mind, body, and soul, but of human beings with other animals and nature, including the universe as a whole. For many, the New Age represented an end to old and dysfunctional dichotomies that separated the mind from the body, spirituality from science, and human beings from nature.

Fourth, related to the emphasis on experience, is a renewed interest in ritual, the performance of certain sets of predetermined actions to bring about a specific set of results, usually for the purpose of change toward the better. From this interest, elements of older spiritualities often found their way into New Age religion. For example, channeling, which many people associate with New Age religion, is related to the practice of mediums, which have always been a part of the occult-metaphysical community.

Fifth is an emphasis on healing any aspect of the self, either spiritually or physically usually by some natural means, giving the New Age movement a therapeutic focus. Many of the practices and rituals of the New Age movement developed as techniques of healing, and healing itself constitutes an extension of transformation.

Finally, harmony, the sixth principle of the New Age, which consists of harmony among body, mind, and soul or any aspect of being, constitutes a further expression of the unity of holism. The emphasis on holism is a way of reaffirming the connectedness of everyone and everything in the universe—a reaction to the many dichotomies that gave rise to so many cultural and social contradictions and ambiguities following World War II.

The New Age movement was precipitated by the massive social changes that occurred in the 1960s and, as such, constitutes a revitalization movement. It occurred at a time when massive numbers of young people were moving out of established churches, or never joined them, because of general disillusionment with the established authorities. It is largely a middle-class movement. However, the New Age movement had precedent. Its origins lay both in the upheavals of the 1960s, many of which were precipitated by post-World War II conditions, and in the spiritual nature and history of the United States itself and in what James R. Lewis and Melton called the "occult-metaphysical community" (also referred to as "esoteric Christianity"), a tradition reaching back to the 18th century.[7] But the New Age differs from historical predecessors, according to Lewis and Melton, because of its millenarian "emphasis on transformation."[8]

The New Age movement is also part of a long-standing counterreligious movement that stands in opposition to mainstream religious expression and spirituality. This counterreligious spirit has always existed in the United States, and there have been predecessors, such as the Theosophical Society, Spiritualism, and New Thought.[9] The New Age movement differs from previous versions of this independent spirituality precisely in its lack of a central organization and the multiplicity of its manifestations, as well as its transformative element. But like those previous movements and spiritualities, it was precipitated by cultural and social changes that challenged the stability of society and the psyches of its members.

The immediate origin of the New Age movement lay in the changes in the United States following World War II and the upheavals of the 1960s.

THE ORIGINS OF THE NEW AGE

Scholars disagree with one another on the precise beginning of the New Age movement. For example, Melton dates it from 1971,[10] but it had definite roots in the volatile atmosphere of the 1960s.

A specific set of circumstances gave rise to the New Age: a major shift in consciousness among the intellectuals following World War II, the increasing affluence in American society, technological innovations, the rise of the Human Potential Movement in psychology, the changes caused by a number of "rights" movements within the country resulting in "the democratization of personhood," and the coming of age of the idealistic Baby Boomer generation. Let us examine each of these factors in turn.[11]

The vanguard of the Baby Boomer generation, those born between 1946 and 1954, grew up in a post-World War II environment of increasing affluence, technological change, unprecedented social change, and spiritual uneasiness.[12] The war epitomized a human nightmare, not only with the loss of life in military engagements, but in the horror created by the Nazi concentration camps, the extermination of millions of people, and the barbarity of the doctrines associated with them and in the very existence of the atomic bomb, a weapon so powerful that it was capable of the annihilation of thousands of people. Because of these troubling events, there was an elevated consciousness following the war and a questioning of basic human values and their meaning in the face of such atrocities. This disturbance of consciousness marked a decided shift that was to become manifest as the 1960s approached.

But accompanying these doubts about the meaning of humanity in the face of so much destruction was also a set of very positive occurrences, including the rise of an unprecedented affluence that finally relieved the economic anxieties of the Great Depression. The middle class rose from a meager 13 percent of the population to an astounding 46 percent of the population, adding to the general optimism. This came about not only due to a recovering economy but because of new advantages, such as education through the G.I. Bill, home ownership made possible by loans to veterans, and the job security that came with the rise in manufacturing and large companies that offered new employment possibilities. After the war, the building of corporate America, which would ultimately lead to the United States becoming a world power, helping to consolidate the cultural view of Americans about the nature of their ideals and their place in the world, occupied much of the activity of much of the adult generation.

While men were off building corporate America, women were giving birth to unprecedented numbers of babies. Between 1946 and 1964, around 78 million new Americans were born—the biggest baby boom ever. The birth of an enormous generation led to a child-centered society with a family orientation. Through the practice of new child rearing methods and ideas, the society moved from a sociocentric society to a society in which self-fulfillment was central to the changes that would take place in the late 1960s.[13] Boomers enjoyed unprecedented childhood attention and the rise of their own subculture separate from that of adults.

One of the key factors in allowing Baby Boomers to think of themselves in a unified way was the rapid rise of television, which provided a horizontal integration of an enormous geographical area. Through the viewing of common shows, both news and entertainment, boomers shared a common American experience, or at least had the illusion of doing so. Because of the parental emphasis on the social aspects of self, boomers also experienced a sense of belonging and unity that they took for granted, but which would begin to fall apart in the 1970s after so many changes. This sense of unity was sought and restored to some degree by the tenets of New Age ideology. Major events, such as the first manned space shot and the assassination of President John F. Kennedy, were shared simultaneously due to the wide coverage of the broadcast media. Thus, the same images were imprinted on the consciousnesses of Baby Boomers everywhere.

Technological innovations were unprecedented as Baby Boomers moved through childhood. Not only the bomb, which posed a threat to all societies, but the development of space exploration in competition with the Soviet Union, the invention of the transistor, and the general emphasis on using technology to create comfort and ease in the home and on the road, all lent an air of possibility and optimism that challenged the undercurrent of doom that arose along with the Cold War between the Soviet Union and the United States and the Cuban missile crisis. Baby boomers faced the possibilities of nuclear annihilation at the same time that they were experiencing the comforts of unprecedented affluence, one of the ironies that came to characterize this generation.

As the vanguard of the baby boom reached maturity, the "democratization of personhood," as Peter Cleçak has called it,[14] occurred in the 1960s and 1970s. First of all, the civil rights movement called attention to the plight of African Americans in the South, and their struggle to obtain the same rights as other Americans was viewed daily on television and, thus, shared by the whole nation, it became a formative part of Baby Boomer consciousness. The civil rights movement also led to disillusionment with the parental generation, whose high ideals were being preached but not lived. Churches, the supposed repository of moral values, did not live up to the ideals they preached, and this was the beginning of a drift away from establishment religion. So when the lives of male Baby Boomers themselves were threatened by the military draft during the Vietnam conflict, boomers used the precedent of civil rights protests as a model for their own antiwar protests. There was also a series of assassinations, ushering in an era of violence, beginning with the assassination of President Kennedy in 1963, followed by Medgar Evers (1963), and the Reverend Martin Luther King, Jr., and Senator Robert Kennedy, both in 1968.

But the democratization of personhood did not stop with blacks or with male conscripts. The women's movement, launched in 1963 with Betty Friedan's *The Feminine Mystique,* became organized and vocal in the early 1970s and led to new visions of liberation and the reassertion of egalitarianism that were always a hallmark of American cultural ideals. It was followed by protests on the part of Native Americans, disabled people, elderly people, and many others until every group in the United States claimed its personhood and changed the nature of American society by doing so. There was also a general shift from seeing the United States as a nation in which all new groups assimilated into the "melting pot" to appreciating the great diversity to be found in the traditions of different ethnic and religious groups. So a positive ethnicity also emerged after the 1960s and led to changes in the educational curriculum of universities and eventually public schools and launched debates about multiculturalism and diversity that continue to this day.

All of these changes, good and bad, major and minor, led to a reevaluation of norms, accompanied by feelings of insecurity and instability in the United States. Along with the culture of protest emerged a counterculture, which became the source for an emerging new consciousness. Adding to the experience of change and offering some solution to it were transactional psychology, whose practitioners and ideas gave rise to the Human Potential Movement, which promised self-fulfillment through self-actualization, an increasing affinity for Eastern religions and practices, such as Zen Buddhism and yoga, and the altered states of consciousness induced by psychedelic drugs introduced to young people at large by Harvard professor Timothy Leary (1920–1996) and his colleague Richard Alpert (b. 1931), among others. These altered states of consciousness formed the basis of a new spirituality rooted in experience of the divine.

These remedies for coping with change also produced many of the early personalities recognized by members of the New Age movement and its historical antecedents.

PERSONALITIES OF THE NEW AGE MOVEMENT

The older spiritual movements with which the New Age is identified with specific founders, leaders, and prophets are all in contrast to the New Age movement itself. The New Age is decidedly nonauthoritarian in nature and consists primarily of individuals seeking ways for the self to be fulfilled or healed in the form of specialist practitioners, classes, pilgrimages, and practices that are fairly specific. Its personalities are seen as teachers or specialists, whose authority is vested in their knowledge but not in their leadership. Thus, the New Age constitutes a conglomeration of individualists seeking out specialists as they need them, setting up a kind of competition among these personalities.

Heelas notes that this situation results in "…voices of authority emanating from experts, charismatic leaders and established traditions being mediated by way of inner experience."[15] New Age personalities tend to be entrepreneurs who provide learning through experience and let movement members pick and choose for themselves in a marketplace of spiritual ideas and practices. There is no single spokesperson, for the very individualistic nature of the movement militates against it. Nevertheless, certain people, some from the past and some from the present, are most associated with the New Age.

Earlier religious movements, such as Spiritualism, Theosophy, and New Thought have lent to the New Age a group of "elders" whose ideas seem similar in some respects to many of those of the New Age or have been picked up and given a renewed life and respectability by members of the New Age movement who have rediscovered them.[16] Among these would be figures such as Madam Helena P. Blavatsky (1831–1891), one of the founders in 1875 of the Theosophical Society, Alice Bailey (1880–1949), a theosophist prophet and author of *The Reappearance of the Christ,* and channeler David Spangler (b. 1945), also from the Theosophical tradition. Another person whose work was rediscovered was Edgar Cayce (1877–1945), a clairvoyant or psychic whose many readings and predictions fascinated people in the United States in the early twentieth century and whose life and readings remain the subject of study even to this day.

Eastern spirituality has always influenced religion in the United States.[17] Influences from Eastern religions include Swami Vivekananda (1863–1902), who founded the Vedanta Society, and Paramahansa Yogananda (1893–1952), who founded the Self-Realization Fellowship and authored *Autobiography of a Yogi,* which was an early influence. Maharishi Mahesh Yogi (b. 1917), who taught Transcendental Meditation (TM) and was a guru to many celebrities, including the Beatles and the Beach Boys. TM was highly influential within the New Age movement. Maharaj Ji (b. 1957), head of the Divine Light Mission originally founded by his father, Hans Ji Maharaj in 1966, also contributed to the New Age movement.

Transactional psychology and the Human Potential Movement lent many of its ideas and practices as well as language to the New Age movement and was the source of much of the emphasis on science and its compatibility with spirituality. The Human Potential Movement had three founders: Abraham Maslow (1908–1970),

Carl Rogers (1902–1987), and Rollo May (1909–1994), who were all also involved in transactional psychology, sometimes called Third Force psychology. These three psychologists came up with the theory of self-actualization with its emphasis on the ability of individuals to transform themselves, and this message carried a lot of weight with members of the Baby Boomer generation just as they were coming of age and searching for new identities. This movement coincided with changes in child rearing and American conceptions of self in a kind of social and cultural synergy. Maslow, in particular, through his writing, had a profound impact on the formation of the New Age movement in the United States. His book, *Religions, Values, and Peak-Experiences* (1964), pointed out the relationship between altered states of consciousness and spirituality that might constitute the basis for all religion.

A "homegrown" contingent emerged from the halls of academe in the form of university professors who were instrumental in introducing various aspects of their own research and understandings into the New Age movement. Among these were Leary and his confederate Alpert, later to become known as Baba Ram Dass (or just Ram Dass for short). These two Harvard professors and some of their colleagues introduced members of the Baby Boomer generation to the altered states of consciousness made possible by the use of psychedelic drugs, such as LSD. Discharged from the university for their careless use of these drugs, they went on to explore other ways of achieving the altered states of consciousness and stumbled upon the practice of meditation as taught by some Indian yogis. While Leary lapsed into cult fame, Ram Dass went on to become one of the best known names among the New Agers, largely through his writings and public appearances. His book, *Be Here Now,* was especially influential.

Also joining the mix from academia, Carlos Castaneda (1925–1998), an anthropologist from the University of California, Los Angeles, became known for a series of books supposedly based on his fieldwork and interviews with Don Juan Matus in Arizona, a Yaqui Indian who taught him shamanism, which Castaneda recounted in *The Teachings of Don Juan: A Yaqui Way of Knowledge* (1968) and a series of sequels that became influential among the Baby Boomers who joined the New Age movement. Discredited as anthropology, his work was a harbinger of an interest in shamanism that was picked up later by Michael Harner, also an anthropologist and author of a legitimate body of ethnographic work done in South America, who popularized shamanism in his 1980 book, *The Way of the Shaman.*

Many of the personalities of the New Age movement used books to spread their ideas and eventually other media as well. Marilyn Ferguson was one of the first to popularize the Age of Aquarius in her book *The Aquarian Conspiracy* (1980), as well as the concept of a global consciousness that was needed to transform society in the coming Aquarian age. She popularized the notion of a "paradigm shift" in human consciousness. Representatives from mainstream religious groups were not immune to the influence of the New Age. For example, Matthew Timothy Fox (b. 1940), an ordained Catholic priest, eventually left the church, founded Creation Spirituality, and in 1983 published *Original Blessing: A Primer in Creation Spirituality.*

Perhaps no single person popularized the New Age movement more than Shirley Maclaine (b. 1934), an actress and writer, beginning with her book, *Out on a Limb* (1983), which was made into a film, and *Dancing in the Light* (1985), followed by other books. Well known because of her stardom in some of the top musical comedies made into movies, when she wrote she raised the general level of awareness of the New Age, although some would also say that she brought much ridicule upon it as well. Although she brought about a general awareness of the New Age, the movement was well under way by the time she made her mark on the public consciousness. Still, the increased media consciousness of the New Age stimulated by Maclaine's books began to manifest itself in the New Age sections in bookstore chains and the proliferation of shops, classes, and practitioners in a vastly expanding spiritual marketplace.

The sheer number of personalities associated with the New Age movement (most of whom cannot be mentioned here) testifies to the depth, popularity, and breadth of the movement. Its beliefs and practices incorporate so many older practices and elements of older spiritualities that the New Age movement has become a great synthesizer of the esoteric, Eastern, and Native American traditions.

BELIEFS AND PRACTICES OF THE NEW AGE MOVEMENT

From an astrological perspective, all of the characteristics of the New Age and the principles defining it are due to the renewal of human energy and values placed into the service of all the learning and experience that has gone on since the last New Age, the Age of Pisces. But since human thought and action may not have caught up with all of the change and accumulated knowledge, the introduction of the new and necessary consciousness and values seems abrupt and even radical. However, the six principles mentioned at the beginning of this essay create the foundations for belief and action that constitute the New Age movement.

Transformation of Self, Society, and the Environment

Transformation, which many scholars identify as central to the New Age movement, takes many different forms, from personal improvement through spiritual practices and self-help programs to workshops at various institutions to direct social action on such issues as animal rights, environmental protection, and poverty. As mentioned above, the Baby Boomer generation was raised with an emphasis on self-fulfillment, which was reinforced through the self-actualization proposed by the Human Potential Movement, creating an element of New Age spirituality that focuses in part on the individual. Transformation is not merely a basic principle but the key goal of the New Age movement, bringing about change for the sake of betterment.

Individual transformation involves a thorough exploration and understanding of the self, which can be obtained through spiritual practices (see below) or through self-help books and programs that teach one the art of transformation. It is no surprise that American bookstores abound with self-help books. Assistance might come from spirit guides of all kinds, through specific practices designed to bring enlightenment, or through cultivating a closer relationship with specific deities.

Complementary to the transformation of the individual and following from it is the transformation of society as a whole. Just as one can work specifically to transform individuals, so can one work to transform things on the social level. For example, some New Agers believe that collective meditation can actually reduce violence in specific areas if done for a long enough time under the right conditions.

Transformation of the environment is deemed by many to be imperative if individuals and societies are to survive. The New Age movement always placed importance on the nature of the physical environment but especially on bringing human beings back into harmony with nature. A distinct difference in New Age thinking, and that which seemed to be dominant in the highly industrialized environment in which it arose, was a turning away from presumed dominance over nature, which was viewed as a breach of the unity of all living things and of all entities in the universe.

Transformation depends on the acquisition of appropriate kinds of knowledge, self-understanding, and action. But the goal of transformation is the end to which all other things are the means. However, without the proper means, transformation cannot take place. Because understanding is a key to transformation, the New Age movement also puts a premium on experience as a source of knowledge.

Experience as the Source of Knowledge

One characteristic of the New Age is its affinity for experience rather than doctrine or dogma. This experience is most often found in altered states of consciousness that open up the perspective and create shifts in values and habits. The spiritual side of self-fulfillment often takes the form of religious devotions: various forms of meditation, yoga, prayer, and channeling.

Meditation, an ancient practice in both Hinduism and Buddhism, has been described by some practitioners as "listening to God" as opposed to prayer, which is "talking to God." Although the methods and purposes of meditation vary, a common effect is to place the practitioner into an altered state of consciousness. Meditation can be therapeutic; it can turn people away from drugs that induce similar states of consciousness and create a sense of calm and reëxamination of one's life. The influence of Eastern religions is most often felt in this practice, with the transformation occurring as a consequence of the experience. The experience itself constitutes empirical evidence of a greater consciousness that all can tap into and become one with.

However, altered states of consciousness can be achieved in many ways, not just the stillness and contemplativeness of meditation, but through exhausting movement and through the use of certain drugs as well. Maslow believed that these experiences, what he called "peak experiences," constituted the very origin of spirituality—that they were universally the basis for all spiritualities, which differed only in particulars.

This affinity for the altered states of consciousness experience also accounts for the rise of interest in shamanism. Real shamans are men and women living in traditional tribal societies who have the ability to heal through their own transformative powers, usually associated with altered states of consciousness achieved through a variety of means. New Age Neo-Shamanism is taught in classes and workshops. In addition to Harner's work in this area, Lynn V. Andrews, who apprenticed herself to Native American shamans, has written a number of books, such as *Medicine Woman* (1981) and *Star Woman* (1986), largely appealing to women.

Often experience can be acquired by attending classes or workshops at established New Age institutions or programs. Esalen Institute, located in Big Sur, California, is one of the oldest New Age centers in the United States. It actually predates the New Age movement, having been founded in 1962. In sum, experience is emphasized over doctrine in the New Age movement.

Ritual and Practice

The experience on which this action is based is achieved through action itself. And the holism or sense of unity that is sought is necessarily related to the kinds of rituals and performances that both accomplish change and lend meaning to that change.

Channeling, or acting as a medium, is the practice of acting as a conduit for information from the spirit world, and it is the practice that most people probably associate with the New Age movement.[18] A medium and author named Jane Roberts is credited with popularizing channeling, a term associated with the New Age. She supposedly brought messages to this world from a personality named Seth in another plane of existence. But many of the practices and rituals of the New Age have been adapted from various spiritual sources that predate the movement itself. The use of mediums is at least as old as Spiritualism, which flourished in the United States in the nineteenth century, and remained a practice among certain individuals long after that movement subsided.

The practices of astrology, reading Tarot cards, numerology, and reflexology are all practices that predated the New Age, some going back centuries. But these have all been retrofitted for use in New Age spirituality, and these have often been combined with other more traditional Eastern religious practices, such as mediation, chanting, fire ceremonies, and so on.

Holism, the Emphasis on Unity

The emphasis on holism, or the unity of body, mind, and spirit, or the unity of self and God, or the unity of self and the universe, in the New Age context represents the rebirth of egalitarianism. Because of the claim that anyone can become transformed, and because this transformation and the experience upon which it is based are meant to unify, the movement may be perceived as egalitarian, creating the conditions in which all human beings are equal. The New Age "implies a rejection of the mainstream and a declaration that New Age ideas and routines are open freely to everyone for the sake of both personal and collective betterment."[19]

Members of the New Age movement, especially those who live in communities, must constantly grapple with the tension between the holistic ideal as the means to unity within the group and the autonomy of the individual. However, the need to affirm the connection to others and to the world is manifested in the creation and maintenance of New Age communities, like Findhorn Foundation in Scotland, Damanhur in Italy, or Ananda in the United States.

Healing and the Therapeutic Focus

One of the most important ways in which transformation can occur, and one of the most important and popular aspects of the New Age that has spread far beyond its own spiritual practitioners, is through healing. Spiritual healing, with roots in both the Christian Science and New Thought traditions, melds together a myriad of healing practices meant to affect both the body and soul. A strong tendency of New Age healing is based on the belief that the mind possesses the ability to heal the body or that certain substances can precipitate healing—crystals or certain metals, such as gold, silver, or copper—can have positive effects on one's spiritual and physical health.

Some healing practices are based on nonwestern healing traditions, including acupressure, acupuncture, and ayurveda. Others have their roots in homeopathic traditions of the West. Some healing practices are rooted in mystical beliefs, such as the use of crystals or certain metals, while others are based loosely on scientific approaches, such as biofeedback, biorhythms, and still others rooted in psychological and physiological approaches, such as the Alexander technique, self-hypnosis, and visualization.

The New Age movement has created and supported a growing concern with preventive medicine and natural remedies. Two popular doctors, Deepak Chopra (b. 1947) and Andrew Weil (b. 1942), represent the bursting of New Age affinity into the mainstream consciousness of the United States. Both regularly appear on television, and both are prolific writers. Chopra is known for combining Eastern and Western medical practices, having been trained in medicine in India and the United States. A student of Maharishi Mahesh Yogi, he was also trained in ayurvedic medicine and Transcendental Meditation. Weil, trained at Harvard Medical School, practices integrative medicine, which emphasizes alternative practices and focuses on prevention and the use of natural remedies.

CONTROVERSIES ABOUT THE NEW AGE MOVEMENT

One of the main reasons why the New Age movement is controversial is its opposition to mainstream religion. To this extent, some people wonder whether the New Age movement constitutes a legitimate religious movement at all.[20] Militating against its legitimate status is newness, its lack of distinct organization, and its tendency to draw people away from mainstream religions.

But there are also those who believe that the New Age movement is a response to the vacuousness of modernity, a product of postmodernity. For example, Carmen Kuhling noting that the New Age "is not a unified social movement or a cultural phenomenon. Rather, it can be characterised as the materialisation of various desires: for integration, for a spiritual life, for connectedness to others, for a union with nature, for health,"[21] goes on to say:

> What is most significant about the New Age is that it can be seen as a response to what people perceive as the spiritual vacuum at the heart of late capitalism. New Age spirituality, an eclectic mix of Eastern mysticism, self-help therapy, paganism, and other philosophies, is not a religious movement per se; it is a response to the secularisation of modern social life or the increasing disenchantment with the world.[22]

Kuhling sees the New Age as a collection of sometimes contradictory elements such as commodification, subversion, and a symptom of postmodernity. In short, "the New Age Movement is a complex and multifaceted movement that exhibits a variety of sometimes contradictory tendencies and agendas," which, because it results in the "proliferation of New Age commodities such as natural foods and cosmetics and spirituality books and seminars" constitute the "exploiting the spiritual vacuum in modern life."[23] Kuhling bases many of her conclusions about the New Age on two studies conducted in Toronto, Canada, and West Cork, Ireland.

The identification of the New Age with commodification or consumerism has also been mentioned by several observers. This aspect of the New Age stems from both the middle-class origins of the movement and the entrepreneurial talents of its practitioners and their prescriptions for self-help, emphasizing the very individualistic nature of the movement. Other critics have also seen the New Age as a movement that encourages narcissism and consumerism.

As Ruth Prince and David Riches note, "The New Age upholds a departure from, indeed a radical turning away from, the social values of the Western mainstream; yet in practice New Agers make the break only partially. There are two opposed senses in which this is so. Either, people entertain New Age notions in limited areas of their lives, whilst otherwise they remain engaged in the mainstream.... Or else, New Agers devote themselves to keeping the mainstream at bay, as when they locate in remote Celtic parts, or gather in communes which outsiders cannot easily penetrate...."[24]

Olav Hammer sees in the New Age movement a vast number of contradictions, some arising from the very principles on which it rests.[25] The claims of New Agers to holism, universalism, and individualism create vague or contradictory messages. For example, while claiming to incorporate universal aspects of all religions, Hammer says, New Agers combine such diverse world views that they cannot actually point out what it is that they all have in common, and many specific beliefs surrounding such concepts as reincarnation, the veneration of the Earth, and other world views are the product of imagination rather than indigenous beliefs. Hammer also notes that many indigenous people resent the use of their religions for New Age commercial purposes, a charge that fits Kuhling's analysis. Hammer also finds contradictions in the simultaneous embrace of science and dismissal of science and in the individualism of the New Age and its attempt to bring together large numbers of people to effect change in the world.

Others see the New Age as having failed in its mission to transform at any level. However, some New Agers would argue that the actual New Age has not yet arrived, and human beings are still involved in catching up with the lessons of the Piscean Age, so that the full effects of the impending transformations cannot yet be seen.

THE FUTURE OF THE NEW AGE MOVEMENT

If we accept Melton's classification of the New Age movement as a "revivalist movement," then we can expect it to fade eventually—only to become another note in the history of religion rather than a permanent fixture of the religious landscape. Part of Bailey's prediction for the coming of the New Age included the "rediscovery of ancient spirituality," "a world religion uniting East and West," "the discovery of the soul by science," and "paranormal abilities, such as telepathy, becoming normal."[26]

So far, the New Age movement seems to be heading in these directions with its adoption and adaptation of shamanism and Native American spiritualities and religious practices, its combining of certain elements from Christianity with those from Hindu and Buddhist practices and beliefs, and the grappling of science and religion for a common ground. However, the paranormal is far from common, unless the presence of so many channelers is evidence that it has become normal. But neither has the New Age shown signs of subsiding.

Almost from the time of its inception, the New Age movement spread to other western countries and led to new interpretations of its basic elements in a variety of cultural milieus. In *Persuasions of the Witch's Craft* (1989), T. M. Luhrmann presented a study of rationality among contemporary young people in England who practiced magic and witchcraft in the evenings and on weekends, while holding down their day-to-day jobs. Prince and Riches studied aspects of the New Age in Glastonbury, United Kingdom, following the Harmonic Convergence in 1987. Carmen Kuhling studied New Age communities in Canada and Ireland. And the New Age literature describes communities in Italy, Japan, and elsewhere. The New Age has even manifested itself on the continent of Africa, where religious revivalism is widespread.

While the exact numbers of people adhering to some form of New Age spirituality is difficult to ascertain because of its somewhat nebulous nature, it is clear that it is now a global phenomenon.

CONCLUSION

If, indeed, the New Age movement is revivalist in nature, then it may very well fade as its carriers in the United States drift back to mainstream churches and/or simply die, giving way to the proclivities of the next generation. However, its basic principle of transformation played a part in raising a consciousness about the role of fulfillment in human life, the ways in which people should relate to one another, and a concern for the natural environment. Self-help, human relations, and ecological sensitivity are apparently permanent concerns as we focus our attention toward the New Age.

The New Age movement has moved beyond the spirituality at its core and expanded to include aspects of culture, such as New Age music, which has become a genre of its own. It could be that the New Age will remain with us longest in a cultural rather than a spiritual form, but even this remains to be seen. The New Age is a movement whose time has come but has not yet gone. It will dissipate as a movement only if there is no longer any need for the particular kind of spirituality and opportunity it makes possible.

NOTES

1. Gerry McGuire Thompson, *The Atlas of the New Age* (Hauppage, NY: Barron's Educational Series, 1999), 7–9, approximates the date as 2010. However, Michael York, *Historical Dictionary of New Age Movements* (Lanham, MD: The Scarecrow Press, 2004), in his chronology mentions December 21, 2012, as the date, citing José Argüelles, who organized the celebration of the Harmonic Convergence, in accordance with the Mayan calendar.

2. Wouter J. Hanegraaff, *New Age Religion and Western Culture: Esotericism in the Mirror of Secular Thought* (Albany: State University of New York Press, 1998), 331. Hanegraaff also cites Marilyn Ferguson, *The Aquarian Conspiracy* (Los Angeles: J.P. Tarcher, 1980); and Matthew Fox, *The Coming of the Cosmic Christ: The Healing of Mother Earth and the Birth of a Global Renaissance* (San Francisco: Harper & Row, 1988), in particular referring to the oppositional thinking about the differences in the two ages.

3. Paul Heelas, *The New Age Movement: The Celebration of the Self and the Sacralization of Modernity* (Oxford: Blackwell, 1996), 18–40.

4. J. Gordon Melton, "New Thought and the New Age," *Perspectives on the New Age,* ed. James R. Lewis and J. Gordon Melton (Albany: State University of New York Press, 1992), 16.

5. Wouter J. Hanegraaff, *New Age Religion and Western Culture: Esotericism in the Mirror of Secular Thought,* sees the major trends of the New Age as four: channeling, healing and personal growth, science, and Neopaganism. Some, such as Sarah M. Pike, *New Age and Neopagan Religions in America* (New York: Columbia University Press, 2004), see Neopaganism as a separate though related movement.

6. See, for example, Susan Love Brown, "God and Self: the Shaping and Sharing of Experience in a Cooperative, Religious Community," in *The Psychology of Cultural Experience,* ed. Carmella C. Moore and Holly F. Mathews (Cambridge: Cambridge University Press, 2001), 173–195.

7. James R. Lewis and J. Gordon Melton, eds., "Introduction," *Perspectives on the New Age* (Albany: State University of New York Press, 1992), xi.

8. James R. Lewis and J. Gordon Melton, eds., *Perspectives on the New Age,* xi. For additional information about the roots of the New Age movement in this occult-metaphysical community, see in James R. Lewis, ed., *The Encyclopedic Sourcebook of New Age Religions* (Amherst, NY: Prometheus Books, 2004), articles by James A. Santucci ("Theosophy and the Theosophical Societies: An Overview," 25–49), Roger E. Olson ("Rudolf Steiner, Esoteric Christianity, and the New Age Movement," 50–62), and Gail Harley ("Paradigms of New Thought

Promote the New Age," 63–80). Also see Pike, *New Age and Neopagan Religions in America,* 39–65, for a narrative account of this same tradition. Catherine Tumber, *American Feminism and the Birth of New Age Spirituality: Searching for the Higher Self, 1875–1915* (Lanham, MD: Rowman & Littlefield, 2002), roots these same traditions in Gnosticism and gives a broad account of New Thought and the role of women in this community. Though Tumber is herself critical of the outcome of this kind of spirituality, her account is very engaging. In James R. Lewis and J. Gordon Melton, eds., *Perspectives on the New Age* (Albany: State University of New York Press, 1992), see J. Gordon Melton, "New Thought and New Age," 15–29; Robert Ellwood, "How New is the New Age?", 59–67.

9. See Lewis, ed., *The Encyclopedic Sourcebook of New Age Religions,* for articles on all of these.

10. J. Gordon Melton, "A History of the New Age Movement," in *Not Necessarily the New Age: Critical Essays,* ed. Robert Basil (Buffalo: Prometheus Books, 1988), 36. Also see Pike, *New Age and Neopagan Religions in America,* 67–88, for a narrative account of how the 1960s ushered in New Age ideas. Her chronology (173–176) actually begins in 1838 with Spiritualism, while York, *Historical Dictionary of New Age Movements,* xix–xxxii, goes all the way back to 2697–2597 BCE, the date of the first acupuncture manual in China. For an almost contemporary account of the development of New Age consciousness, see Robert Wuthnow, *Experimentation in American Religion: The New Mysticisms and Their Implications for the Churches* (Berkeley: University of California Press, 1978).

11. J. Gordon Melton sees the New Age movement as beginning in England and being exported to the United States. See his "New Thought and the New Age," in *Perspectives on the New Age,* ed. Lewis and Melton, 20–21. Melton specifically ties the rise of New Age thought to the "light" groups of the Universal Foundation and its Universal Link network and the influx of Asian religious practitioners with the end of the Asian Exclusion Act, although two of the most important religious figures from the East, Swami Vivekanana, who attended the World's Parliament of Religions in 1893 and established the Vedanta Society in 1897, and Paramahansa Yogananda, who came to the United States in 1920 to attend the International Congress of Religious Liberals and founded the Self-Realization Fellowship in 1925, had their influence much before that time. The particular events identified by Melton took place within a larger American cultural context without which the New Age movement would not have emerged with such force and may not have emerged at all.

12. See Susan Love Brown, "Baby Boomers, American Character, and the New Age: A Synthesis," in *Perspectives on the New Age,* ed. Lewis and Melton, 87–96, for a discussion of the relationship between generation and American character in the New Age in the context of a particular religious community.

13. For the study that demonstrates this shift in American concepts of self between generations see Joseph Veroff, Elizabeth Douvan, and Richard A. Kulka, *The Inner American: A Self-Portrait from 1957–1976* (New York: Basic Books, 1981).

14. See Peter Clecak, *America's Quest for the Ideal Self: Dissent and Fulfillment in the 60s and 70s* (New York: Oxford University Press, 1983).

15. Heelas, *The New Age Movement,* 21.

16. For the writings of these and other forerunners, see Lewis, *The Encyclopedic Sourcebook of New Age Religions,* 443–613. These include selections written by José Argüelles, Alice Bailey, H. P. Blavatsky, Emma Curtis Hopkins, David Spangler, Rudolf Steiner, Swami Vivekananda, and others.

17. See Andrea Grace Diem and James R. Lewis, "Imagining India: the Influence of Hinduism," in *Perspectives on the New Age,* ed. Lewis and Melton, 48–58.

18. For a more detailed discussion of channeling see Elijah Siegler, "Marketing Lazarus: A Rational Choice Theory of Channeling," in *The Encyclopedic Sourcebook of New Age Religions,* ed. Lewis, 174–191.

19. Ruth Prince and David Riches, *The New Age in Glastonbury: The Construction of Religious Movements* (New York: Berghahn Books, 2000), 6.

20. For example, see D. Groothuis, *Unmasking the New Age* (Downer's Grove, IL: Intervarsity Press, 1986); D. Groothuis, *Confronting the New Age* (Downer's Grove, IL: Intervarsity Press, 1988).

21. Carmen Kuhling, *The New Age Ethic and the Spirit of Postmodernity* (Cresskill, NJ: Hampton Press, 2004), vii.

22. Ibid., vii.

23. Ibid., 168. Kuhling's claim that there is not much literature that deals with the New Age "in terms of the social, historical, political, and cultural context in which the movement has emerged" (25) is not the case. In the Further Reading section at the end of this essay see Brown 1992, Lewis 2004, Lewis and Melton 1992, Pike 2004, Ellwood 1994.

24. Prince and Riches, *The New Age in Glastonbury,* 5.

25. Olav Hammer, "Contradictions of the New Age," in *The Encyclopedic Sourcebook of New Age Religions,* ed. Lewis, 409–424.

26. This list is taken from Belinda Whitworth, *New Age Encyclopedia: A Mind, Body, Spirit Reference Guide* (Franklin Lakes, NJ: New Page Books, 2003), 22.

FURTHER READING

Brown, Michael. *The Channeling Zone: American Spirituality in an Anxious Age.* Cambridge, MA: Harvard University Press, 1997.

Brown, Susan Love. "Baby Boomers, American Character, and the New Age: A Synthesis." In *Perspectives on the New Age.* Edited by James R. Lewis and J. Gordon Melton. Albany, NY: State University of New York Press, 1992, 87–96.

Cleçak, Peter. *America's Quest for the Ideal Self: Dissent and Fulfillment in the 60s and 70s.* New York: Oxford University Press, 1983.

Ellwood, Robert S. *The Sixties Spiritual Awakening: American Religion Moving from Modern to Postmodern.* New Brunswick, NJ: Rutgers University Press, 1994.

Ferguson, Marilyn. *The Aquarian Conspiracy: Personal and Social Transformation in the 1980s.* Los Angeles, CA: J.P. Tarcher, 1980.

Hanegraaff, Wouter J. *New Age Religion and Western Culture: Esotericism in the Mirror of Secular Thought.* Leiden: E.J. Brill, 1996.

Heelas, Paul. *The New Age Movement: The Celebration of the Self and the Sacralization of Modernity.* Oxford: Blackwell, 1996.

Lewis, James R., ed. *The Encyclopedic Sourcebook of New Age Religions.* Amherst, NY: Prometheus Books, 2004.

Lewis, James R., and J. Gordon Melton, eds. *Perspectives on the New Age.* Albany, NY: State University of New York Press, 1992.

Pike, Sarah M. *New Age and Neopagan Religions in America.* New York: Columbia University Press, 2004.

Prince, Ruth, and David Riches. *The New Age in Glastonbury: The Construction of Religious Movements*. New York: Berghahn Books, 2000.

Thompson, Gerry McGuire. *The Atlas of the New Age*. Hauppage, NY: Barron's Educational Series, 1999.

Whitworth, Belinda. *New Age Encyclopedia: A Mind, Body, Spirit Reference Guide*. Franklin Lakes, NJ: New Page Books, 2003.

York, Michael. *Historical Dictionary of New Age Movements*. Lanham, MD: The Scarecrow Press, 2004.

Contemporary Shamanism

Dagmar Wernitznig

Nowadays, the term *shamanism* has acquired multifaceted meaning and is utilized extensively in academic and nonacademic contexts. Increasingly, contemporary shamanism is also labeled *neo-shamanism*. Occasionally, contemporary shamanism is called "constructed" or "dislocated" shamanism, thus, juxtaposing what is usually described as "traditional" or "organic" shamanism. Without a doubt, shamanism is popular today and appropriated extensively for a diversity of disciplines and life styles. For example, the term shamanism occurs in several contexts, as diverse as advertising, philosophy, and weekend seminars.

The prevalent interest in shamanism could be largely due to its amorphous, sometimes even ambivalent, character. It is especially this heterogeneous appearance that attracts the attention to shamanism in numerous circles. Shamanism seems to signify various ideas and images to many different people, while at the same time eluding specific meaning. In order to comprehend contemporary shamanism, it is imperative to investigate briefly what is usually referred to as "traditional" or "organic" shamanism.

Generally speaking, shamanism is an ancient and intercultural phenomenon, and shamans are considered to be archetypal figures. Although academic, foremost anthropological, analyses emphasized Siberian shamanism as a paradigmatic example, the transcultural character of shamanism—with striking parallels to animism, paganism, or totemism—was never ignored. As Europeans first encountered the prototypical concept of shamanism in Siberia, the Tungus-based term *shaman* turned into an interdisciplinary trope.

Etymologically, the term *shaman* is believed to derive from the so-called Tungus (ic)—a language, culture, and tribe of Eastern Siberia. The actual origin of the term remains disputed. Theories involve the Pali *samana,* which might have developed from the Chinese *shamen,* whose Sanskrit version is *sramaṇa.* This suggests that the term *śaman* was projected onto Siberian language groups and cultures and did not originally evolve from there.

The Tungusic term can be further differentiated between the Siberian word *shaman* and the Sanskrit word *saman*. The most common translation for *shaman* is "inner heat," which usually links the shaman figure with the profession of the blacksmith, for *saman* it is "song." The prefix *sa* is usually translated as "to know," but *shaman* also denotes a person who is in a state of excitement and agitation. Comprehensive linguistic roots are

- Tungusic—*śaman*
- Pali—*samaṇa*
- Sanskrit—*sramaṇa*
- Chinese—*shamen*
- Vedic—*śram* ("to heat oneself")
- Hindu—*tapas* ("heat" or "power")
- Turkic—*kam*
- Yakuts—*oyuna*
- Samoyeds—*tadibey*
- Yukaghirs—*alma*
- Buriat—*buge*

This diverse linguistic background indicates that the practice of shamanism was very much determined by regional dialects of individual tribes as well as by geographic locations. Furthermore, the perception of shamanism was heavily influenced by outside observers—or intruders—like ethnographers. Especially with reference to shamanism in North America, the term medicine (wo)man is also frequently used. Through course of time, the terminology dealing with shamanism has experienced a vast generalization. It came to relate to concepts of witchcraft, sorcery, transvestism, and tricksterism. This terminological ambiguity offers a loophole for many contemporary practitioners and their claim to traditional variants of shamanism.

Shamans could be either male or female. The overemphasis on male, especially Siberian, shamans might be a result of predominantly male scholarship that initially dealt with shamanism. If at all, gender restrictions were primarily bound to particular geographic regions. In Korea, for example, shamans overwhelmingly, though not exclusively, were and still are women. Additionally, notions of shamanic transvestism or transgenderism defy clear-cut classifications.

Most commonly, anthropological circles refer to organic shamanism as a kind of ur religion, involving primal aspects like (re)birth, illness, and death. The contemporary sociological definition of functional differentiation, where different social functions are attached to specific professions, was not inherent in tribal shamanism. In today's vocabulary, the traditional shaman had to fulfill the role of a "multitasker": priest, medical doctor, psychoanalyst, seer, philosopher, warrior, artist, mystic, and politician. Originally, the tasks of a shaman included various secular and religious aspects. Within the tribe or clan, shamans were everything from spiritual counselor to provider of healing remedies. The concept of the medicine (wo)man, for example, epitomizes this connotation of spiritual *and* medical practices.

The principal role of the shaman was to mediate between the natural and the supernatural worlds to the point of using strategies of deception or manipulation pertaining to shamans' interaction with their physical surroundings and their spectators. For instance, the shaman could employ the art of ventriloquism. Shamans held a pivotal position in the social order of the tribal group they belonged to, yet at the same time lived the lives of public outcasts. For example, in some societies, the shaman, while having to mystically ensure that wild game was available for tribal hunters, was—due to this special status—not entitled to join the actual hunting parties. Having both religious as well as secular influence, they were feared and respected at the same time. Their responsibility for coherence and balance in the tribal environment resulted in a more or less strong sociopolitical voice. Thus, shamans were curators of the communal infrastructure of their tribe. By negotiating between spiritual and physical worlds, they were not only figures of authority, but also trickster figures for their peers. The shaman learned to live both in a central position in clan hierarchy and on the margins of clan society. Within the tribal context, shamans fulfilled their numerous tasks by utilizing particular tools and acts of performance. The standard repertoire of shamanic talents included chanting and singing, dancing and drumming. The paraphernalia of shamans, consisting of drums, masks, rattles, bones, pipes, feathers, and mirrors, for example, had simultaneously symbolic meaning and practical purposes.

Shamanic expertise was not simply limited to curing people, but included personifying an interpreter between the (meta)physical world and mankind. This involved meteorological knowledge as well as clairvoyance, for instance. Predicting and—as a further consequence—interfering with the future were especially important in terms of hunting, weather conditions, and natural catastrophes. In nonliterate societies, shamans, treasuring their tribal cultural heritage, also personified the intellectual property and folkloristic archive of their community. As keepers of stories and narrators of myths, they were responsible for guaranteeing their group's cultural survival.

There were several ways for shamans to receive their "call." Amongst the most common conditions to determine the vocation of a shaman are listed: exceptional physical appearance like a birthmark or an extra digit, legacy (i.e., "hereditary shamanism," passed on from parent or grandparent to their offspring), and the impact of experiences like illness or visionary dreams. Most significant factors with disease and visions were "out-of-body," "near-death," and "fragmentation/dismemberment" experiences. In many cases, an essential element in visions was the process of the shaman-to-be being taken apart and put together again by spirits. Overwhelmingly, initiation to the shamanic craft could not deliberately be planned. Most shamans were reported to have initially refused the gift, because of the hazards and sacrifices involved. Shamanic power, which was usually discovered during or after puberty, additionally, was very precarious. It could be lost through careless or incorrect behavior, or it could become destructive and turn against the shaman.

The mental conditions of shamans have been subject to a lot of professional debates. Because of shamans' practices of trance and/or ecstasy—mostly based on the usage of hallucinogenic drugs—Western observers often assumed shamans to be mentally ill or emotionally unstable. Claude Lévi-Strauss is credited with redefining the discourse about shamanic mental health. Lévi-Strauss claimed that shamans, rather than being psychopathic members of the tribe, embodied the role of what—by Western standards—could be compared to a psychoanalyst in tribal societies. This assumption is mirrored by C. G. Jung's notion of shamanism as a therapeutic model in psychoanalysis. Lévi-Strauss's approach, later on, has increasingly been criticized as being too structuralist.

The shaman's counseling duties involved the physical as well as psychosomatic well-being of tribal members. A commonly described concept in Western literatures of shamanic beliefs is the so-called "loss or damage of the soul" or "possession by spirits." Thereby, the shaman could rely on ritualistic or magic antidotes, such as, for instance, séances, to instigate the patient's recovery.

One of the most prominent books about shamanism, undoubtedly, is Mircea Eliade's *Shamanism: Archaic Techniques of Ecstasy.* The French original *Le Chamanisme et les Techniques Archaïques de l'Extase* appeared in 1951, the English translation was published in 1964. Investigating shamanism from an overwhelmingly religious point of view, Eliade, a historian of religions from Romania, provided a synopsis of shamanism in terms of its global universality, while at the same time also highlighting individual variants of local shamanisms. As the term "ecstasy" is considered to be too sensationalist in certain contexts, sometimes "trance" is chosen as an alternative in post-Eliade scholarship. "Trance," however, is not an uncomplicated choice, either, because it also implies behaviorisms of possession.

Particularly in the Western hemisphere of the 1960s and its so-called counterculture, there emerged an enormous fascination with and curiosity about anything remotely connected to shamanism. Perhaps the most notorious figure associated with Westernized or dislocated shamanism is Carlos Castaneda. Studying anthropology at the University of California, Los Angeles, Castaneda claimed to have become acquainted with an enigmatic Yaqui informant, called Don Juan. According to Castaneda, Don Juan was residing in the rural areas of Mexico and Arizona. In his several best-seller books, Carlos Castaneda described his experiences as an apprentice to his sorcerer-teacher Don Juan. Castaneda's flamboyant tales about hallucinogens, visions, and paranormal encounters catered to the interests of his readers. At the same time, his fabricated, evidence-free texts triggered critical responses. Castaneda's critics, foremost among them Richard de Mille, deconstructed the Don Juan books by seriously questioning aspects of authenticity and liability. Negative criticism of Castaneda's writing particularly zeroes in on issues of postcolonial hegemony and its tendency to distribute accounts of indigenous knowledge as an undecipherable and opaque conglomerate of hearsay and fiction. According to Vine Deloria, Jr., "[t]he Don Juan books were just what young whites needed to bolster their shattering personal identities[.]"[1]

Since the 1960s, a number of writers, taking their cues from Castaneda's books, produced shamanic adventure stories as quasi-autobiographical accounts. These texts, nevertheless, were presented as fact. Perhaps the most prominent name amongst those is Lynn V. Andrews. Like Castaneda, Andrews cited shamanic teachers, called Agnes Whistling Elk and Ruby Plenty Chiefs of Manitoba, Canada. These shamans and their rather unorthodox practices, however, were unknown to the official First Nations Communities in Manitoba. As early as 1987, for example, Andrews was sarcastically declared a so-called "Plastic Medicine Woman" by the Mohawk Nation of Akwesasne. Recently, Andrews expanded her quest for shaman informants to Australia, rivaling yet another semishamanic writer, Marlo Morgan. Again, there is no evidence for Andrews's Australian encounters with local variants of shamanism, and Aboriginal and Torres Strait Islander peoples were equally surprised and annoyed by her distorted depictions of indigenous spiritualities.

Critical debates about these writings tend to overshadow the perceptions of the reading public regarding these books. Books by chic shaman authors have prolific editions and distribution. Their readership is selective in consuming fictional stories with factual moments whenever convenient. There seems to exist a silent agreement between contemporary writers about shamanism and their audience that neoshamanic products like books or workshops, for example, can be utilized without having to tackle questions of validity. Customers particularly appreciate the "anything goes" element of neoshamanic items and services.

In most cases, contemporary shamanism—both writers and practitioners—is closely associated with the New Age. New Age is an umbrella term for a smorgasbord of various beliefs and life styles: channeling and crystals, parapsychology and alternative medicine, Wicca, and astrology. Although the New Age spread all over the United States, prototypical New Age environments are particularly concentrated on the West Coast and in the Southwest. The predominant targets for New Age products are upscale, urban, middle-class citizens. Personal growth, individual enlightenment, and spiritual self-help are the most commonly propagated New Age themes.

Self-realization is also the most popular premise in contemporary shamanism. Books and weekend seminars are the standard products to supply this demand. Michael J. Harner is closely affiliated with workshops to instruct consumers in contemporary shamanism. An anthropologist by training, Harner conducted field studies in Ecuador and Peru in the 1950s, where he was reportedly introduced to shamanism. Afterward, he studied North American shamanism. In Harner's biography, a noticeable gap exists between his final anthropological book, *Hallucinogens and Shamanism* (1973), and his first handbook on contemporary shamanism, *The Way of the Shaman: A Guide to Power and Healing* (1980). This seven-year period most likely signifies Harner's personal reinvention of himself as a coach in contemporary shamanism. In 1983, Harner opened the Center for Shamanic Studies in New York, which was moved to Mill Valley, California, and renamed The Foundation for Shamanic Studies two years later. There, the so-called Harner Method of Shamanic Counseling is taught to promote shamanism. Although the headquarters of Harner's training academy for contemporary shamanism are in the United States, his workshops are conducted on an intercontinental basis, with Western and Central Europe as particular target zones. Workshops for all levels of shamanic disciples, ranging from beginners to advanced, are offered. Harner's methodology of so-called Core Shamanism heavily relies on Shamanic State of Consciousness (SSC). This state can supposedly be achieved through drumming, chanting rhythms, or practicing meditation techniques. Workshop participants are further advised to search for their spirit helpers or power animals via imaginative journeys. Harner's prided patent is the so-called Dream Canoe, a mixture of emotional bondage and initiation ceremonies as well as group therapy dynamics, where crowd activity and individual experience are subtly synthesized.

Naturally, contemporary shamanism is confronted with a plethora of critical responses. Native American poets and scholars, for example, oppose what they prefer to call *whiteshamanism*. The phrase *whiteshamanism,* sometimes also spelled *white shamanism,* was created by Geary Hobson (Cherokee). In addition to Hobson, other critics include Wendy Rose (Hopi-Miwok), Leslie Marmon Silko (Laguna Pueblo), and Vine Deloria, Jr. (Standing Rock Sioux). Native critique especially emphasizes postcolonial implications of modern or synthesized shamanism, which is considered to be diametrically opposed to organic shamanism. They argue that the appropriation of indigenous spiritualities in general and of Native American religions specifically is yet another form of cultural imperialism.

Critics like those mentioned regard contemporary shamanism as the final stage of colonization—the usurpation of cultural heritage and spiritual knowledge, following territorial annexation. Moreover, they believe that non-Native interpretations of shamanism reinforce stereotypical images of Native peoples, fostering a particularly monolithic and prehistoric iconography of Native Americans and other indigenous groups around the world. The most important concept here is a dichotomy of primitive versus civilized worlds, which stigmatizes Native peoples as ancient loincloth wearers in industrialized societies. Such ethnocentrism is particularly evident in the journey from ignorance to wisdom related by white shamans, who almost always portray themselves as "out-shamaning" their Native teachers in the end. Expressively one-dimensional by supplying an all-white perspective, the overwhelming majority of shamanic products eclipse the so-called (indigenous) Other. Teachings of contemporary shamanism both recruit new disciples and generate new (white) shamans. Several former apprentices of well-known contemporary shamans have entered shamanic careers themselves. For instance, Sandra Ingermann, originally studying at Harner's Foundation for Shamanic Studies, has in turn engaged in writing about self-help shamanism and invented her technique of Soul Retrieval.

Additionally, evaluations of contemporary shamanism from a Native point of view focus on the sellout boom of indigenous cultures, with the fiercest controversies centering around sacred sites. Places like Chaco Canyon in New Mexico, for example, are commercialized by contemporary shamanism for spiritual tourism. Amongst the many negative side effects created by shamanic souvenir hunters are not only the cultural showcasing of inhabitants of such places, but also the environmental pollution of local sceneries.

While organic shamanism is gradually disappearing on a global scale, dislocated shamanism enjoys immense popularity by copyrighting a synthetic alternative to traditional shamanic practice. The compartmentalization of religions and lifestyles is an integral ingredient of contemporary shamanism. Contemporary shamans and their disciples are very eclectic in both filtering out and amalgamating individual aspects of several belief systems. This cloning of particular types of shamanisms is customized according to personal needs and preferences. Thus, contemporary shamanism is often accused of being orchestrated and self-absorbed. Unlike organic shamanism, which is overwhelmingly directed towards a clan or tribe, contemporary shamanism is designed to be less phylogenetic. As an organized "ism" that can be purchased during a weekend seminar, contemporary shamanism is also criticized for lacking in-depth achievements. Generally, the long phases of apprenticeship and the aggravating existence of trial and error of tribal shamans is missing from contemporary shamanic practice. Indeed, contemporary shamans are sometimes associated with hedonism and simulation. Skeptics of contemporary shamans stress the artificiality of instant, effortless, and financially tailored shamanic enlightenment. They are suspicious of the simplistic formulas of contemporary shamanism and its profit-oriented priorities. Consequently, the exclusively materialistic clientele of contemporary shamans is attributed with myopia, complacency, and apolitical credos. Either believing or portraying themselves as genuinely shamanic, whiteshamans have made it a general norm to not respond to such critiques.

Although obsolete, the succeeding two Resolutions[2] capture the controversial nature of contemporary shamanism:

APPENDIX

RESOLUTIONS ON THE PRACTICE OF SHAMANISM BY NON-NATIVE PEOPLES

RESOLUTION OF THE 5TH ANNUAL MEETING OF THE TRADITION ELDERS CIRCLE

Northern Cheyenne Nation, Two Moons' Camp
Rosebud Creek, Montana
October 5, 1980.
It has been brought to the attention of the Elders and their representatives in Council that various individuals are moving about this Great Turtle Island and across the great waters to foreign soil, purporting to be spiritual leaders. They carry pipes and other objects sacred to the Red Nations, the indigenous people of the western hemisphere.

These individuals are gathering non-Indian people as followers who believe they are receiving instructions of the original people. We, the Elders and our representatives sitting in Council, give warning to these non-Indian followers that it is our understanding this is not a proper process, that the authority to carry these sacred objects is given by the people, and the purpose and procedures are specific to time and the needs of the people.

The medicine people are chosen by the medicine and long instruction and discipline are necessary before ceremonies and healing can be done. These procedures are always in the Native tongue; there are no exceptions and profit is not the motivation.

There are many Nations with many and varied procedures specifically for the welfare of their people. These processes and ceremonies are of the most Sacred Nature. The Council finds the open display of these ceremonies contrary to these Sacred instructions.

Therefore, be warned that these individuals are moving about playing upon the spiritual needs and ignorance of our non-Indian brothers and sisters. The value of these instructions and ceremonies is questionable, may be meaningless, and hurtful to the individual carrying false messages. There are questions that should be asked of these individuals:

1. What nation does the person represent?
2. What is their Clan and Society?
3. Who instructed them and where did they learn?
4. What is their home address?

If no information is forthcoming, you may inquire at the address listed below, and we will try to find out about them for you. We concern ourselves only with those people who use spiritual ceremonies with non-Indian people for profit. There are many other things to be shared with the four colors of humanity in our common destiny as one with our Mother the Earth. It is this sharing that must be considered with great care by the Elders and the medicine people who carry the Sacred Trusts, so that no harm may come to people through ignorance and misuse of these powerful forces.

Signed,
Tom Yellowtail
Wyoloa, MY 59089.
Larry Anderson
Navajo Nation
PO Box 342
Fort Defiance
AZ 86504.
Izadore Thom
Beech Star Route
Bellingham
WA 98225.
Thomas Banyacya
Hopi Independent Nation
Shungopavy Pueblo
Second Mesa
via AZ 86403.
Philip Deere (deceased)

Muskogee (Creek) Nation (in tribute).
Walter Denny
Chippewa-Cree Nation
Rocky Boy Route
Box Elder
MT 59521.
Austin Two Moons
Northern Cheyenne Nation
Rosebud Creek
MT.
Tadadaho
Haudenasaunee
Onondaga Nation
via Nedrow, NY 13120.
Chief Fools Crow (deceased)
Lakota Nation (in tribute).
Frank Cardinal, Sr.
Chateh, PO Box 120
Assumption, Alberta
Canada TOM OSO.
Peter O'Chiese
Entrance Terry Ranch
Entrance, Alberta
Canada.

AIM (AMERICAN INDIAN MOVEMENT) RESOLUTION

Sovereign Diné Nation
Window Rock, AZ
May 11, 1984.
Whereas the Spiritual wisdom which is shared by the Elders with the people has been passed on to us through the creation from time immemorial; and

Whereas the spirituality of Indian Nations is inseparable from the people themselves; and

Whereas the attempted theft of Indian ceremonies is a direct attack and theft from Indian people themselves; and

Whereas there has been a dramatic increase in the incidence of selling Sacred ceremonies, such as the sweat lodge and the vision quest, and of Sacred articles, such as religious pipes, feathers and stone; and

Whereas these practices have been and continue to be conducted by Indians and non-Indians alike, constituting not only insult and disrespect for the wisdom of the ancients, but also exposing ignorant non-Indians to potential harm and even death through the misuse of these ceremonies; and

Whereas the traditional Elders and Spiritual leaders have repeatedly warned against and condemned the commercialisation of our ceremonies; and

Whereas such commercialisation has increased dramatically in recent years, to wit:

- the representations of Cyfus McDonald, Osheana Fast Wolf, and Brooke Medicine Ego, all non-Indian women representing themselves as "Sacred Women," and who, in the case of Cyfus McDonald, have defrauded Indian people of Sacred articles;
- A non-Indian woman going by the name of "Quanda" representing herself as a "Healing Woman" and charging $20 for sweat lodges;
- Sun Bear and the so-called "Bear Tribe Medicine Society," who engage in the sale of Indian ceremonies and Sacred objects, operating out of the State of Washington, but traveling and speaking throughout the United States;
- Wallace Black Elk and Grace Spotted Eagle, Indian people operating in Denver, Colorado, charging up to $50 for so-called "Sweat Lodge Workshops;"
- A group of non-Indians working out of Boulder, Colorado, and throughout the Southwest, and audaciously calling itself "Vision Quest, Inc.," thereby stealing the name and attempting to steal the concept of one of our most spiritual ceremonies;

Therefore, let it be resolved that the Southwest AIM Leadership Conference reiterates the position articulated by our Elders at the First American Indian Tribunal held at D.Q. University, September 1982, as follows:

Now, to those who are doing these things, we send our third warning. Our Elders ask, "Are you prepared to take the consequences of your actions? You will be outcasts from your people if you continue these practices" … Now, this is another one. Our young people are getting restless. They are the ones who sought their Elders in the first place to teach them the Sacred ways. They have said that they will take care of those who are abusing our Sacred ceremonies and Sacred objects in their own way. In this way they will take care of their Elders.

We Resolve to protect our Elders and our traditions, and we condemn those who seek to profit from Indian Spirituality. We put them on notice that our patience grows thin with them and they continue their disrespect at their own risk.

NOTES

1. Vine Deloria, Jr., *God Is Red: A Native View of Religion* (Golden, CO: Fulcrum, 1994), 38.
2. As these cannot be identified as official authorities, responsible for permissions pertaining to these Resolutions, the main reference source for citations are the reprints quoted in Ward Churchill, *Fantasies of the Master Race: Literature, Cinema and the Colonization of American Indians* (Monroe, ME: Common Courage Press, 1992), 223–28.

FURTHER READING

Atkinson, Jane M. "Shamanisms Today." *Annual Review of Anthropology* 21 (1992): 307–30.
Brown, Michael F. "Shamanism and Its Discontents." *Medical Anthropology Quarterly* 2/2 (1988): 102–20.

————. *The Channeling Zone: American Spirituality in an Anxious Age*. Cambridge, MA: Harvard University Press, 1997.

Devereux, George. "Shamans as Neurotics." *American Anthropologist* 63 (1961): 1088–90.

Diószegi, Vilmos, and Mihály Hoppál, eds. *Shamanism in Siberia*. Budapest: Akadémiai Kiadó, 1978.

Durkheim, Emile. *The Elementary Forms of Religious Life: A Study in Religious Sociology*. Translated by Joseph Ward Swain. London: George Allen and Unwin, 1915.

Eliade, Mircea. *Shamanism: Archaic Techniques of Ecstasy*. Translated by Willard R. Trask. London: Routledge & Kegan Paul, 1964.

Flaherty, Gloria. *Shamanism and the Eighteenth Century*. Princeton, New Jersey: Princeton University Press, 1992.

Frazier, Kendrick. *People of Chaco: A Canyon and Its Culture*. New York: Norton, 1986.

Hoppál, Mihály, and Otto von Sadovszky, eds. *Shamanism: Past and Present*. Budapest: Ethnographic Institute, 1989.

Hultkrantz, Åke. "A Definition of Shamanism." *Temenos* 9 (1973): 25–37.

Lévi-Strauss, Claude. *Structural Anthropology*. Translated by Claire Jacobson and Brooke Grundfest Schoepf. New York: Basic Books, 1963.

Shirokogorov, Sergej M. *Psychomental Complex of the Tungus*. London: Kegan, Paul, Trench, Trubner, 1935.

Taussig, Michael. *Shamanism, Colonialism and the Wild Man: A Study in Terror and Healing*. Chicago: University of Chicago Press, 1987.

Vitebsky, Piers. *The Shaman*. London: Macmillan, 1995.

Wallis, Robert J. *Shamans/Neo-Shamans: Ecstasies, Alternative Archeologies and Contemporary Pagans*. London: Routledge, 2003.

Wernitznig, Dagmar. *Going Native or Going Naïve? White Shamanism and the Neo-Noble Savage*. Lanham, MD: University Press of America, 2003.

The Worship of the Goddess in Feminist Spirituality in the United States

Cynthia Eller

The feminist spirituality movement emerged concurrently with the second wave of feminism in the late 1960s and early 1970s in the United States. It represented an attempt to create a uniquely feminist religion, one that empowered individual women and at the same time nurtured a society-wide revolution away from male dominance and the exploitation of nature. With this quest in mind, spiritually minded feminists were quickly drawn to the evolving Neopagan movement, and more narrowly to one of its subreligions: witchcraft, or Wicca. The Neopagan movement is extremely diverse, but most Neopagans worship a central Goddess, and this feature was very appealing to feminists in search of an alternative to the male monotheism of established religions, especially Judaism and Christianity, in the United States.

The feminist spirituality movement might have developed as simply another variant of Neopaganism, but it quickly distinguished itself from its Neopagan peers by its eclecticism, its zeal for independence, and, most of all, its separatism. Most feminist spirituality groups did not accept male participation in any form. They declared that they were exploring "the female mysteries" and that "male energy" would distract them from this mission. Moreover, they took the rather heterodox view—for Neopagans—that it was perfectly acceptable for them to worship female deities alone and to provide no role for male gods, not even as subordinate figures. These choices made spiritual feminists such mavericks in the world of Neopaganism that it is fair to say that the feminist spirituality movement emerged as its own religion, albeit one closely allied with Neopaganism.

The feminist spirituality movement peaked in the 1980s, when it introduced its message—that God was a woman and that all women partook of the divinity of the Goddess—to an uninitiated audience. Today, most adult women with feminist inclinations have been exposed to the basic ideas of feminist spirituality, so the movement has lost some of its revolutionary edge, though not its devoted following. Because of its loose structure and the difficulty in drawing any firm lines in the amorphous religious landscape occupied by the feminist spirituality movement, it is impossible to say how many women today are practitioners of this new religion. In the 1970s and early 1980s, when it was a struggle for women to define themselves as both feminist and spiritual, the very difficulty of the task resulted in a vibrant and comparatively unified movement. Today, feminism is a less visible and vocal cultural force, and Neopaganism is increasingly acceptable as a viable religious alternative, so it has sometimes been the path of least resistance for spiritual feminists to accept a niche for themselves as the feminist variant of Neopaganism.

HISTORY OF THE FEMINIST SPIRITUALITY MOVEMENT

From the beginning, the feminist spirituality movement straddled different social worlds. On the one hand, it was a form of feminism, aligned with "cultural feminism"—the effort to develop new, nonpatriarchal cultural forms—as opposed to "political feminism": the effort to secure political gains and legal rights for women within current power structures. On the other hand, feminist spirituality was an alternative religion born most immediately from the ferment of the antiestablishment 1960s counterculture, and more distantly from the long history of Western occult societies and their practice of ritual, magic, and divination.

Three strands of influence affected the initial emergence of the feminist spirituality movement in the early 1970s: secular feminism, Jewish and Christian feminism, and the presence of women—particularly women with a growing feminist consciousness—within existing Neopagan religions. The principal aims of the feminist movement of the 1960s were secular and political: reproductive rights, rights for women in the workplace, and nondiscriminatory marriage and divorce laws. But as the feminist movement gathered steam, it took on a profound significance for many of its participants, and the critique they mounted of patriarchal society went ever deeper. Eventually they felt driven to ask the "big questions" about sexism: What was the cause of male dominance? Was it inevitable? Were women different from men, and if so, how? Should women merely fight for the opportunity to compete in patriarchal society, or should they use their uniquely feminine traits and experiences to create a different type of world, better for all? Big questions became religious questions: first, because feminists sought to understand the role religion played in creating and maintaining male-dominant societies; and second, because the very depth and breadth of these "why" questions, along with individuals' profound, life-transforming commitment to the feminist movement, took on a religious dimension.

Spiritual feminists often conceptualized this turning toward spirituality as a natural development in which consciousness-raising (CR) groups evolved into feminist spirituality groups. CR groups, developing first under the guise of "rap sessions" or "bitch sessions" in the late 1960s, were loosely structured gatherings in which small groups of women gathered to share their experiences, searching for common threads of sex discrimination.[1] Certainly the dynamic of a small, all-female group bent on investigating female identity was common to both CR groups and spiritual feminist gatherings, and this similarity helped to provide a bridge between the two for secular feminists who were initially uncertain about dabbling in spiritual matters.

Jewish and Christian feminists felt no such hesitancy about addressing religious questions. For them, the greater leap was from established religion into alternative religion. Already comfortable with religious language—and, depending on their specific religious background, with ritual—Jewish and Christian feminists took the sometimes difficult step of rejecting the religious certainties that they were taught and venturing into new theological and spiritual territory. Even today, there is significant shared history between the feminist spirituality movement and Jewish and Christian feminism, and also a surprising amount of shared belief and ritual. Fundamentally, what separated those Jewish and Christian feminists who remained within established religions from those who entered the realm of Neopagan religious creativity was their differing opinions about whether or not established religions could be successfully transformed. Those who became spiritual feminists finally concluded that efforts at reform from within Judaism or Christianity were either doomed to failure or not worth the effort, given the profound inadequacies of established religions, and so they searched for religious alternatives.

The most famous step out of Jewish and Christian feminism into feminist spirituality was a literal step, one taken by Mary Daly (b. 1928), a prominent Catholic theologian and author of increasingly radical feminist critiques of Christianity. Her first book, *The Church and the Second Sex* (1968), was a rather mild criticism of Christianity. But her opposition to established religion accelerated with *Beyond God the Father* (1973) and ran right off the rails of established religion with *Gyn/Ecology* (1978) and her subsequent publications. In 1971, Daly was invited to preach at The Memorial Church of Harvard University, the first woman given this honor. In her sermon, "The Women's Movement: An Exodus Community," Daly formally took leave of established religion, declaring, "We [women] cannot really belong to institutional religion as it exists. It isn't good enough to be token preachers.... Singing sexist hymns, praying to a male god breaks our spirit, makes us less than human. The crushing weight of this tradition, of this power structure, tells us that *we do not even exist.*" At the conclusion of her sermon, Daly walked out of the church in protest, inviting the other women present to depart with her.[2]

Upon abandoning male-dominant religions, some Jewish and Christian feminists joined the ranks of secular feminists, but many felt a need to replace the patriarchal religion they abandoned with one that was woman-affirming. Though Daly never became a leader in the feminist spirituality movement, as soon as she left Christianity she began speaking of witchcraft as women's proper religious heritage, motivating other women to search out avowed witches and learn more about their religious beliefs and practices. But even when Jewish and Christian feminists did not explicitly recommend witchcraft or Neopaganism to their disgruntled sisters, they implicitly did so by focusing their theological critique of western monotheistic religions on the maleness of God. If God's apparent manhood, evident in the male pronouns used to speak of him, was to be removed, only two options short of atheism remained: either speak of God in gender-neutral ways or use female images and pronouns for God at least as often as male ones, if not to the exclusion of male terms altogether. Jewish and Christian feminists often experimented with feminine terms for God within the context of their own religious traditions, finding Bible passages that spoke of God as Mother or referred to God's wisdom, Sophia, as a divine female being. Others longed for something less apologetic and more revolutionary, resolving that only exclusively female language for God could hope to undo the damage of the unrelieved androcentrism of millennia of western religious tradition.

This they found in witchcraft, which, as fleshed out by British occultist Gerald Gardner (1884–1964), involved worship of a goddess (though usually a male god too) and central religious roles for women as her priestesses. Gardner began his public career as a witch in the 1950s. By the 1970s, when American feminists increasingly found witchcraft attractive, Gardner's movement was already splintered into several denominations centered around different leaders, liturgies, and sacred lores. Gardner's form of witchcraft, and those descended from it, typically claimed a connection with ancient British paganism. These traditions typically included elaborate initiations and other occult practices, understanding themselves as secret societies with privileged access to efficacious magic and divination.

Gardnerian witchcraft was far too stodgy and authoritarian for most feminists seeking alternatives to established religions. But it still played a role in the development of feminist spirituality, in part because individual Gardnerian witches wished to bring their Wiccan practice into line with their own developing feminist principles. These women provided an entry point for other feminists intent on exploring the spiritual possibilities of witchcraft as a gynocentric (woman-centered) religious tradition.

At least as important in the development of feminist spirituality, however, was the broader Neopagan movement. Especially in the United States, witchcraft was not limited to Gardner and his former disciples, nor was Neopaganism limited to witchcraft. Religious innovation was the order of the day for members of the Sixties counterculture, and numerous Neopagan groups claimed allegiances to any and all pagan—or even nonpagan—religions they could find, making their own eclectic assemblages of deities, rituals, and beliefs, unified around an all-embracing nature worship.[3] It was an ideal milieu for spiritually minded feminists, offering them both freedom and resources to create their own female-centered religion. Spiritual feminists found themselves up against certain orthodoxies in Wicca, such as the presence of male deities in the pantheon and men in the ritual circle, but Neopaganism was so fluid and diverse in the early 1970s that spiritual feminists were hardly alone in experimenting with new forms of magic and ritual. The female separatism of feminist spirituality was unique within the world of Neopaganism, and it attracted criticism from some Neopagans, but no one was in any position to enforce any rules that would prevent the formation of female-separatist Neopagan groups.

One of the main people who propelled the feminist spirituality movement along its way was Zsuzsanna Budapest (b. 1940), a Hungarian refugee living in Los Angeles, California, in the late 1960s. Budapest took her surname from the city she left behind. She brought with her the taste for political activism and radical social change that led to her participation in the failed Hungarian revolution of 1956, and transferred it to an enthusiasm for the women's movement. As the women's movement quickly became Budapest's life, she saw a need for a women's religion to ground and motivate feminist politics. But unlike many of her contemporaries, she had a prior acquaintance with paganism. Budapest was a "hereditary witch," initiated into witchcraft by someone who claimed to have been similarly initiated in an unbroken line leading back to pre-Christian times in Europe. Specifically, Budapest said that she had been initiated into witchcraft by her mother, Masika Szilagyi, who in turn had been initiated by Victoria, a household servant.[4]

Whatever religious resources Budapest brought with her from Hungary, it is clear that by the time she founded the Susan B. Anthony Coven No. 1 (named after American suffragist and nineteenth-century feminist leader Susan B. Anthony) in Los Angeles in 1971, she drew on other sources as well, including other forms of witchcraft and Neopaganism, and elements of the New Age movement then taking root in California. Budapest boldly declared that witchcraft was women's religion, and she, along with a small group of similarly motivated women, began to celebrate the solstices and equinoxes and initiate other women into their form of feminist witchcraft. They were tremendously successful. During the 1970s, over 700 women were initiated as witches by the Susan B. Anthony Coven No. 1, and Budapest presided over large public rituals, sometimes with more than 100 participants. Budapest inspired feminists in other cities across the United States to form their own covens. The movement proliferated rapidly, partly because feminists were given tacit permission to invent their own rituals within the rather spare parameters laid down by pioneers like Budapest.[5]

The Susan B. Anthony Coven No. 1 announced its religious and political intentions in the form of a manifesto that captures many of the themes that later characterized the feminist spirituality movement:

> We believe that feminist witches are wimmin who search within themselves for the female principle of the universe and who relate as daughters to the Creatrix.
>
> We believe that just as it is time to fight for the right to control our bodies, it is also time to fight for our sweet womon souls.
>
> We believe that in order to fight and win a revolution that will stretch for generations into the future, we must find reliable ways to replenish our energies. We believe that without a secure grounding in womon's spiritual strength there will be no victory for us.
>
> We believe that we are part of a changing universal consciousness that has long been feared and prophesized by the patriarchs.
>
> We believe that Goddess-consciousness gave humanity a workable, long-lasting, peaceful period during which the Earth was treated as Mother and wimmin were treated as Her priestesses. This was the mythical Golden age of Matriarchy.
>
> We believe that wimmin lost supremacy through the aggressions of males who were exiled from the matriarchies and formed the patriarchal hordes responsible for the invention of rape and the subjugation of wimmin.
>
> We believe that female control of the death (male) principle yields hummin evolution.
>
> We are committed to living life lovingly towards ourselves and our sisters. We are committed to joy, self-love, and life-affirmation.

We are committed to winning, to surviving, to struggling against patriarchal oppression.

We are committed to defending our interests and those of our sisters through the knowledge of witchcraft: to blessing, to cursing, to healing, and to binding with power rooted in woman-identified wisdom.

We are opposed to attacking the innocent.

We are equally committed to political, communal, and personal solutions.

We are committed to teaching wimmin how to organize themselves as witches and to sharing our traditions with wimmin.

We are opposed to teaching our magic and our craft to men until equality of the sexes is reality.

Our immediate goal is to congregate with each other according to our ancient woman-made laws and to remember our past, renew our powers and affirm our Goddess of the Ten-thousand Names.[6]

The manifesto reflected the themes of female separatism, the worship of a single Goddess known by many names and in many guises, belief in a past era of matriarchy, and the use of magic and ritual as both a means of women's empowerment and a tool for initiating social and political change.

Though Budapest played an important role in the birth of the feminist spirituality movement, the movement was not centered around a single charismatic leader. Many influential leaders were important, and even though the rank and file admired the brightest stars in their firmament, the antiauthoritarianism of both Neopaganism and radical feminism was so prevalent that feminist spirituality could never have become a personality cult.

That having been said, one of the most significant influences on the feminist spirituality movement after Budapest was Starhawk (b. 1951), another Californian who combined interests in witchcraft and feminism. Starhawk, born Miriam Simos, was raised Jewish, but from an early age she was fascinated by magic and the occult. At the same time she hoped to find a theological grounding for her own sense that the divine inhered in the natural world. She pursued witchcraft first, finding teachers in the San Francisco Bay Area, but she yearned for a more explicitly feminist version of witchcraft. Eventually, she created one. Spurred on her journey by a chance encounter with Budapest and the Susan B. Anthony Coven No. 1, Starhawk wrote an introduction to witchcraft that strongly underscored the religion's reverence for women and the female principle and the importance of women's leadership. *The Spiral Dance* (1979) sold thousands of copies and Starhawk gained fame as a spokesperson for Neopaganism in general and feminist spirituality in particular. Starhawk did not exclude men from the practice of witchcraft, as did many other spiritual feminists. However, since she asserted that female-only groups and rituals had their place, and because she regarded witchcraft's ground-level feminism as one of its most attractive aspects, she effectively became a leader in the feminist spirituality movement.[7]

Budapest and Starhawk both identified themselves as witches and, by extension, as Neopagans. But many feminists who wished to plumb the religious depths of their feminist commitment or to find an alternative to the established religions were not willing to identify themselves as witches. They were simply women honoring the Goddess, wherever they could find her. In the 1970s and 1980s, most Neopagans were still devoted to reviving pre-Christian pagan religions that had a definite pedigree: usually British, though sometimes Norse, Greco-Roman, or Egyptian. Neopagans most often regarded themselves as reviving the religions of their (mostly white) ancestors. In contrast, spiritual feminists were, from the beginning, less geographically bound in their search for the divine feminine. To the Neopagan favorites of Diana or Cerridwen, spiritual feminists added Hindu, Buddhist, and Taoist goddesses, not to mention every goddess they could find in Native American and African pantheons. Spiritual feminists were similarly prepared to adopt religious practices and preoccupations from the New Age, from channeling disembodied spirits, to observing auras, to investigating their past lives. To the extent that feminist spirituality developed from a solid core, it was that of Wicca. But spiritual feminists' voracious hunger for images and experiences of the divine feminine made the movement, from its inception, unabashedly syncretistic.

SOCIOLOGICAL STRUCTURE OF THE FEMINIST SPIRITUALITY MOVEMENT

As a religion committed to individual creativity and highly suspicious of any form of top-down leadership, the feminist spirituality movement never developed a central organization that monitors the activities of its constituent groups. Though people made efforts to create national-level resource agencies—most notably, the Re-formed Congregation of the Goddess—none managed to represent the plethora of feminist spirituality groups active in the United States. Indeed, many spiritual feminists choose to practice alone. They identify themselves as spiritual feminists, Neopagans, or witches, they practice magic, and they may set up altars or meditate or observe the solar and lunar holidays. Despite their solitude, they are part of a wider world of feminist spirituality, gaining legitimacy for their choices through the many books, magazines, retreats, and other gatherings that unite spiritual feminists into a modestly cohesive group.

Many spiritual feminists practice their religion with small groups of like-minded women. Even solo practitioners have often been in a group at some time if they no longer are now. The style of these groups varies enormously. Some gather to experiment with trance states and direct communion with the Goddess while others resemble a book club. Spiritual feminist groups come together and fall apart quite readily, though some maintain a steady core of members for ten or more years, supporting one another, celebrating events in each other's lives, and marking the turning of the seasons with rituals to the Goddess.

Spiritual feminists take many routes to find one another and form small groups. A woman interested in practicing in a group may advertise at a feminist bookstore, in a spiritual feminist publication, or online to find others who live in her area. Adult education programs, especially ones oriented toward New Age topics, may offer courses in feminist spirituality that later become ritual groups when their official term has ended. Interestingly, another avenue to the formation of a feminist spirituality group is through a church or synagogue. More liberal denominations, like the United Church of Christ or Reform Judaism, may sponsor study groups exploring feminine aspects of the divine in Christianity or Judaism, and these may evolve into feminist spirituality groups, either with or without official sanction. The Unitarian Universalist Association sponsors a large and active organization, the Covenant of Unitarian Universalist Pagans, that regularly organizes workshops, study groups, and ritual circles, some of which restrict their membership to women and operate effectively as spiritual feminist groups. Especially now that feminist spirituality is no longer a brand new player on the religious scene, the line between Jewish and Christian feminism on the one hand and feminist spirituality on the other is somewhat blurred. Early on, spiritual feminists were often driven by a deep hostility toward established religions and wanted to discard anything that reminded them of western monotheistic traditions. Meanwhile, Jewish and Christian feminists who decided to stay within their traditions wished to have that choice reinforced by others who had made the same decision. Today Jewish and Christian feminists typically feel less threatened, and other spiritual feminists are more accepting and less judgmental of the multiple allegiances that such women maintain.

Like the rest of the Neopagan community, spiritual feminists also mingle at large summer festivals devoted to drumming circles, workshops on everything from reading Tarot cards to dowsing, and, of course, large public rituals. Some of these festivals are composed entirely of self-identified spiritual feminists interested in learning more about ritual, magic, and the Goddess from others further along the path than themselves. But spiritual feminists also congregate at Neopagan festivals, meeting in female-only groups, and at lesbian feminist festivals, where they take the opportunity to address spiritual topics and share sacred space with other spiritual feminists. Spiritual feminists also meet and make ritual with one another by signing up for one of the many "goddess pilgrimages" now offered by more experienced spiritual feminists. The most popular destinations for goddess pilgrimages are Great Britain or the Mediterranean, particularly Malta, Greece, and Turkey. The Neolithic town of Çatalhöyük in Turkey, currently under excavation, is one such pilgrimage site since its first excavator, James Mellaart, interpreted frescos and figurines there as evidence that the town's population practiced a goddess-based religion and reckoned kinship matrilineally. Minoan Crete is also very popular for goddess pilgrimages since its first excavator, Sir Arthur Evans, also described the culture he unearthed as goddess-worshipping and matrilineal. But spiritual feminists can also join pilgrimages to Mexico, Poland, or virtually any location where it is believed that there are sites sacred to the Goddess. And since most spiritual feminists believe that goddess religion was the universal religion of the human race for most of our history, such sites are indeed everywhere.

The feminist spirituality movement also functions as a sort of virtual community, bonded together through books, magazines, newsletters, and email lists as much as through face-to-face contact. The movement gives permission for individual women to take their own spiritual investigations seriously and to perceive themselves as part of a legitimate feminist and spiritual enterprise.

BELIEFS OF THE FEMINIST SPIRITUALITY MOVEMENT

The feminist spirituality movement holds almost all its beliefs lightly. From the beginning, it took a very pragmatic approach to religious belief, supporting those beliefs that empower women and dismissing those that do not. Women with a wide range of religious beliefs cooperate with one another, regarding this variation in belief as mainly a personal matter. Nevertheless, feminist spirituality has a definite belief structure. Deviations from it may be accepted or dismissed as irrelevant, but a central spiritual feminist theology defines the values of feminist spirituality and distinguishes it from other religions.

The principal beliefs of the feminist spirituality movement are all contained in its vision of the Goddess, she who is the heart of the universe and exists as the divine within each woman. Spiritual feminists conceive of the Goddess in a number of ways that appear contradictory at a superficial level, but are not felt as contradiction by her worshippers. She is often referred to as the Great Goddess, the Great Mother, the Creatrix—all of which give rise to an impression of Goddess monotheism. Indeed, spiritual feminists usually speak of the Goddess in singular terms. Yet the Goddess is also worshipped—indeed is far more frequently worshipped—in her various polytheistic aspects. One prevalent version of the Goddess's aspects is Trinitarian: she is virgin (or maiden), mother, and crone, a division meant to illustrate that she is not merely a fertility goddess or a wise old woman, but a goddess who manifests characteristics of all the phases of a woman's life. (In keeping with the movement's generally very positive attitude toward sexuality, it is frequently stressed that the term "virgin" simply means unmarried, a woman who belongs to herself and no one else, rather than a woman who has not experienced sexual intercourse.)

The polytheism of the feminist spirituality movement extends further than this, however. Any female deity in any religion worldwide is considered an "aspect" or "manifestation" of *the* Goddess, and in these many guises spiritual feminists most often interact with the Goddess. A woman may choose to worship the Greek goddess Demeter to connect with the concept of motherhood or with Artemis to grow in strength and independence. She may call on Pele, the Hawaiian goddess of the volcano, or Kali, Hindu goddess of destruction, if she is working through feelings of rage. Spiritual feminists are sometimes criticized for lifting these deities out of their cultural and religious contexts. Spiritual feminists are rarely troubled by this. They tend to believe that, for example, when Tibetans developed iconography and mythology around the goddess Tara, they were expressing their experience of the Great Goddess, the original deity, in the only context they knew, that of Buddhism. For a spiritual feminist to embrace Tara, then, is not to appropriate a Buddhist goddess but to celebrate the fact that the Goddess is everywhere. If anything, when Tara becomes a spiritual feminist deity, it is felt that she is returning to her original matrix, that of the Great Goddess.[8]

The Goddess is a radically immanent deity, present in all things and accessible through all things. Spiritual feminists frequently remark that the Earth is the body of the Goddess and that women connect with the Earth through their experiences of their own bodies and their experiences of nature. The Goddess *is* nature, and nature is sacred: she celebrates her sexuality and gives birth to everything. Spiritual feminists see the Goddess as constantly changing, ever-renewed, moving endlessly through the cycles of the seasons and the ages. The quality of belief in this Goddess is thus significantly different from that of belief in the transcendent God found in most Western religious traditions. Spiritual feminists stress that one need not have faith in the Goddess because one can experience her directly. Starhawk responds to the question "do you believe in the Goddess?" as follows: "People often ask me if I *believe* in the Goddess. I reply 'Do you believe in rocks?' It is extremely difficult for most Westerners to grasp the concept of a manifest deity. The phrase 'believe *in*' itself implies that we cannot *know* the Goddess, that She is somehow intangible, incomprehensible. But we do not *believe* in rocks—we may see them, touch them, dig them out of our gardens, or stop small children from throwing them at each other. We know them; we connect with them."[9] For many spiritual feminists, however, the idea of the Goddess is enough: just to regard the divine as somehow like them, to feel that ultimate power is female, is spiritually profound.

Adding strength to this epiphany is the spiritual feminist belief that our human ancestors all recognized the Goddess as the supreme deity of the universe and that it was she who was worshipped millennia before anyone ever dreamed up the idea of a male God. Spiritual feminists conceive of this era of universal goddess worship as a golden age in which human beings lived in peace with themselves, their environment, and their neighbors. It is typically reconstructed as a time when women had access to social power (if not holding an actual monopoly on social power) and were revered as a reflection of the divine. Moreover, spiritual feminists believe that this was a time when "female" values—nurturance, cooperation—held sway. Spiritual feminists generally argue that during this long age of the Goddess writing, mathematics, and agriculture developed, and that only relatively recently has the religion and civilization of the Goddess been destroyed by male-dominant cultures.[10]

Though this era of Goddess worship and gynocentrism was supposedly universal, spiritual feminists most often tell the story with respect to the cultures of the Mediterranean. In this part of the world, beginning around 3000 BCE, patriarchal invaders imposed male dominance and a divine sanction for it in the form of an omnipotent male deity. The demise of Goddess worship was necessary for the success of the patriarchs' mission, spiritual feminists argue, because women who knew they were living reflections of a powerful Goddess would never assent to men controlling the world. Armed violence in the short run, and ideological indoctrination in the form of patriarchal religion in the long run, sealed the patriarchy's triumph and forced the Goddess religion underground.[11] However, even under the patriarchal religions of Judaism and Christianity, say spiritual feminists, Goddess worship continued as a minority religion among the peasant populations of Europe. This religion was so successful in winning the hearts and minds of the common folk that, according to spiritual feminists, European Christianity had to take drastic measures to snuff it out. These efforts were the witch persecutions of the medieval and early modern periods. The figure typically given by spiritual feminists for the number of men, women, and children burned as witches in Europe during the sixteenth and seventeenth centuries is nine million, the great preponderance of these being women.[12] However, spiritual feminists are quick to add that not all of those persecuted for witchcraft were actually practitioners of paganism or Goddess worship. Most were sadly the victims of the patriarchs' need to consolidate their power. Women who did not fit neatly into the categories allotted to them under male domination were accused of witchcraft and then murdered for their supposed crimes, so that the potential revolution of women could be contained and patriarchal rule secured. Thus, the "Burning Times" stand for spiritual feminists as the single most blatant case of misogyny in Western history.

The understanding of spiritual feminists is that we continue to live in a patriarchal society today, and if women are no longer burned as witches, that is because of luck and persistent rebellion rather than reform by either the ruling patriarchs or ordinary men. However, the final installment of feminist spirituality's sacred history is not the present, but the future. Spiritual feminists hope for a time when society will return to the life-loving values of the Goddess, and just as often dread a planetary catastrophe brought on by the abuse of the environment through technology and the abuse of women, children, and minorities by ruling males. For spiritual feminists, we hover at the edge of apocalypse, and the days of the present order are numbered: either the patriarchy will destroy us all or we will at the last moment extricate ourselves from the bonds of male domination and usher in a new golden age of the Goddess.

Spiritual feminists exhibit considerable variation regarding their beliefs in the Goddess, in her many manifestations in religions around the world, and in the nature of prehistoric societies that worshipped her. Even more strikingly, spiritual feminists have a wide range of beliefs about whether they believe in the Goddess at all, or in any history of her former universality. So long as spiritual feminists affirm the basic values associated with the Goddess—principally, the value of women and nature and the importance of living in peace—this lack of unity in belief rarely creates any dissension in the movement. Spiritual feminists expect that women will bring their own beliefs and understandings about the Goddess to the ritual circle, and so long as individual spiritual feminists can commune with one another, issues of "belief" will not divide them.

PRACTICES OF THE FEMINIST SPIRITUALITY MOVEMENT

The central practices of the feminist spirituality movement involve ritual and magic or, most often, a combination of the two. Feminist witches conduct regular rituals on the solstices, equinoxes, and cross-quarter days between them, and sometimes on the new and full moons as well. Other spiritual feminists, less influenced by Wicca and Neopaganism, may meet on a biweekly or monthly basis following the Gregorian rather than the lunar calendar. For those who follow the solar cycle (the "Wheel of the Year"), rituals differ depending on the season. Winter is a time for looking inward while summer is a time for dance and revelry. Whenever rituals are held, however, they mostly exhibit the same basic structure, beginning with the opening of the circle and ending with its closing. Often an altar is constructed in the middle of the ritual space, covered with flowers, candles, fruit, seashells, crystals, figurines of the Goddess, and any other objects that participants consider important. The ritual begins as all participants stand in a circle. The ritual leader or leaders go to each of the four compass points, beginning with the east and moving counterclockwise, holding a ritual object (usually a knife or wand). Energies and aspects of the Goddess associated with each direction are invoked and the ritual space is formally consecrated. Once the circle is formally cast, no one leaves it until it is formally closed. The ritual progresses with a series of songs, chants, readings, meditations, and dances. At some point participants usually make an effort to "raise energy" by holding hands, breathing together, and chanting or singing with increasing tempo and volume until the energy has reached its peak. The energy is then "sent" to its desired object (the end of patriarchy, the health of the earth, healing for a sick friend) and grounded (participants place their hands on the ground and gradually relax their breathing). Often participants will go around the circle, with each woman lighting a candle and announcing a wish to the group, those wishes ranging from "an end to the oppression of women" to "a new lover" and "money to pay the rent." Wishes are answered with shouts of "blessed be!" from the other participants. Some spiritual feminist groups are more psychotherapeutic in orientation and spend the majority of their ritual time going around the circle making wishes reflecting their current emotional or relational struggles and asking for the assistance of the group. The circle is closed in the opposite direction from which it was opened, and the goddesses are thanked and dismissed. After the circle is closed, participants usually share a meal, discuss the ritual, and talk companionably with one another.[13]

The raising and sending of energy in the context of a ritual circle is regarded as a form of magic within feminist spirituality, but other forms of magic are practiced as well, and most do not require group participation. Indeed, magic is often practiced alone, with the creation of protective charms or the binding of the powers of one's enemies, or in practicing forms of divination, from reading tea leaves to gazing into crystal balls. Some spiritual feminists make their living from the practice of magic, producing candles, herbs, oils, and other magical supplies and training others in their proper use.

The mechanisms of magic are explained differently by different individuals in the feminist spirituality movement. The most straightforwardly psychological interpretation of magic offered by spiritual feminists is that it works by triggering the subconscious mind. Magic, and the material devices it relies upon, focuses one's thoughts and energy on the desired event so that it will more likely come to pass. For example, a woman may sew a red heart-shaped charm, fill it with herbs, and place it under her pillow, in the belief that it will bring love into her life. When love does come into her life, she may say that it could just as well have happened had she sewn a green rectangular charm and that, if the red one was more efficacious, it was only because her mind was trained for years to associate red with love. What really produced the desired result was her determination to have it.

Another interpretation of magic given by spiritual feminists, this one with a cosmological basis, suggests that magic works because it moves patterns of energy in accord with the practitioner's desires. According to this view, everything in the universe is connected by energy. And though it may seem to the conventional Western mind-set that someone could not protect her house from a tornado if it happens to be in the storm's path, feminist spirituality answers that the energy of the tornado and the energy of the individual mind are composed of the same substance and may therefore communicate with one another. Again, the focus is on one's mind, and not on the magical props used to trigger it, but the idea that the mind has powers to control not only one's own behavior but also other people and objects by virtue of their interconnection is superadded in this view of magic.[14]

A third understanding of magic among spiritual feminists is that actual causal connections exist between the magical props used and the ends sought. Thus, if a woman wants love, a green rectangular charm will never do, but neither will a red heart-shaped one unless it is filled with the proper herbs and oils and charged with the proper ritual actions. In this interpretation, the practitioner physically creates a charm that will bring her lover to her. For those who understand magic in this way, the magical act, not merely the intention behind it or the changes it creates in one's consciousness, effects the desired result. To illustrate, one feminist witch told me that she made a charm to keep the police away and placed it in her freezer. For over a year, the police gave her no trouble, but then one day a highway patrol officer pulled her over and gave her a speeding ticket. Puzzled and confused, she drove home, only to find that the electrical power to her house was out and everything in her freezer, including the charm, had thawed.

Whatever the immediate goal of the magic practiced by spiritual feminists, its overall importance in the feminist spirituality movement lies in the feeling of control it gives individual practitioners. Especially for women raised to believe that they have little control over their destinies, it is enormously freeing to have magical tools with which one can guide one's life. Spiritual feminists frequently comment on the difference between forms of prayer they learned in established religions, which required them to humbly request favors from a "big man in the sky," versus the practice of magic in the feminist spirituality movement, which involves women more actively taking their fate into their own hands.

FUTURE OF THE FEMINIST SPIRITUALITY MOVEMENT

The feminist spirituality movement was born out of a unique intersection of needs, interests, and available religious resources that characterized a certain group of women in the 1970s and 1980s in the United States. To the extent that those needs, interests, and religious resources remain today, the feminist spirituality movement continues to thrive. However, much has changed since the movement's inception, and, with its trademark flexibility, the feminist spirituality movement has found ways to accommodate these changes.

The sometimes angry separatism that characterized early manifestations of feminist spirituality is less common today. This is partly because spiritual feminists have less cause to defend their choice to practice in female-only groups, now that that choice is more firmly established as a viable one. But it also reflects a mellower phase in the feminist movement as a whole. The revolutionary fires do not burn as brightly as they once did. Whether this is because the feminist movement succeeded or failed is a matter of enormous contention, but feminism simply does not grab headlines and scandalize ordinary folk the way it did at the time the feminist spirituality movement first came into being. Though individual women still come to the feminist spirituality movement in a spirit of religious rebellion, feminist spirituality is no longer the freshest face among alternative religions, or even among Neopagan ones. The feminist spirituality movement still encourages individual religious creativity, but newcomers are clearly arriving in a land where many of the customs and traditions are already set in place.

Perhaps most significant for the future of the feminist spirituality movement is the spirit of détente between it and the broader Neopagan movement. When feminist spirituality first came into being, it was decidedly at odds with much of the Neopagan mainstream: it was more free-form, less bound to occult tradition, more inclusive of a variety of religious and New Age traditions, and, of course, considerably less interested in making any space for men or maleness. Furthermore, many participants in the feminist spirituality movement never would have considered becoming involved had the movement not been a feminist religion. Women with scant interest in or attraction to alternative spiritualities sometimes found their way into feminist spirituality simply because this was where their sister feminists were active.

This is less true today. Women who have no appetite for the occult rarely become involved in feminist spirituality. As a result, the feminist spirituality movement is more unapologetically pagan than before and less hesitant to involve itself in the subculture of alternative religions on an equal footing with others. Because it does not distance itself as much from other forms of Neopaganism, the feminist spirituality movement is somewhat less distinctive. In the future it may or may not maintain a separate identity. It might gradually define itself as simply one form—though a very female-centered form—of Neopaganism.

NOTES

1. For a history of the CR movement, see Anita Shreve, *Women Together, Women Alone: The Legacy of the Consciousness-Raising Movement* (New York: Fawcett Columbine, 1989).

2. For details on this event, see Ursula King, *Women and Spirituality: Voices of Protest and Promise* (New York: New Amsterdam, 1989), 170; Mary Daly, "After the Death of God the Father: Women's Liberation and the Transformation of Christian Consciousness," in *Womanspirit Rising: A Feminist Reader in Religion,* ed. Carol P. Christ and Judith Plaskow (San Francisco: Harper and Row, 1979), 57.

3. This period of neopagan religious innovation is well documented in Margot Adler, *Drawing Down the Moon: Witches, Druids, Goddess-Worshippers, and Other Pagans in America Today* (Boston: Beacon Press, 1979).

4. Zsuzsanna Budapest, *The Holy Book of Women's Mysteries: Feminist Witchcraft, Goddess Rituals, Spellcasting, and Other Womanly Arts* (Berkeley: Wingbow Press, 1989), 258–64.

5. Ibid., xi–xviii. As Budapest recounts it, she selected Susan B. Anthony's name for her coven after she learned that Anthony once answered a reporter's question about the afterlife by saying "When I die I shall go neither to heaven nor to hell, but stay right here and finish the women's revolution." Budapest reasoned that Anthony could be feminist spirituality's "guardian spirit," its "Lady of the Coven" (xviii).

6. Z. Budapest, *The Holy Book of Women's Mysteries, Part One* (Oakland, CA: Susan B. Anthony Coven No. 1, 1979), 9–10.

7. *The Spiral Dance* has been reissued twice, each time with extensive comments on the original text that illustrate the continued development of Starhawk's thinking about Wiccan belief and practice.

8. Cynthia Eller, *Living in the Lap of the Goddess: The Feminist Spirituality Movement in America* (Boston: Beacon Press, 1995), 67–74, 77–78, 132–34.

9. Starhawk, *The Spiral Dance: A Rebirth of the Ancient Religion of the Great Goddess* (San Francisco: Harper and Row, 1979), 77.

10. Vicki Noble, *Shakti Woman: Feeling our Fire, Healing our World. The New Female Shamanism* (San Francisco: HarperSanFrancisco, 1991), 227–28; Marija Gimbutas, *The Civilization of the Goddess: The World of Old Europe* (San Francisco: HarperSanFrancisco, 1991), 308–21.

11. Some spiritual feminists regard this story as a helpful myth; others believe it is an accurate historical account of human religion and civilization. Spiritual feminists are not alone in believing that human societies have undergone a major shift from being female-centered and goddess-worshipping to being male dominant and god-worshipping. Beginning in the late nineteenth century, many scholars put this theory forward as a scientific certainty [see Cynthia Eller, *Motherright* (Berkeley: University of California Press, forthcoming)]. Though spiritual feminists offer much evidence in support of this theory of original Goddess worship and its defeat via a patriarchal revolution, none of this evidence is convincing [see Cynthia Eller, *The Myth of Matriarchal Prehistory: Why an Invented Past Won't Give Women a Future* (Boston: Beacon Press, 2000)]. It is thus more accurate to regard this story as a myth or sacred history, rather than as history per se.

12. This figure is almost certainly inaccurate. It was first asserted by Matilda Joslyn Gage in *Woman, Church and State*, originally published in 1893. Historians of this era [for example, E. William Monter, *European Witchcraft* (New York: Wiley and Sons, 1969), 73] offer much more modest estimates, some as low as 100,000—which is still, of course, very high.

13. Starhawk, *Spiral Dance*, 55–75; Eller, *Living in the Lap of the Goddess*, 93–103.

14. Starhawk gives a basic introduction to this understanding of magic in *The Spiral Dance*, 18.

FURTHER READING

Adler, Margot. *Drawing Down the Moon: Witches, Druids, Goddess-Worshippers, and Other pagans in America Today.* Boston: Beacon Press, 1979.

Budapest, Zsuzsanna. *The Holy Book of Women's Mysteries.* Berkeley, CA: Wingbow Press, 1986.

Christ, Carol P. *Rebirth of the Goddess: Finding Meaning in Feminist Spirituality.* Boston: Addison-Wesley, 1997.

Eller, Cynthia. *Living in the Lap of the Goddess: The Feminist Spirituality Movement in America.* Boston: Beacon Press, 1995.

———. *The Myth of Matriarchal Prehistory: Why an Invented Past Won't Give Women a Future.* Boston: Beacon Press, 2000.

Gimbutas, Marija. *The Civilization of the Goddess: The World of Old Europe.* Edited by Joan Marler. San Francisco: HarperSanFrancisco, 1991.

Purkiss, Diane. *The Witch in History: Early Modern and Twentieth-Century Representations.* New York: Routledge, 1996.

Rountree, Kathryn. *Embracing the Witch and the Goddess: Feminist Ritual-Makers in New Zealand.* New York: Routledge, 2003.

Salomonsen, Jone. *Enchanted Feminism: The Reclaiming Witches of San Francisco.* New York: Routledge, 2002.

Sjöö, Monica, and Barbara Mor. *The Great Cosmic Mother: Rediscovering the Religion of the Earth.* San Francisco: Harper and Row, 1987.

Starhawk. *The Spiral Dance: A Rebirth of the Ancient Religion of the Great Goddess.* San Francisco: Harper and Row, 1979.

Wicca, Witchcraft, and Modern Paganism

Douglas E. Cowan

INTRODUCTION

Nine men and women gather in a midtown apartment, not far from a major shopping mall. It is February 1, and, just as they have for many years, the group has come to celebrate the Wiccan sabbat known as Imbolc, the ritual bidding farewell to winter and looking forward to the return of spring. On the street below, rush hour traffic begins to wane and the noise drops away. The moon rises, its light gleaming off the polished windows of high-rise office buildings. Inside the apartment, the living room furniture has been pushed to the side and the room cleaned thoroughly. Soft music greets those who gather, and the sweet scent of incense hangs in the air. A circle has been carefully chalked on the hardwood floor, and tall candles mark the cardinal points of its compass, the four directions. They provide the only light in the room, and in their midst sits an altar, with various ritual tools arranged carefully on a deep blue altar cloth. As the moment for the ritual draws near, a feeling of expectation grips those in attendance, and two women begin to chant gently. Welcomed into the circle with a kiss, the members of the coven hold hands as their High Priestess grasps her *athame*—her ritual knife—and begins the opening invocation. "I call upon thee, O guardians of the watchtowers of the East, spirits of air and intellect, to witness our rites and to safeguard our circle." As she speaks, she draws a pentagram in the air before her, imagining as she does lines of pale blue fire.[1] As she finishes the last line of the pentagram, her coven responds as one, "So mote it be."

On that same night, in a number of different cities and towns across the continent, other Pagans gather. Unlike the midtown coven, however, these are all women, and no one in this group has ever met face-to-face. Any two of them could pass on the street and neither would be the wiser. They met through an Internet discussion forum for beginning Witches, one that advertised a safe place to identify as Witches. For several months, they have been meeting online, struggling to plan a ritual they can perform together. Tonight will be the first. One of them has written a simple ritual script and distributed it by e-mail to the others in the group. Different members have chosen to play different roles, with no one acting as High Priestess. Some will call the quarters, others will offer the charge to the Goddess and the God, and another will lead an online visualization exercise designed to bring their disparate energies into harmony. Seated at their computers, each participant prepares a few essentials—candles to represent the Goddess and the God, incense, and bowls of earth and water. One by one, they log in to the private chat room. As they enter their usernames and passwords, a message scrolls slowly up the screen.

> *Welcome to our circle. This is a place of perfect love and perfect trust. All who live as daughters of the Goddess are welcome here. The sun has set in this ancient grove, and the shadows deepen on the edges of the firelight. Find a place and prepare yourself for what is to come.*

As each member enters, her name appears on the screen, and she is greeted by those already in the chat room/ritual grove. When it is time for the ritual to begin, the appointed leader types:

> ::Lady Onyx rises and approaches the altar. She picks up her athame and motions her circle sisters to rise. She raises her athame::

> *<Onyx>* In this place, we walk between the worlds, and in this time, we step outside of time… This night, we invoke the Goddesses of old: Isis the protector of visions, and Brighid, the bringer of wisdom.
> *<ALL>* SO MOTE IT BE.

No one hears the words of the others. Only the glowing text on the screen signifies their presence and participation. Like many modern Pagan rituals, theirs is less an established sacred place than a sanctuary of the imagination, a shared vision of their ritual that they are convinced connects them one to another.

Not all experiences of modern Paganism are so gratifying, so potentially fulfilling as these. Many other Wiccans, Witches, Druids, and Ásatrúer lead what amounts to double lives. Though their religions are officially recognized in the United States and Canada, the growing popularity of Wicca and Witchcraft has not completely eclipsed the stigma that remains attached to them. Many Pagans remain "in the broomcloset," afraid to reveal their religious choices to friends and family. And, when they do try to stand in the truth of their own beliefs, they are often marginalized. During one ritual celebration, for example, Pagans in Lancaster, California, were accosted by evangelical Christians who gathered around their circle praying, reading Bible verses aloud, and blaring Christian music from a SUV parked nearby. Though only three blocks away, it took local police more than four hours to respond to the Pagans' complaints of harassment.[2] At the largest military post in the United States, members of the Fort Hood Open Circle, one of the first official Wiccan groups approved by the U.S. Army, had to contend with evangelicals "calling the base and threatening to stage a march in town and disrupt the rituals,"[3] as well as threats of federal hearings from a prominent House representative.[4] Numerous Pagan students have been suspended from school or threatened with suspension for activities ranging from wearing a pentacle to carrying books like Silver RavenWolf's popular *Teen Witch,* to simply admitting they are Wiccan.[5]

According to many of its adherents, as well as media commentators and academic analysts, modern Paganism is among the fastest growing cluster of religious traditions in North America, Great Britain and parts of Europe, and Australia.[6] Through film and television, it is prominent in popular culture. Though there is some indication that the market has flattened, for the last decade-and-a-half modern Paganism has been among the fastest growing sections in bookstores such as Borders, Barnes and Noble, and Chapters.

An introductory essay such as this cannot hope to do justice to the vast panoply of emergent religious belief and practice that constitutes modern Paganism: Witches and Wiccans, whether connected to established lineages, eclectically oriented covens, or working their magic as solitaries; non-Wiccan Goddess worshippers who follow a variety of paths ranging from Northern European paganism to the pantheons of Greece, Rome, Egypt, and Africa; New Druids and Celtic Reconstructionists—the former interested in revitalizing the spirit of what they believe was the religious practice of pre-Roman Britain, the latter only in reconstructing what can be known from the extant historical record; Ásatrúer and Odinists, followers of Norse heathenism, who are often and inaccurately painted as violent and reactionary in their beliefs; syncretistic Pagan practitioners, such as Jewish Witches and Christo-Wiccans, who are often marginalized by both constituent communities; and eclectic nature worshippers who gather under the organizational auspices of institutions like the Unitarian Universalist Association. Indeed, one of the major problems that confronts academic analysts who try to map either modern Paganism or the various phenomena of the so-called "New Age movement" is that neither displays rigid enough doctrinal, practical, ritual, historical, or sociological boundaries to allow for easy categorization.[7] While recognizing that modern Paganism encompasses far more belief systems, ritual practices, and traditional lineages than just Wicca or Witchcraft, because these are arguably the most well-known in North America, this chapter focuses primarily on these as two examples of modern Paganism.

Rather than an easily definable set of beliefs and practices, it is, perhaps, most useful to think of modern Paganism as a family of related religious traditions, some of which are more traditional in their outlook and appearance, while others are experimental, innovative, and, in the eyes of traditionalists, not a little rebellious. Many Wiccan and Witchcraft traditions, however, though they may have changed and adapted over the years, trace their origins to a retired British civil servant named Gerald Brousseau Gardner (1884–1964).

Gardner spent most of his working life in southeast Asia, working as a tea planter, on a rubber plantation, and later as a customs official for the British government. Among other things, Gardner was an ardent amateur archeologist and folklorist. He retired to England in 1936, and claims that he was initiated into a traditional Witchcraft coven in 1939, just before the start of World War II. According to Wiccan lore, during the war Gardner was an instrumental part, if not the instigator, of what is known as "Operation Cone of Power"—as many as four separate rituals that were conducted by Witches in southern England to deter the impending invasion of Great Britain by Germany.[8] After the war, Gardner wrote about the "Old Religion," first under a pseudonym,[9] and then under his own name. In 1951, the last of the Witchcraft Acts in Britain was repealed, and Gardner came fully out of the broom-closet. Though there is considerable dispute about Gardner's sources—whether he really was initiated into the New Forest Coven or simply invented Wicca from the stock of religious knowledge he possessed[10]—there is no denying that his influence, along with that of people like Raymond Buckland, who is credited by many with bringing Gardnerian Witchcraft to the United States in the early 1960s, and Janet and Stewart Farrar, who published a recension of Gardner's principal ritual text, the *Book of Shadows,* in the mid-1980s, was instrumental in the growth of modern Witchcraft in the late twentieth century.

MODERN PAGAN BELIEFS AND RITUALS

Modern Pagan Beliefs

Two principal factors make it difficult to generalize about modern Pagan beliefs: (a the difference in groups that cluster (and are clustered) under the modern Pagan rubric; and (b) the open source character of modern Pagan belief itself, which, even within groups that are nominally similar, manifests in both experimental and tradi-tional ways. Groups such as Gardnerian and Alexandrian witches,[11] for example, consider the balanced polarity of male and female membership in a ritual group essential to the magical success of the group. Others, such as Dianic Witches, often regard the presence of any male energy as dangerous to the safety and integrity of their ritual circle. While many modern Witches still hold fast to the maxim that "only a witch can make a witch"[12]—and, in its more restricted form, that only a male Witch can initiate a female Witch, and vice versa—others have embraced the practice of self-initiation, which has generated a thriving literature within modern Paganism.[13]

That said, however, there are certain general characteristics that set modern Pagan-ism apart as a distinct religious family.[14] Though most Pagans live in urban and sub-urban settings,[15] all have a love, indeed a reverence, for nature that they believe has been either accidentally lost or actively discarded by other religions. For many mod-ern Pagans, the natural world itself is a sentient and sacred entity, and invokes within them an imaginative, a ritual, and in many cases a political connection. Ritual practice, spellwork, and daily Pagan living are guided by belief in a spiritual imma-nentalism and the ethical principle of reciprocity—that the world around them is spiritually vital and active, and that they can participate in and affect that world. These effects, however, are managed within the boundaries of what many refer to as the Law of Threefold Return, that is, whatever one puts out into the world, whether positive or negative, will return threefold.

Most modern Pagans devote themselves to one or more gods or goddesses, often basing their choice on an affinity for certain pantheons—Celtic, Norse, Greek,

Egyptian, and so forth—and an intuitive sense that they have been called or chosen by particular gods or goddesses within those pantheons. Broadly speaking, and allowing for the idiosyncrasy that marks much of modern Pagan belief and practice, gods and goddesses are conceptualized in two ways. On the one hand, in a manner analogous to some Hindus' belief that all manifestations of the divine are simply emanations of the one reality or Brahman, many modern Pagans believe that the various gods and goddesses on whom they call in ritual and magic are "merely aspects of an all-pervasive divinity, and the particular god or goddess invoked represents only a facet of that divinity."[16] This explains the belief among many modern Pagans that the number of gods and goddesses with whom one can work is unlimited, or the ability to draw on the energies of disparate deities depending on the particular situation or need. On the other hand, for some Wiccans and Witches every deity from every pantheon represents a separate and distinct divine entity, existing and operating independently. "If," as I have noted elsewhere, "in the first instance, the names of gods and goddesses are facets of a single divine diamond, in the second understanding each deity represents a different, unique jewel."[17]

Though all of this may seem a bit odd to the outside observer, the Farrars point out that "witches are neither fools, escapists not superstitious."[18] Indeed, "if witchcraft did not have a coherent rationale, such people could only keep going by a kind of deliberate schizophrenia."[19] For the Farrars, as for other modern Pagans, the world as we see and experience it is only one level of reality, for many the most mundane level. This understanding is hardly limited to modern Paganism; for centuries Roman Catholicism had its various levels of existence in heaven and hell, and Buddhism and Hinduism have their multiple domains of *samsaric* existence. Unfortunately for most of the Western world, modern Pagans maintain, the scientific revolution managed to convince us that the physical plane of existence is the only level of reality—a claim many Wiccans and Witches seek actively to challenge. Some even talk about Witchcraft as an empirical science, fully aligned with the latest discoveries in physics, biology, and astronomy. "When I speak of Witchcraft as a science," writes Laurie Cabot, a well-known American Witch, who also calls herself the "Official Witch of Salem" and who has named her Witchcraft lineage the Science Tradition, "I use the word *science* in its strictest form."[20] She continues:

> Witchcraft is a system based on hypotheses that can be tested under controlled conditions. Magical spells are step-by-step experiments that produce statistical results from which we can derive our success rates. The physical sciences maintain that a 32 percent success rate establishes the validity of a hypothesis. When I teach the science of Witchcraft based on the Hermetic laws, my students' experiments show a 50 percent and often a 75 to 90 percent success rate.[21]

Since, according to modern Pagan belief, everything in the universe—visible and invisible—is intimately connected, and any appearance of separation merely the social and cultural residue of the so-called scientific revolution, it follows logically that there ought to be mechanisms by which those connections can be accessed and influenced. This is one function of modern Pagan ritual and magical practice.

Modern Pagan Ritual

Modern Pagan ritual serves a variety of purposes, both religious and psychosocial: honoring and worshipping the gods and/or goddesses to which individual Pagans or groups are dedicated; teaching and initiating in a particular tradition; raising and releasing energy that is then directed toward specific purposes; and spellworking, which is generally practiced with very specific intent. The psychosocial benefits of ritual within a group that is working well are, among others, interpersonal bonding, as well as world view maintenance and reinforcement. In modern Paganism, the ideal is that every participant will take responsibility for his or her own spiritual growth and skill development. Unlike many Christian churches, the congregants are not spectators watching a performance presented by the pastoral staff. Rather, because they tend to work in much smaller groups, in ideal circumstances the high level of commitment and participation expected of all group members strengthens the bonds between those in the circle. These positive experiences, as well as the inevitable discussion that takes place after, reinforce the modern Pagan world view.

Although different groups have subtle differences, Wiccan and Witchcraft traditions follow a liturgical year that is divided into two principal ritual patterns: the *sabbats,* four "greater" and four "lesser" festivals based on the yearly seasonal cycle and celebrated on the solstices, equinoxes, and the midpoints between, and the *esbats,* 13 ritual meetings that follow the monthly lunar cycle. A few of the sabbats coincide with well-known Christian festivals, and modern Pagans contend that the Christian church simply appropriated the festival observances of the peoples it converted and adapted old ways to a new faith. Samhain, for example, which many Wiccans regard as the Pagan new year, is celebrated on Hallowe'en, the eve of All Saints' Day. Yule, or the Midwinter festival, occurs on the winter solstice, and is, perhaps, the best known of the Pagan sabbats because of its association with Christmas.[22] Ostara, which is celebrated on or around the vernal equinox, is named for Eostre, a Teutonic fertility goddess and according to many modern Pagans the etymological source of the English word, Easter. Pagans read different theological emphases into these ritual patterns, and there is no "orthodox" interpretation of what is known as the "wheel of the year."

Some groups meet only for the sabbats, while others take every opportunity to gather for ritual and companionship. For some, every ritual celebration is a closed event; only those initiated into the tradition and a part of the group may attend. Other groups regularly invite the public to their sabbat celebrations, especially the more well-known sabbats such as Beltaine, Samhain, and Yule. This illustrates another of the tensions in modern Paganism. Though many practitioners point with pride to the growth of traditions such as Wicca and Witchcraft, and in many cases at least tacitly equate growth with legitimacy, others are troubled by a commercialization that they believe is diluting the core of Pagan belief and practice, but without which the growth they applaud would be difficult if not impossible.

One ritual practice attracts non-Pagan attention more than any other, though it is actually performed far less often than might be imagined: the Great Rite of the

Wiccan and Witchcraft traditions, the *hieros gamos,* the sacred marriage. Though it was abandoned by a number of traditions as hopelessly patriarchal and implicitly abusive,[23] the Great Rite remains a central ritual in both Gardnerian and Alexandrian Witchcraft.[24] It consists of actual or symbolic sexual union between two coven members, who embody the union of the Goddess and the God. By all accounts, performance of the actual Great Rite occurs relatively infrequently, and the chosen couple either leave the circle and return once intercourse is completed or are left together in the circle by the rest of the coven. Far more often, indeed as a fundamental element of many Wiccan and Witchcraft rituals, the Great Rite is performed symbolically, or "in token." Kneeling before the High Priestess, the High Priest elevates a ritual chalice, which symbolizes the female principle in the divine complementarity. Standing above him, the High Priestess, who functions in the coven as *prima inter pares,* the first among equals, inserts her athame (the male principle) into the chalice. As the Farrars point out: "The couple enacting the Great Rite are offering themselves, with reverence and joy, as expressions of the God and Goddess aspects of the Ultimate Source. 'As above, so below.' They are making themselves, to the best of their ability, channels for the divine polarity on *all* levels, from physical to spiritual. That is why it is called the *Great* Rite."[25]

The Open Source Character of Modern Pagan Belief and Practice

Searching for a way to conceptualize the eclectic and often confusing nature of modern Paganism, I borrowed a concept from computer programming and suggested that they are an *open source* family of religious traditions.[26] As I contend in *Cyberhenge,* "*open source traditions* are those which encourage (or at least do not discourage) theological and ritual innovation based on either individual intuition or group consensus, and which innovation is not limited to priestly classes, institutional elites, or religious *virtuosi.*"[27] Closed source traditions, on the other hand, the quintessential example of which is the Church of Scientology, do not permit any form of theological or ritual innovation on the part of practitioners.

The open source character of modern Paganism displays itself in numerous ways. Some practitioners combine deity elements from different traditional pantheons to generate their own eclectic, syncretistic family of gods and goddesses. The Temple of Sekhmet, for example, is a small, adobe shrine in the Nevada desert 60 miles northwest of Las Vegas. Designed as a temple to the Egyptian goddess, Sekhmet, the shrine has become something of a pilgrimage spot for modern Pagans, given its proximity to the sprawling Nellis Air Force Base complex and the mysterious, heavily guarded, and officially unacknowledged testing site known around the world as Area 51. Besides Sekhmet, however, there are also statues of another Egyptian goddess (and Sekhmet's sister), Bast, a Native American Earth Mother, the Buddhist goddess of compassion Kuan Yin, and a painting of Mary modeled on the Virgin of Guadalupe. Although some have questioned the ethics of this kind of appropriation of spiritual resources,[28] the modern Pagan understanding that everything in the universe is connected means, by extension, that everything is available for use by all.

Some Wiccans not only appropriate the spiritual and ritual resources of other traditions, but invent their own as need, circumstance, and inspiration dictate. Writing about being "Web witches," for example, popular Pagan authors Patricia Telesco and Sirona Knight encourage their readers to develop not only their own relationships with various deities, but their own gods and goddesses as well. "This sounds a little silly," they write, "but given some serious thought, there's no reason why we cannot create new mythologies based on the world as it is today and the techno-tools in it."[29] They suggest that technologically inclined Pagans might "choose to venerate Snap (the God of microwaved foods), Click (the computer mouse Goddess), Popup (the Goddess of toasters and toaster ovens), Ram and Rom (the computer twin Gods), Bit and Byte (the computer twin Goddesses), or Wireless (the spirit of cell phones)."[30] In the context of the emergence and development of modern Pagan belief and practice, this kind of innovation is a question worth pondering. As G. L. Ebersole points out in his discussion of myth, history, and the various relationships between the two, mythologies "are not timeless and static structures but dynamic agents in the ongoing process of the creation and maintenance of a symbolic world of meaning."[31] And, as I have noted elsewhere:

> [Knight and Telesco] illustrate tension between two distinct innovative subcultures within modern Paganism, what I have called the research-oriented and the fantasy-oriented. Research-oriented subcultures regard some measure of historical accuracy in both Pagan belief and practice (insofar as these may be determined) as central to the reconceptual or reconstructive religious enterprise; historical accuracy in fantasy-oriented subcultures, on the other hand, is less important and, as Knight and Telesco amply demonstrate, for these the potential canon of belief and practice is expanded considerably.[32]

MODERN PAGAN ORGANIZATION AND WORKING PRACTICE

Solitaries and Working Groups

In broad terms, modern Pagan working practice occurs in two ways: as a solitary, working alone whether by chance or by choice, or in community, working as part of a more formal ritual group. The basic unit of modern Pagan social organization, ritual working groups are called by a variety of names. Following its conceptual inspiration in Robert Heinlein's science fiction novel, *A Stranger in a Strange Land*,[33] for example, for 40 years the Church of All Worlds, the oldest officially recognized modern Pagan group in North America, called its working groups "nests" and "proto-nests," a group of which may join together as a "branch." Ásatrúer gather together in "kindreds" or "hearths" for their ritual practices, which are called *blots* and *sumbels*.[34] Druids congregate in "groves" and "henges,"[35] while Wiccans and Witches, the most well-known of modern Pagans, tend to belong to "covens" or "circles."

"The coven," writes Starhawk in *The Spiral Dance,* one of the most influential modern Pagan texts of the past few decades, "is a Witch's support group, consciousness-raising group, psychic study center, clergy-training program, College of Mysteries, surrogate clan, and religious congregation all rolled into one."[36] Usually a relatively small group, especially when compared to some of the large congregations that gather in churches, synagogues, and mosques across the United States, the members of a coven often have a much more intimate relationship than that experienced by congregants in these other religious traditions. Given the still marginalized status of modern Paganism in many parts of the country, this intimacy is hardly surprising, born as it is from the religious bond the members feel in the Craft, as well as the trust they place in one another in order to share their beliefs and rites together. Unless they are related by lineage and commitment to a particular tradition—Gardnerian, for example, or Alexandrian—each coven functions as an autonomous group, responsible only to its members and to a set of principles founded on the most basic of Wiccan precepts, the Wiccan Rede: "An it harm none, do as thou wilt."[37] Usually guided by a High Priestess (and, in some but not all cases, a High Priest), they meet to perform rituals on the sabbats and esbats, to raise and release energy for spellworking when one or more of the coven feel the need, and to study and teach, which leads to the initiation of new coven mates.

Although they may belong to the same general tradition, it is important to note that, in keeping with the open source character of modern Paganism, not all groups function in similar ways. Indeed, disagreements over the interpersonal and organizational dynamics of ritual working groups have led to the disintegration of more than one coven, grove, or circle.[38] Sometimes, those who leave covens under strained circumstances never return to ritual group work. Instead, they choose to continue their magical lives as solitaries, answering only to themselves, their personal understanding of the modern Pagan path, and the demands of the particular deities to whom they are dedicated.

Some commentators suggest that most modern Pagans will spend at least a portion of their magical careers working alone.[39] The legitimacy of solitary practice, however, especially if one has never been a member of a coven or circle, is one of the most contentious issues between solitary Pagans and Pagan working groups. As I have noted elsewhere (in the context of the benefits offered by online interaction among modern Pagans), even though a solitary may have been initiated into a variety of traditions, many "feel that coveners (or those who practice in other kinds of ritual working group) consider them 'second-class Pagans,' as though they are somehow less authentic or less committed to the modern Pagan path if they are not part of a working lineage."[40] On the other hand, according to Scott Cunningham (1956–1993), whose books are extremely influential among modern Pagan solitaries, Wiccans should never feel "second-class" because they choose to work alone.

> Never feel inferior because you're not working under the guidance of a teacher or an established coven. Don't worry that you won't be recognized as a true Wiccan. Such recognition is important only in the eyes of those giving or withholding it, otherwise it is meaningless. You need only worry about pleasing yourself and developing a rapport with the Goddess and God.[41]

Two aspects are important to point out here: (a) the personal gnosticism that is characteristic of many modern Paganisms, which is in tension with (b) an incipient orthodoxy that claims to distinguish "authentic" from "inauthentic" Paganism. There is no overarching organizational authority to impose an orthodoxy on modern Pagan belief and practice, no standardized set of sacred texts to which practitioners may turn to ground them, and no practical limit to the stock of spiritual resources available for sampling and synthesis. So many modern Pagans feel free, essentially, to make up their religion as they go along. Thus, Cunningham's concept of "you need only worry about pleasing yourself" epitomizes the tacit agreement among many (arguably most) modern Pagans that the intuitive, intentional construction of one's own religious beliefs and the feeling of personal gnosis by which that construction is authorized are the principal criteria that determine genuine Pagan practice.

Despite modern Pagan openness to creativity and experimentation, there are signs that an incipient orthodoxy emerges when practitioners either feel that other Pagans are not taking their Paganism seriously or disapprove of the particular way in which some Pagans choose to construct their religious belief and practice. Sociologically speaking, the first group would be called "free riders," or "nightstand Pagans," those who bought a few books, who decided to call themselves Wiccans or Witches, but who have not demonstrated any significant commitment to a modern Pagan practice. They choose, in effect, to be Pagan because Paganism has a certain cultural attraction at the moment. The issue of an incipient orthodoxy, on the other hand, shows up when, despite the apparent and professed openness of modern Pagans, some religious choices appear to transgress the boundary between appropriate and inappropriate Pagan belief. This is seen most clearly when some modern Pagans incorporate Christian symbols, liturgical and devotional practice, or deity figures into their Paganism. Going so far as to call themselves Christian Witches, Christo-Wiccans, or Christopagans, the problem this presents for the open source egalitarian-ism of modern Paganism is discussed in the last section.

Larger Organizations

Paganism has organizations larger than covens and groves. These constitute ongoing attempts to institutionalize modern Paganism. The Church of All Worlds (CAW), for example, founded by Tim Zell (b. 1942), who now goes by the name Oberon Zell-Ravenheart,[42] was incorporated in 1968 as the first official modern Pagan Church in the United States and was officially chartered with the Internal Revenue Service two years later. The CAW is based on a principal belief called "the Gaia thesis" that all life on Earth is interconnected, indeed has its origin in "a single, fertil-ized cell."[43] According to Zell-Ravenheart, "the Gaia thesis, which is globally unifying and comprehensive, is *the* fundamental myth in Pagan culture ... the first unifying myth waiting to be universally adopted: the notion that we are all children of the same Mother."[44] Indeed, for members of the CAW, "everything that's wrong with our modern culture can be traced to our forgetting of this fundamental notion."[45] For more than 30 years, Zell-Ravenheart and his "waterkin," the word they use to describe fellow members of the CAW, published their ideas, artwork, poetry, and rituals in *The Green Egg*, which grew from a single mimeographed sheet to a respected journal in the modern Pagan community before closing due to financial pressure in 2001. Currently, though, with about three dozen nests and proto-nests in the United States, and affiliates in Australia, Europe, and on the Internet, the CAW remains one of the most well-known modern Pagan organizations in North America.

On the summer solstice in 1975, a confederation of covens was organized "to increase cooperation among Witches and to secure for Witches and covens the legal protection enjoyed by members of other religions."[46] According to Margot Adler, "thirteen covens and several solitary Witches ratified the Covenant of the Goddess (COG),"[47] the name by which the organization has been known ever since. A year earlier and after lengthy discussion, a group calling itself the Council of American Witches produced "The Principles of Wiccan Belief," a document that sought to lay the foundation for a larger modern Pagan organization. Beset by the differences that almost inevitably emerge when a group of strong individualists gather, the Council of American Witches was unable to organize efficiently or successfully beyond that.[48] "The Principles of Wiccan Belief," though, remain important for the larger organization of modern Paganism. COG, on the other hand, has had considerably more impact.

From its beginning, COG was clear that it had no authority to dictate policy to modern Pagans regarding belief, ritual, practice, or organization. Rather, it works on behalf of its membership to educate the public, to issue ministerial credentials, and to facilitate communication and cooperation among modern Pagans across North America and beyond. Perhaps its most public accomplishment to date was to participate as one of more than 200 religious groups cosponsoring the 1993 World Parliament of Religions in Chicago, Illinois. Pagan participation at the Parliament, however, did not go unnoticed. Indeed, it was a lightning rod for the real issues of religious difference that often lay hidden beneath declarations of tolerance. First, though a full participant in the Parliament, COG was denied permission by the city of Chicago to host a large ritual, a Full Moon dance, in Grant Park, near the conference hotel. When COG sought the help of both the American Civil Liberties Union and Parliament organizers, park officials relented, apologized, and permitted the ritual to take place. Indeed, Judy Harrow, a Gardnerian Witch and former first officer of the Covenant of the Goddess, points out that the ritual took place in precisely the same location as the 1968 Chicago police riot and became thereby a healing and reclaiming act.[49] Later that week, though, COG was in the news again, when several Greek and Russian Orthodox delegates withdrew from a variety of scheduled events, "citing the 'distinctive participation of certain quasi-religious groups.'"[50] Though unnamed, the Orthodox Christians clearly meant the modern Pagans. "As a result of both those things," recalls Harrow, "instead of being lost in the shuffle of this huge multireligious event, we ended up having attention focused on us. We became the hot topic. We became what the grapevine was buzzing about."[51] Most of COG's work is carried out through local councils, such as Northern Dawn in Minnesota, Pronghorn Moon in California, and Dogwood in Georgia. There is also an educational program dedicated to helping young people who are interested in modern Paganism, especially those who become interested through pop cultural products such as films like *The Craft* and television series such as *Charmed* and *Buffy the Vampire Slayer.*

As modern Pagans have come out of the broomcloset, both personally and culturally, many have discerned the need for a more professionalized and educated clergy to serve the growing Pagan population responsibly. Both the open source character of modern Paganism and the ready availability of mail-order (and e-mail-order) ministerial credentials have created a situation where anyone, regardless of training, skill, or even the most basic understanding of the helping professions, can become ordained and present themselves as priest or priestess, pastoral counselor, and teacher.[52] To address this, Harrow and a number of her colleagues founded Cherry Hill Seminary (CHS), which is designed not to teach the principles of magic, but the professional skills of pastoral care and counseling. That is, CHS is not a coven, and does not offer the degree of training one would receive in a coven setting. Rather, CHS is organized to respond to the needs of those who feel called to a more intentional ministry among modern Pagans, something that CHS founders regard as inevitable as modern Paganism grows in popularity. "The focus of CHS," reads the online description, "is to teach those specialized skills and knowledge necessary for serving in positions of community leadership: as a pastoral counselor, a chaplain, in public relations, as social services liaison, as a minister for public rites of passage, in interfaith work and in any other roles in which s/he will interact with governmental agencies and the non-Pagan community."[53] Though there are minimal residency requirements, in that students are expected to take part in a number of "on-campus intensives," most of the CHS curriculum is offered online. Logging in to courses such as "Human Development in a Pagan Context," "Children in Contemporary Paganism," and "Psychology of Religion Applied to Paganism," students and instructors interact via discussion forums and chat rooms, disseminate lectures and other course material electronically, and submit coursework through e-mail.

Modern Paganism on the Internet

While recognizing its undeniable advantages as well as its disadvantages, computer-mediated communication is one important way in which many modern Pagans interact both locally and globally. From a few online covens to hundreds of Yahoo! discussion forums, from relatively simple "My Wiccan Web Pages," that do little more than replicate modern Pagan material cut and pasted from other sites, to elaborate and original information spaces such as The Witches' Voice,[54] which is arguably the largest and most comprehensive Internet site devoted to modern Paganism, Wiccans, Witches, Druids, and Ásatrúer have successfully colonized their own portions of cyberspace. Though online Paganism is fraught with the same frustrations and limitations as any other computer-mediated communication—hardware or software failure, server overload or inaccessibility, the decontextualized nature of the communication itself, which not infrequently results in misunderstanding and damaged relationships—it is also clear that for many Pagan practitioners who go online regularly, the Internet provides significant benefit, especially in (a) the potential for modern Pagan community, and (b) the performance of modern Pagan identity.[55]

Though the social and cultural profile of modern Paganism has risen substantially in recent years, those who find themselves drawn to particular Pagan paths are still likely to experience a sense of isolation and alienation if there is no Wiccan or Witch to speak with locally. The nearest coven or ritual working group may be hundreds of miles away, or the potential Pagan may live in circumstances that preclude seeking out more direct contact. In these cases, the Internet is a tremendous boon, and many who use it regularly speak eloquently about the benefits of communicating with other modern Pagans, if only through the computer. As I note elsewhere, "one very common aspect of discussion threads among modern Pagans online, especially newcomers to the various traditions, is the sense of relief they display when participants find like-minded Wiccans, Witches, Druids, or Ásatrúer with whom they can exchange information, trade gossip and opinion, or share a sense of community."[56] With nearly 1600 members, for example, from Karlsuhe to Istanbul, Ontario to Arkansas, and Jordan to Wales, participants in the Yahoo! group Beginners Wicca regularly comment on the benefit they derive from their Internet communication. Although some may regard the modern Pagan Web as little more than "a global notice board for the privileged,"[57] its value cannot be underestimated for members of a religious community that still faces occasional marginalization and to which significant social stigma is still attached.

Thus, taking into account all the caveats about cyberpredation, the Internet also becomes a relatively safe environment for potential practitioners to "try on" their Paganism, to experiment with and, in many cases, establish a modern Pagan identity. Relatively few modern Pagans disclose significant personal information online. Thus, using Pagan rather than mundane names, they carry on conversations, express (or impose) opinion, present themselves as authorities wearing only the masks that they themselves have chosen. Who is to know whether "Lady Spiritwind" is the revered Wiccan elder she claims to be or simply an interested teenager playing an online role? On the other hand, if a young person is truly interested in the Pagan path, perhaps as a result of his love for famous fantasy author J. R. R. Tolkien, entering a discussion forum as "Treebeard" allows him to test the waters, without inviting undue attention to his emerging Pagan interests. As I observed in *Cyberhenge:*

> Through interaction in discussion groups, alt-lists, and chat rooms, identity testing and the reinforcement of modern Pagan authority occurs in readily identifiable discursive loops. Participants test their modern Pagan identities online as a function of moving from internal resonance [an affinity for modern Paganism] to external performance and conformation [the demonstration of one's modern Pagan affiliation]; other participants reinforce their identity as modern Pagan authorities by answering questions, providing resources, and weighing in on any topic available.[58]

CONTROVERSIES WITHIN THE CIRCLE AND WITHOUT

The history of many religious movements can be written from the perspective of the controversies that mark their emergence, development, and, in many cases, decline and disappearance. In the case of modern Paganism, consider three such controversies that have continued, and arguably will continue, to haunt its growth in North America: (a) misperceptions arising from lingering cultural stigma, ignorance, and fear, and which are often exacerbated by irresponsible media reporting and dedicated countermovement activity; (b) the sociological problem of generations succeeding one another through the passage of time, and the inevitable effect on the growth of a religious movement; and (c) the logical problems inherent in open source religion and the surfacing of an incipient orthodoxy among modern Pagans.

Common Myths: The Problem of Misperception

The single misperception that Wiccans and Witches work most diligently to dispel is that they do not worship Satan. This, however, is also arguably the most common misperception that continues to pervade uninformed discussion about modern Paganism. On the one hand, Pagans argue that, because Satan is a Christian theological construct and they are not Christians, charges that Witches and Wiccans worship Satan are absurd. Not only do they not worship him, they do not even believe he exists. On the other hand, taking a page from the infamous *Malleus Maleficarum,* the fifteenth-century manual for prosecuting suspected witches, many Christian opponents of modern Paganism contend either that Wiccans and Witches are simply lying or that they are deluded, either they worship Satan or they do so implicitly because Satan is the architect of all "false religion."[59] Not surprisingly, this kind of misinformation and prejudice has some very real consequences for modern Pagans.

First, it forces many to remain "in the broomcloset," afraid to reveal themselves as Wiccans or Witches precisely because they do not want to be accused of being Satan worshippers. Although she lives in a rural area known for its tolerance of new and alternative lifestyles, for example, one Wiccan solitary wrote that her reading of countercult author Texe Marrs pushed "all my panic buttons." "I no longer wanted to be out of the broom closet, with the risk of meeting someone like the author of this book. Fear, anger, and anger at being afraid have invaded my life in a way I have never experienced."[60] Second, it places Pagan parents in the precarious position of losing custody or visitation during divorce proceedings, a situation C. Barner-Barry cites as "one of the primary fears of Pagans who are parents of minor children."[61] Third, numerous Pagans have experienced workplace harassment, denial or termination of employment, and physical abuse on the basis of their religious beliefs.[62]

Linked to the uninformed belief that Witches or Wiccans worship Satan is the concomitant belief that they are practitioners of black magic and that they curse or cast spells on those whom they regard as enemies. Both of these contravene the most basic tenets of Pagan ethics—the Wiccan Rede and the Law of Threefold Return. In her excellent treatment of modern Paganism as a "minority faith in a majoritarian America," Barner-Barry chronicles a number of incidents in which schoolchildren, for example, were expelled or suspended for allegedly cursing or hexing their teachers and classmates. "The interesting thing about such cases," writes Barner-Barry, "is the readiness of school authorities to take seriously the ability of a student to cast effective spells or hex others;" teachers and principals "seemed startlingly ready to act on their personal superstitions with no real proof that an offense had been committed."[63] With the exception of television programs such as *Charmed, Bewitched, Sabrina the Teenage Witch,* and, to a lesser degree, *Buffy the Vampire Slayer,* the North American entertainment industry has done little to dispel the popular image of the witch as a harbinger of evil. With relatively few exceptions, Hollywood still regards the "wicked witch" as a screen staple, depicting her as capriciously dangerous (e.g., *The Craft*), homicidal (e.g., *The Blair Witch Project, Hocus Pocus*), or, in the case of any number of popular horror films, sexually predatious.

For hundreds of years, inappropriate sexual license was a common charge leveled at New Religious Movements (NRMs), and the various streams of modern Paganism are no exception. Three factors particularly contribute to the persistence of this misperception. First, dating back nearly 1000 years, a lengthy history of accusations of sexual predation against alleged Witches ensures that these charges are never far beneath the surface.[64] Second, many modern Pagans prefer to perform their rituals in the nude, or "sky-clad," and these rituals occasionally involve both sexual reference (e.g., the *hieros gamos,* or the Great Rite) and ecstatic dance, neither of which have escaped popular treatments of Wicca and Witchcraft.[65] Third, there is a tradition of sex magic in modern Paganism that derives from both its generally sex-positive attitude and the roots some Pagan groups have in ceremonial and ritual magic.[66]

Pagan Youth: The Problem of Generations

Sexuality and socialization are the lightning rods for the problem of Pagan generations. That is, how do Pagans keep their children safe from sexual predation while maintaining the generally sex- and body-positive atmosphere that characterizes modern Paganism as a whole, and how do they retain their youth as Wiccans, Witches, or Druids when these youth grow up and begin to ask their own religious questions?[67]

Before there was a discernible second-generation of modern Pagans, nudity at Pagan festivals and rituals was commonplace. Many Pagans regard clothing as both a barrier to a more intimate experience of nature and a material marker of the sex- and body-negative attitude of culturally dominant religions like Christianity. Nudity, on the other hand, whether general or ritualistic, signifies a healthy acceptance of the body as natural. As Sarah Pike notes in her work on modern Pagan festivals, quoting one Pagan: "A naked man has to be walking an inflated dinosaur to get anyone to pay attention to him."[68] With more and more children attending festivals, however, some organizers have felt the need to structure both clothing-optional portions of the event—some rituals are designated sky-clad, for example—and areas of the venue where clothing is not required. While many adult ritual groups still work sky-clad, family-style covens and circles have largely abandoned the practice, both to protect the youth from predation and to protect themselves from the kind of persecution described above.

Whether these youth will ultimately remain on the modern Pagan path is the question of religious socialization faced by every faith and tradition. It is worth remembering that, in the early years of modern Paganism in North America, most Wiccans or Witches had made the choice to convert from some other faith. Countless testimonies both in print and online reprise the participants' discomfort and unhappiness in the religion to which they were born, which is usually Christianity, and their sense of relief, of liberation, of "coming home" to a truer self when they discovered modern Paganism. From a sociological perspective, there is no reason to believe that this process of rebellion, rejection, seekership, and eventual conversion to an alien faith would not manifest within modern Paganism as well. That is, there is always the potential that modern Pagan youth will find their religious upbringing similarly unsatisfying and choose other paths—even fundamentalist Christian— which brings us to the final tension.

Christo-Pagans: The Problem of Open Source Religion

"If someone wants to blend pantheons of a couple of trads," writes one modern Pagan to an online discussion forum, "if that's what feels right to them, then so be it."[69] Barring strict reconstructionists, whose beliefs and practices are intentionally limited to what is historically demonstrable, a significant number of modern Pagans would agree with this comment. Indeed, Pagan primers are replete with suggestions for syncretizing and synthesizing elements of different pantheons.[70] This toleration holds until modern Pagan practitioners incorporate Christian symbols, practices, or deity figures into their modern Paganism. Then modern Paganism appears decidedly less tolerant.

In a 1996 editorial in *SageWoman*, a popular Pagan magazine, the editor revealed that in the midst of her Pagan practice she occasionally "[reaches] out to an old friend"—Jesus.[71] Though she was quick to reassure her readers that "the Goddess is here with me, as She has been since I was a little girl,"[72] reactions from a number of those readers was swift and unequivocal. "How dare you?!" wrote one reader named Autumn Storm, "I can think of nothing more tastelessly bizarre or despicably inappropriate than tossing out your reconciliation with christianity to readers who have supported this MATRIFOCAL, PAGAN, GODDESS magazine for ten years!"[73] While other readers were shocked at the outpouring of anger and vitriol, a number called for the editor to step down, though she did not. Rather, a year later, she published a retrospective on the conflict and pointed out that only about ten percent of the letters contained this kind of harsh criticism. Twice as many, she noted, were from readers "who were already holding these two traditions together in [their] hearts."[74] A similar controversy erupted in 2004, when *SageWoman* published a series of articles on prayer and invocation, and included a reference to "prayer beads," something to which a former Catholic convert to Paganism took particular exception. Though the article was entitled "Garlands for the Goddess: The Magic of Christian Prayer Beads,"[75] one reader expressed her concern "that this is Catholicism in disguise," and was "left wondering if *SageWoman* is, in fact, a *truly* Pagan magazine."[76] Comments such as these notwithstanding, there is some evidence that the synthesis of Christian and modern Pagan belief and practice appears to be growing.[77]

CONCLUSION

Whether the family of religious practitioners, groups, and movements that cluster under the rubric of modern Paganism are or remain among the fastest growing NRMs in North America is open to question. As a "minority faith in a majoritarian America" modern Pagans face an almost inevitable marginalization from elements of the dominant religion and culture. Despite this, however, Witches and Wiccans now conduct prison ministries, perform hospital chaplaincy, and serve on municipal interfaith councils. Modern Paganism is recognized as a valid religious belief by various branches of the government, including the military, and Wiccans in the armed forces are currently lobbying for permission to place pentagrams on the headstones of Pagan soldiers killed in action. It is clear, however, that for hundreds of thousands of Witches, Wiccans, Druids, Goddess-Worshippers, and Ásatrúer, the myriad paths of pre-Christian religions exercise a powerful call.

NOTES

1. Although there are a few basic frameworks, the details of modern Pagan ritual are often as varied as the groups that practice and range from detailed liturgies that are linked to particular traditions to *laissez-faire* constructions that exemplify both the creativity and the open source character of modern Paganism. See, for example, J. Farrar and S. Farrar, *Eight Sabbats for Witches, and Rites for Birth, Marriage and Death* (Custer, WA: Phoenix Publishing, 1981); J. Farrar and S. Farrar, *The Witches' Way: Principles, Rituals and Beliefs of Modern Witchcraft* (Custer, WA: Phoenix Publishing, 1984); S. Farrar, *What Witches Do: A Modern Coven Revealed*, 3rd ed. (Custer, WA: Phoenix Publishing, 1991).

2. City News Service, "Pagans," April 30, 2002, retrieved through LexisNexis; Reuters, "Witches say Christians Violated their Rights,"April 30, 2002; retrieved through LexisNexis.

3. H. Rosin, "An Army Controversy: Should the Witches Be Welcome? Flap over Wiccans Tests Military's Religious Tolerance," *Washington Post,* June 8, 1999, A01.

4. Ibid.

5. S. RavenWolf, *Teen Witch: Wicca for a New Generation* (St. Paul, MN: Llewellyn Publications, 1998). On instances of discrimination against Pagan students, see, for example, A. Gumbel, "Brandi the Teenage Witch—A True Story (Not that You'll Believe It)," *The Independent (London),* January 5, 2001, 1, 7; R. La Ferla, "Like Magic, Witchcraft Charms Teenagers," *The New York Times,* February 13, 2000, Sec. 9, 1; C. Rouvalis, "Witches and Wardrobes: Wicca Practitioners Support Brownsville Student in the Wearing of Symbolic Pentacle," *Pittsburgh Post-Gazette,* September 27, 2000, D-1. For an excellent discussion of the broader spectrum of discrimination against modern Pagans, see C. Barner-Barry,

Contemporary Paganism: Minority Faith in a Majoritarian America (New York: Palgrave Macmillan, 2005).

6. For at least a decade, and citing a wide variety of sources, many contemporary Pagans claim that their family of religious traditions—though most particularly Wicca—are among the fastest growing in the world; see, for example, R. Buckland, *Witchcraft from the Inside: Origins of the Fastest Growing Religious Movement in America,* 3rd ed. (St. Paul, MN: Llewellyn Publications, 1995); P. W. Curott, *Book of Shadows: A Modern Woman's Journey into the Wisdom of Witchcraft and the Magic of the Goddess* (New York: Broadway Books, 1998); R. Grimassi, *Spirit of the Witch: Religion and Spirituality in Contemporary Witchcraft* (St. Paul, MN: Llewellyn Publications, 2003); M. M. NightMare, *Witchcraft and the Web: Weaving Pagan Traditions Online* (Toronto: ECW Press, 2001); RavenWolf, *Teen Witch;* E. Restall Orr, *Druid Priestess: An Intimate Journey through the Pagan Year* (London: Thorsons, 1998). This general claim has been picked up and repeated without question by news media ranging from the mainstream press to online news services; see, for example, K. Burke, "No Rest for the Wicca—Growing Pagan Population Shows its Political Spirit," *Sydney Morning Herald,* June 30, 2003, News and Features, 3; J. Kiddle, "Every Witch Way," *The Scotsman,* October 31, 2005, 10; P. Rice, "In October, Spotlight Focuses on Neopagan Beliefs," *St. Louis Post-Dispatch,* October 27, 2001, 20; K. Winston, "The Witch Next Door," Beliefnet, www.beliefnet.com/story/155/ story_15517.html (accessed January 6, 2006); S. Woodward, "Paths to Paganism," *The Sunday Oregonian,* October 27, 2002, L01. It has been deployed by evangelical Christians as yet and again another dire cultural alarm, further evidence of the spiritual decline of late modern society; see, for example, B. Alexander, *Witchcraft Goes Mainstream* (Eugene, OR: Harvest House Publishers, 2004); T. Baker, *Dewitched: What You Need to Know about the Dangers of Witchcraft* (Nashville: Transit Books, 2004). And, finally, it has been reproduced almost without any further interrogation in recent academic publications on contemporary Paganism; see T. Foltz, "The Commodification of Witchcraft," in *Witchcraft and Magic: Contemporary North America,* ed. H. A. Berger (Philadelphia: University of Pennsylvania Press, 2005); D. Waldron, "Witchcraft for Sale! Commodity vs. Community in the Neopagan Movement," *Nova Religio* 9, no. 1 (2005): 31–48. For critical evaluations of these claims, see D. E. Cowan, "Count the Candles and Divide by Two: Methodological Considerations in the Quantification of Modern Paganism" (paper presented at the annual meeting of the Society for the Scientific Study of Religion, Rochester, NY, November 2005); D. E. Cowan, *Cyberhenge: Modern Pagans on the Internet* (New York and London: Routledge, 2005), especially 84–87, 193–198; D. E. Cowan, "Too Narrow and Too Close: Some Problems with Participant Observation in the Study of New Religious Movements," *Method & Theory in the Study of Religion* 10 (1998): 391–406.

7. Though they are written from a range of perspectives and vary substantially in quality, for a variety of academic and popular explorations of modern Paganism, see, for example, M. Adler, *Drawing Down the Moon: Witches, Druids, Goddess-Worshippers, and Other Pagans in American Today,* rev. ed. (Boston: Beacon Press, 1986); H. A. Berger, *A Community of Witches: Contemporary Neo-Paganism and Witchcraft in the United States* (Columbia, SC: University of South Carolina Press, 1999); H. A. Berger, E. A. Leach, and L. S. Shaffer, *Voices from the Pagan Census: A National Survey of Witches and Neo-Pagans in the United States* (Columbia, SC: University of South Carolina Press, 2003); J. Blain, D. Ezzy, and G. Harvey, eds., *Researching Paganisms* (Lanham, MD: AltaMira Press, 2004); C. S. Clifton, ed., *Living Between Two Worlds: Challenges of the Modern Witch* (St. Paul, MN: Llewellyn Publications, 1996); C. S. Clifton, ed., *The Modern Craft Movement: Witchcraft Today, Book One* (St. Paul, MN:

Llewellyn Publications, 1997); Cowan, *Cyberhenge;* M.D. Faber, *Modern Witchcraft and Psychoanalysis* (London and Toronto: Associated University Presses, 1993); S. Greenwood, *Magic, Witchcraft and the Otherworld: An Anthropology* (Oxford: Berg, 2000); W. J. Hanegraaff, *New Age Religion and Western Culture: Esotericism in the Mirror of Secular Thought* (Leiden and New York: E.J. Brill, 1996); P. Heelas, *The New Age Movement: The Celebration of the Self and the Sacralization of Modernity* (Oxford: Blackwell Publishers, 1996); R. Hutton, *The Triumph of the Moon: A History of Modern Pagan Witchcraft* (Oxford: Oxford University Press, 1999); R. Hutton, *Witches, Druids, and King Arthur* (London: Hambledon and London, 2003); T.M. Luhrmann, *Persuasions of the Witches' Craft: Ritual Magic in Contemporary England* (Cambridge, MA: Harvard University Press, 1989); S. Magliocco, *Witching Culture: Folklore and Neo-Paganism in America* (Philadelphia: University of Pennsylvania Press, 2004); K. Marron, *Witches, Pagans, & Magic in the New Age* (Toronto: Seal Books, 1989); L. Orion, *Never Again the Burning Times: Paganism Revived* (Prospect Heights, IL: Waveland Press, 1995); S.M. Pike, *Earthly Bodies, Magical Selves: Contemporary Pagans and the Search for Community* (Berkeley and Los Angeles: University of California Press, 2001); S.M. Pike, *New Age and Neopagan Religions in America* (New York: Columbia University Press, 2004); J. Salomonsen, *Enchanted Feminism: The Reclaiming Witches of San Francisco* (London and New York: Routledge); G.G. Scott, *Cult and Countercult: A Study of a Spiritual Growth Group and a Witchcraft Order* (Westport, CT: Greenwood Press, 1980); M. York, *The Emerging Network: A Sociology of the New Age and Neo-Pagan Movements* (Lanham, MD: Rowman & Littlefield Publishers, 1995).

8. See P. Heselton, *Wiccan Roots: Gerald Gardner and the Modern Witchcraft Revival* (Somerset, UK: Capall Bann Publishing, 2000), 226–260.

9. In 1949, Gardner published *High Magic's Aid,* an historical novel, under the pseudonym, Scire. Following the repeal of the Witchcraft Acts, he published openly *Witchcraft Today* in 1954 and *The Meaning of Witchcraft* in 1959. See G.B. Gardner, *High Magic's Aid* ([1949] Hinton, WV: Godolphin House, 1996); G.B. Gardner, *Witchcraft Today* ([1954] New York: Citadel Press, 2004); G.B. Gardner, *The Meaning of Witchcraft* (London: Aquarian Press, 1959).

10. On this dispute, see Hutton, *Triumph of the Moon,* 205–252; A. Kelly, *Crafting the Art of Magic: Book 1* (St. Paul, MN: Llewellyn Publications, 1991).

11. In what some modern Pagans have come to regard as British Traditional Witchcraft, though there is dispute even about this, Gardnerians are those who are initiated into and follow the Pagan path laid down by Gardner, considered by most the founder of the modern Witchcraft movement. Alexandrians, on the other hand, are adherents of the tradition established by Alex Sanders (1926–1988) and his wife and high priestess, Maxine (b. 1946), after they came into possession of a copy of Gardner's *Book of Shadows* (Farrar and Farrar, *The Witches' Way,* 245). On Gardner, see P. Crowther, *High Priestess: The Life & Times of Patricia Crowther* (Custer, WA: Phoenix Publishing, 1998); Farrar and Farrar, *The Witches' Way;* Gardner, *High Magic's Aid;* Gardner, *Witchcraft Today;* Gardner, *The Meaning of Witchcraft;* Heselton, *Wiccan Roots;* Hutton, *Triumph of the Moon.* On Sanders, see Crowther, *High Priestess;* Farrar, *What Witches Do;* J. Johns, *King of the Witches: The World of Alex Sanders* (New York: Coward-McCann, 1970).

12. Farrar and Farrar, *The Witches' Way,* 244; cf. R. Buckland, *The Witch Book: The Encyclopedia of Witchcraft, Wicca, and Neo-paganism* (Detroit: Visible Ink Press, 2002), 254–256.

13. See, for example, S. Cunningham, *Wicca: A Guide for the Solitary Practitioner* (St. Paul, MN: Llewellyn Publications, 1988); Farrar and Farrar, *The Witches' Way*, 244–250; M. Green, *A Witch Alone: Thirteen Moons to Master Natural Magic* (London: Thorsons, 1991).

14. In an effort to more carefully differentiate modern Paganism as a distinct religious culture, a few scholars have begun to consider it from a theological standpoint, rather than the historical or sociological. Though he eschews the qualifier "modern" or "contemporary," York contends that the majority of religious traditions around the world either have Pagan roots or manifest Pagan religious behavior. Paper, on the other hand, takes York to task for not following his argument through to its logical conclusion. See J. D. Paper, *The Deities Are Many: A Polytheistic Theology* (Albany: State University of New York Press, 2005); M. York, *Pagan Theology: Paganism as a World Religion* (New York: New York University Press, 2003).

15. See H. A. Berger, E. A. Leach, and L. S. Schaffer, *Voices from the Pagan Census: A National Survey of Witches and Neo-Pagans in the United States* (Columbia, SC: University of South Carolina Press, 2003).

16. Cowan, *Cyberhenge*, 71.

17. Ibid., 72.

18. Farrar and Farrar, *The Witches' Way*, 105.

19. Ibid., 105.

20. L. Cabot and T. Cowan, *Power of the Witch* (New York: Delta Books, 1989), 150.

21. Ibid., 150–151. For other attempts to conceptualize modern Pagan practice as an empirical science, see P. E. I. Bonewits, *Real Magic: An Introductory Treatise on the Basic Principles of Yellow Light*, rev. ed. (York Beach, ME: Red Wheel/Weiser, 1989); W. H. Keith, *The Science of the Craft: Modern Realities in the Ancient Art of Witchcraft* (New York: Citadel Press, 2005).

22. According to the Farrars, "The Christian Nativity story is the Christian version of the theme of the Sun's rebirth, for Christ is the Sun-God of the Piscean Age. The birthday of Jesus is undated in the Gospels, and it was not till AD 273 that the Church took the symbolically sensible step of fixing it officially at midwinter, to bring him in line with the other Sun-Gods (such as the Persian Mithras, also born at the Winter Solstice" (Farrar and Farrar, *Eight Sabbats for Witches*, 137–138). See also J. Matthews, *The Winter Solstice: The Sacred Traditions of Christmas* (Wheaton, IL: Quest Books, 1998).

23. See, for example, Salomonsen, *Enchanted Feminism*, 180–181.

24. See Farrar and Farrar, *Eight Sabbats for Witches*, 48–54.

25. Ibid., 49, emphases in the original.

26. See Cowan, *Cyberhenge*, 30–35. The open source revolution in computer programming, which led to the invention and ongoing development of the Linux operating system, for example, is based on the principle that the source codes, the basic building blocks of computer software, are available to everyone. This allows each user to tailor the software to his or her very specific needs. Closed source programming like Microsoft products, on the other hand, do not allow this kind of access, and the software must be used exactly as it is supplied by the manufacturer.

27. Ibid., 30.

28. See, for example, L. Aldred, "Plastic Shamans and Astroturf Sundances: New Age Commercialization of Native American Spirituality," *American Indian Quarterly* 24, no. 3 (2000): 329–352.

29. S. Knight and P. Telesco, *The Cyber Spellbook: Magick in the Virtual World* (Franklin Lakes, NJ: New Page Books, 2002), 48.

30. Ibid., 48).

31. G.L. Ebersole, *Ritual Poetry and Politics of Death in Early Japan* (Princeton: Princeton University Press, 1989), 6.

32. Cowan, *Cyberhenge,* 40–41.

33. R.A. Heinlein, *Stranger in a Strange Land* (New York: Putnam, 1961).

34. A *blot* is a ritual exchange with the gods, usually of mead or ale. In the same way that the sharing of food and drink builds and strengthens the relationships between human beings, Ásatrúer believe that this exchange reinforces their relationship with the gods. A *sumbel,* on the other hand, is a series of ritualized toasts, often accompanied by boasts, oaths to the gods, and the reading or recitation of the *Eddas,* the sacred texts of Norse heathenry. On various aspects of northern European paganism and heathenry, see Adler, *Drawing Down the Moon,* 273–282; J. Blain, *Nine Worlds of Seid-Magic: Ecstasy and Neo-Shamanism in North European Paganism* (London and New York: Routledge, 2002); G. Harvey, *Contemporary Paganism: Listening People, Speaking Earth* (New York: New York University Press, 1997), especially 53–68; G. Harvey, "Heathenism: A North European Pagan Tradition," in *Paganism Today,* ed. C. Hardman and G. Harvey (London: Thorsons, 1996); J. Kaplan, "The Reconstruction of the Ásatrú and Odinist Traditions," in *Magical Religion and Modern Witchcraft,* ed. J.R. Lewis (Albany: State University of New York Press, 1996).

35. For a variety of perspectives on modern Druidry, see P. Carr-Gomm, *The Elements of the Druid Tradition* (Shaftesbury, UK: Element, 1991); P. Carr-Gomm, *In the Grove of the Druids: The Druid Teachings of Ross Nichols* (London: Watkins Publishing, 2002); P. Carr-Gomm, ed., *The Druid Renaissance: The Voice of Druidry Today* (London: Thorsons, 1996); Harvey, *Contemporary Paganism: Listening People, Speaking Earth,* especially 17–34; E.E. Hopman and L. Bond, *People of the Earth: The New Pagans Speak Out* (Rochester, VT: Destiny Books, 1996), especially 1–34; R. Hutton, *Witches, Druids and King Arthur* (London and New York: Hambledon and London, 2003), especially 239–258; P. Shallcrass, "Druidry Today," in *Paganism Today,* ed. C. Hardman and G. Harvey (London: Thorsons, 1996).

36. Starhawk, *The Spiral Dance: A Rebirth of the Ancient Religion of the Great Goddess* (San Francisco: Harper and Row, 1979), 35.

37. On the Wiccan Rede and modern Pagan ethics, see C.S. Clifton, "What has Alexandria to do with Boston? Some Sources of Modern Pagan Ethics," in *Magical Religion and Modern Witchcraft,* ed. Lewis, 269–275; S.T. Rabinovitch and M. Macdonald, *An Ye Harm None: Magical Morality and Modern Ethics* (New York: Citadel Press, 2004).

38. See, for example, A-M. Gallagher, "Woven Apart and Weaving Together: Conflict and Mutuality in Feminist and Pagan Communities," in *Daughters of the Goddess: Studies of Healing, Identity, and Empowerment,* ed. W. Griffin (Lanham, MD: AltaMira Press, 2000), 42–58; S.L. Reid, "Witch Wars: Factors Contributing to Conflict in Canadian Neopagan Communities," *The Pomegranate* 11 (Winter 2000): 10–20.

39. Cabot and Cowan, *Power of the Witch,* 111–112; S.L. Reid, "Solitary," in *The Encyclopedia of Modern Witchcraft and Neo-Paganism*, ed. S. Rabinovitch and J. Lewis (New York: Citadel Press, 2002), 252.

40. Cowan, *Cyberhenge,* 82–83.

41. Cunningham, *Wicca,* 53–54. On Cunningham himself, see D. Harrington and D. Regula, *Whispers of the Moon: The Life and Work of Scott Cunningham, Philosopher-Magician, Modern-day Pagan* (St. Paul, MN: Llewellyn Publications, 1997). On solitary Pagan practice, see also, for example, R. Beth, *Hedge Witch: A Guide to Solitary Witchcraft* (London: Robert Hale, 1990); R. Beth, *The Wiccan Path: A Guide for the Solitary Practitioner* (Freedom, CA: The Crossing Press, 1990); S. Cunningham, *Living Wicca: A Further Guide for the Solitary*

Practitioner (St. Paul, MN: Llewellyn Publications, 1993); F. De Grandis, *Goddess Initiation: A Practical Celtic Program for Soul-Healing, Self-Fulfillment, and Wild Wisdom* (New York: HarperSanFrancisco, 2001); S. RavenWolf, *Solitary Witch: The Ultimate Book of Shadows for the New Generation* (St. Paul, MN: Llewellyn Publications, 2003).

42. See Hopman and Bond, *People of the Earth,* 217–223; V. Vale and J. Sulak, *Modern Pagans: An Investigation of Contemporary Pagan Practices* (San Francisco: Re/Search Publications, 2001), 130–153. Zell-Ravenheart's own understanding of the modern Pagan path is best exemplified in O. Zell-Ravenheart and the Grey Council, *Grimoire for the Apprentice Wizard* (Franklin Lakes, NJ: New Page Books, 2004).

43. Zell-Ravenheart, in Vale and Sulak, *Modern Pagans,* 137.

44. Ibid., 137.

45. Ibid., 137.

46. "About the Covenant of the Goddess," www.cog.org/aboutcog.html (accessed January 16, 2006). See also Adler, *Drawing Down the Moon,* 103–105; Hopman and Bond, *People of the Earth,* 249–280; Vale and Sulak, *Modern Pagans,* 94–107.

47. Adler, *Drawing Down the Moon,* 103.

48. See Ibid., 101–103

49. J. Harrow, personal communication with author, January 21, 2006.

50. D. Lattin, "World Conference of Religions Tests Tolerance for Fringe Faiths," *San Francisco Chronicle,* September 2, 1993, A1.

51. Harrow, in Hopman and Bond, *People of the Earth,* 253.

52. On the specific problems with this, especially as they relate to online ordination and the instantiation of modern Pagan identity, see Cowan, *Cyberhenge,* 88–90, 185–191.

53. "FAQ," http://cherryhillseminary.org/faq.html (accessed January 17, 2006).

54. See www.witchvox.com.

55. For a fuller discussion of modern Paganism on the Internet, see Cowan, *Cyberhenge.*

56. Ibid., 199.

57. Sant, "Paganism and the Net: Oil and Water?" *Circle Network News* 62 (Winter 1996): 18.

58. Cowan, *Cyberhenge,* 172.

59. For a variety of evangelical countercult responses to modern Paganism, see Alexander, *Witchcraft Goes Mainstream;* Baker, *Dewitched;* C.S. Hawkins, *Witchcraft: Exploring the World of Wicca* (Grand Rapids, MI: Baker Books, 1996); C.S. Hawkins, *Goddess-Worship, Witchcraft and Neo-Paganism* (Grand Rapids, MI: Zondervan, 1998); D. Hunt, *Occult Invasion: The Subtle Seduction of the World and the Church* (Eugene, OR: Harvest House Publishers, 1998); B. Larson, *Larson's Book of Spiritual Warfare* (Nashville: Thomas Nelson, 1999); B. Larson, *Satanism: The Seduction of American's Youth* (Nashville: Thomas Nelson, 1989); T. Marrs, *Texe Marrs Book of New Age Cults and Religions* (Austin, TX: Living Truth Publishers, 1990); W. Schnoebelen, *Wicca: Satan's Little White Lie* (Chino, CA: Chick Publications, 1990).

60. L.J. Doerksen, "Book review of *New Age Cults* by Texe Marsden [sic]," *Hecate's Loom* 29 (Lammas 1995): 37–38.

61. Barner-Barry, *Contemporary Paganism,* 116; cf. 116–127.

62. Ibid., 147–171.

63. Ibid., 132.

64. See, for example, L. Paine, *Sex in Witchcraft* (New York: Taplinger Publishing Company, 1972); B. Walker, *Sex and the Supernatural: Sexuality in Religion and Magic* (N.p.:

Castle Books, 1970); G. Wellesley, *Sex and the Occult* (New York: Bell Publishing Company, 1973).

65. See, for example, A. Kemp, *Witchcraft and Paganism Today* (London: Brockhampton Press, 1993).

66. See, for example, A. Crowley, L.M. Duquette, and C.S. Hyatt, *Enochian World of Aleister Crowley: Enochian Sex Magic* (Tempe, AZ: New Falcon Publications, 1991); U.D. Frater, *Secrets of Sex Magic: A Practical Handbook for Men and Women* (St. Paul, MN: Llewellyn Publications, 1995); J.G. Hughes, *Celtic Sex Magic For Couples, Groups, and Solitary Practitioners* (Rochester, VT: Destiny Books, 2001); S. Knight, *Moonflower: Erotic Dreaming with the Goddess* (St. Paul, MN: Llewellyn Publications, 1996); D.M. Kraig, *Modern Sex Magick: Secrets of Erotic Spirituality* (St. Paul, MN: Llewellyn Publications, 1998); P.B. Randolph, *Sexual Magic,* trans. R. North (New York: Magickal Childe Publishing, 1988); N. Schreck and Z. Schreck, *Demons of the Flesh: The Complete Guide to Left Hand Path Sex Magic* (London: Creation Books, 2002).

67. For an excellent collection of essays on this topic as it concerns a variety of NRMs, see S.J. Palmer and C.E. Hardman, eds., *Children in New Religions* (New Brunswick, NJ, and London: Rutgers University Press, 1999); see especially H.A. Berger, "Witches: The Next Generation," 11–28.

68. Pike, *Earthly Bodies, Magical Selves,* 204; cf. 203–207.

69. Erin, electronic communication to Celtic-Cauldron, Yahoo! discussion group (November 15, 2002).

70. On some of the problems with this, see P.B. Thomas, "Re-Imagining Inanna: The Gendered Reappropriation of the Ancient Goddess in Modern Goddess Worship," *The Pomegranate: The International Journal of Pagan Studies* 6, no. 1 (2004): 53–69.

71. A.N. Niven, "Living the Dream: Editorial Musings," *SageWoman* 35 (Autumn 1996): 4.

72. Ibid., 4.

73. Autumn Storm, Letter to the editor. *SageWoman* 36 (Autumn 1996): 85.

74. A.N. Niven, "The Rattle Begins with a Response from Anne to the Ongoing Controversy about Jesus and the Goddess…" *SageWoman* 39 (Autumn 1997): 80–81.

75. C.D. Cooper, "Garlands for the Goddess: The Magic of Pagan Prayer Beads," *SageWoman* 64 (2004): 27–33.

76. J. Canaway, Letter to the editor. *SageWoman* 64 (2004): 84–85.

77. A number of online discussion forums have been formed that are dedicated to the synthesis of aspects of Christianity and Paganism. See also R.E. Kuykendall, "Where Christian Liturgy and Neo-Pagan Ritual Meet," in *Magical Religion and Modern Witchcraft,* ed. Lewis, 327–337; C.J. Manning, "Embracing Jesus *and* the Goddess: Towards a Reconceptualization of Conversion to Syncretistic Religion," in *Magical Religion and Modern Witchcraft,* ed. Lewis, 299–326; C. McColman, *Embracing Jesus and the Goddess: A Radical Call for Spiritual Sanity* (Gloucester, MA: Fair Winds Press, 2001); N.C. Pittman, *Christian Wicca: The Trinitarian Tradition* (N.p.: 1st Books Library, 2003); The Reverend B, "Priestess and Pastor: Serving Between the Worlds," in *Living Between Two Worlds: Challenges of the Modern Witch,* ed. C.S. Clifton (St. Paul, MN: Llewellyn Publications, 1996), 61–86.

FURTHER READING

Adler, M. *Drawing Down the Moon: Witches, Druids, Goddess-Worshippers, and Other Pagans in American Today.* Rev. ed. Boston, Beacon Press, 1986.

Berger, H. A. *A Community of Witches: Contemporary Neo-Paganism and Witchcraft in the United States.* Columbia, SC: University of South Carolina Press, 1999.

Berger, H.A., E.A. Leach, and L.S. Shaffer. *Voices from the Pagan Census: A National Survey of Witches and Neo-Pagans in the United States.* Columbia, SC: University of South Carolina Press, 2003.

Blain, J., D. Ezzy, and G. Harvey, eds. *Researching Paganisms.* Lanham, MD: AltaMira Press, 2004.

Buckland, R. *The Witch Book: The Encyclopedia of Witchcraft, Wicca, and Neo-paganism.* Detroit: Visible Ink Press, 2002.

Cowan, D.E. *Cyberhenge: Modern Pagans on the Internet.* New York and London: Routledge, 2005.

Farrar, S. *What Witches Do: A Modern Coven Revealed.* 3rd ed. Custer, WA: Phoenix Publishing, 1991.

Heselton, P. *Wiccan Roots: Gerald Gardner and the Modern Witchcraft Revival.* Somerset, UK: Capall Bann Publishing, 2000.

Luhrmann, T.M. *Persuasions of the Witches' Craft: Ritual Magic in Contemporary England.* Cambridge, MA: Harvard University Press, 1989.

Magliocco, S. *Witching Culture: Folklore and Neo-Paganism in America.* Philadelphia: University of Pennsylvania Press, 2004.

Paper, J.D. *The Deities Are Many: A Polytheistic Theology.* Albany: State University of New York Press, 2005.

Pike, S.M. *Earthly Bodies, Magical Selves: Contemporary Pagans and the Search for Community.* Berkeley and Los Angeles: University of California Press, 2001.

———. *New Age and Neopagan Religions in America.* New York: Columbia University Press, 2004.

RavenWolf, S. *Teen Witch: Wicca for a New Generation.* St. Paul, MN: Llewellyn Publications, 1998.

Salomonsen, J. *Enchanted Feminism: The Reclaiming Witches of San Francisco.* London and New York: Routledge, 2002.

Vale, V., and J. Sulak. *Modern Pagans: An Investigation of Contemporary Pagan Practices.* San Francisco: Re/Search Publications, 2001.

York, M. *Pagan Theology: Paganism as a World Religion.* New York: New York University Press, 2003.

Zell-Ravenheart, O., and the Grey Council. *Grimoire for the Apprentice Wizard.* Franklin Lakes, NJ: New Page Books, 2004.

Learning about Paganism

Helen A. Berger

Neopaganism is not a religion of "the Book," but a religion of books. It is through the printed word and within the past decade through Web sites that most Neopagans learn about their religion. Since most American Neopagans are solitary practitioners,[1] books, Web sites, and public teachers are particularly important in transmitting information about the religion. Covens, groves, and groups are important as well, as they were traditionally the source of training and continue to be one of the sources for new adherents to learn about the religion. But Neopagans are readers, and even those trained in groups, nonetheless, read books about their religion, mythology related to their spiritual practice, and the spiritual practices of indigenous peoples. Through writing books, publishing magazines, maintaining Web sites, leading workshops, and organizing festivals, Neopagan elders and groups most clearly make their mark on the religion.

Neopaganism encompasses different traditions or spiritual paths. Some of these traditions are oriented toward a particular historic and geographic area. For example, Druids focus on historic Celtic practices, and Ásatrú worship the Norse pantheon. Others, such as Gardnerians or Alexandrians, perpetuate the teachings of a particular individual. Gardnerians trace their lineage back to the original coven of Gerald Gardner (1884–1964). Each Gardnerian teacher was herself or himself trained in a coven that traces back to either Gardner or someone within his original coven. Gardner is credited with creating Wicca in the 1930s in Great Britain.[2] Alexandrians trace their history back to Alex Sanders (1926–1988) who received training in Gardnerian Wicca, then created a variant. Several different forms of Wicca are practiced in the United States. When I began my research in 1986, Neopagans commonly used the terms *Witch* and *Wiccan* interchangeably. Today a distinction is usually made between Witches and Wiccans; only those trained in an initiatory tradition are considered Wiccans. Some individuals, however, are self-initiated, having learned about Wicca through books and the Internet.

It is a cliché among Neopagans and scholars of Neopaganism that an exception can be found to almost any generalization about the religion and its practitioners.

This is because Neopaganism has no central organization or dogma to determine theology, practice, or even membership. Most forms of Neopaganism are experiential; that is, they emphasize individuals' unmediated encounters with the spiritual world gained in or outside of ritual through a series of techniques, such as meditation, drumming, or dancing. Each person is considered an authority on her or his own spiritual experience and hence on her or his interpretation of and relationship with the divine, the other world, or the mystical. Douglas Cowan,[3] applying a computer term, has dubbed Neopaganism an "open source" religion. Open source programming is "software for which the basic building blocks—the source code—is freely available for modification.… Open source traditions are those which encourage (or at least do not discourage) theological and ritual innovation based on either individual intuition or group consensus, and which innovation is not limited to priestly classes, institutional elites, or religious virtuosi."[4] Because of the lack of dogma and the belief in each person having direct access to the divine, anyone can contribute to and change Neopagan practices and beliefs. However, in practice most groups and individual practitioners have many similarities.[5] These similarities often result from individuals having read the same books, attended the same festivals, and participated in the same Internet sites and chat rooms.

Traditionally Witchcraft, Wicca, and other forms of Neopaganism are taught in covens for Witches, groves for Druids, or other groups for other forms of Neopaganism. Knowledge is passed down by elders in the religion to newcomers. These groups tend to be small, easily formed, and easily terminated, although people remain within the same social circles, resulting in former coven mates sometimes continuing to work together, even forming a new coven or group after the old one disbands. Normally for Witches and Wiccans—and commonly among other forms of Neopaganism—teaching within groups is given at no charge to learners. Among Wiccans it is considered the duty of those who have been trained without cost in a coven to in turn teach others for free. Although teaching remains free within most if not all covens, some Witches are now charging for training in courses given outside the coven. In *Voices from the Pagan Census*[6] my colleagues and I found that most American Neopagans, in theory, support the concept of paid clergy. Few, however, give money to support clergy or organizations. Most of the money exchanged for learning is through courses at adult education centers, at occult bookstores, through the mail, or on the Internet. In some cases training occurs at festivals or retreats.

Coven and group learning continues today, but with the growth of solitary practitioners such learning is more and more the minority form of training. The success of publications and ultimately other forms of media in spreading information about the religion has ramifications for the methods of training among the next cohort of practitioners. As Douglas Ezzy[7] demonstrates, this has resulted, on the one hand, in the democratization of instruction. Any one with a library card, or more recently access to the Internet, can learn about most if not all Neopagan traditions. On the other hand, such learning is devoid of face-to-face relationships as exist in covens and instead becomes mediated by the market. The growth of market relationships is further evidenced by the number of teachers who charge for lessons.[8] Spiritual teachers requiring payment is still controversial within Neopagan circles but, nonetheless, is increasingly common. Less controversial are Witches and other Neopagans writing how-to books, some of which are popular enough to generate an income. Journals and magazines, which often play an important role within the Neopagan movement, may sometimes generate money for those who produce them but at other times are subsidized by groups and have not been able to generate money.

BOOKS AND MAGAZINES

Green Egg, which was published by the Church of All Worlds (CAW) from 1968 until 2001, played a central role in helping to create the nascent Neo-Pagan movement out of a set of spiritual ideas including the notions of nature as sacred, the divine as immanent, and a belief in an alternative reality. Most of these spiritual paths also invoke multiple deities, or at least the god and the goddess. *Green Egg* popularized the term "Neo-Pagan," giving the movement its name, and more importantly through its articles and its policy of publishing unedited letters gave the movement a public forum.[9] The magazine was also a recruitment tool for CAW, which takes it name from the classic science fiction novel of 1961 by Robert Heinlein, *Stranger in a Strange Land.* CAW's form of Neopaganism combines elements of libertarianism, science fiction, and environmentalism.[10] The magazine made editor Tim Zell (b. 1942) into a major figure in the Neopagan world, who is often quoted in other Pagan's publications and is a welcome speaker at Neopagan gatherings.

Other groups subsequently began newsletters and magazines, each of which contributed to the creation of a national, and at times an international, community of Neopagans. *WomanSpirit,* which began publication in 1974, was the earliest to appeal to the growing women's spirituality movement.[11] "Put out four times a year from Oregon the writing staff consisted of changing collectives of women in different states and so reflected the ferment that women were experiencing across the county. It provided a forum for women to explore their spirituality through poetry, art, prose, discussions, and descriptions of women's rituals that were growing in popularity."[12] Other journals, for example, *SageWoman,* followed *WomanSpirit's* lead in providing information and a forum for the women's spirituality movement. Although not all within the women's spirituality movement are Neopagans—some remaining firmly within Judaism or Christianity—an important section of this movement are Feminist Witches.[13] Zsuzsanna Budapest (b. 1940), a Hungarian immigrant who helped to create a women's only form of Wicca, in which the goddess was worshipped to the exclusion of the god force, was one of the earliest and strongest voices of Feminist or Dianic Witchcraft. Budapest gained notoriety after *Ms. Magazine* featured a story about her being arrested for reading Tarot cards, which at the time was illegal in California, the state where she lived. The article also helped to spread information about the growing feminist spirituality movement. In *The Grandmother of Time* Budapest, remembering her first goddess circle with six friends, asserted that the other women "just came to try it out, to find out if it had any validity for feminist women. We did agree that we cannot work toward liberation as long as our inner selves remain unchanged. Liberation has to begin inside; liberation has to be getting past the fears of taking our own power."[14] For Dianic Witches, the goddess is the symbol of women's empowerment. The veneration of the goddess is intertwined with women's growing awareness of their subjugation in Western culture.

Traditionally Wicca was based on balancing male and female energies. Gardner spoke of the perfect coven being 13: the high priestess, six men and six women. Budapest not only eliminated the need for gender balance but provided a different mythology for the circle of the year—one that eliminated the need for god. In traditional Wiccan mythology the god is transformed from the goddess's son born to her at Yule (December 21), to her consort at Beltaine (May 1), her dead lover at Samhain (October 31), and ultimately in rebirth the following Yule to her son again. The changes in the relationship between the goddess and the god mirror changes in nature from the stirring of life in the midst of winter, to fertility in spring, to death in the fall, and ultimately to rebirth the following spring. Within Dianic Witchcraft the cycle of the year focuses only on the changes of the Goddess from maid, to mother, to crone. Budapest also questioned the Rule of Return. The Wiccan Rede—do as thou will as long as thou harm none—and its corollary—whatever you send out will be returned three times—are the bases of ethical behavior within the religion. Budapest argued that if a Witch cannot curse she cannot cure and that women are justified in cursing rapists and abusers.[15]

Although influenced by Wicca, women-only Witchcraft groups came into conflict with more traditional Witchcraft groups.[16] Some of the early conflict was displayed in the letters to *Green Egg*.[17] Although tensions continue to exist between women's only or feminist Witchcraft and more traditional Witchcraft, these have decreased over the years. Miriam Simos (b. 1951), who is better known by her magical name Starhawk, was an important figure in decreasing these tensions. In her first book, *The Spiral Dance*,[18] Starhawk bridged the gap between traditional Wicca and Feminist Witchcraft. Starhawk is an initiated Witch trained both in the Faery Tradition, a form of Wicca, and in Feminist Witchcraft by Budapest. Starhawk is one of the founders of the Reclaiming Tradition, which is feminist, activist, nonhierarchical, and inclusive of both men and women. In the *Spiral Dance* and in her subsequent books, *Dreaming the Dark* and *Truth and Dare*,[19] Starhawk was interested in spreading information about Witchcraft, not specifically teaching the Reclaiming Tradition. In her introduction to the *Spiral Dance* she states: "The myths, underlying philosophy and 'thealogy'[20] ... in this book are based on the Faery Tradition. Other Witches may disagree with details, but the overall values and attitudes expressed are common to all of the Craft."[21]

Starhawk's presentation of Witchcraft blends the Feminist Witches' emphasis on the Goddess with Wiccan rituals, magical practices, and ethics. In describing the Goddess's meaning for men and women within Witchcraft, Starhawk writes:

> The Goddess is the "end of desire," its origin and its completion. In Witchcraft, desire is itself seen as a manifestation of the Goddess. We do not seek to conquer or escape from our desires—we seek to fulfill them.... Fulfillment becomes, not a matter of self-indulgence, but of self-awareness. For women, the Goddess is the symbol of the inmost

self, and the beneficent nurturing, liberating power within woman.... The Goddess does not limit women to the body; She awakens the mind and spirit and emotions. Through Her, we can know the power of our anger and aggression, as well as the power of our love ... for a man the Goddess as well as being the universal life force is his own hidden female self.... He may chase Her forever, and She will elude him, but through the attempt he will grow, until he too learns to find Her within.[22]

Like Feminist Witches, Starhawk views the goddess as empowering to women, putting them in touch not only with images of nurturing, loving women but also with female warriors. However, unlike Budapest's model of goddess worship, for Starhawk men too are included. According to Starhawk the goddess is not just part of women, but is part of men as well. As with all forms of Witchcraft the female aspect of the divine is referred to as the goddess. She is perceived as encompassing many different goddesses from different pantheons and cultures, or as a projection of an aspect of all women and men. Although Starhawk gives priority to the goddess, the god is not ignored. She tells us: "In the women's movement, Dianic separatist Witchcraft has become the fashion, and some women may have difficulty understanding why a feminist would bother with the Horned God at all. Yet there are few if any women whose lives are not bound up with men, if not sexually and emotionally then economically. The Horned God represents powerful, positive male qualities that derive from deeper sources than the stereotypes and violence and emotional crippling of men in our society."[23] Like the goddess, the god can encompass many different deities or symbolize manhood. The Horned God imagined by Starhawk provides a feminist image of manhood.

The Spiral Dance sold over 300,000 copies.[24] Starhawk's influence pervades the Neopagan movement, although not everyone agrees with her. For example, the image of the god provided by Starhawk is not supported by all Witches and certainly not all Neopagans. Ásatrú who worship the Norse gods do not blend them into one and are more likely to view these gods in less feminist terms, seeing them in their warrior aspect. Starhawk does not speak for all Witches. Nonetheless, her work is widely read within the Neopagan movement and permeates much of the language used, even if at times individuals may not be aware of it. In my fieldwork in the northeastern United States I often heard people use Starhawk's words as their own, either having forgotten that they had read them or having absorbed them from conversations with others.

Margot Adler's *Drawing Down the Moon* was published the same year as *Spiral Dance.* Adler (b. 1946), a reporter for National Public Radio and an initiated Witch, provided an overview of the movement in the United States. The book was important, both in giving a positive public face to the movement and for its discussion of many different forms of Neopaganism in addition to Witchcraft or Wicca. She also provided a list of resources for those interested in learning more about the religion. Unlike Starhawk, Adler did not provide rituals or magical workings as part of her book.

The Spiral Dance, like other books at the time, such as *The Feminist Book of Lights and Shadows* written by Budapest and other members of her coven, provided a conduit for people to learn about the magical, mystical, and ritual practices of Witchcraft without receiving coven training. Starhawk included a discussion of how to run a coven, useful to both those who were coven-trained and those who were not coven-trained but wanted to start their own group. The book also discussed rituals and magical workings, which could be done by anyone even without coven training.

Starhawk, Adler, and Budapest's books were not the first on Wicca, Witchcraft, or Paganism. Gerald Gardner published books on the religion shortly after the British laws against Witchcraft were revoked in 1951.[25] Nonetheless, Starhawk, Adler, and Budapest are important because they mark the beginning of a larger process— the popularization of Witchcraft through books. Some publishing houses, such as Llewellyn have specialized in occult, New Age, and alternative books. Among those books published by Llewellyn, the work of two authors were particularly important in Witchcraft—Scott Cunningham (1956–1993) and Silver RavenWolf (b. 1956).

In *Wicca: A Guide for the Solitary Practitioner* and *Living Wicca: A Further Guide for the Solitary Practitioner*, Cunningham forcefully advocated and provided information for individuals to practice Witchcraft alone, without coven training. His are not the only books advocating this approach. Thousands of how-to books on Witchcraft, and to a lesser degree other forms of Neopaganism, exist. Some are on specific topics, such as how to raise a Pagan child or run a coven. But many repeat in slightly different words what is often referred to as Wicca 101, involving a basic outline of the eight sabbats at the beginning and height of each season; the esbats or moon phases; and instruction on how to cast a circle, call the direction (east, south, west, and north), raise energy for magical workings, and close the circle. These books all are accused of giving individuals the illusion that they are trained Witches or Pagans without really providing the depth of training and supervision available in covens and other groups. Traditionally in Wiccan covens the High Priestess and High Priest determine when neophytes are ready to be initiated and when they are then ready to receive their second and third degrees. Within Wicca, three degrees indicate levels of spiritual attainment within a particular tradition. Solitary practitioners sometimes eschew degrees but at other times determine themselves when they are ready to go on to the next level. On the one hand, some elders are concerned that these individuals are not properly trained, but nonetheless will attempt to train others, resulting in a watering down of the religion. On the other hand, many solitary practitioners believe that they are not accorded the proper respect within Neopagan circles.[26] Because Neopaganism is a religion in which each person can create his or her own form of Paganism, and no accrediting body determines who is or is not properly trained, no one can be excluded from the religion or stopped from teaching. Each person is ultimately the authority on his or her own spiritual path and relationship with the divine. Some solitary practitioners prefer to be coven-trained but live in an area in which they are unable to find a coven or at least one that they prefer and that is willing to accept them. Other solitaries prefer working alone and developing what they feel is their own form of practice.

Silver RavenWolf's books targeted preteens and teenagers interested in Witchcraft. The books provided a basic background in Witchcraft, rituals, ritual tools, magical workings, and ethics. In *Teen Witch* RavenWolf, for example, prior to providing a love spell, enumerated how these spells could not or should not be used. She informed her reader that a Witch must never violate another's free will and hence should not do a spell to make a particular person fall in love with her or him. If the Witch does, the relationship will be doomed. A Witch must never attempt to win another person's significant other. And "you cannot own another person. A person doesn't 'belong' to you like a piece of property. Witches never give away their 'shields' to another person. You always retain your personal power."[27] RavenWolf then provided a spell for bringing love to the spell maker—that is, bringing her or him in contact with eligible people. RavenWolf's discussion of how to use love magic was consistent with Wiccan beliefs and practices. Her books contained spells, some of which were geared toward the young, like the crabby teacher or exam spell, and others that were common within the Neopagan community, like healing spells to help others or oneself recover from an illness. RavenWolf also gave advice to teens on how to live, such as the suggestion that one never give away one's personal power in a relationship or that illegal drugs and alcohol do not mix with magic.

In my recent study with Ezzy on teenage Witches in the United States, England, and Australia,[28] a number of the young Witches mentioned reading one or more of RavenWolf's books when they began exploring Witchcraft. Some were embarrassed to admit this, having come to see RavenWolf's works, as one of them phrased it "too fluffy bunny," that is, too lightweight. Others felt that she provided them with a foray into the world of Witchcraft in a language they could understand. RavenWolf is the best known, but only one of the many authors who orients their publications towards teenagers. Unlike RavenWolf, some authors write books completely of spells, particularly love spells geared toward teenage girls. Publishers code these books with pink or lavender covers to signal that they are oriented toward girls and young women.

Teenagers often do not have the option of being coven-trained. Judy Harrow[29] recommends that teachers do not permit underage individuals whose parents are not Pagans into their covens because this might make the group legally vulnerable. Amber K,[30] on the other hand, recommends that coven leaders speak to the underage seeker's parents or guardian to get their approval, which if given should be put in writing. Both Harrow and K are concerned with the legal ramifications of training underage seekers without parental consent. Teenagers who are interested Witchcraft or any other form of Paganism often have no alternative but to learn about it from books or the Internet, either alone or with a few friends.

Many in the religion are offended by the more flagrant popular books on Witchcraft, whether geared toward teenagers or to adults, which focus almost exclusively on spells. Although a minority, one-third of Neopagans in the *Pagan Census* stated that they find popularization of the religion a problem.[31] For some this problem is the diluting of the religion by books and Web sites. For others they are concerned about the public perception of their religion—fearing that the emphasis on casting spells in some of these books will not reflect well on them or help them get their religion recognized within interfaith councils and in the law courts. Witches and other Neopagans have experienced discrimination. Recently, for example, two Witches, divorced and involved in a custody battle over their only son, were enjoined by the court not to teach the child their religion.[32] The initial court ruling was overturned on appeal, but the case indicates that Witches and other Neopagans continue to experience discrimination.[33]

Most of the books published about Neopaganism are about Wicca or Witchcraft. In part, this is because it is the most popular form of Neopaganism.[34] The current interest in Witchcraft was spurred by the popular media, for example, the feature film *The Craft* and television shows such as *Buffy the Vampire Slayer*, in which one of the characters, Willow, is a Witch, and *Sabrina the Teenage Witch*. In our study of teenage Witches in the United States, England, and Australia, Ezzy and I found that although only a few said that they explored Witchcraft after seeing one of these shows, they all watched at least one episode. Televisions shows, movies, and books constitute a general background that helps to fuel the interest in Witchcraft, or at least on spell work. Most of those who begin exploring Witchcraft, and bought some books, did not become Witches or join another form of Neopaganism. The young people who do become Witches tend to graduate from spell books to more serious literature.[35]

Non-Wiccan Paganism also generated books. Isaac Bonewits (b. 1949), who is an important voice in Druidism, published his undergraduate thesis on magic in 1989. The book did not present the basic principles of Druidism, but instead focused on the practice of magic, his theory behind magic, and his critique of what he considered hubris among other Neopagan authors. Bonewits's book and his writings in *Green Egg* and other Neopagan journals made him a respected voice within Neopaganism and the founder of one branch of Druidism, ÁrnDraíocht Féin (ADF), which translates from the Gallic as our own Druidism. Bonewits broke from the New Reformed Druids of North America (NRDNA) to create the ADF, largely over the issue of clergy training. The ADF has a very well developed training program for each of its three specialists: the Druid, who is the leader; the Bard, or storyteller; and the Ovate, or soothsayer. Interestingly, one can move both up and down in accreditation, indicating an increase or perceived decrease in learning. The NRDNA continues to exist, and other splinter groups developed out of the ADF. Furthermore, other forms of Druidism exist, some of which are not Pagan.[36] Amazon.com alone lists over 800 books on Druidism, most of which, like those on Witchcraft, are how-to books. Somewhat fewer books are listed on Heathenry or Ásatrú. Nonetheless, Amazon.com lists more than 500 books on this spiritual path, most of which provide basic information on its beliefs and practices.

Books are a major form of transmission of information to neophytes of all forms of Neopaganism. But, face-to-face interactions remain important. As noted earlier, most contemporary Neopagans consider themselves solitary practitioners. In some instances, this means that the individuals practice alone—combining what they learned from books and the Internet with what they may learn from a class or by attending a festival. But, at other times, being a solitary practitioner has another meaning. In West Chester, Pennsylvania, where I teach, there was until it disbanded about a year ago a group of solitary practitioners, led by a woman and a man who did not take the title High Priestess and High Priest. They insisted that they were not a coven but just a group of solitary practitioners. The group celebrated the sabbats, at times celebrated the esbat, and had classes to learn about techniques for entering altered states, mythology about the holidays, and various beliefs. Although the group had many of the hallmarks of a coven they did not initiate neophytes, bestow degrees, or claim to train individuals in a particular form of Witchcraft or Paganism. Similarly, in our research on teen Witches, we found that most of our respondents are solitary practitioners even though they often practice with other Witches, by attending classes and participating in student Pagan or Wiccan clubs and at times by training with particular Wiccan or Witchcraft traditions. They define themselves as solitary practitioners because they remain in control of their own spirituality and are eclectic, taking insights from different sources—including the Internet, books, teachers, and other Neopagans. This does not mean that the various traditions of Witchcraft and other forms of Neopaganism are no longer relevant. Although the majority claim to be solitaries, 48 percent report that they do work in groups.[37]

THE INTERNET

The Internet has become one of the major sources of information on Neopaganism and a venue through which Neopagans can interact. Cowan reminds us that the Internet, while permitting interaction among participants, is not open to all.[38] Computers are not equally distributed among nations or within nations. Social class, education, age, and gender all determine the likelihood of individuals having access to and using the Internet for more than just checking e-mail. M. Macha NightMare, a Reclaiming Witch and well-known Pagan author asserts:

> The web allowed community to be created where none had been. The anonymity of online communications liberated witchen folks to express their thoughts and feelings and experiences in relative safety … so in a sense the Web became our church.… It has allowed previously fragmented groups to find each other and previously isolated people to find community. It has fostered the growth of Pagan rights organizations, Pagan publishing, organizing in general, and mobilization of Pagan safety and civil rights The Net has provided us with unlimited resources to learn about our ethnic and cultural heritage, to reconstruct ancient rites, and to bond around these sharings.[39]

NightMare mentions several benefits that the Internet provides Pagans: a place to foster community, a source of information, and a network through which to organize. Erik Davis also suggested that the Internet could provide an alternative "universe" in which to do ritual.[40] Witchcraft in particular, but also most forms of Paganism, are experiential religions. The focus is more on experiencing an alternative universe than in holding a set of beliefs or participating in a set of activities. To what degree does the Internet meet all of these promises—fostering community, providing information, being a source for organizing, and furnishing an alternative universe in which to do ritual?

In our study of teenage Witches, Ezzy and I found that most young people use the Internet as an alternative encyclopedia, although more turn first to books and then to the Internet. Few were involved in chat rooms, and those who were only occasionally participated in discourse—more often choosing to lurk than write. But those who did participate in chat rooms felt that they were part of a community. For some it was important to realize that they were not alone and to have their beliefs confirmed by others. Others established friendships on the Internet, at times meeting people in person whom they befriended in chat rooms. Still others learned of local events that were listed on electronic bulletin boards and became more involved in their local community. Cowan warns that on the Internet individuals can conceal their true identity and more easily lie than in everyday interactions. But, he suggests, the Internet affords those who are thinking about or are in the early stages of becoming a Neopagan a no-risk chance to try on the identity. The individual can remain in the "broom closet" with all those outside the Internet forever, or until she or he is comfortable with her or his new identity.[41]

The Internet also permits individuals to take on the role of teacher. This has both positive and negative effects. Positively, all participants can provide information, tell about their own spiritual quests, and hope to influence the larger religion by their writing on the Internet. Young Witches who are students in their daily lives can become or attempt to become respected teachers on the Internet.[42] Negatively, information is not vetted on the Internet; both good and bad suggestions and information are equally available. In addition, as Cowan illustrates, individuals because of either lack of time or lack of knowledge sometimes just cut and paste, often without noting that the material is not originally theirs, resulting in the same information being presented on a number of Web sites, at times out of context.[43]

The Internet does provide a community especially for solitary practitioners. For example, individuals who live in rural areas where there are no other Neopagans, or at least none whom they know, can communicate on the Internet. It is also a way to network, meeting others in your local area, and learning about festivals, open rituals, and groups. Witchvox.com is one of the largest and most respected sites on the Internet for Pagans. It provides pages for Neopagans from different nations around the world, as well as pages for adults, teens, and children. There are pages of information about different forms of Neopaganism, organizations, and local gatherings. Individuals, groups, and companies can advertise on the site. They have articles about current Neopagan issues. Thousands of sites exist for all forms of Neopaganism. Not all of them are active; more are started than are maintained.

Some groups exist only in cyberspace, but these are rare. Cowan found that many of the cyber covens were teaching covens—that is, they did not perform rituals but promised to teach neophytes about Wicca. It was unclear how successful any of these were. He found that many of these sites had not been updated in two or more years and their links were not functional. Cowan questions whether a cyber coven can survive without any face-to-face interactions. Some groups meet in cyberspace as well as in mundane space. The Internet meetings help to create cohesion by permitting interactions in between face-to-face meetings and linking those who can only rarely attend in-person meetings, because they either have moved away or have family or work obligations that make it difficult for them to regularly attend the larger group. Some of these groups define their cyber meetings as online covens. In her dissertation on a Reclaiming coven in the northeastern United States, Pam Detrixhe documents the use of online interactions among one group that also has face-to-face meetings several times a year. Conflicts arose in this group over decisions made at the face-to-face meetings that some members were unable to attend. Some suggested that all decisions should be based on online discussions. The online aspect of the group helped to create both cohesion and tensions. But, nonetheless, the group would either have not existed or been very different without the inclusion of the online meetings.[44]

Only a few of the cyber covens that Cowan explored attempted to do the central component of coven work—rituals—online. He discovered that "in terms of their content … online rituals differ very little from their off line counterparts."[45] He notes that they follow the same basic format, of creating a sacred circle, calling the quarters, invoking the same goddesses and gods. They often use the same texts as a basis for ritual. As he argues: "with the exception of problems related specifically to Internet technology—from frozen servers, to unexpected 'fatal errors' in one's operating system, to cats who jump on the keyboard and drop the user unceremoniously from the chat room—even pre and post-ritual chatter is indistinguishable from that which occurs off-line. That is, there is nothing inherently special about online ritual, other than … it gathers together those who might not otherwise meet."[46] Cowan agrees with NightMare, Telesco and Knight, and Davis that the Internet can potentially offer an alternative format for rituals, but in his extensive research he found none that has actually met this potential. [47]

Organizing against discrimination and to fight for their civil rights is another use of the Internet mentioned by NightMare. Information about discrimination and a call to write letters are often posted on Pagan Web sites and sent out on Pagan listserves. Lady Liberty League, the legal arm of Circle Sanctuary, maintains a Web site listing current cases of discrimination again Pagans. As many studies[48] show, Neopagans as a group are well-educated and middle-class—a cross-section of American society that tends to be more likely to participate in letter-writing campaigns than lower-class and less-educated people. The Internet is well suited for instantly and inexpensively organizing these campaigns.

FESTIVALS AND WITCH CAMPS

Prior to the widespread use of the Internet, festivals and camps were the main venues that gave Neopagans opportunities to create community. Festivals are large gatherings of Neopagans that normally occur in the spring and summer, although a few take place in the fall. The festivals are organized by Neopagan umbrella groups like Earthspirit Community, Elf Lore, Circle Sanctuary, and Covenant of the Goddess

(COG). The festivals are typically held outside, often at camping grounds or children's summer camps prior to their opening for the season. They have elements of both spiritual retreat and summer camp atmosphere for adults.[49] When entering a festival, one commonly sees people dressed in ritual robes, medieval styled garb, tie-dyed T-shirts and jeans, or skyclad—that is, naked or seminaked. Some individuals who need to hide their identity in their work lives revel in decking themselves out in Pagan jewelry—necklaces, bracelets, earrings with pentagrams, or images of goddesses. Most festivals boast a merchants' row with stalls selling a variety of Pagan-related goods and services, such as crystals, jewelry with Pagan symbols, massages, or herbal remedies for common ailments. A ritual fire, which is normally lit at the beginning of the festival and kept burning until the end, becomes the center of festival life. Rituals open and close the festivals and are held several times a day. Usually one large ritual a day occurs that most people attend. Workshops also take place throughout the day on a variety of topics. Some explore spiritual practices such as mask making, astral projection, and ritual construction. Others are organized as discussion groups to explore common problems within Neopaganism, such as how to raise a Pagan child, coming out of the broom closet, or dealing with religious discrimination. Meals are usually communal and participants are expected to volunteer for jobs around the camp—from working in the kitchen to helping with parking. Conflicts arise over people not meeting their obligations or participating in behavior that is offensive. This can vary from throwing cigarette butts into the ritual fire to making unwanted sexual advances to other participants.[50]

Neopagans come from across the United States and sometimes from abroad to attend festivals. There they meet others and exchange information, see rituals performed, and take workshops. Normally one group or tradition will lead a particular ritual. Others may learn some techniques, poetry, or ritual ideas from that group and then incorporate them into their own practice. Ideas are also exchanged throughout the day, as Neopagans sit around the central fire, dance, sing, and chat with one another. Most Neopagans do not attend festivals, and solitary practitioners are less likely to attend than those who are in groups.[51] Nonetheless, the impact of the festivals, in terms of sharing information and building networks, is greater than the numbers who attend, because people bring what they learned back to their local communities.[52] The effect of festivals is felt least by those who are the most isolated from their local communities. They are the least likely to attend the festivals and the least likely to interact with others who attended.

In addition to festivals, which bring together most if not all forms of Paganism, camps are organized to teach particular Pagan traditions. The Reclaiming Tradition is well known for their Witch Camps, which are offered in nine states in the United States—California, Florida, Georgia, Michigan, Missouri, Pennsylvania, Texas, Vermont, and Virginia. Reclaiming also has Witch Camps in Canada and Europe. The Witch Camps developed from classes offered in the San Francisco Bay Area, initially by Starhawk and a member of her coven, Diane Baker, in 1980. The initial classes, which took place over a six-week period, were so popular that new teachers were recruited to meet the demand. Requests by those who lived too far away to attend the classes resulted in Witch Camps starting in 1985. The camps are an intensive week of classes, rituals, and group living. Participants are encouraged to take what they learn back to their local communities and teach others. The camps teach the Reclaiming form of Witchcraft, which is feminist, activist, and focused on self-transformation.[53]

The Reformed Congregation of the Goddess, International (RCG-I), also hosts a Witch Camp for Dianic Witches. These camps, which are weekend retreats, are less intense than those offered by Reclaiming. The organization, however, also offers the Cella course in Priestess training, which is done in part by correspondence and in part by face-to-face interactions over a one- to six-year period. Diana's Grove, another Dianic group, also offers Witch Camps and correspondence courses that can be completed either in person at the Witch Camps or online.[54]

In addition to festivals and Witch Camps, two annual women's music gatherings are important: The National Women's Music Festival and the Michigan Womyn's Music Festival. Both are held in the summer. They include Women's Spirituality and Goddess worship workshops, often led by well-known Neopagans, such as Adler, Budapest, and Jade River, one of the founders of the RGC-I.[55] Because there is an elective affinity between Neopagans and other groups, such as those interested in recreating historical periods, the New Age, science fiction, and fantasy literature, Neopagan teachers can often be found at Renaissance fairs, New Age gatherings, and science fiction conventions.[56]

CONCLUSION

The traditional path to Witchcraft and other forms of Paganism was through covens, groves, or groups. These collectives remain important in training initiates, but are becoming less central as more individuals practice alone or with one other person. Books, which since the spread of Neopaganism in the 1960s and 1970s were important in transmitting the religion to the next cohort, are even more important. As the religion grew in popularity, more books were produced that present spell work with little concern for other aspects of the religion. Since the 1990s, with positive images of teenage Witches appearing in movies like *The Craft* and subsequent television shows, bookstore shelves have seen an increasing number of books geared toward teenagers. Concerns were raised by many in Neopagan communities that this resulted in a diluting of the religion. Some speculate that the market in popular works on Witchcraft and Neopaganism is decreasing.[57] What this will ultimately mean for the religion is not clear. It is possible that the market is so saturated with introductory spell books that few if any more can be marketed. An increasing number of young people may be turning to the Internet for their information and therefore buying fewer books. My own research on teenage Witches suggests that, like their elders, they are readers. Teenage Witches search the Internet, at times participating in chat rooms, but they also read books, often those they find recommended on the Internet. Many of them read the classic works, such as those by Starhawk, Adler, Crowley, and Cunningham, and are not interested in spell books.

Although most Neopagans practice alone, a Neopagan community does exist; it is not on the whole a face-to-face community, but one that could best be described as a community of interest: people who are loosely linked through their shared concerns. Neopagans meet on the Internet, at festivals, and at other gatherings. These are venues for teaching and learning about the religion, mythology, and techniques for getting into an altered state of consciousness in order to come in contact with the spiritual world. Some individuals have become noted teachers through writing books, editing journals, running festivals, and organizing umbrella organizations. Others are known as teachers only on a small scale in their own local community where they work with a few people each year in their coven. Since Neopaganism has no accrediting agencies, anyone can become a teacher—but not all who teach are respected and not all well-known. Learning about Neopaganism is often multifaceted; people take lessons, participate on the Internet, and read widely on mythology, anthropology, and Witchcraft. However, as an increasing number of people become Pagans outside of training groups they are more likely to be eclectic—combining different strands of Paganism as they choose. Almost counterintuitively this has resulted in not greater variety but less, as Neopagans rely on the same books and Internet sites for information on how to do a ritual and engage with the other world.

NOTES

1. Helen A. Berger, Evan A. Leach, and Leigh S. Shaffer, *Voices from the Pagan Census: Contemporary: A National Survey of Witches and Neo-Pagans in the United States* (Columbia, SC: The University of South Carolina Press, 2003).

2. Ronald Hutton, *The Triumph of the Moon: A History of Modern Pagan Witchcraft* (Oxford: Oxford University Press, 1999).

3. Douglas E. Cowan, *Cyberhenge: Modern Pagans on the Internet* (New York: Routledge, 2005).

4. Ibid., 29–30.

5. Helen A. Berger, *A Community of Witches: Contemporary Neo-Paganism and Witchcraft in the United States* (Columbia, SC: The University of South Carolina Press, 1999).

6. Berger et al., *Voices*.

7. Douglas Ezzy, "The Commodification of Witchcraft," *Australian Religious Studies Review* 14, no. 1 (2001): 31–44.

8. Tanice G. Foltz, "The Commodification of Witchcraft," in *Witchcraft and Magic: Contemporary North America,* ed. Helen A. Berger (Philadelphia: University of Pennsylvania Press, 2005), 137–168.

9. Margot Adler, *Drawing Down the Moon* (Boston: Beacon Press, 1978); J. Gordon Melton, *The Encyclopedia of American Religions* (Wilmington, NC: McGrath Publications, 1978).

10. Helen A. Berger, "Witchcraft and Magic," in *Witchcraft and Magic,* ed. Berger, 28–54.

11. Wendy Griffin, "Webs of Women: Feminist Spiritualities," in *Witchcraft and Magic,* ed. Berger, 55–80.

12. Wendy Griffin, personal communication, October 20, 2005.

13. Cynthia Eller, *Living in the Lap of the Goddess: The Feminist Spirituality Movement in America* (New York: Crossroads, 1993).

14. Zsuzsanna E. Budapest, *The Grandmother of Time: A Women's Book of Celebrations, Spells, and Sacred Objects for Every Month of the Year* (San Francisco: Harper and Row, 1989), 15.

15. Wendy Griffin, "Goddess Spirituality and Wicca in the West," in *In Her Voice, Her Faith: Women Speak on World Religions,* ed. Arvind Sharma and Katherine Young (Boulder, CO: Westview Press, 2002), 243–282.

16. Eller, *Living;* Griffin, "Webs of Women: Feminist Spiritualities," in *Witchcraft and Magic,* ed. Berger, 55–80.

17. Adler, *Drawing.*

18. Starhawk, *The Spiral Dance: A Rebirth of the Ancient Religion of the Great Goddess* (San Francisco: Harper & Row Publishers, 1979).

19. Starhawk, *Dreaming the Dark: Magic, Sex and Politics* (Boston: Beacon Press, 1982); Starhawk, *Truth or Dare: Encounters with Power, Authority, and Mystery* (San Francisco: Harper and Row, 1987).

20. Thealogy is a term that was first used by Naomi Goldenburg to denote a theology based on the goddess instead of God.

21. Starhawk, *Spiral,* 11.

22. Ibid., 84–85.

23. Ibid., 95.

24. Jone Salomonsen, *Enchanted Feminism: The Reclaiming Witches of San Francisco* (London and New York: Routledge Press, 2002).

25. Gerald Gardner, *Witchcraft Today* (London: Rider, 1954); Gerald Gardner, *The Meaning of Witchcraft* (London: Aquarian Press, 1959).

26. Berger et al., *Voices.*

27. Silver RavenWolf, *Teen Witch: Wicca for a New Generation* (St. Paul, MN: Llewellyn Publications, 1999), 133.

28. Helen A. Berger and Douglas Ezzy, *Teen Witches: The United States, England, and Australia* (New Brunswick, NJ: Rutgers University Press, forthcoming).

29. Judy Harrow, "Other People's Kids: Working with the Underaged Seeker," in *Modern Rites of Passage: Witchcraft Today, Book Two,* ed. Chas S. Clifton (St. Paul, MN: Llewellyn Publications, 1994).

30. Amber K, *Covencraft: Witchcraft for Three or More* (St. Paul, MN: Llewellyn Publications, 1998).

31. Berger et al., *Voices.*

32. Kevin Corcoran, "Paganism Ruling Stirs Outcry," *Indianapolis Star,* May 27, 2005.

33. Michele McNeil, "Parent can Share Wicca with Son," *Indianapolis Star,* August 18, 2005.

34. Berger et al., *Voices.*

35. Berger and Ezzy, *Teenage Witches.*

36. Berger, "Witches and Neopagans."

37. Berger et al., *Voices.*

38. Cowan, *Cyberhenge.*

39. NightMare, *Witchcraft,* 24.

40. Erik Davis, "May the Astral Plane Be Reborn in Cyberspace," *Wired* 3, no. 7 (1995): 126–133, 174–181.

41. Cowan, *Cyberhendge.*

42. Helen A. Berger and Douglas Ezzy, "The Internet as Virtual Community: Teen Witches in the United States and Australia," in *Religion Online: Finding Faith on the Internet*, ed. Lorne L. Dawson and Douglas E. Cowan (New York and London: Routledge, 2004).

43. Cowan, *Cyberspace.*

44. Pam Detrixhe, "Shape-Shifting 'Religion': Witchen Identities as Post-Modern Exemplum" (unpublished dissertation, Philadelphia: Temple University, 2005).

45. Cowan, *Cyberspace,* 127.

46. Cowan, *Cyberspace,* 127–128.

47. NightMare, *Witchcraft;* Patricia Telesco and Sirona Knight, *The Wiccan Web: Surfing the Magic on the Internet* (New York: Citadel Press, 2001); Davis, "May the Astral Plane."

48. See, for example, Berger et al., *Voices;* Margot Adler, *Drawing Down the Moon: Revised and Expanded Edition.* (Boston: Beacon Press, 1986); Danny L. Jorgensen and Scott E. Russell, "American Neo-Paganism: the Participants' Social Identities," *Journal for the Scientific Study of Religion* 38, no. 3 (September 1999): 325–338.

49. Sarah M. Pike, *Earthly Bodies, Magical Selves: Contemporary Pagans and the Search for Community* (Berkeley, CA: The University of California Press, 2001).

50. Ibid.

51. Berger et al., *Voices.*

52. Pike, *Earthly Bodies;* Adler, *Drawing.*

53. Salomonsen, *Enchanted;* Detrixhe, "Shape-Shifting."

54. Foltz, "Commodification."

55. Ibid.

56. Berger, *A Community.*

57. Phyllis Curott, "A Canary in the Culture War Coal Mines," www.witchvox.com (accessed October 2 , 2005).

FURTHER READING

Adler, Margot. *Drawing Down the Moon: Revised and Expanded Edition.* Boston: Beacon Press, 1986.

Bado-Fralick, N. *Coming to the Edge of the Circle: A Wiccan Initiation Ritual.* Oxford: Oxford University Press, 2005.

Berger, Helen A. *A Community of Witches: Contemporary Neo-Paganism and Witchcraft in the United States.* Columbia, SC: The University of South Carolina Press, 1999.

Berger, Helen A., ed. *Witchcraft and Magic: Contemporary North America.* Philadelphia: University of Pennsylvania Press, 2005.

Berger, Helen A., and Douglas Ezzy. *Teen Witches: United States, England, and Australia.* New Brunswick, NJ: Rutgers University Press, forthcoming.

Berger, Helen A., Evan A. Leach, and Leigh S. Shaffer. *Voices from the Pagan Census: Contemporary: A National Survey of Witches and Neo-Pagans in the United States.* Columbia, SC: The University of South Carolina Press, 2003.

Cowan, Douglas E. *Cyberhenge: Modern Pagans on the Internet.* New York: Routledge, 2005.

Crowley, Vivianne. *Wicca: The Old Religion in the New Millennium.* London: Thorsons, 1996.

Eller, Cynthia. *Living in the Lap of the Goddess: The Feminist Spirituality Movement in America.* New York: Crossroads, 1993.

Griffin, Wendy. *Daughters of the Goddess: Studies in Healing, Identity, and Empowerment.* Walnut Creek, CA: AltaMira Press, 2000.

Hutton, Ronald. *The Triumph of the Moon: A History of Modern Pagan Witchcraft.* Oxford: Oxford University Press, 1999.

Luhrmann, T.M. *Persuasions of the Witch's Craft: Ritual Magic in Contemporary England.* Cambridge, MA: Harvard University Press, 1989.

NightMare, M. *Witchcraft and the Web.* Toronto: ECW Press, 2001.

Pike, Sarah M. *Earthly Bodies, Magical Selves: Contemporary Pagans and the Search for Community.* Berkeley, CA: The University of California Press, 2001.

Salomonsen, Jone. *Enchanted Feminism: The Reclaiming Witches of San Francisco.* London and New York: Routledge Press, 2002.

Starhawk. *The Spiral Dance: A Rebirth of the Ancient Religion of the Great Goddess.* San Francisco: Harper & Row Publishers, 1979.

York, Michael. *The Emerging Network: A Sociology of the New Age and Neo-Pagan Movements.* London: Rowman and Littlefield, 1995.

New and Alternative Religions in the United States: Ritual and Neopaganism

Adrian Harris and M. Macha NightMare

INTRODUCTION

Most of this essay has been entirely cowritten by M. Macha NightMare and Adrian Harris. For the section on *Neopagan Ritual in Practice,* however, we wanted to offer a more personal expression of this experiential spirituality. To that end, NightMare speaks there of her own experience of the Reclaiming Tradition.

As practicing Neopagans, we temper many years of experience with academic understanding to craft our perspective on this fascinating topic. Because Neopagans honor personal experience above any human authority or tradition, this diverse practice is in constant flux. As a result, whatever we write dates quite quickly. But rather than count this as a problem, we consider it as a mark of the vigor of the movement.

Neopaganism is one of the fastest growing New Religious Movements in the United States, and ritual is its primary expression. Both terms are somewhat problematic, and fixing a meaning of either seems an invidious task.

Given that *any* attempt at definition will necessarily be selective and blur subtleties, we offer our own as a guide that describes *most* Neopagan ritual, but note that it is an evolving practice.

A Neopagan ritual is a process played out through performance. It is set apart from the mundane and involves physical activity and symbolic verbal or nonverbal communication expressed through multiple sensory modalities. Some Neopagan ritual intends to engage with "ultimate reality" or mystical powers and takes place in the context of a heightened emotional state.

HISTORY OF NEOPAGAN RITUAL

...in the absence of ritual, the soul runs out of its real nourishment, and all kinds of social problems then ensue.

—*Malidoma Patrice Some*[1]

Although some Neopagans claim links with ancient traditions, most celebrate the creative potential of following eclectic new spiritual paths. The tongue-in-cheek suggestion that there are as many Neopagan belief systems as there are Neopagans is not so far from the truth: New "traditions" constantly emerge, and existing practices are in flux. Mapping a history of such a varied landscape is tricky, but there are sufficient landmarks to show the lay of the land. Different Neopagan rituals share family resemblances and emerge from a common stock. In addition, most Neopagans venerate more than one deity, draw on ancient myths, weave magic (variously defined), and often believe in reincarnation.

Neopagan rituals draw inspiration from many myths and stories, both ancient and modern. However, the most common influences are the pre-Christian religions of northwestern Europe, ancient Egypt, Rome, and Greece. Whereas most Neopagans use the past as a creative resource, Neopagans called Reconstructionists attempt to revive or emulate earlier faiths as closely as possible.

To guide you through this complex landscape, we explore four intersecting pathways in the history of Neopagan ritual: Neopaganism as a "Nature religion," British Traditional Wicca (BTW), reconstructed traditions, and feminist spirituality.

NEOPAGANISM AS A NATURE RELIGION

Terminology is confusing and changeable, but most commentators on Neopaganism refer to it as a "Nature religion," a term that has been used extensively since the early 1970s to designate indigenous folk religions that make Nature their symbolic focus. Those who practice such religions venerate both "external nature and our own physical embodiment."[2] We see this veneration repeatedly expressed in Neopagan ritual; however, other influences complicate this practice.

Another term often used is "Earth-based spirituality." This term, along with "Nature religion," usually designates the various Neopagan traditions and does not imply indigenous folk religions, "ethnic" religions, or reconstructed religions.

In the world of international interfaith organizations, indigenous and tribal religions are considered to be Pagan, while contemporary revivals and reconstructions fall under the general term of Neopaganism.

BRITISH TRADITIONAL WICCA

Wicca, also known as "the Craft," is the most common form of Neopaganism in the United States and provides the foundation of most Neopagan ritual. It began with Gardnerian Wicca in the United Kingdom during the late 1940s and was soon joined by the offshoot Alexandrian Tradition. A third generation of Wiccan traditions later emerged, which included Raymond Buckland's Seax-Wicca.

The origins of Wicca remain in debate, but we can draw some conclusions regarding its ritual. Two linked influences are apparent: the Western Occult Tradition and Freemasonry. The Western Occult Tradition remained hidden for many years, but during the Reformation and Enlightenment periods it manifested in the founding of Rosicrucian and Masonic organizations.

Aidan Kelly plausibly proposes that the Western Occult Tradition led to the emergence of Modern Druids, the Theosophical Society, Wicca, and the New Age movement.[3] Furthermore, the rituals, symbolism, and terminology of Freemasonry were "absorbed into ... the rituals of the neopagan witchcraft movement."[4]

The influence of the Western Occult Tradition leads to what Harvey calls "the Gnostic temptation" in Neopaganism.[5] Because much of its ritual structure is taken from this esoteric tradition, some Neopagans sometimes "do or say things which denigrate matter."[6] He suggests that this influence might create a kind of "schizophrenia" in Neopagans who celebrate Nature yet seek transcendence.[7]

Susan Greenwood draws the related conclusion that the purpose of some modern witchcraft is more about enabling personal growth than creating a deeper relationship with Nature.[8]

The extent of the influence of BTW on North American Neopagan ritual is difficult to gauge. We note two points of discussion. First, although conventional wisdom has it that BTW came to the United States in the 1960s, evidence suggests that it arrived much earlier. Chas Clifton suggests that two Americans, independently of one another, brought Craft, as it is called, to the United States from England.[9] One, a career military man named Ed Fitch, anonymously published a book called *Rituals of the Pagan Way / A Book of Pagan Rituals*[10] that was widely used by American Neopagans for many years. The other, the late Joe Wilson, was stationed in England during his term in the U.S. Air Force. When he returned to the United States, Wilson carried on extensive correspondence with the late Robert Cochrane/Roy Bowers in England; copies of these letters have also been widely circulated, informally, throughout the American Pagan community. Both Fitch and Wilson subsequently published books and other writings about Witchcraft and shamanism in the United States.

Second, a North American Pagan revival was emerging well before British Craft arrived. Victor and Cora Anderson were practicing a form of witchcraft in Oregon as early as the 1930s. Originally called Faery tradition, later changed to Feri to distinguish it from other Craft traditions of similar names, their rituals were a synthesis of several strands, drawing heavily on Appalachian folk magic from Cora's childhood in northern Alabama, as well as African, Pictish, Yezidi from the Middle East, Hawaiian Huna sources, and Silva Mind Control.

As noted above, the Western Occult Tradition and Freemasonry had an early influence on British Wicca, and there is a long history of Freemasonry and lodges in the United States. Many elements from Freemasonry appear in contemporary Craft rituals. Among them are the symbol of the pentacle, or five-pointed star, the use of the phrases "Blessed Be," and, to seal a spell and assure its efficacy, "So mote it be." Ritual roles such as the Masonic "tyler" have become the "Man in Black" or the "Summoner" in Craft. The binding and blindfolding at initiation is part of both Masonic and Craft ritual, as is the swearing of an oath, although the specifics of the oath itself differ.[11]

Contemporary Craft traditions, based on a Wiccan, or BTW, format, include elements from Native American spiritualities, New Age, Buddhist, Hindu and other religions, as well as the human potential movement.

RECONSTRUCTED TRADITIONS

As Neopaganism grew in visibility and popularity, and as mongrel Americans of mixed genetic and ethnic heritage, instead of seeking assimilation into the mainstream of American culture, sought their (mostly) European roots, Neopagans began to reconstruct ancient Pagan traditions. Drawing from history, anthropology, mythology, and folklore, and using texts when available, people created rituals and traditions that addressed their personal ethnic and national heritages.

Perhaps the most widespread of the reconstructed traditions are various forms of Druidry and Celtic reconstructionism. Among other notable traditions are Hellenismos (reconstructed Greek religion), Nova Roma (reconstructed Roman religion), Kemetic (Egyptian), Polonia (Polish folk tradition), Canaanite-Phoenician, and Sumerian, as well as Stregheria, or Italian Witchcraft. Some practitioners of Asatru, a Norse Paganism whose adherents call themselves Heathens, fall under the broader classification of Neopagan; however, many Heathens consider their religion to be ethnic rather than a Nature religion or an Earth-based spirituality.

The rituals of these traditions are often performed in the language of the original practitioners, or a language as closely resembling the original as it is possible to know.

FEMINIST SPIRITUALITY

Neopaganism has always had a countercultural feel and to some extent is a reaction to patriarchal religions. Not surprisingly, Second Wave Feminism (SWF) in the 1970s took an interest in Neopagan ritual. An important element for women in the women's liberation movement was the acceptance of, love of, and respect for the female body. SWF fostered an appreciation of the values of roles such as motherhood, weaving, and cooking, traditionally performed by women. Women's overlooked history suggested to some that there had been a golden age of matriarchy in the distant past. Lacking adequate evidence, this theory has not withstood scrutiny; however, it served as a compelling emotional unifying force at the time, and perhaps continues to do so. Most importantly, many feminists found tremendous healing, support, and comfort in having a feminine image of the divine. Thus was born goddess spirituality.

Because Witches in popular culture were portrayed as ugly old hags unworthy of respect, early feminists "reclaimed" this word and applied it to themselves. In addition, mainstream religions were essentially male-oriented and male-dominated, further alienating women from the religions in which they were reared. Thus, the format—and the glamour—of BTW was wedded to a goddess-focused spirituality. Neopagans whose ritual style is based on BTW and whose rites center solely on goddesses are known as Dianics.

This development meant that, for some at least, Neopagan ritual became political. Margot Adler concludes that the only political Neopagan group of significant size is the "thousands of women from Greenham Common[12] to New York to California who are combining political action with women's spirituality and earth reverence."[13] Key influences are Starhawk and the Reclaiming Tradition, Z. Budapest, and archaeologist Marija Gimbutas. Feminist spirituality is generally nonhierarchical, creates eclectic detraditionalized rituals, and celebrates radically embodied notions of spirituality. Ronald Hutton believes that integrating the women's spirituality movement into the Craft was "America's most distinctive single contribution to that witchcraft."[14]

One notable result of the growth of Feminist spirituality is a rise in political and environmental activism among Neopagans that has led to the emergence of "Eco-Pagan" rituals described below in "Neopagan Counterculture" and "The Power That Connects."

KEY ASPECTS OF NEOPAGAN RITUAL

It is a consciousness-altering technique, the best there is.

—Alison Harlow[15]

When most people think of Neopagan ritual, they think of exotic rites involving fire, chanting, flowing robes, and ecstatic dancing. They would not be wrong, for these words do describe elements of many Neopagan rituals. Neopagan rituals share many elements in common, yet are astounding in their variety and endless creativity.

Broadly, Neopagan rituals are celebrations (e.g., festivals), veneration (e.g., shrines), rites of passage (c.g., initiations), or an attempt to shift existing patterns (e.g., spellwork). Many mix these somewhat simplified distinctions.

Neopagan rituals may be private or public, political, personal, or both. They may involve hundreds or just one person.

At one end of this spectrum lies public ritual. Such events include festival celebrations organized by one of the larger Neopagan organizations, such as Circle Sanctuary in Wisconsin or EarthSpirit in Massachusetts, or a political ritual to highlight an environmental or social issue.

The antinuclear protests at Lawrence Livermore National Laboratory in California in the early 1980s, where protesters prepared for action with a dramatic burning of a wicker man, exemplify political ritual. The action itself very effectively combined protest with ritual as participants wove a giant web entangling police efforts to break up the group.

Public rituals are open to anyone and are advertised; semipublic rituals are by invitation only. These are usually celebratory events that take place in someone's home, in a larger rented property, or on private land.

Most such rituals are part of a gathering that may last a day or a couple of weeks. Over the course of a week-long festival, there may be many rituals. There is an opening ritual and a closing ritual, with several more specifically focused rituals, such as coming-of-age rituals for young and old people, handfastings, etc., in between.

In her study of such festival events in the United States, Sarah Pike notes how important they are to creating a counterculture because they offer a shared reality that is very different from what Neopagans experience in their everyday lives.[16]

Pike's study gives a fascinating example of how festival goers use ritual dance to gain a more positive attitude toward their bodies. She provides an evocative description of a Fire dance ritual at Starwood, one of the largest Neopagan festival gatherings:

> ...once the fire is lit there is no leader, no orchestration, no focus of attention, and the ritual develops its own organic forms. Emerging structures and patterns are unplanned and unspoken, taking shape in the interplay of drums and movement.[17]

The ritual continues through the night and a few will greet the sunrise with dance. The ritual dance Pikes describes exemplifies several aspects of Neopagan ritual in general. Because ritual space is safe, it is liberating: The dancers can fully express themselves because they are free from sexual harassment or social comment. As a result, participants come to "trust their bodies in ways that are new for them."[18] This trust allows participants to explore unfamiliar dimensions of physical expression: they move in different ways, finding new relationships between body and space that can transform the self.

Pike's personal experience of the ritual dance hints at its power:

> Upon entering the circle, I was overwhelmed by heat and smoke and mesmerized by the drums, and I began to feel a sense of oneness with the dancers and drummers ... The endless circling facilitated our disorientation in time and space. It was this disorientation that played with the boundaries between self and other that made possible the feeling of union with others.[19]

Surrendering to the power of the ritual fire can bring a profound shift in how participants experience their bodies that remains long after the festival has ended. One festival dancer explained how "ritual dance may also be used to work on personal issues which are too threatening or deeply buried to address in our everyday consciousness. Emotions which have been repressed ... can be allowed expression and worked through in the safe space created by dance."[20]

The festival culture is somehow more "real" because it embodies an ideal reality and offers heightened experiences. Ritual is an essential part of the process of creating this magical reality. An understanding of how this is achieved emerges in the course of this chapter.

Although festival culture is important, the majority of Neopagan rituals are private events involving small groups of close friends. Compatible people come together for ongoing ritual work, usually but not always under the guidance of a high priestess, high priest, or both. Sometimes several people with no training or outside guidance will form a ritual group and work from a book. These groups are called covens, groves, nests, cells, or other similar terms. They work together and grow, magically and spiritually, over a period of years, during which time their relationships bond.

Their understandings of ritual and its effect on their lives and the world deepens. They consider themselves as family.

Individual circumstances may make solitary ritual the only option; however, some deliberately choose to work alone. In principle, an individual ritual can achieve anything a larger one can, and most Neopagans work alone at least occasionally. Common examples are rituals that are focused on an altar or shrine, which are usually part of Neopagan personal practice. An altar typically holds sacred objects symbolizing the season and will change with each Festival. (See "Neopagan Ritual in Practice" below.) A shrine is an altar to a specific deity and serves as a way of venerating and building a relationship with them.

LIMINAL SPACE

Almost all Neopagan rituals take place within a "sacred circle," one notable exception being altar and shrine work. Altar and shrine work typically occur outside a circle because they are not usually concerned with raising power nor do they require protection. The circle may be physically marked out, but usually the participants "cast" a circle by visualizing it and using words, gestures, and tools to aid that visualization. (See "Neopagan Ritual in Practice" below.) The circle creates a sacred space, "between the worlds and beyond time" in which the ritual can occur.

Different people understand the sacred circle in different ways. For some Neopagans the circle is there to protect and ward off intrusion, while others cast a circle to help focus the power raised by the ritual. Still others explain it as being like a mixing bowl that serves both functions.

The circle also serves other functions. We can usefully describe the sacred circle as a "liminal" space. A limen is literally a threshold or sill, so a liminal space is one that is betwixt and between—neither one place nor another. The liminal space of the sacred circle marks a space that is outside normal social roles, responsibilities, rules, and even modes of thought. As a result, the circle provides the potential for great freedom and creativity.

Neopagans use the format of a circle for many reasons. When people come together to talk, they instinctively tend to group themselves into a circle, and humans circle round hearth fires. Circles are egalitarian, with no single person being above, below, or aside from everyone else. Circles are found in Nature in such things as tree trunks, flowers, the sun and the moon. Earth circles the Sun. Most significantly, perhaps, the horizon is circular. If you can see the horizon, you are always in the center of a vast circle. So the magic circle is a microcosm, a smaller version of the world. The center or focal point of a circle is like an umbilicus, the point between inside and outside, between life and death, between the world of matter and the world of spirit, the portal between the worlds.

ALTERED STATES

One result of the entry into the liminal space of the sacred circle is a shift away from more usual states of consciousness. This shift may be subtle or profound.

Some Neopagan rituals do not create altered states of consciousness. A handfasting (marriage), for instance, ritually sanctifies and celebrates the commitment of two (or more) people to each other in the presence of their loved ones. A ritual marking a change in the seasons is essentially celebratory in nature. It is aesthetic, but may not require a powerful ritual. An initiation or therapeutic ritual, however, is designed to have a profound psychological impact on the participants.

How does Neopagan ritual create an altered state of consciousness?

There are many sacred technologies that can shift us to a heightened state of awareness, and Neopagan ritual uses most of them. The most common are guided meditation, breathwork, and the powerful combination of rhythm, movement, and dance. We discuss these techniques in more detail in "Neopagan Ritual in Practice," below.

Some Neopagans use entheogens[21] and sexual intercourse in rituals, but neither is common practice. Many Neopagans are explicitly critical of any use of entheogens, believing that they are too unpredictable and tend to confuse rather than enlighten. When they are used, entheogens are generally part of a personal ritual in a shamanic tradition.

The popular idea that Neopagan ritual regularly involves sexual activity is unfounded. Although sexual contact between consenting partners does occur in private rituals, it is by no means common.

Gardnerian Wicca traditionally used scourging at every ritual, but this is unusual today. Traditional Wiccan initiations still include gentle scourging of the back. Although this was primarily intended to symbolize purification, the practice does have physiological effects that change consciousness. Scourging draws blood to the surface of the skin and thereby reduces blood flow to the brain, resulting in a light trance.

SYMBOLS

For Victor Turner symbols are "the basic building-blocks" of ritual.[22] Rituals speak to us at a deep level and use a language that we intuitively understand—the language of symbols.

Starhawk describes a simple street ritual that took place during the Genoa protests in 2001:

> We brew up a lovely magical cauldron—a big pot full of water from sacred places and whatever else women want to add: rose petals, a hair or two, tobacco from a cigarette, anything that symbolizes the visions we hold of a different world.[23]

Simply having the image of a strong, self-reliant goddess on an altar during ritual provides a more empowered attitude on the part of female participants. Worshippers place upon their altars images of deities that show qualities, strengths, and characteristics they admire and seek to emulate. This incorporation reaches deep within the psyche to assist people to develop those qualities within themselves. Bright, colorful flowers on a Springtime altar remind us of life's renewal. A harvest altar heaped with the bounty of the fields and orchards conveys a sense of abundance without a word being spoken. Photographs of and small articles belonging to our departed loved ones ("Beloved Dead") on altars commemorating the dead bring them closer to us in spirit.

A symbol most Witches and Wiccans associate with their religion is the encircled pentacle, which symbolizes different things to different practitioners. However, one basic understanding corresponds the five points of the pentacle to the elements— Air, Fire, Water, Earth, and Spirit. The symbol that binds most Druids is the *awen* ("inspiration"), a circle containing three "bars of light" converging toward three dots. Such symbols as the pentacle and the *awen* help create a group identity.

CREATING RITUALS

Most religious ritual relies on the legitimating authority of tradition. The ritual has been performed in a particular way for many years; this is taken to guarantee its authenticity. Changes to such rituals require a special dispensation from a recognized spiritual authority, and if it is not performed properly it may be deemed ineffective.

But Neopagan rituals are unusual in that they are very often self-consciously created for the occasion.[24] Neopagans do not recognize *any* human as a spiritual authority and judge the effectiveness of a ritual entirely in terms of personal experience. (See "The Importance of Personal Experience," below.) Some Neopagans specialize in creating effective ritual, often understanding it as a form of sacred art.[25]

As we can see, this is a very flexible practice, and there is a wide range of practice from reconstructed rituals, through rituals of specific Neopagan traditions to eclectic workings.

Reconstructed and "traditional" rituals are usually carefully structured while the eclectic workings may be spontaneous. Eclectic rituals are, however, highly variable, and many are carefully planned and tightly structured.

RECONSTRUCTED RITUALS

A minority of Neopagans seek to reconstruct and recreate ancient rituals as accurately as possible. Their efforts are challenging, because adequate research into the ancient practice may be unavailable or conflicting and, of course, what was acceptable in a past culture may not be acceptable today.

Some Nordic Neopagans seek to recreate the rituals of pre-Christian Northern Europe that are described in medieval Icelandic literature and other sources. Rituals of reconstructed traditions are often conducted in the language of the parent religion, i.e., Celtic and Druid rituals in Gaelic or Hellenic rituals in Greek. In addition, they may wear clothing, jewelry, and accessories like those worn in the time and place that the tradition was previously practiced.

"TRADITIONAL" RITUALS

There are many different "traditions" in Neopaganism, including various forms of Wicca, Witchcraft, and Druidry. Using fairly common basic structures, each tradition has its particular style of working ritual. Although a Wiccan would recognize the structure of a Druid ritual, and vice versa, they would also be aware of significant differences. There are variations in language and symbols, the degree of formality, how the group invokes the sacred, which deities are celebrated, and even the timing of rituals. These differences give the rituals of each tradition different voices, character, and nature.

Rituals in these traditions are still being created and constantly evolving, but each works with the appropriate symbolic vocabulary.

ECLECTIC RITUALS

Many Neopagans choose to practice outside any recognized tradition. Instead, they freely combine aspects of many practices—both sacred and secular. Although Eclectics do look to the existing Neopagan traditions for inspiration, they might weave in Eastern religious practices, ideas from the human potential movement, and aspects of performance art.

BODY AND NATURE

Because most Neopagans consider their practice to be that of a Nature religion, a sensual relationship to nature lies at the heart of the spiritual practice. Deity is immanent in the physical world, and both the earth and the body are considered sacred. For Neopagans the natural environment is a fundamental source of spiritual truth: Jone Salomonsen noticed that the ritual symbols used by Reclaiming Witches in San Francisco are grounded in "ordinary human life and the human body, sexuality and parenting, as well as the earth and the seasonal cycles of the natural world."[26] This is typical of Neopagan practice in general.

The celebration of the passage of the seasons—the "Wheel of the Year"—structures the annual cycle of Neopagan ritual practice, and the deities venerated are understood as being immanent in Nature. (See "Neopagan Ritual in Practice," below.)

Ritual theorists have long recognized that the body is fundamental to ritual. Because we experience ritual in a heightened emotional state, a gesture or physical movement becomes loaded with symbolic power: what would be a simple wave of the arm in everyday space becomes an invitation to deity in the sacred circle.[27]

It is useful to understand ritual as a kind of bodywork that can be profoundly healing. Pike's discussion of ritual dance (see "Key Aspects of Pagan Ritual," above) provides a good example, while Salomonsen believes that ritualizing has the power "to deeply alter the consciousness and embodied thinking of western people."[28]

NEOPAGAN COUNTERCULTURE

By now it may be apparent that Neopagan ritual has strong countercultural dimensions. Neopaganism grew up in the counterculture 1960s and 1970s, and, although today its increasing popularity may be drawing it toward the mainstream, Neopagan practitioners continue to question social norms, just as counterculture enthusiasts did 30 or 40 years ago.

This aspect of Neopaganism is perhaps most apparent in the closely related Eco-Pagan and the women's spirituality movements. Eco-Pagans partly express their spirituality through environmental activism and rituals of resistance. For Eco-Pagans belief in the sacredness of Earth leads inevitably to political action. The rituals of the women's spirituality movements are similarly intended to create a space of resistance. According to Kay Turner, the feminists using these rituals believe them to be the most "radical affirmation of the revolutionary potential of the feminist movement."[29]

In patriarchal societies, which have been the norm worldwide for centuries, if not millennia, female children are socialized in ways that are not always in their best interests. Nor are they in the best interests of male children. These mores often inhibit, if not prohibit, women from expressing their full potential as humans. For instance, women were taught to defer to males, to "play dumb," and to be subservient. Married women could not have their own bank accounts, hold separate property, make decisions affecting their own bodies and reproduction, or establish credit independently of their husbands. Even worse, patriarchal societies tend to condone abusive behavior towards women. They teach the young that women are less worthy of respect than men. One of the major appeals of goddess spirituality and Dianic Witchcraft to women is the healing and empowerment that can be gained from the rituals. Encountering feminine images of the divine is a source of tremendous validation for women.

CROSSOVERS

By no means would all those in the women's spirituality movement identify as Neopagans, and neither are all environmental activists Eco-Pagans. But these connections exemplify the importance of crossovers between Neopaganism and other groups. There are also significant overlaps with the New Age movement, as well as Eastern, Native American, and African diasporic religions.

IMPORTANCE OF PERSONAL EXPERIENCE

As we noted above, Neopagans assess their ritual entirely in terms of personal experience, and religious authority is grounded in the self rather than any external institutions. Peter Beyer suggests that having personal experience as a "final arbiter of truth or validity" is a defining feature of Neopaganism.[30] Neopaganism is based not on belief, but on practice. As Adler says, Neopagan beliefs are "not based on creed, they are based on process, they are based on ceremony."[31] We could go so far as to say that many Neopagans have no fixed belief system and our practice evolves from life as lived.

NEOPAGAN RITUAL IN PRACTICE

To better illustrate Neopagan ritual practice, Macha provides a personal view of her experience of a Witchcraft ritual in San Francisco. *Macha writes:* Here's a glimpse of a Witchen[32] seasonal celebration honoring the dead:

> Three guests of the host covens sit in the living room of an apartment in anticipation of our first "real Witches' sabbat." Preparations are going on in the penthouse above us. Now and then someone descends the stairs to fetch something or to tell us it won't be long before we start. None of us has met one another until this night. When the ritual space is ready, a priestess comes downstairs and tells us to remove our clothes, for this ritual, being "traditional," is skyclad, meaning that all celebrants are clad by the sky, or naked.
>
> Then she blindfolds each of us and leads us up the stairs. When we reach the door to the ritual room, we are told to put our hands upon the shoulders of the person in front of us. We walk in, we know not where. We are instructed to keep our hands on the shoulders of the person in front of us, to chant the words, "Set sail. Set sail," while swaying to the rhythm of the chant. We are going to the Isle of the Ever Young, the land beyond the mists, the place on the other side of the veil where the spirits of the dead live, for it is Samhain, the most sacred night of the year.

This is how I remember the first private ritual I was ever invited to attend. Of course, there was much more to the ritual than the little I have described. I am guessing that one of the first questions the reader might have is "what about this skyclad[33] business?"

In all my readings about Witchcraft up until that time I had read that Witches performed their rituals in the nude. There is more than one reason for this custom. One is that there is no visible difference in class or social status among unclothed people; the prince and the pauper are the same, just men. Another reason is that clothing can restrict the free flow of energy, and one of the things we cultivate in ritual is energy flow.

As you might expect, I was nervous about taking off my clothes with a bunch of strangers. The only person I knew before that night was the woman who invited me. The company was mixed gender. My nervousness was not so much because I was uncomfortable with nudity as a concept, or that I felt shame about the naked human body. It was not because I had a moral objection to nudity. It was because of my shyness about body image and whether my body was beautiful. But because I was blindfolded, I could let go of my apprehensions.

Nowadays, with the many changes that Witchcraft has undergone as we have emerged from the broom closet, fewer people seem to worship skyclad. Even at that time (1975), there were occasions when people wore ritual robes when they circled. Nighttime outdoor rituals always required robes for warmth. Some covens worked robed rather than skyclad, only occasionally going skyclad for very specific rituals. Today we find people in various kinds of dress, stages of undress, or nude.

The point of these changes in clothing or doffing of clothing altogether is that they tell our hearts and minds that we are about to go into sacred space. We are preparing to shift our consciousness from the mundane to the magical. We are beginning to engage what in Reclaiming Tradition is called "child self." [34]

Ritual preparation is every bit as important as performing the ritual itself. We clean and rearrange and prepare our ritual spaces before our rites. We sweep, vacuum, dust, put away extraneous things, and clear up clutter. We clean old candle wax from holders; we wash and polish. We spread altar cloths on tables, and we find the right vase for flowers, greenery, and feathers. We select candles in the colors we want to use and the best incense for the purpose of a particular ritual.

When I do these things, when I set up a space in my home for working magic, when I get into it, I begin to build the ritual. Once the space and tools are cleaned, I withdraw to prepare my body with a purificatory bath or shower. I might choose to immerse myself in a particular herb or salt bath and to anoint myself with a special oil or lotion. Sometimes I will burn a candle, sometimes light incense in our bathroom. Once I am clean and robed, I return to the ritual space to set up the altars.

Ritual Roles

In many Witchcraft traditions, each coven has a high priestess and a high priest, or perhaps only one or the other. The shorthand terms used are HPS and HP. The covens in my tradition (Reclaiming), however, are based on group priest/esshoods where specific priestly roles are rotated or shared. We use the word priest/ess as both a noun and a verb, and we use it when we are speaking of any gender.

So a woman or a man is the priestess or priest who "priest/esses" a ritual when she or he assumes a specific role that moves the ritual along. In this essay I use those terms. In large public rituals we have other assigned roles, sometimes called "rehearsed participants." However, in small group work we have no need of these other roles.

Other traditions have such roles as a Maiden, who assists the HPS. A Man in Black or Summoner may give notice of meetings, guard the entrance to the circle, and admit individuals into the sacred space that has been created. In Reclaiming, we are all standing in circle together, and it is from that point that we all create sacred space around ourselves, rather than entering a space that has been erected by others. No one style is right or wrong: different styles appeal to different people.

Purification

Before a person can enter a sacred space, she must be ritually clean. She needs to let go of any cares and worries she may carry from her life before she enters the circle. I have already discussed purification. Here I mention some other methods we use to ritually purify ourselves and each other.

The most common method of purification is with water and salt. Salt is added to water and stirred until it is dissolved. Then the solution may be sprinkled on each person. Or the bowl may be passed to each person in turn so she may perform her own personal ablutions. Or a priest/ess might anoint each celebrant with consecrated oil, usually on the brow. A saltwater purification may involve anointing the brow, lips, heart, palms, or other parts of the body.

Another form of purification, called censing, is done with smoke. The priest/ess may use a bundle of burning sage, an abalone shell, or other nonflammable container with burning cedar, Indian sweet grass, or rosemary. Or she may burn frankincense, myrrh, copal, or other incense in a swinging censer on a chain. Incense smoke is also used to consecrate people and objects, or to "charge" them. Consecration sanctifies and dedicates an object or person to a specific purpose and is different from purification.

Regardless of whether one enters from outside a sacred space created by others or one is already within the space created with others, an act of purification precedes the ritual.

Creating Sacred Space

Creating sacred space means ritually erecting a safe space where those within can focus exclusively on the work at hand. This can be done in any number of ways. Many Witches use the besom, or Witch's broom, to sweep a space of negative energies, thus purifying the physical space where the circle will be. If the ritual space has already been set up, a challenger may confront each individual seeking to enter with a question before admittance is granted and the person steps over a broom that marks the circle's threshold.

A circle is a temporary mandala. It can be drawn on the floor or ground, with paint, tape, chalk, colored powders, corn meal, seeds, or flower petals or traced in the sand on a beach. This act is called "casting," or erecting, a circle.

Some covens may circumambulate the space with salt water and incense before the actual casting is done. They may draw the circle with a wand, staff, stang (two-pronged staff specific to some traditions), or sword.

Once the circle has been cast, the ritualists are "between the worlds."

Once a circle has been cast, it should not be broken. Small children, dogs, and cats seem to be able to go in and out of a circle without disturbing the containment that the circle provides, but adults, who are there to participate fully and not to passively observe, must honor the sanctity of the circle by remaining inside until the circle is ritually opened, or taken down, by a priest/ess. The hosts will usually advise people just before beginning a ritual to give them time to use the bathroom. If there is some exceptional reason why one must leave before the ritual is complete, he can be "cut out" by tracing a portal on the periphery and stepping through it. When outside the circle, the door is closed by retracing the portal in reverse. Some covens might have a designated person such as the Man in Black, tyler, or dragon who will help anyone who needs to leave and reenter the circle. This ritualistic "cutting" and "closing" prevents the energy being used in the circle from "leaking" out, and it also assures the continued focus on the matter at hand by other celebrants.

Altars and Tools

The most practical purpose for having altars in ritual spaces is to hold the tools that will be used, including candles, salt and water, incense, blade and wand, chalice or cup, and pentacle, all usually set out upon an altar cloth. Altars serve our aesthetic sensibilities when they display images of deities, statuary, natural objects such as shells, feathers, rocks, flowers, and/or seasonal greenery. By taking care in choosing what is put on the altars, a mundane, even ugly, place can be transformed into a place of beauty.

Altars are built for specific purposes. Some Pagan traditions have a very specific altar layout: each item has its prescribed place. The same deity iconography—statuary, paintings, photographs—is used at each gathering. Or every altar may be a new work of art.

The specific purpose of the ritual suggests which items are put upon the altar, which incense burned, what color candles lit, what deity(ies) invited, and whose witness or aid is sought. Creating an altar for a Moon ritual brings to bear a slightly different sensibility than creating one to celebrate a maiden's first blood. A Yule altar will contain slightly different items from those found on a Beltaine (Mayday) altar. Choice of color, flowers, imagery, incense, and other variables enhance the sacred space and aid the work.

The number and placement of altars differ from group to group and from one ritual to another. Dianic circles tend to set their altars in the center of the ritual space. Some groups have one altar in the North and three other "point candles" in the Quarters, while others will have four altars, one for each element, the most common elemental correspondences being East to Air, South to Fire, West to Water, and North to Earth.

These seemingly more housekeeping-type activities have a part to play in making the best, most efficacious, most powerful, moving magic.

Grounding and Centering

Once all celebrants have formed a circle, a priest/ess leads a short meditation to "ground and center" everyone. This commonly involves holding hands in a circle, closing the eyes, and breathing deeply together. She may also lead a guided meditation. These practices allow celebrants to drop their mundane cares and concerns.

In my tradition, we use the image of the tree of life as our body, with roots extending down into the deep, dark Earth and branches reaching to the sky. A group becomes a sacred grove of trees all standing together and shading each other. At the conclusion of grounding and centering, all are ready to focus on the ritual and nothing else.

Sacred Technologies To Change Consciousness and "Raising Energy"

Neopagan worshippers of the Old Gods, of Gaia, of Mother, have an array of techniques to advance their personal and collective spiritual practices. In seeking to tread a path in balance, harmony, and respect for Nature, Neopagans use these technologies of the sacred to help shift consciousness and to aid and fortify magic.

The most obvious means of effectuating change are rhythm and drumming, breathwork, chants, song, and vocalization, as well as dance, movement, gesture, and asana.[35] Cleaning and preparing the ritual space, indoors or out, initiates the process of using sacred technology to change consciousness.

All, some, or none of these sacred technologies can be found in an individual rite. Some things may not work as well for one person as others. For instance, I can shift into a magical consciousness in my bedroom, which is already an intimate and sanctified space in my life, almost immediately by lighting quarter candles and perhaps incense. On the other hand, one friend of mine never uses candles except when working with others who do. He does not erect altars either.

Some people use fasting and/or entheogens to enhance their practice. For others—for reasons of health, their own moral consciences, predisposition, or the legal climate—fasting or ingestion of mind-altering substances is not an option.

A drummer may set the pace and guide the dancing, singing, or chanting. Or a group may use rhythm in a way for everyone to participate. They may have an assortment of rattles, tambourines, sistrums, castanets, finger cymbals, drums, and other rhythm instruments for all celebrants to join in the rhythm making. A common technique for "raising energy" is dancing, unless there are celebrants who cannot indulge in vigorous exercise.

Whichever of these techniques are employed in a particular rite, they are all part of a common treasure.

"Cakes and Wine"

At the end of a ritual, all share a drink and some food. This part of ritual is called cakes and wine, cakes and ale, the feast, or some other similar term. This traditional term may be inaccurate if the group does not use alcoholic beverages in its rituals. Alternatively, there may be more than one communal cup going around so that those who cannot indulge in alcoholic substances are still part of this communal toast. This communal breaking of bread allows for socialization and fun.

One or more priest/esses bless the beverage and food to consecrate it for consumption. The chalice and plate of food are usually passed around the circle deosil (clockwise), sometimes with a blessing such as "May you never thirst" or "May you never hunger." Cakes and wine are not necessarily limited to those two substances; many rituals, especially large sabbat celebrations, include an entire shared meal. In our tradition, cakes and wine are potluck, with everyone expected to bring something to eat or drink to share.

Sharing food and drink also helps us to "ground" after people have raised a lot of energy. This is an important element, since people who are not grounded well enough, who are not safely back into their everyday reality, can have problems negotiating life outside. They may find it difficult to drive or navigate. Their awareness of the mundane is compromised, and they are therefore vulnerable in the outside world.

Post-Ritual Evaluation

No ritual is complete without an evaluation. How did it go? What happened for you? What worked? What did not work? What should be repeated another time? What should be revised, and what should be abandoned because it did not work at all? I do not think it is fair to try to analyze a ritual until it has been given a chance to work its effect. Therefore, this should not be done until at least 24 hours have elapsed.

Critiquing a ritual does not mean criticizing the priest/ess(es) and their acts. Rather, critique tells how each individual experienced the ritual—what felt good, what sent a thrill through one's body, and what fell flat. This not only helps the process of integrating the experience into one's life, it also helps the ritual designers to know what is effective for others.

Each ritual should be approached with respect, awareness, and an open heart and mind to allow for the full experience that good rituals can provide.

THE PURPOSE OF NEOPAGAN RITUAL

> The purpose of ritual is to change the mind of the human being. It's sacred drama in which you are the audience as well as the participant and the purpose of it is to activate parts of the mind that are not activated by everyday activity.
>
> —*Sharon Devlin*[36]

All humans perform rituals of many kinds every day. Sacred ritual is what we humans do to create a sense of sacredness in an otherwise seemingly dull mundane world. We set aside a special time and place to focus on the spiritual aspects of our lives. Our ancestors may have used sacred drama to help us attain a sense of oneness with the cosmos. Ritual, which may have evolved from sacred drama, can help us access parts of ourselves that our rational minds normally obscure. Ritual can help us to attune ourselves to the cycles of Nature. Ritual can help us bypass our minds and experience our intuitive selves and our bodies in new and different ways.

When people think of Witchcraft, one of the first things they think of is magical spells. Spells are intended to effect change in our personal lives and in the world, changes such as healing, protection, or abundance. Neopagans ritualize their spells by "charging," or empowering, them in the sacred circle. Although spellwork is done in the context of ritual, not every ritual involves the casting of spells. Nor does every Neopagan perform spells. However, often the principles of good spellwork—intent, harmonization, and attuning to the forces of Nature—are applied in rituals done for other reasons.

Many rituals are celebrations, marking an event in a very conscious and intentional fashion. These rites of passage are discussed in detail below. Other rituals are designed to help the ritualists to go deeper within themselves or to explore farther beyond the boundaries of their individual selves. Rituals foster bonding with the others in the circle and help transcend separateness. Rituals can lead to a deeper understanding of deity. The rituals called sabbats are celebratory in nature. They celebrate the seasons and the turning of the Wheel of the Year. Other rituals may be designed to bring people closer to a particular deity, to bring about personal insights or transformation, or to facilitate a deeper emotional and/or spiritual experience.

SPEAKING TO OUR OTHER SELVES

One fundamental purpose of Neopagan ritual is to allow the conscious mind to get in touch with other levels of awareness. Because ritual uses symbolism across a wide range of senses, it allows us to communicate with powerful parts of ourselves that do not use verbal language. These are often just those aspects of our being that have been most neglected.

As feminist priestess Z. Budapest said: "The purpose of ritual is to wake up the old mind in us, to put it to work. The old ones inside us, the collective consciousness, the many lives, the divine eternal parts, the senses and parts of the brain that have been ignored. Those parts do not speak English. They do not care about television. But they do understand candlelight and colors. They do understand nature."[37]

For many Neopagans this is a vital need not served in any other way by Western culture, and this is part of our drive to ritualize. Kelly feels that

> You do a ritual because you need to, basically, and because it just cuts through and operates on everything besides the "head" level … since ritual is a need, and since the mainstream of Western civilization is not meeting this need, a great deal of what's happening these days is, simply, people's attempts to find ways to meet this need for themselves.[38]

Ritual uses all the senses to achieve this: Incense, food, colorful images, robes or body paint, music, especially drums, dancing, and set gestures. All these elements have symbolic significance that our more instinctive, nonverbal awareness will readily understand.

Timothy Leary is attributed on several Web sites and in Neopagan discussion as having said that "Ritual is to the internal sciences what experiment is to the external sciences."[39] This is especially true for Neopagans, who, as we noted earlier, *deliberately create* their rituals. By using the sacred techniques of many spiritual paths and adopting ideas from many human disciplines, Neopagans attempt to construct rituals that will communicate with deeper levels of the self.

Some suggest that ritual is a way of "thinking" through the body. Richard Schechner believes that "Rituals don't so much express ideas as embody them. Rituals are thought-in/as-action."[40] For Performance theorist Deirdre Sklar, movement is "a corporeal way of knowing." She believes that the body knowledge that comes through movement cannot be spoken about because it uses the "vocabulary" of sensations.[41]

Speaking to our other selves is perhaps most important at times of personal change, so they are marked with *rites of passage.*

RITES OF PASSAGE

Among the rites of passage celebrated for individuals are the following: presentation, naming, and blessing rituals for babies; first-blood rituals; a boy's transition to manhood; commitment ceremonies, handfastings, and/or weddings; eldering, croning (ritualizing a woman's coming to the age of wisdom and repose), and saging (ritualizing a man's coming into his age of wisdom and repose); dying and death; funerals and memorials.

Human life is defined by moments of transition: Birth, marriage, and death are the most familiar in Western culture, and Neopagans ritually mark such events. But Neopagans, like those in other times and places, honor more subtle life changes.

The principal rite of passage people usually think of in connection with Witchcraft is the initiation rite. This is done when a person commits herself to a chosen path. Some traditions have rites of passage for dedications, preparatory steps to full initiation. In such traditions, subsequent rituals are performed to acknowledge members' attainment of elevations, usually called First, Second, and Third Degrees. These degrees mean that members have acquired successively higher (or deeper) levels of knowledge and skill.

Arnold van Gennep first used the term "rites of passage" in 1908,[42] and, although his theory may oversimplify the complex process of ritual transition, it remains useful. He identified three stages in every rite of passage: (1) The process begins with the key participant being separated from her/his normal life in preparation for (2) entering liminal space. We have already noted the importance of liminal space above. (3) The final phase is reintegration into society in a new role.

According to van Gennep, different rituals emphasize different phases. The separation phase is more important in death rites, while reintegration is key in handfasting. The liminal phase is the most important part of an initiation, as this is where an initiate will be tested and taught secrets of the Tradition.

Van Gennep noted common elements of these rites, including simulated death and resurrection, and a symbolic passage through an opening or across a threshold. We have seen how these motifs are used in "Neopagan Ritual in Practice."

In some tribal initiation ceremonies participants may be isolated in the liminal space for a long period of time. Victor Turner describes the close bonding that occurs between people in liminal space as *communitas.*[43] Before leaving van Gennep, it is worth considering a key critique of his theory. Bruce Lincoln claimed that his theory describes only the structure of *male* rites. He noted several differences in traditional tribal women's initiations that challenge the van Gennep model: Women are usually initiated individually, so they have no opportunity to develop *communitas,* and there is little in the way of new knowledge communicated to them. The whole process can be seen as an "opiate for an oppressed class," constructing social control rather than facilitating transformation.[44] Lincoln's work is relevant to Neopagan ritual precisely because it does not apply: Neopagan rituals, whether for women or men, celebrate and facilitate transformation, rather than construct control.

THE POWER THAT CONNECTS

Neopagan ritual can put us back in touch with "the wisdom of the body," a deep knowledge of our connection with the other-than-human world. We believe this reconnection can help us heal our relationship with the planet.

Most Neopagans would agree that modern life has led to increasing alienation from nature and from one another, and that ritual can—at least temporarily—shift our awareness to a more connected state. Adler believes that the whole purpose of ritual is "to end, for a time, our sense of human alienation from nature and from each other."[45]

Alexei Kondratiev expresses his belief that "attunement to the natural world" is the main contribution Neopaganism can make to the modern world. This attunement "is not just an intellectual understanding about what nature is good for" but rather "a gut feeling."[46]

In *Key Aspects of Neopagan Ritual* we noted how ritual dance can help resolve personal issues about our bodies, enabling a deeper emotional sensitivity and a greater understanding of bodily needs.[47]

Ritual reconnection may not only be with our bodies or the other-than-human world, but also with the ancestors. Ancestral reconnection is perhaps most apparent in rites of passage and during Samhain celebrations—the Neopagan "Day of the Dead." (See "Neopagan Ritual in Practice" above.)

Ritual can also help connect us at a social level. A feeling of *communitas* emerges during a ritual that helps bond social groups. It is common for Neopagans to describe a feeling of "coming home" when they first discover this particular path. Oz's experience of her first Neopagan ritual is typical: "Tears ran down my face. I felt a tremendous emotion as though after a long search I had finally found my people again."[48] The power of ritual to bond and inspire a group is used by Eco-Pagans, especially in preparation for a protest action. In her book *Sacred Land, Sacred Sex: Rapture of the Deep,* Dolores La Chapelle states,

> One of the primary biological functions of ritual behavior is to make it easier … for individuals to become synchronized for group action. This action might be directed toward some environmental challenge that cannot be met by individual action.[49]

Bron Taylor describes how some rituals at Earth First! camps use drumming and dancing in a similar way to those described by Pike, above. During these rituals "some activists report mystically fusing with the cosmos, 'losing themselves' and their sense of independent ego, as they dance into the night."[50]

Less ecstatic rituals take place to support activist comrades. Typically, a conventional circle is formed and energy is "drawn-down from the moon, from the four directions, and most commonly from earth itself." Taylor notes that both forms of ritual are typically coordinated by Wiccan priestesses, but our experience suggests a more eclectic range of practice.

CONTROVERSIES AND ISSUES

The Origins of Neopaganism

Eclectic Neopagan ritual draws on spiritual paths from many lands. Although this adds to the richness of our practice, there are accusations of cultural appropriation. Most discussions focus on Native American cultures, but others—notably perhaps Aboriginal Australian—are also appropriated. This is a complex and sensitive issue to tackle in a short space, but in essence the concern is that Neopaganism appropriates aspects of another people's culture.[51] Those who have honored an ancient path for centuries see their most sacred traditions misrepresented, used, or abused by people who have no understanding of their true meaning.

According to Native American scholar Lisa Aldred, this "imperialistically nostalgic fetishization" is an expression of a consumerist attitude to spirituality.[52]

While many share Aldred's view, the issues around cultural appropriation are complex and attitudes vary. Some Native Americans recognize the possibility of genuine cultural exchange. Many tribal groups do not object to teaching outsiders, but insist that they learn spiritual practices within a total cultural context and respect any restrictions that are placed on sharing knowledge.

Sam Gill believes that while it is appropriate for people "to be inspired by and influenced by other traditions," "[t]o do so superficially and to claim special knowledge of the source tradition is to engage in what can only be termed domination and conquest."[53]

Some accusations of cultural appropriation are due to misunderstanding: Neopaganism has a complex history, and aspects found in common with Native American traditions—like the quartered sacred circle—have evolved independently. In fact, a great deal of Neopagan ritual can be exonerated from any accusation of cultural appropriation: traditional Wicca and Witchcraft focus on European traditions, as does Heathenry (Northern Traditions) and most Druidry.

However, eclectic Neopagan ritual and Neo-Shamanism do draw on Native Americans traditions, and in many cases the accusations are sound. Although many Neopagans remain ignorant of the issues, others are working to develop a greater respect for the traditions from whom they might wish to borrow.

There is a danger that if Neopagans avoid working with any tradition that is not their own, their rituals will become "whiter and whiter."[54] In a world where cultures constantly mingle and cross-fertilize, this seems like a mistake.

As Starhawk says, "The edge where different systems meet is always fertile ground, in culture as well as in nature."[55]

But we must tread carefully as everyone loses when the rot of cultural appropriation sets in. Without cultural context a sacred practice is drained of meaning, and, even if it still functions, it is irrevocably distorted. As Paula Gunn Allen, Laguna Pueblo author and teacher, says, "You cannot do Indian spirituality without an Indian community … it's physical and social and spiritual and they're fused together."[56]

Some propose that the way forward is to develop genuine cultural sharing which "involves interaction with the whole of a person and community, reciprocal giving and receiving, sharing of struggle as well as joy, receiving what the community wants to give, not what we want to take."[57]

Oren Lyons, a traditional chief of the Onondaga Nation expresses a similar sentiment: "We've got real problems today, tremendous problems which threaten the survival of the planet. Indians and non-Indians must confront these problems together, and this means we must have honest dialogue, but this dialogue is impossible so long as non-Indians remain deluded about things as basic as Indian spirituality."[58]

The key is to be clear about what counts as appropriation and what is genuine sharing. Whenever colonialism or neocolonialism creates an unequal distribution of power then appropriation is likely to occur. If Neopagans are to work with spiritual integrity, we need to educate ourselves about the issues, abandon any practice that is legitimately refused to us, and develop rituals based on the cultural richness that remains. As we proceed with openness, honesty, and respect, we believe Neopagans will discover opportunities for real cultural sharing.

The Growth in Neopaganism

Neopaganism is one of the fastest growing religions in the United States. How are Neopagans coping with this prodigious growth? Several questions must be faced in the future: As more and more people want to perform ritual in the Nature they revere, what damage might ensue? Will Neopaganism lose its depth if it becomes a more popular, casual practice? Can a sizable religion function without more structure and hierarchy?

There are already Neopagan organizations that own and manage land for the community to practice ritual outdoors. This has worked well to date, and this model can be expected to alleviate pressures on the land. Permanent ritual structures are also appearing, including replica shrines created by reconstructionist traditions. For instance, Pagan landowners erect stone circles to the *vanir* (Norse Earth deities); others construct labyrinths. Also, there is a permanent shrine with a statue of Hekate in Index, Washington.

Neopagans typically worship in their homes, backyards, parks, woods, and beaches. Because of the intimate nature of Neopagan rituals and the small size of congregations, Neopagans seldom have need of large indoor ritual space. When needed, however, Neopagans rent halls, frequently at Unitarian Universalist Association buildings.

Ritual and Priesthood

Neopaganism is a moving target. In recent years the complexion of Neopaganism has been changing at a rapid pace. One result of this growth has been the emergence of a priest/esshood and a laity not seen before in countercultural movements. This development is appropriate in some of the reconstructed traditions, but it proves problematical in Witchen circles where all participants are capable of and empowered to perform any ritual role.

There are people who share a general Neopagan world view yet have no desire to pursue studies, training, or deeper involvement. However, they wish to share the seasonal celebrations with others and to have someone preside at their life passages. Ritual groups have arisen that produce public sabbat celebrations to meet this need.

In addition, Neopagan seminaries are beginning to train those who are called to service in ministry skills. Students learn about other forms of Neopaganism than their own tradition, in interfaith organizations, secular law as it affects religion, public liturgy, pastoral skills, requirements, and other relevant subjects. Although no Neopagan *must* minister to others in order to practice her tradition, it is important for those who are called to be well equipped to answer the call.

In addition to the aforementioned communal Neopagan land where Neopagans can live, work, study, and gather for festivals, parents are creating camps and schools for children and adolescents, as well as homeschooling.

Neopagans are greying, so they are beginning to look at ways to meet the needs of an aging community. More gatherings are taking place indoors where there are amenities like beds and indoor plumbing. Easier access allows for more comfortable participation of older—and very young—Neopagans in community activities. There is almost no infrastructure in terms of hospitals, facilities for the disabled or elderly, communal buildings, and cemeteries.

With thought and care and creativity, Neopagans will evolve in unique ways consistent with this unique religious response. The future of Neopaganism is wide open.

CONCLUSION

Victor Turner believed that 1960s counterculture, like the Neopagan ritual it inspired, sought the transformational power of "the liberated and disciplined body itself, with its many untapped resources for pleasure, pain, and expression."[59]

Schechner thinks Turner's optimism was probably unjustified.[60] But is it? Many Neopagans believe their rituals can have a profoundly transformative power, and the steady growth of the movement suggests it addresses a deep social need.

The West stands at a point of transition and challenge: Neopagan ritual offers itself as a paradoxical guide in these strange days—the path of an "ancient-future religion," drawing on the past, but working in the present towards a bright and sustainable future.

NOTES

1. Malidoma Patrice Somé, *Ritual: Power, Healing, and Community* (New York: Penguin/Compass, 1993), 1.

2. Joanne Pearson, Richard Roberts, and Geoffrey Samuel, eds., *Nature Religion Today* (Edinburgh: Edinburgh University Press, 1998), 1.

3. Aidan Kelly, "Western Occult Tradition," in *Encyclopedia of Cults, Sects, and New Religions,* ed. James L. Lewis, 2nd ed. (New York: Prometheus Books, 2002), 791–792.

4. Lewis, ed., *Encyclopedia of Cults, Sects, and New Religions,* 344.

5. Graham Harvey, *Listening People, Speaking Earth: Contemporary Paganism* (London: Hurst and Co., 1997), 138.

6. Ibid., 139.

7. Ibid.

8. Susan Greenwood, "The Nature of the Goddess: Sexual Identities and Power in Contemporary Witchcraft," in *Nature Religion Today,* ed. Pearson, Roberts, and Samuel, 109.

9. Chas S. Clifton, personal communications with the authors.

10. "Both are different titles for essentially the same body of rites. These are the core of the Pagan Way, and were designed and published as 'public domain.'" Ed Fitch and Janine Renee, *Magical Rites from the Crystal Well* (St. Paul, MN: Llewellyn Publications, 1988), 146.

11. Ronald Hutton, *The Triumph of the Moon: A History of Modern Pagan Witchcraft* (Oxford: Oxford University Press, 1999), 54–57.

12. Greenham Common was the site of a U.S. Air Force base in England. In 1981 a women's peace camp was established there in protest at the deployment of cruise missiles. Over the next 19 years women at the camp drew on Goddess spirituality to support their protest. The camp closed on September 5, 2000, after 19 years of a continuous presence. It is now being transformed by the Greenham Common Trust into Greenham Common Park.

13. Margot Adler, *Drawing Down the Moon: Witches, Druids, Goddess Worshippers and Other Pagans in America Today,* revised and expanded ed. (New York: Penguin Books, 1986), 414.

14. Hutton, *The Triumph of the Moon,* 341.

15. Adler, *Drawing Down the Moon,* 198.

16. Sarah M. Pike, *Earthly Bodies, Magical Selves: Contemporary Pagans and the Search for Community* (Berkeley, CA, and London: University of California Press, 2001), 19–20.

17. Ibid., 183.

18. Ibid., 198.

19. Ibid., 186.

20. Ibid., 197.

21. An entheogen is a substance the ingestion of which creates an experience of the deity. For instance, the intoxication produced by wine can offer an experience of Dionysus (i.e., the Maenads). Other substances believed to provide divine insight are peyote buttons and amanita muscaria mushrooms. Traditional "Witches' flying ointment" is made of carefully combined plant substances known for both their soporific and stimulating properties.

22. Victor Turner, *The Ritual Process: Structure and Anti-Structure* (Ithaca, NY: Cornell University Press, 1969), 19.

23. Starhawk, *Webs of Power: Notes from the Global Uprising* (Gabriola, B.C.: New Society Publishers, 2002), 103.

24. See "Invented Rituals" in Catherine Bell, *Ritual: Perspectives and Dimensions* (New York: Oxford University Press, 1997), 223–242.

25. See Sabina Magliocco, "Ritual Is My Chosen Art Form: The Creation of Ritual as Folk Art among Contemporary Pagans," in *Magical Religion and Modern Witchcraft*, ed. James R. Lewis (Albany, NY: State University of New York Press, 1996), 93–119.

26. Jone Salomonsen, *Enchanted Feminism: Ritual, Gender and Divinity among the Witches of San Francisco* (London and New York: Routledge, 2002), 14.

27. Catherine Bell, "The Ritual Body," in *Ritual Theory, Ritual Practice* (Oxford: Oxford University Press, 1992), 93–117.

28. Salomonsen, *Enchanted Feminism*, 211.

29. Kay Turner, "Contemporary Feminist Rituals," in *The Politics of Women's Spirituality*, ed. Charlene Spretnak (Garden City, NY: Anchor Books, 1982), 222.

30. Peter Beyer, "Globalisation and the Religion of Nature," in *Nature Religion Today*, ed. Pearson, Roberts, and Samuel, 17.

31. Ellen Evert Hopman and Lawrence Bond, *People of the Earth: The New Pagans Speak Out* (Rochester, VT: Destiny Books, 1995), 342.

32. The adjective "Witchen" refers to Craft rituals of all kinds, whether they are BTW (Wiccan) or not.

33. Unclothed, nude, clad in the sky.

34. See Starhawk, *The Spiral Dance* (San Francisco: HarperSanFrancisco, 1979), for an explanation of "Younger Self," one of the Three Souls.

35. An *asana* is a sacred pose or posture used in yoga.

36. Adler, *Drawing Down the Moon*, 141.

37. Ibid., 198.

38. Ibid., 161.

39. http://www.spiritmoving.com/resources/ritual.htm; http://www.rawilsonfans.com/articles/neurologic.htm; http://www.mozuna.com/quotes.htm

40. Richard Schechner, *Performance Studies: An Introduction* (London and New York: Routledge, 2002), 50.

41. Deirdre Sklar, "Can Bodylore Be Brought to Its Senses?" in *Journal of American Folklore* 107, no. 423 (Winter 1994): 9–22.

42. Arnold Van Gennep, *The Rites of Passage* (Chicago: University of Chicago Press, 1960 [1908]).

43. Victor Turner, *The Ritual Process: Structure and Anti-Structure* (Ithaca, NY: Cornell University Press, 1991), 128–129.

44. Bruce Lincoln, *Emerging from the Chrysalis: Rituals of Women's Initiation* (New York and Oxford: Oxford University Press, 1991), 105. Although in the 1981 edition Lincoln suggests that such rituals are a valuable means to provide meaning to women's oppression (1981, p. 107), his revised edition is highly critical of this process (1991, p. 112).

45. Adler, *Drawing Down the Moon*, 162.

46. Hopman and Bond, *People of the Earth*, 25.

47. Pike, *Earthly Bodies, Magical Selves*, 198.

48. Oz, "An Insider's Look at Pagan Festivals," in *The Modern Craft Movement: Witchcraft Today, Book One*, ed. Chas S. Clifton (St. Paul, MN: Llewellyn Publications, 1992), 40.

49. Dolores La Chapelle, *Sacred Land, Sacred Sex: Rapture of the Deep* (Silverton, CO: Finn Hill Arts, 1988), 154.

50. Bron Taylor, "Earth and Nature-Based Spirituality (Part II): From Earth First! and Bioregionalism to Scientific Paganism and the New Age," *Religion* 31 (2001): 228.

51. See Christina Welch, "Appropriating the Didjeridu and the Sweat Lodge: New Age Baddies and Indigenous Victims?" in *The Encyclopaedic Source Book of the New Age,* ed. James Lewis (New York: Prometheus Press, 2004), 349–375.

52. Lisa Aldred, "Plastic Shamans & Astroturf Sun Dances: New Age Commercialization of Native American Spirituality," *American Indian Quarterly* 24, no. 3 (2000): 329–332.

53. Sam Gill, in "The Power of Story," *American Indian Culture and Research Journal* 12, no. 3 (1988): 69–84.

54. Starhawk, *The Spiral Dance,* 202.

55. Ibid.

56. Jane Caputi, "Interview with Paula Gunn Allen," *Trivia* 16/17 (Fall 1990): 50.

57. Myke Johnson, "Wanting to be Indian: When Spiritual Searching Turns into Cultural Theft," in *Belief Beyond Boundaries: Wicca, Celtic Spirituality, and the New Age,* ed. Joanne Pearson (copublished by Milton Keynes, UK: The Open University, and Hants, UK: Ashgate Publishing, 2002), 287.

58. Ward Churchill, with M. Annette Jaimes, *Fantasies of the Master Race: Literature, Cinema and the Colonisation of American Indians* (Monroe, ME: Common Courage Press, 1992), 216–217.

59. Turner, quoted by Schechner, *Performance Studies.*

60. Ibid., 62.

FURTHER READING

Adler, Margot. *Drawing Down the Moon: Witches, Druids, Goddess Worshippers and Other Pagans in America Today.* Revised and expanded edition. New York: Penguin Books, 1986. Revised and expanded edition forthcoming.

Bell, Catherine. *Ritual Theory, Ritual Practice.* Oxford: Oxford University Press, 1992.

Beyer, Peter. "Globalisation and the Religion of Nature." In *Nature Religion Today.* Edited by Joanne Pearson, Richard Roberts, and Geoffrey Samuel. Edinburgh: Edinburgh University Press, 1998.

Blain, Jenny, Douglas Ezzy, and Graham Harvey, eds. *Researching Paganisms.* Walnut Creek, CA: AltaMira Press, 2004.

Bonewits, Isaac. *Rites of Worship: A Neopagan Approach.* Berkeley, CA: Dubsar House Publishing, 2003.

Clark Roof, Wade, ed. *Contemporary American Religion.* New York: Macmillan Reference USA, 2000.

Clifton, Chas S., and Graham Harvey, eds. *The Paganism Reader.* London and New York: Routledge, 2004.

Eliade, Mircea, ed. *Encyclopedia of Religion.* New York: Macmillan Publishing Company, 1987.

Frisk, Trudy. "Paganism, Magic, and the Control of Nature." *The Trumpeter: Journal of Ecosophy,* 14, no. 4 (1997).

Griffin, Wendy, ed. *Daughters of the Goddess: Studies of Healing, Identity, and Empowerment.* Walnut Creek, CA: Alta Mira Press, 2000.

Grimes, Ronald L. *Deeply into the Bone: Re-Inventing Rites of Passage.* Berkeley: University of California Press, 2000.

Lewis, James L., ed. *Magical Religion and Modern Witchcraft.* Albany: State University of New York Press, 1996.

Magliocco, Sabina. *Witching Culture: Folklore and Neo-Paganism in America.* Philadelphia: University of Pennsylvania Press, 2004.

Melton, J. Gordon. *The Encyclopedia of American Religions.* Detroit: Gale Research, 1993.

NightMare, M. Macha. *Witchcraft and the Web: Weaving Traditions Online.* Toronto: ECW Press, 2001.

Rabinovitch, Shelley, and James Lewis. *The Encyclopaedia of Modern Witchcraft and Neo-Paganism.* New York: Citadel Press, 2002.

Starhawk. *Dreaming the Dark: Magic, Sex & Politics.* 15th Anniversary Edition. Boston: Beacon Press, 1997.

———. *The Spiral Dance.* 20th Anniversary Edition. San Francisco: HarperSanFrancisco, [1979] [1989], 1999.

Victor Turner, *The Ritual Process: Structure and Anti-Structure.* Ithaca, NY: Cornell University Press, 1969.

The Witches' Voice, www.witchvox.com.

York, Michael. *Pagan Theology: Paganism as a World Religion.* New York: New York University Press, 2003.

Selected Bibliography

Bach, Marcus. *They Have Found a Faith*. Indianapolis, IN: Bobbs-Merrill, 1946.

———. *Strange Sects and Curious Cults*. New York: Dodd, Mead and Co., 1962.

Barker, Eileen, ed. *New Religious Movements: A Perspective for Understanding Society*. New York and Toronto: The Edwin Mellen Press, 1982.

———. *New Religious Movements: A Practical Introduction*. London: HMSO, 1989.

Beckford, James A. *Cult Controversies: The Societal Response to New Religious Movements*. London and New York: Tavistock Publications, 1985.

Bednarowski, Mary Farrell. *New Religions and the Theological Imagination in America*. (Bloomington and Indianapolis, IN: Indiana University Press, 1989.

Braden, Charles S. *These Also Believe: A Study of Modern American Cults and Minority Religious Movements*. New York: The Macmillan Co., 1949.

Bromley, David G., and J. Gordon Melton, eds. *Cults, Religion & Violence*. Cambridge: Cambridge University Press, 2002.

Bromley, David G., and Lewis F. Carter, eds. *Toward Reflexive Ethnography: Participating, Observing, Narrating*. Amsterdam and New York: JAI, 2001.

Bromley, David G., and Jeffrey K. Hadden, eds. *Religion and the Social Order: The Handbook on Cults and Sects in America*. Vol. 3, Part A. Greenwich, CT, and London: JAI Press Inc., 1993.

Bromley, David G., and Jeffrey K. Hadden, eds. *Religion and the Social Order: The Handbook on Cults and Sects in America*. Vol. 3, Part B. Greenwich, CT, and London: JAI Press Inc., 1993.

Bromley, David G., and Phillip E. Hammond, eds. *The Future of New Religious Movements*. Macon, GA: Mercer University Press, 1987.

Chryssides, George D. *Exploring New Religions*. London and New York: Cassell, 1999.

Chryssides, George D., and Margaret Wilkins, eds. *A Reader in New Religious Movements*. London and New York: Continuum, 2006.

Clark, Elmer T. *The Small Sects in America*. New York: Abingdon Press, 1949.

Clarke, Peter B., ed. *Encyclopedia of New Religious Movements*. London and New York: Routledge, 2006.

Daschke, Dereck, and W. Michael Ashcraft, eds. *New Religious Movements: A Documentary Reader*. New York: New York University Press, 2005.

Davis, Derek H., and Barry Hankins, eds. *New Religious Movements and Religious Liberty in America.* Waco, TX: Baylor University Press, 2003.

Dawson, Lorne L. *Comprehending Cults: The Sociology of New Religious Movements.* New York: Oxford University Press, 1998.

Dawson, Lorne L., ed. *Cults and New Religious Movements: A Reader.* Malden, MA, and Oxford: Blackwell Publishing, 2003.

Ellwood, Robert S., Jr. *Religious and Spiritual Groups in Modern America.* Englewood Cliffs, NJ: Prentice-Hall, Inc., 1973.

Festinger, Leon, Henry W. Riecken, and Staley Schachter. *When Prophecy Fails.* Minneapolis, MN: University of Minnesota Press, 1956.

Fichter, Joseph H., ed. *Alternatives to American Mainline Religions.* Barrytown, NY: Unification Theological Seminary, 1983.

Foster, Lawrence. *Religion and Sexuality: Three American Communal Experiments of the Nineteenth Century.* New York and Oxford: Oxford University Press, 1981.

Galanter, Marc. *Cults and New Religious Movements Task Force Report of the American Psychiatric Association.* Washington, D.C.: American Psychiatric Press, Inc., 1989.

Gallagher, Eugene V. *The New Religious Movements Experience in America.* (Westport, CT: Greenwood Press, 2004.

Glock, Charles Y., and Robert N. Bellah, eds. *The New Religious Consciousness.* Berkeley, CA, Los Angeles, CA,. and London: University of California Press, 1976.

Hall, John R., Philip D. Schuyler, and Sylvanie Trinh. *Apocalypse Observed: Religious Movements and Violence in North America, Europe and Japan.* London and New York: Routledge, 2000.

Hammond, Phillip E., ed. *The Sacred in a Secular Age: Toward Revision in the Scientific Study of Religion.* Berkeley: University of California Press, 1985.

Jacobs, Janet. *Divine Disenchantment: Deconverting from New Religions.* Bloomington and Indianapolis, IN: Indiana University Press, 1989.

Jenkins, Phillip. *Mystics and Messiahs: Cults and New Religions in American History.* New York: Oxford University Press, 2000.

Kanter, Rosabeth M. *Commitment and Community: Communes and Utopias in Sociological Perspective.* Cambridge, MA: Harvard University Press, 1972.

Kaplan, Jeffrey, and Heléne Lööw, eds. *The Cultic Milieu: Oppositional Subcultures in an Age of Globalization.* Walnut Creek, CA: Alta Mira Press, 2002.

Lewis, James R. *Legitimating New Religions.* New Brunswick, NJ: Rutgers University Press, 2003.

Lewis, James R., ed. *The Oxford Handbook of New Religious Movements.* New York: Oxford University Press, 2003.

Lewis, James R., and Jesper Aagaard Petersen, eds. *Controversial New Religions.* New York: Oxford University Press, 2005.

Lucas, Phillip Charles. *The Odyssey of a New Religion: The Holy Order of MANS from New Age to Orthodoxy.* Bloomington, IN: Indiana University Press, 1995.

Lucas, Phillip Charles, and Thomas Robbins, eds. *New Religious Movements in the 21st Century: Legal, Political, and Social Challenges in Global Perspective.* New York and London: Routledge, 2004.

McCloud, Sean. *Making the American Religious Fringe: Exotics, Subversives, and Journalists, 1955–1993.* Chapel Hill, NC, and London: University of North Carolina Press, 2004.

Melton, J. Gordon. *Biographical Dictionary of American Cult and Sect Leaders.* New York: Garland Publishing Co., 1986.

Melton, J. Gordon, ed. *The Encyclopedia of American Religions.* Wilmington, NC: Consortium Books, 1978.

Melton, J. Gordon, ed. *The Encyclopedic Handbook of the Cults.* New York: Garland Publishing Co., 1986.

Miller, Timothy, ed. *When Prophets Die: The Postcharismatic Fate of New Religious Movements.* Albany, NY: State University of New York Press, 1991.

Moore, R. Laurence. *Religious Outsiders and the Making of Americans.* New York: Oxford University Press, 1986.

Needleman, Jacob. *The New Religions.* Garden City, NY: Doubleday and Co., 1970.

Needleman, Jacob, and George Baker, eds. *Understanding the New Religions.* New York: The Seabury Press, 1978.

Nova Religio: The Journal of Alternative and Emergent Religions. Published by University of California Press four times a year.

"Ontario Consultants on Religious Tolerance," http://religioustolerance.org.

Palmer, Susan J. *Moon Sisters, Krishna Mothers, Rajneesh Lovers: Women's Roles in New Religions.* Syracuse, NY: Syracuse University Press, 1995.

Palmer, Susan J., and Charlotte E. Hardman, eds. *Children in New Religions.* New Brunswick, NJ: Rutgers University Press, 1999.

Partridge, Christopher. *New Religions: A Guide.* Oxford: Oxford University Press, 2004.

Poewe, Karla, and Irving Hexham. *New Religions as Global Cultures.* Boulder, CO: Westview Press, 1996.

"The Religious Movements Homepage Project @ The University of Virginia," http://religious-movements.lib.virginia.edu.

Richardson, James T., ed. *Conversion Careers: In and Out of the New Religions.* London: Sage Publications, 1978.

———, ed. *Regulating Religion: Case Studies from Around the Globe.* New York: Kluwer Academic/Plenum Publishers, 2004.

Robbins, Thomas. *Cults, Converts, and Charisma: the Sociology of New Religious Movements.* London, Newbury Park, CA: Sage Publications, 1988.

Robbins, Thomas, and Dick Anthony, eds. *In Gods We Trust: New Patterns of Religious Pluralism in America.* 2nd ed. New Brunswick, NJ: Transaction Publishers, 1990.

Robbins, Thomas, and Susan Palmer, eds. *Millennium, Messiahs, and Mayhem.* London: Routledge, 1997.

Rothstein, Mikael, and Reender Kranenborg, eds. *New Religions in a Postmodern World.* Aarhus, Denmark: Aarhus University Press, 2003.

Saliba, John A. *Understanding New Religious Movements.* Grand Rapids, MI: Eerdmans, 1996.

Stark, Rodney, ed. *Religious Movements: Genesis, Exodus, and Numbers.* New York: Paragon House Publishers, 1985.

Stark, Rodney, and William Sims Bainbridge. *The Future of Religion: Secularization, Revival, and Cult Formation.* Berkeley and Los Angeles: University of California Press, 1985.

Wallis, Roy. *The Elementary Forms of the New Religious Life.* London: Routledge and Kegan Paul, 1984.

Wallis, Roy, ed. *Sectarianism: Analyses of Religious and Non-Religious Sects.* New York: John Wiley and Sons, 1975.

Wessinger, Catherine. *How the Millennium Comes Violently: From Jonestown to Heaven's Gate.* New York: Seven Bridges Press, 2000.

Wessinger, Catherine, ed. *Women's Leadership in Marginal Religions: Explorations Outside the Mainstream.* Urbana and Chicago, IL: University of Illinois Press, 1993.

Wilson, Bryan R. *Sects and Society: A Sociological Study of the Elim Tabernacle, Christian Science and Christadelphians.* Berkeley: University of Calif. Press, 1961.

Wilson, Bryan R. *The Social Dimensions of Sectarianism: Sects and New Religious Movements in Contemporary Society.* New York: Oxford University Press, 1992.

Wilson, Bryan R., and Jamie Cresswell, eds. *New Religious Movements: Challenge and Response.* New York and London: Routledge, 1999.

Wuthnow, Robert. *The Consciousness Reformation.* Berkeley: University of California Press, 1976.

Wuthnow, Robert. *Experimentation in American Religion: The New Mysticisms and Their Implications for the Churches.* Berkeley and Los Angeles, Calif.: University of California Press, 1978.

Zablocki, Benjamin, and Thomas Robbins, eds. *Misunderstanding Cults: Searching for Objectivity in a Controversial Field.* (Toronto, Buffalo, New York, and London: University of Toronto Press, 2001.

Zaretsky, Irving I., and Mark P. Leone, eds. *Religious Movements in Contemporary America.* Princeton, NJ: Princeton University Press, 1974.

Index

About the Editors and Contributors

EDITORS

Eugene V. Gallagher is the Rosemary Park Professor of Religious Studies at Connecticut College. He is the author of *Divine Man or Magician? Celsus and Origen on Jesus* (1980), *Expectation and Experience: Explaining Religious Conversion* (1990), *The New Religious Movements Experience in America* (2004), and, with James D. Tabor, *Why Waco? Cults and the Battle for Religious Freedom in America* (1995), as well as articles on ancient Mediterranean religions and contemporary new religious movements.

W. Michael Ashcraft is Associate Professor of Religion at Truman State University in Kirksville, Missouri. He is the author of *The Dawn of the New Cycle: Point Loma Theosophists and American Culture* (2002) and coeditor with Dereck Daschke of *New Religious Movements: A Documentary Reader* (2005). He is currently conducting research for a book on the history of the study of new religions.

CONTRIBUTORS

Yaakov Ariel is Professor of Religious Studies at the University of North Carolina at Chapel Hill. He is the author of a number of books and articles on Christian-Jewish relations in the modern era. His book, *Evangelizing the Chosen People: Missions to the Jews in America,* has won the American Society of Church History Outler prize.

Mary Farrell Bednarowski is Professor Emerita of Religious Studies at United Theological Seminary of the Twin Cities. She is the author of three books, among them *New Religions and the Theological Imagination in America* (1989), and has a long-standing interest in various forms of theological innovation in American religion especially as it is related to issues of gender.

Helen A. Berger is Professor of Sociology at West Chester University of Pennsylvania. She is the author of *A Community of Witches: Contemporary and Neo-Paganisms Witchcraft in the United States* (1999), coauthor of *Voices from the Pagan Census: A National Survey of Witches and Pagans in the United States* (2003), and editor of *Witchcraft and Magic: Contemporary North America* (2005). She is now completing a book on teenage witches on three continents with Douglas Ezzy.

David G. Bromley is Professor of Sociology and Religious Studies at Virginia Commonwealth University. His most recent books are *Teaching New Religious Movements* (Oxford, 2007), *Defining Religion: Critical Approaches to Drawing Boundaries Between Sacred and Secular* (Elsevier Science/JAI Press, 2003), *Cults, Religion and Violence* (Cambridge University Press, 2001), and *Toward Reflexive Ethnography: Participating, Observing, Narrating* (Oxford: Elsevier Science/JAI Press, 2001).

Susan Love Brown is Associate Professor of Anthropology at Florida Atlantic University and also teaches in the Public Intellectuals and the Women's Studies programs. She is the editor of *Intentional Community: An Anthropological Perspective* and has written a number of articles about Ananda Village, a California New Age community with branches in Oregon, Washington, and Italy.

James D. Chancellor is the W.O. Carver Professor of World Religions at The Southern Baptist Theological Seminary and Professor of Religion at The Philippine Baptist Theological Seminary. He is the author of *Life in the Family: An Oral History of the Children of God* published by Syracuse University Press and has written numerous journal articles and book chapters.

George D. Chryssides is Senior Lecturer in Religious Studies at the University of Wolverhampton, England. His publications include *The Advent of Sun Myung Moon* (London: Macmillan, 1991), *Exploring New Religions* (London: Cassell, 1999), and *Historical Dictionary of New Religious Movements* (Metuchen, NJ: Scarecrow Press), as well as contributions to various anthologies and journals.

Mary Ann Clark is a lecturer in the University of Houston system where she teaches courses in Religious Studies, Humanities, and Anthropology and is the coordinator of the Council of Societies for the Study of Religion. She is the author of *Where Men are Wives and Mothers Rule: Santería Ritual Practices and Their Gender Implication* (2005). She has also published numerous journal articles and book chapters.

Douglas E. Cowan is Assistant Professor of Religious Studies and Social Development Studies at Renison College/University of Waterloo. In addition to numerous scholarly articles and chapters, he is the author of *Cyberhenge: Modern Pagans on the Internet* (Routledge, 2005), *The Remnant Spirit: Conservative Reform in Mainline Protestantism* (Praeger 2003), and *Bearing False Witness? An Introduction to the Christian Countercult* (Praeger 2003).

Robert S. Cox is Head of Special Collections and Adjunct Professor of History at the University of Massachusetts Amherst. He is author of *Body and Soul: A*

Sympathetic History of American Spiritualism (Charlottesville: University of Virginia Press, 2003) and editor of *The Shortest and Most Convenient Route: Lewis and Clark in Context* (Philadelphia: APS, 2004).

Daniel Cozort is Professor and chair of the Department of Religion at Dickinson College, in Carlisle, Pennsylvania, where he teaches about the religions of India and Native America. He is the author of *Unique Tenets of the Middle Way Consequence School, Highest Yoga Tantra, Buddhist Philosophy, Sand Mandala of Vajrabhairava,* and *Imagination and Enlightenment* and a documentary film, *Mandala: Sacred Circle of Vajrabhairava,* as well as book chapters and articles.

Dereck Daschke is Associate Professor of Philosophy and Religion at Truman State University in Kirksville, Missouri. He is coeditor of *New Religious Movements: A Documentary Reader*(2005). He has published frequently on ancient Jewish apocalypticism and prophecy, including "Mourning the End of Time: Apocalypses as Texts of Cultural Loss" in *Millennialism from the Hebrew Bible to the Present* (2002) and "'Because Of My Grief I Have Spoken': The Psychology of Loss in 4 Ezra" in *Psychology and the Bible* (2004).

Dell deChant is an Instructor and the Associate Chair in the Department of Religious Studies at the University of South Florida. He is also on the faculty of the Honors College at USF. He is the author of *The Sacred Santa: The Religious Dimensions of Consumer Culture* (2002) and coauthor of *Comparative Religious Ethics: A Narrative Approach* (2001). He has also published numerous journal and encyclopedia articles and book chapters on New Religious Movements.

Brenda Denzler works full-time as a writer at the University of North Carolina at Chapel Hill and part-time as an independent scholar with an interest in marginal religious phenomena and movements. She is the author of *The Lure of the Edge: Scientific Passions, Religious Beliefs, and the Pursuit of UFOs* (2001). She is also the author of several presentations and papers on the UFO community.

Jacob S. Dorman currently holds the Mellon Postdoctoral Fellowship at Wesleyan University's Center for the Humanities. His book on black Israelites and the discourse of civilization during the Harlem Renaissance is forthcoming from Oxford University Press.

Cynthia Eller is Associate Professor of Women and Religion at Montclair State University. She is the author of *Am I a Woman? A Skeptic's Guide to Gender* (2003), *The Myth of Matriarchal Prehistory: Why an Invented Past Won't Give Women a Future* (2000), *Living in the Lap of the Goddess: The Feminist Spirituality Movement in America* (1995), and the interactive textbook *Revealing World Religions* (2005).

Robert Ellwood is Distinguished Emeritus Professor of Religion at the University of Southern California and is the author of several books, including *Religious and Spiritual Groups in Modern America* and *Alternative Altars.* He lives in Ojai, California, and has served as vice president of the Theosophical Society in America.

Ina Johanna Fandrich is an independent scholar living in New Orleans. She is the author of *The Mysterious Voodoo Queen, Marie Laveaux: A Study of Powerful Female Leadership in Nineteenth-Century New Orleans* (Routledge 2005).

Ron Geaves is Professor of Religious Studies in the Department of Theology and Religious Studies at University College Chester. His research interests focus around the transmigration of Indian traditions to the West. He has published two monographs and several journal articles in this area, including *Sufis of Britain (2000)*. His most recent publications are *Islam and the West post 9/11* (2004) and *Aspects of Islam* (2005). He has just completed a monograph on Śaivite traditions in Diaspora to be published in 2006. He has known Prem Rawat since 1969 and has already published four journal articles concerning his activities.

Terryl L. Givens is Professor of Literature and Religion and holds the James A. Bostwick Chair of English at the University of Richmond. He is the author of the prize-winning *Viper on the Hearth: Mormons, Myths and the Construction of Heresy* (Oxford 1997), *By the Hand of Mormon: The American Scripture that Launched a New World Religion* (Oxford 2003), and *The Latter-day Saint Experience in America* (Greenwood 2004), in addition to articles and chapters on Romanticism, Literary Theory, and religious studies.

Adrian Harris has been a Practicing Pagan since 1990 and is currently conducting postgraduate research into Eco-Pagan ritual at the University of Winchester, UK. He has written several articles and book chapters, including "Sacred Ecology" in *Paganism Today* (Harper Collins, 1996) and "Dragon Environmental Network" in *The Encyclopaedia of Modern Witchcraft and Neo-Paganism* (Citadel Press, 2002).

Michael Homer is a practicing trial lawyer in Salt Lake City. He is a member of the Board of State History (appointed by Governor Michael Leavitt in 1997) and has been Chair since 2003. He has published four books, 13 chapters in books, and over 70 articles on historical and legal subjects. He is the recipient of the David Kirby Best Article Award from the Arthur Conan Doyle Society, the Lowell L. Bennion Editor's Award by *Dialogue, A Journal of Mormon Thought,* the T. Edgar Lyon Award of Excellence by the Mormon History Association, and The John Whitmer Historical Association Best Article Award. His most recent book, *On the Way to Somewhere Else: European Sojourners in the Mormon West,* was published by Arthur H. Clark Company in 2006.

Dawn L. Hutchinson is an instructor of religion at Christopher Newport University. She has authored entries in the *Encyclopedia of Religion, Communication, and Media, The Handbook for the Study of Religion, Encyclopedia of Religious Freedom,* and *The 21st Century Encyclopedia of the World's Religions.*

Jeffrey Kaplan is Associate Professor of Religion and the Director of the University of Wisconsin Oshkosh Institute for the Study of Religion, Violence and Memory. He serves as book review editor and serves on the Editorial Boards of the journals *Terrorism and Political Violence* and *Nova Religio.* He is the author or editor of 11 books on religious violence and millenarian terrorism: *Millennial Violence: Past, Present and Future* (2002), *The Cultic Milieu* (2002), *Encyclopedia of White Power: A Sourcebook on the Radical Racist Right* (2000), *Beyond The Mainstream: The Emergence Of Religious Pluralism In Finland, Estonia And Russia* (2000), *The Emergence of an Euro-American Radical Right* (coauthored with Leonard Weinberg) (1998), and *Radical Religion in America: Millenarian Movements From the Far Right to the Children of Noah* (1997). His latest book, *Religious Resurgence and Political Violence*, will be published in 2006. In addition, he has authored numerous articles, encyclopedia entries, and book reviews that have appeared in a multidisciplinary range of peer reviewed academic journals.

Philip Lamy is Professor of Sociology and Anthropology at Castleton College in Castleton, Vermont. He is the author of *Millennium Rage: Survivalists, White Supremacists, and the Doomsday Prophecy* (1996). His articles and commentary on New Religious Movements and countercultures have appeared in professional journals, edited volumes, and the mass media, including *Time Magazine, The London Times, Wired Magazine,* National Public Radio, and the BBC.

David Christopher Lane is a Professor of Philosophy at Mount San Antonio College and a Lecturer in Religious Studies at California State University, Long Beach. He is the author of *The Radhasoami Tradition* (1992), *Exposing Cults* (1992), *The Making of a Spiritual Movement* (1983), and *The Unknowing Sage* (1993). He has also produced several films, including *Moving Water, Digital Baba,* and *Truth Lies.* On a more personal note, Lane won the world bodysurfing championship in 1999 and the International Bodysurfing Championships in 1997, 1998, 2000, and 2004.

Scott Lowe is professor and chair of the Department of Philosophy and Religious Studies at the University of Wisconsin–Eau Claire. He is the author of *Mo Tzu's Religious Blueprint for a Chinese Utopia* and *Da: The Strange Case of Franklin Jones* (with David Christopher Lane) as well as numerous articles and book chapters on Chinese religions and alternative religions in the West.

David W. Machacek is associate director of Humanity in Action, a New York–based not-for-profit organization that sponsors international educational programs on minority issues and human rights, and Visiting Assistant Professor of Public Policy at Trinity College in Hartford, Connecticut. He is coauthor of *Soka Gakkai in America: Accommodation and Conversion* and coeditor of *Global Citizens: The Soka Gakkai Buddhist Movement in the World.* His articles have appeared in *Nova Religio, Sociology of Religion, Research in the Social Scientific Study of Religion, Journal of Oriental Studies,* and *Journal of Church and State.*

J. Gordon Melton is the Director of the Institute for the Study of American Religion and is a research specialist with the Department of Religious Studies at the University of California–Santa Barbara. He is the author of a number of books on American religion including the *Encyclopedia of American Religions* (7th ed., 2003), *The*

Encyclopedic Handbook of the Cults in America (1992), and *Finding Enlightenment: Ramtha's School of Ancient Wisdom* (1998).

Michael L. Mickler is Professor of Church History and Vice President of Unification Theological Seminary. He is the author of *40 Years in America: An Intimate History of the Unification Movement in America, 1959–1999* (2000), *A History of the Unification Church in America, 1959–74* (1993), and *The Unification Church in America: A Bibliography and Research Guide* (1987), as well as articles and reviews on the Unification Church and other movements.

Timothy Miller is Professor of Religious Studies at the University of Kansas. He is the author of *Following In His Steps: A Biography of Charles M. Sheldon* (Tennessee, 1987), *American Communes, 1860–1960: A Bibliography* (Garland, 1990), *The Hippies and American Values* (Tennessee, 1991), *The Quest for Utopia in Twentieth-Century America* (Syracuse, 1998), *The 60s Communes: Hippies and Beyond* (Syracuse, 1999), and editor of *When Prophets Die: The Postcharismatic Fate of New Religious Movements* (State University of New York Press, 1991) and *America's Alternative Religions* (State University of New York Press, 1995), as well as articles in many journals and in the popular press.

Rebecca Moore is Associate Professor of Religious Studies at San Diego State University. She is the author of *Voices of Christianity: A Global Introduction* (2005), and coeditor of *Peoples Temple and Black Religion in America* (2004). She is Co-General Editor of *Nova Religio: The Journal of Alternative and Emergent Religions.* She has also published several journal articles and book chapters on the subject of Peoples Temple and Jonestown.

Douglas Morgan is professor of history at Columbia Union College in Takoma Park, Maryland. He is author of *Adventism and the American Republic: The Public Involvement of a Major Apocalyptic Movement* (2001).

M. Macha NightMare is an author, ritualist, and all-round Pagan webweaver. She presents at colleges, universities, and seminaries and teaches about death and dying and Neopagan public ritual at Cherry Hill Seminary, the first and only seminary serving the Neopagan community. (www.machanightmare.com.)

Kathleen Malone O'Connor is an Assistant Professor of Religious Studies at the University of South Florida where she specializes in Islamic studies. She has published in *Folklore: An Encyclopedia of Beliefs, Customs, Tales, Music, and Art, Journal of the American Academy of Religion,* and the *Encyclopedia of the Qur'an.* She has contributed chapters to *Black Zion: African American Religious Encounters with Judaism, Anthropology and Theology: Gods, Icons, and God-talk,* and *Studies in Middle Eastern Health.*

James T. Richardson is Director of the Grant Sawyer Center for Justice Studies and director of the Judicial Studies graduate degree program for trial judges at the University of Nevada, Reno. His latest book is *Regulating Religion: Case Studies from*

Around the Globe (Kluwer, 2004). He has published over 200 articles and chapters, as well as ten books, mostly about various aspects of New Religious Movements.

Robin Rinehart is Associate Professor of Religious Studies at Lafayette College, where she also directs the Asian Studies program. She is the author of *One Lifetime, Many Lives: The Experience of Modern Hindu Hagiography* (Oxford 1999), editor of *Contemporary Hinduism: Ritual, Culture, and Practice* (ABC-CLIO 2004), and has also published journal articles and encyclopedia entries.

E. Burke Rochford Jr. is Professor of Sociology and Religion at Middlebury College in Vermont. He is author of *Hare Krishna in America* and the forthcoming *Hare Krishna Transformed* to be published in 2007 by New York University Press. He has also published numerous articles and book chapters on the Hare Krishna movement and new religions.

Rosamond C. Rodman is an Assistant Professor of Religious Studies at Macalester College, in St. Paul, Minnesota. She works on intersections of Bible and American culture.

Nora L. Rubel is Visiting Assistant Professor of Religious Studies at Connecticut College. Trained in American religious history, she has published articles on African American religion and contemporary Judaism.

John K. Simmons, Professor of Religious Studies and chairperson of the Department of Philosophy & Religious Studies at Western Illinois University, is the creator of the popular "Beliefs and Believers" teleclass. He publishes regularly in the area of women-led, New Religious Movements in late nineteenth and early twentieth century American history, including the coauthored book, *Competing Visions of Paradise: The California Experience of 19th Century American Sectarianism.* Recent articles include "Eschatological Vacillation in the Mary Baker Eddy's Presentation of Christian Science" in *Nova Religio* and "Vanishing Boundaries: When Teaching About Religion Becomes Spiritual Guidance in the Classroom" in *Teaching Theology and Religion.*

Robert H. Stockman is an instructor for the Department of Religious Studies at DePaul University, Chicago, Illinois, and Director of the Institute for Baha'i Studies in Evanston, Illinois. He is the author of *The Baha'i Faith in America: Origins, 1892–1900, Vol. 1, The Baha'i Faith in America: Early Expansion, 1900–1912, Vol. 2,* and *Thornton Chase: The First American Baha'i.* He has also published 25 articles on Baha'i topics.

Bron Taylor is Samuel S. Hill Ethics Professor at the University of Florida, where he teaches in the interdisciplinary graduate program in religion and nature. He has written widely about religious environmental movements and nature religions. His books include *Ecological Resistance Movements: The Global Emergence of Radical and Popular Environmentalism* (SUNY 1995) and the *Encyclopedia of Religion and Nature*

(Continuum 2005), and he is the editor of the *Journal for the Study of Religion, Nature, and Culture.*

Suzanne Thurman is an independent scholar and former history professor who now manages intellectual property portfolios for IPWatch. She has published extensively on the Shakers. Her book, *"O Sisters Ain't You Happy?": Gender, Family, and Community Among the Harvard and Shirley Shakers, 1781–1918,* won a *Choice* Outstanding Academic Book Award in 2002.

Arthur Versluis is Professor of American Studies at Michigan State University. He is editor of the journal *Esoterica* and author of numerous books, including *Restoring Paradise* (State University of New York Press 2004) and *The New Inquisitions: Heretic-hunting and the Origins of Modern Totalitarianism* (Oxford University Press 2006).

David L. Weddle is Professor of Religion and chair of the Department at Colorado College. He is the author of *The Law As Gospel: Revival and Reform in the Theology of Charles G. Finney* (1985). He has published journal articles on Jonathan Edwards, Christian Science, and Jehovah's Witnesses, as well as review essays on law and religion. His entries on Jehovah's Witnesses appear in *The Encyclopedia of Protestantism* and the *Encyclopedia of Religion.*

Dagmar Wernitznig is an Associate Fellow with the Rothermere American Institute, University of Oxford. She is the author of *Going Native or Going Naive?: White Shamanism and the Neo-Noble Savage* (University Press of America 2003).

Catherine Wessinger is professor of the history of religions at Loyola University New Orleans. She is Co-General Editor of *Nova Religio: The Journal of Alternative and Emergent Religions.* She is the author of *Annie Besant and Progressive Messianism* (1988), and *How the Millennium Comes Violently: From Jonestown to Heaven's Gate* (2000), as well as articles on New Religious Movements. She has edited *Women's Leadership and Marginal Religions: Explorations Outside the Mainstream* (1993), *Religious Institutions and Women's Leadership: New Roles Inside the Mainstream* (1996), and *Millennialism, Persecution, and Violence: Historical Cases* (2000). Her current projects include collecting oral histories relating to the Branch Davidian case and editing the *Oxford Handbook on Millennialism.*

Melissa M. Wilcox is Assistant Professor of Religion and Director of Gender Studies at Whitman College. Author of *Coming Out in Christianity: Religion, Identity, and Community* and coeditor (with David W. Machacek) of *Sexuality and the World's Religions,* she is currently working on a book entitled *Spirituality and Sex in the City: Queer Religiosities in Practice and Theory.*

Jane Williams-Hogan is the Carpenter Chair Professor of Church History at Bryn Athyn College where she also teaches sociology. She is the author of *Swedenborg e le Chiese Swedenborgiane* (2004). She has also published journal articles, encyclopedia articles, and book chapters.

Jeff Wilson is a doctoral candidate in Religious Studies at the University of North Carolina at Chapel Hill. A specialist on Buddhism in America, he is the author of *The Buddhist Guide to New York* (2000) and numerous articles and book chapters on the subject. Wilson is a Contributing Editor to *Tricycle: The Buddhist Review.*

Joseph Dylan Witt is a Ph.D. student in the Religion and Nature Graduate Program at the University of Florida. He has contributed to the journal *Worldviews* and serves as the Managing Editor for the *Journal for the Study of Religion, Nature and Culture.*